Architektur   jovis   Rausch

EINE POSITION ZUM ENTWERFEN   A POSITION ON ARCHITECTURAL DESIGN

Architek

HERAUSGEGEBEN VON EDITED BY

THOMAS ARNOLD
PAUL GRUNDEI
CLAIRE KARSENTY
ELKE KNOESS

TEXTE VON ESSAYS BY

THOMAS ARNOLD
BAR
ANTJE BUCHHOLZ
TORSTEN FRANK
GUNDA FÖRSTER
MATTHEW GRIFFIN
WOLFGANG GRILLITSCH
PAUL GRUNDEI
SUSANNE HOFMANN
ANDREW HOLMES
ÇAGLA ILK
MARTIN KALTWASSER
LUTZ KANDEL
CLAIRE KARSENTY
BIRGIT KLAUCK
HARALD KLOFT
ELKE KNOESS
FOLKE KÖBBERLING
ANUPAMA KUNDOO
THOMAS KUTSCHKER
WINFRIED PAULEIT
MATTHIAS REESE
MARC RIES
ROBERT SLINGER
CHRISTIAN TECKERT
AXEL THALLEMER
JULIAN VINCENT

jovis

Inhalt / Contents

07	Rudolf Schäfer **GRUSSWORT	GREETING**
08	k_studio: Thomas Arnold, Paul Grundei, Claire Karsenty, Elke Knoess **EDITORIAL**
14	**BUCHSTRUKTUR	BOOK ORGANISATION**
16	Studentenprojekt	Student project: Franziska Laue **ORGANIC BANK**
20	Studentenprojekt	Student project: Julian Breinersdorfer **DOG BITES TAIL**
24	Studentenprojekt	Student project: Schadi Weiss **BACKPACK FULL OF ILLUSION**
28	Birgit Klauck **ZUKÜNFTIGE BILDUNGSARCHITEKTUR	NEW EDUCATIONAL ARCHITECTURE**
36	Axel Thallemer **RAUMGESTALT UND DESIGNSTRATEGIEN IN DER UNIVERSITÄREN LEHRE FÜR DAS 21. JAHRHUNDERT	"RAUMGESTALT" AND DESIGN STRATEGIES IN UNIVERSITY TEACHING FOR THE 21ST CENTURY**
48	Andrew Holmes **NACHRICHTEN UND ARRANGEMENTS	MESSAGES AND ARRANGEMENTS**
56	Studentenprojekt	Student project: Katharina Rüter **INSIDE OUT & DAMPFBANK**
60	Andrew Holmes **OHNE BESONDERES ZIEL	NO PARTICULAR PLACE TO GO**
64	Werkzeug	Tool **COLLAGE**
66	Matthias Reese **ZEICHNEN MIT DER MAUS	DRAW WITH THE MOUSE**
72	Christian Teckert **ARCHITEKTUREN DES RAUMS	ARCHITECTURES OF SPACE**
84	Werkzeug	Tool **SHADOWPLAY**
86	Studentenprojekt	Student project: Michael Reiss **TRANSFER 1 & 2**
90	Studentenprojekt	Student project: Daniel Theiler **SUSHIBOX**
92	k_studio: Elke Knoess **PERFORMATIVE ARCHITEKTUR	PERFORMATIVE ARCHITECTURE**
100	BAR: Base for Architecture and Research **SHIFTING THE VIEW – DOCUMENTATION OF THE COMMONPLACE**
104	Werkzeug	Tool **REISEN 1	TRAVEL 1**
106	Studentenprojekt	Student project: Benedikt Tulinius **THE HALL OF VARIETY**
110	Antje Buchholz **ASIA FOOD LAND BERLIN**
114	Werkzeug	Tool **REISEN 2	TRAVEL 2**
116	k_studio: Elke Knoess **ISTANBUL, KONSTANTINOPEL, BYZANZ: HYBRID CITY**
118	Martin Kaltwasser / Folke Köbberling **ISTANBUL: SELF-SERVICE-CITY**
130	Çagla Ilk **STADT ALS PROFIT	CITY AS AN INTEREST**
134	Robert Slinger **STÄDTEBAULICHES ENTWERFEN AN DER SCHNITTSTELLE DER UNSCHÄRFE	URBAN DESIGN AT THE INTERFACE OF UNCERTAINTY**
144	k_studio: Claire Karsenty **KOMPLEX DENKEN	COMPLEX THINKING**
148	Studentenprojekt	Student project: Christoph Jantos **HYBRID: TEMPTATIONS**

152	Studentenprojekt | Student project: Robert Burghardt **[AUSBRUCH AUS DEM] GEFÄNGNIS FÜR INTELLEKTUELLE**	218	k_studio: Paul Grundei **AKTIVE TRÄUME | ACTIVE DREAMS**
156	k_studio: Thomas Arnold **ZEITZEICHNUNG | TIME DRAWING**	222	Wolfgang Grillitsch **1:1**
160	Studentenprojekt | Student project: Doreen Smolensky **PALACE SCREENING**	232	Harald Kloft **TRAGWERKSPLANUNG GEKRÜMMTER FORMEN | ENGINEERING CURVED SHAPES**
164	Thomas Kutschker **DIE DUNKLEN LICHTER | THE OBSCURE LIGHTS**	244	Torsten Frank **RAUMNETZE | SPATIAL NETS**
170	Marc Ries **RAUM, MACHT UND IHR GEGENTEIL IN STANLEY KUBRICKS „FULL METAL JACKET" | SPACE, POWER AND ITS OPPOSITE IN STANLEY KUBRICK'S "FULL METAL JACKET"**	250	Studentenprojekt | Student project: Jo Staudt **URBAN CURRENTS**
		254	Studentenprojekt | Student project: Daniel Krüger **BIBLIOTHEK NONSTOP**
178	Winfried Pauleit **TEKTIEREN | "TEKTIEREN"**	258	Werkzeug | Tool **MATERIALEXPERIMENTE | MATERIAL EXPERIMENTS**
184	Gunda Förster **NICHTS | NOTHING**	260	Werkzeug | Tool **MATERIALEXKURSION | MATERIAL EXCURSION**
190	Werkzeug | Tool **LICHTMODELL & LICHTZEICHNUNG | LIGHT MODEL & LIGHT DRAWING**	262	Anupama Kundoo **AUF DAS MATERIAL KOMMT ES AN | MATERIAL MATTERS**
192	Werkzeug | Tool **LICHTFILM | LIGHT FILM**	270	Julian Vincent **BIONIK UND ARCHITEKTUR | BIOMIMETICS AND ARCHITECTURE**
194	Werkzeug | Tool **PERFEKTER RAUM | THE PERFECT SPACE**	276	Studentenprojekt | Student project: Stefan Endewardt **ERFAHRISATOR & THE SKY-BASE-PROJECT**
196	Studentenprojekt | Student project: Felix Sommerlad **MOLESTAGE**	280	Matthew Griffin **ARCHITEKTUR AUSDEHNEN | EXPANDING ARCHITECTURE**
200	Susanne Hofmann **SPÜRBARE ARCHITEKTUR | SENSUOUS ARCHITECTURE**	290	k_studio: Lutz Kandel **DER NEUE ARCHITEKT | THE NEW ARCHITECT**
210	Werkzeug | Tool **WORKSHOP HAUT | WORKSHOP SKIN**	296	**SEMESTERTHEMEN, VORTRÄGE & GASTKRITIKER | TOPICS, WORKSHOPS, LECTURES & GUEST CRITICS**
212	Studentenprojekt | Student project: Ines Wegner **TRANSFER 1 & 2**	298	**AUTOREN | AUTHORS**
216	Werkzeug | Tool **WORKSHOP TOUCH**		

IMPRESSUM
IMPRESSUM

© 2005 by Jovis Verlag GmbH
Das Copyright für die Texte liegt bei den Autoren. Das Copyright für die Abbildungen liegt bei den Photographen bzw. bei den Bildrechteinhabern. / Copyright for the texts by the authors. Copyright for the pictures by the photographers and holders of the picture rights.
Alle Rechte vorbehalten / All rights reserved

Dank an / Thanks to: TU Berlin, Fakultät 6
für die finanzielle Unterstützung/ for financial support

Herausgeber / Editors:
Thomas Arnold, Paul Grundei, Claire Karsenty, Elke Knoess
TU Berlin, Fakultät 6, Fachgebiet Entwerfen und Baukonstruktion
Prof. Lutz Kandel
Koordination / Coordination: Stefan Haas
Mitarbeit und Satz / Collaboration and Layout: Marie Harms, Christoph Jantos, Michael Reiss, Felix Sommerlad, Jo Staudt, Ariane Wiegner
Dank an / Thanks to: Jan Patrick Bastian, Anne Doose, Franziska Laue
Bildbearbeitung / Picture Editing: Hanna Rohrbach, Nick Kaindl

Allgemeine Beratung und Redaktion deutsche Texte /
General advice and Editing of German texts:
Architectural Affairs, Berlin

Redaktion englische Texte / Editing of English texts: (Ilk, Kloft, Kundoo): Erik Smith, Berlin
Übersetzung Deutsch - Englisch / Translation German - English:
Ian Cowley, Berlin; SAW Communications, Dr. Sabine A. Werner, Mainz:
Anthony Vivis, Dr. Suzanne Kirkbright
Übersetzung Englisch–Deutsch / Translation English–German:
Stephanie Rupp, Berlin; SAW Communications, Dr. Sabine A. Werner, Mainz: Norma Keßler
Redaktion englische Übersetzungen / Editing of English translations: (Editorial, Teckert): Erik Smith, Berlin

Grafisches Konzept / Layout concept: all&slothrop
Druck und Bindung / Printing and binding: bookwise, München

Bibliographische Information der Deutschen Bibliothek:
Die Deutsche Bibliothek verzeichnet diese Publikation in der Deutschen Nationalbibliographie; detaillierte bibliographische Daten sind im Internet über http://dnb.ddb.de abrufbar.
Bibliographic information published by Die Deutsche Bibliothek:
Die Deutsche Bibliothek lists this publication in the Deutsche Nationalbibliographie; detailed bibliographic data are available in the Internet at http://dnb.ddb.de.

Jovis Verlag
Kurfürstenstr. 15/16, 10785 Berlin
www.jovis.de

ISBN 3-936314-45-4

BILDNACHWEIS
ILLUSTRATION CREDITS

Alle Abbildungen sind Eigentum der Technischen Universität Berlin, außer den unten angeführten. / All images are copyrighted to the Technical University of Berlin except those listed below.
Umschlagbild / Front cover image: Bettina Schriewer, k_studio

S. 110-113: Filmstills aus „Asia Food Land" von Antje Buchholz und Kilian Schmitz-Hübsch
S. 118-129: Kaltwasser / Köbberling
S. 134: Stanley Cursiter: "The Sensation of Crossing the Street" (1913), Öl auf Leinwand, 51 x 61 cm, reproduziert mit Genehmigung von Mr. William Hardie
S. 135: "Wells Cathedral tracing-floor", gezeichnet von John Harvey, reproduziert mit Genehmigung von Ms. Eleanor Harvey
S. 164-169: Filmstills aus „Die dunklen Lichter" von Thomas Kutschker
S. 184-189: Gunda Förster
S. 232-243: Harald Kloft
S. 244-245: AGS Leichtbauten, gezeichnet von Ulrike Müller
S. 246-249: Corocord Raumnetz GmbH
S. 262-269: Andreas Daffner
S. 281+285 links: Petra Dörsam
S. 280-289: Matthew Griffin

Rudolf Schäfer

Grußwort / Greeting

Die dramatisch reduzierten Perspektiven der Bautätigkeit in Deutschland und die sich gleichzeitig radikal verändernden Strategien im Umgang mit Immobilien erfordern, ebenso wie der sogenannte Bologna-Prozess, ein kritisches und kreatives Überdenken der Berufsperspektiven von Architekten und ihrer universitären Ausbildung.

Ich begrüße diese Publikation, weil sie ein aktuelles thematisches Diskussionsfeld entwickelt, das die oben genannten Ausgangsbedingungen zum Anlass nimmt, um über Inhalte und Ziele einer heutigen Architekturausbildung aktiv nachzudenken.

Die Präsentation von Studienarbeiten im Fachgebiet Entwerfen und Baukonstruktion von Prof. Lutz Kandel, die Textbeiträgen von fachgebietsnahen, außenstehenden Fachleuten gegenübergestellt werden, knüpft an die Tradition einer integrativen und prozessorientierten Lehre an, die das Studienmodell "Projektstudium" im Diplomstudiengang Architektur der Technischen Universität Berlin in den letzten Jahrzehnten ausgezeichnet hat.

Die hier dargestellte, aufwendige Diskussion zur Architekturausbildung macht in ihrer Vielschichtigkeit auch deutlich, dass das Architekturstudium weiterhin zeit- und damit betreuungsintensiv bleiben wird. Dieser Betreuungsaufwand wird zunehmend im Rahmen universitärer Forschung diskutiert und dargestellt werden müssen. Eine derartige Publikation kann ein Schritt in diese Richtung sein.

The dramatic reducing of prospects for architectural activity in Germany as well as the radically changing strategies when dealing with real estate calls for – as with the so-called Bologna process – a critical and creative re-examination of the professional opportunities for architects and their university education.

I welcome this publication because it develops an up-to-date discussion of a topical subject that takes the above-mentioned conditions as a basis for active reflection on the contents and aims of today's architectural training.

The presentation of students' projects in the special field of design and building construction supervised by Prof. Lutz Kandel is contrasted with text contributions by qualified outside experts. This approach dovetails with the tradition of integrative and process-oriented tuition that, during recent decades, has distinguished the framework of "project-based study" for an undergraduate degree in architecture at the Technische Universität Berlin.

The complex discussion of architectural training that is presented here also clarifies by means of its diversity how studying architecture will continue as a time-consuming and intensive supervision-based programme. This level of supervision will increasingly have to be discussed and illustrated in the context of university research. This publication can be a step in that direction.

k_studio: Thomas Arnold, Paul Grundei, Claire Karsenty, Elke Knoess

Editorial

Dieses Buch reflektiert ein aktuelles Lehrkonzept der Architektur-Entwurfsgrundlehre, das in einem Studio an der Technischen Universität Berlin, dem k_studio, am Fachgebiet Entwerfen und Baukonstruktion von Professor Kandel umgesetzt wurde. Es zeigt methodische Schritte dieses Lehrkonzepts sowie ausgewählte Arbeiten von Studierenden und stellt ihnen zahlreiche Positionen und Projekte interner und externer Fachleute aus dem Umfeld des k_studios gegenüber. Aufgabe des k_studios ist es, Grundkenntnisse der Entwurfslehre an rund einhundert Studierende in den ersten beiden Studienjahren zu vermitteln. Dafür haben wir als ständige wissenschaftliche Mitarbeiter in den letzten vier Jahren gemeinsam mit wechselnden Kollegen und Kolleginnen aus einem Netzwerk interessierter Fachleute ein offenes Lehrkonzept entwickelt, das auf eine vielfältige, forschende und experimentelle Lehrmethodik unter Verwendung zeitgemäßer Bearbeitungs-, Visualisierungs- und Kommunikationstechniken ausgerichtet ist. Wir möchten als k_studio eine offene und breit gefächerte Diskussion unterstützen, die Fragen und Antworten zur Zukunftsfähigkeit der Profession, zur Architektur- und Stadtentwicklung und zu aktuellen Vernetzungsstrategien mit anderen Wissensbereichen definiert.

Buchstruktur

In diesem Buch werden Arbeiten von Studierenden präsentiert, die nicht nur die notwendige Aneignung der Entwurfswerkzeuge vor Augen führen, sondern auch eine eigenständige Sprache erkennen lassen. Anhand dieser Beispiele werden die prozesshafte Arbeitsweise des k_studios und die diversen Semesterthemen erörtert und beschrieben. Von einer 1:1-Aktion vor Ort bis zu theoretischen Projekten zeigen wir ohne Hierarchie die Vielfalt der Eingriffe, die das k_studio auszeichnet. Ergänzend dazu wird der methodische Hintergrund anhand der vermittelten „Werkzeuge" auf eigenen Doppelseiten erläutert. Daneben stehen Arbeiten und Texte externer Referenten und Kritiker: Nicht nur Architekten kommen zu Wort, sondern auch Theoretiker, Konstrukteure, Wissenschaftler und Künstler.[1] Hier spiegeln sich die Diskussions- und Referenzsysteme des Studios wider. Vier Einzelbeiträge der Herausgeber/innen heben bestimmte Aspekte der Lehre hervor und verknüpfen die weiteren Beiträge. Der Aufbau dieses Buches bietet dem Leser einen Leitfaden für die „Navigation", erlaubt aber auch eine freie und vielfältige Lesart der präsentierten Themen. Auch wenn sich der Entwicklungsprozess in seiner Komplexität nicht linear definieren lässt, soll an seinem Ende ein Bild der Aktivitäten und der Gedankenwelt des k_studios entstanden sein.

Hintergründe

In Deutschland und vor allem in Berlin steckt das Berufsbild der Architekten seit einigen Jahren in einer krisenartigen Umbruchsituation. Planungsleistungen für Hochbauten konzentrieren sich zunehmend auf bekannte und erfahrene Architekturbüros.

Editorial

This book addresses the current teaching methodology of a foundation course of architectural design, as practised by the k_studio at the Chair of Architectural Design and Construction led by Professor Kandel at Berlin's Technical University. It illustrates the course's pedagogical approach and presents selected works by students, setting them alongside numerous positions and projects by both independent and in-house experts from within and around the studio. The objective of the k_studio is to impart the basics of architectural design to around 100 students during their first two years of study. Over the past four years, we have developed as the core team of lecturers an open-ended teaching methodology that is augmented by colleagues drawn from a network of interested experts. Our multifaceted, research-oriented, and experimental teaching approach makes use of contemporary techniques of revision, visualisation and communication. The k_studio would like to provoke a frank, broad-based discourse on the profession's future prospects, including the development of architecture and the city, as well as current strategies of knowledge transfer from and to other disciplines.

Book Structure

In this book, we present works by students that reveal not only the necessary incorporation and synthesis of architectural design skills, but also even suggest the existence of an original independent voice. These examples are used to describe and discuss the k_studio's process-based way of working as well as the various themes that are investigated during the semesters. From 1:1 actions on-site to theoretical positions, the diverse array of interventions of the k_studio is presented without any particular hierarchy. In addition, the methodological background is explained in relationship to the acquired 'skills' at some length. Presented along this are the works and texts of independent lecturers and critics: not only architects are given a voice, but also theoreticians, construction specialists, scientists and artists.[1] Here, the studio's discourse and referential systems are reflected. Four individual contributions by the editors highlight specific aspects of the teaching and link the remaining contributions. This book's structure offers the reader a guide for orientation, as well as a free and varied way of reading the themes presented here. Even if the developmental process of the book in all of its complexity cannot be defined in linear terms, by the end it should give readers a picture of the k_studio's activities and world of concepts.

Contexts

In Germany and especially in Berlin, the state of the architectural profession has for the past few years been caught up in a period of crisis-like radical change. Assignments for building projects increasingly concentrate around well-known and

Parallel dazu hat sich eine lebendige Szene von jungen Gestaltern entwickelt, die in vielerlei Ausdrucksformen eine aktive Debatte zu Architektur- und Stadtplanungsfragen führt – allerdings außerhalb der traditionellen Architekturinstitutionen. Die öffentliche Diskussion kreist endlos um institutionelle Strategien wie das „Planwerk Innenstadt", während eine Vielzahl von jungen Büros in ökonomischen Nischenbereichen neuartige Ideen und Raumkonzepte entwickelt und mit geringem finanziellen Aufwand umsetzt. Gleichzeitig beginnt in den teilweise noch bis vor kurzem mit Millionen aus öffentlichen Mitteln hergerichteten Plattenbausiedlungen der Abriss. Wie reagiert die Lehre auf diese veränderten Rahmenbedingungen für Architekten?

Unser wichtigstes Anliegen ist es, die Unverzichtbarkeit von Vielfältigkeit und Offenheit der Lehre im Hinblick auf das aktuelle Berufsbild herauszustellen. Wir wenden uns gegen die in den europäischen Universitäten gegenwärtig stattfindende Reduktion der Studienziele auf eine bautechnische Grundausbildung.[2] Wir möchten stattdessen deutlich machen, dass Architekten die derzeitige Krise des Berufsstandes viel eher überwinden können, wenn sie sich ihrer Fähigkeiten als Integratoren bewusst werden, die unterschiedliche Positionen zu einer gemeinsamen Idee zusammenfügen können; wenn sie zunehmend in der Lage sind, Projekte selbst zu entwickeln; wenn sie wirkliche Forschung betreiben und wenn diese Fähigkeiten auch weiterhin von Anfang an in der Lehre vermittelt werden.

Lehrmethodik

Unsere Arbeit in der Grundlehre besteht darin, mit den Studierenden ihre eigenen räumlichen Themen zu entwickeln, diese zu testen und zu kommunizieren. Die Vermittlung handwerklicher Fähigkeiten findet vor dem Hintergrund dieses Ziels fortwährend statt. Bezugsfelder für Architektur sind dabei nicht nur gebaute Räume der Stadt oder eines Gebäudes, sondern alle Informationen, die zu den kulturellen, gesellschaftlichen und politischen Rahmenbedingungen beitragen, mit denen wir leben. In der Vernetzung mit anderen Wissensbereichen werden auch die Grenzen dieser Profession bewusst in Frage gestellt.

Mit einigen Begriffen können wir wesentliche Aspekte unserer Lehre beschreiben:
- Beobachten: Genaues Beobachten, Analysieren, ist immer unumgänglich und erfordert jeweils angepasste Werkzeuge.
- Notieren: Der Entwurf ist auch eine Forschungsarbeit. Jede Forschung benötigt exakte Messergebnisse und sorgfältig entwickelte Medien zur Dokumentation.
- Referenzen: Referenzen aus vielerlei Ressourcen sind wichtige Quellen und kontinuierliche Dialogpartner der Entwurfsarbeit.
- Experimente: Erst mit der Anordnung ergebnisoffener Experimente kann die „Forschungsarbeit Entwurf" zu neuen, nicht vorhersehbaren Ergebnissen führen.
- Maßstab 1:1: Viele räumliche Hypothesen können nicht hinlänglich in modellhaften Simulationen überprüft werden, sondern müssen im Maßstab 1:1 unter Einsatz der im Entwurfskonzept wirklich vorgesehenen Werkstoffe getestet werden. Die Arbeit im Maßstab 1:1 lehrt auch, Produktionsbedingungen zu berücksichtigen.
- Kommunizieren: Architekten sind Kommunikatoren. Sie müssen Entwürfe in unterschiedlichen Stadien mit verschiedenartigen Dialogpartnern vermitteln, um Arbeits-

highly experienced architectural practises. Parallel to this, a lively scene of young designers has developed, producing a multiplicity of expressive forms that drive an active debate on architecture and city planning – outside the traditional institutional framework. Public debate revolves endlessly around institutional strategies such as "Planwerk Innenstadt Berlin", whilst a multitude of young studios in economic niche markets develops innovative ideas and spatial concepts that are carried out on a very tight budget. Simultaneously, demolition commences in residential complexes of "prefabricated apartment blocks", some of which were only recently reconstructed with public funding at a cost of millions. How does teaching architecture respond to these radically altered contexts for architects?

Our most important objective is to apply the indispensable variety and openness of the teaching programme to the current picture of the architectural profession. We oppose the trend, which is current in several European universities, of cutting back students' aspirations to basic training in building construction.[2] Instead, we would like to stress the fact that architects are much more likely to overcome the current crisis in their professional status at an earlier stage, if they become aware of their skills as integrators, who are capable of unifying the most diverse positions; if they are increasingly able to develop projects on their own; if they undertake viable research of their own; and if these skills continue to be from forward on communicated in the teaching programme.

Teaching Methodology

Our work in teaching the fundaments consists of developing with the students their own spatial themes, as well as testing and communicating them. Conveying mechanical skills takes place in the context of this objective. What is relevant to architecture is not simply constructed spaces in a city or a building, but all the information that contributes to the social and political conditions in which we live. In networking with other disciplines, the boundaries of the profession are also called into question.

We can describe the essential features of our instruction with a few terms:
- Observing: exact observation – or analysis – is always indispensable, and requires the skills appropriate to a given situation.
- Notations: Design is also a work of research. Every act of research demands exact measurement and carefully developed media for documentation.
- References: References from a mass of different resources are important sources and continuous partners for dialogue in design work.
- Experiments: Because of the open-ended nature of its experiments the "design research work" can produce unforeseeable results.
- 1:1 Scale: Many spatial hypotheses cannot be checked adequately in model simulations, but have to be tested on a 1:1 scale using the real materials envisaged in the design concept. Working on the 1:1 scale also teaches one to take production conditions into account.
- Communication: Architects are communicators. In order to create successful working processes, they must convey designs during different stages of develop-

prozesse erfolgreich gestalten zu können. Angewandte Visualisierungsmethoden sind Kommunikationsträger.

- Prozesshaftes Arbeiten: Komplexe Forschungen entstehen in kontinuierlichen Arbeitsabläufen, deren Zwischenergebnisse fortlaufend kommuniziert und bewertet werden. Die Gestaltung des Arbeitsprozesses ist Teil der Forschung.

- Wahrnehmungsorientierung: Alle Wirkung entsteht letztlich in der Wahrnehmung, in der physischen wie auch der kulturellen, in der individuellen wie auch der kollektiven Rezeption.

- Reisen: Studienreisen dienen nicht nur zur Anschauung fremder Kulturen, sondern sind Testfelder für eine ganz alltägliche Arbeitspraxis, die durchaus nicht auf den Studienort Berlin beschränkt ist.

„Lehre basiert auf Vertrauen. Der Lehrende öffnet sich der Zukunft, indem er den Studierenden vertraut und die Entwicklung von Dingen unterstützt, die noch unsichtbar sind; eine sich entwickelnde Sensibilität, die mit heutigen Maßstäben gemessen werden kann. (...) Eine gute Schule behütet und unterstützt eine Art des Denkens, welche von allem ausgeht, was heute bekannt ist, um energiegeladen in das Unbekannte zu springen, im Vertrauen auf die Ansprüche der nächsten Generation, die per Definition der heutigen Logik widersprechen."[3]

Danksagung

Wir möchten unserem Professor Lutz Kandel für das Vertrauen danken, das er als Lehrstuhlinhaber in uns setzt, und für die gestalterische Freiheit, die wir unter seiner wohlwollenden Beobachtung nutzen konnten. Dieses Buch erscheint kurz vor seiner Pensionierung als Hochschullehrer wie auch vor der Pensionierung seiner langjährigen Sekretärin, Christine Neute, die wir ebenfalls dankend erwähnen möchten. Danken möchten wir unseren zahlreichen externen Referenten und Gastkritikern[4] und unseren Kollegen, die das k_studio als wissenschaftliche Mitarbeiter oder Lehrbeauftragte zeitweilig ergänzt haben: Barbara Böhm, Rudolf Zimmermann, Philipp von Matt, Cornelia Schluricke und Gabor Stark. Dank gilt ebenso unseren studentischen Mitarbeitern, die im Regelfall für zwei Jahre im Team mitgearbeitet haben oder noch mitarbeiten und die Lehre tatkräftig unterstützen: Katja Barthmuss, Gesa Büttner, Uwe Dahms, Stefan Haas, Marie Harms, Anne Heusmann, Svea Heinemann, Yan Humbert, Christoph Jantos, Philipp Kring, Sven Morhard, Anja Müller, Beate Schmiegel, Johannes Staudt, Dag Thies, Daniel Wahl, Ariane Wiegner.[5]

ANMERKUNGEN

(1) Liste der Vorträge siehe Seite 296

(2) Die spezifischen Rahmenbedingungen der Studienordnung Architektur an der Technischen Universität Berlin haben mit dem „Projektstudium" günstige Voraussetzungen für ein fächerübergreifendes, kontinuierliches und integratives Studienmodell geboten. Alle Qualifikationen in Nebenfächern sollten hierbei durch die Integration in die Entwurfsprojekte des Hauptfachs „Entwerfen und Baukonstruktion" erworben werden. Im Herbst 2005 werden auch hier neue Bachelor- und Master-Studiengänge eingeführt. Bei stark gekürzten Lehrkapazitäten sieht die Studienordnung im dreijährigen Bachelor-Studium ein vereinfachtes Grundlagenprogramm vor, das integrative und experimentelle Lehrkonzepte weitgehend reduziert und die Ausbildung in zunehmend isolierten Fächern auf bautechnische Grundkenntnisse konzentriert. In einer Art Rückbesinnung auf konservative Ausbildungstraditionen gilt nunmehr für das Bachelor-Studium die „employability", die „Anstellbarkeit" des jungen Bachelors im Architekturbüro, als Studienziel, während im Rahmen der (konsekutiven) Master-Studien diverse Spezialisierungen angeboten werden sollen.

(3) Mark Wigley. In: *Architectural Design*, Volume 74, Nr. 5, Sept./Okt. 2004, S. 13ff.

(4) Zu den Gastkritikern siehe auch Übersicht auf Seite 297

(5) Zur Zusammensetzung des Teams siehe auch Grafik auf Seite 297

ment to various partners for dialogue. Applied methods of visualisation are vehicles for communication.

- Process-style Working: Complex research projects arise in continuous working processes, whose interim results are continually communicated and assessed. Creating a working process is an integral part of research.
- Perceptual Orientation: In the final analysis, all effects issue from one's perception, in physical, cultural, individual as well as collective reception.
- Travel: Study trips are useful not only to see foreign cultures first hand, but as testing grounds for routine working practices that are not confined to Berlin alone.

"Education is all about trust. The teacher embraces the uncertain future by trusting the student, supporting the growth of something that cannot yet be seen, an emergent sensibility that cannot be judged by contemporary standards. A good school fosters a way of thinking that draws on everything that is known in order to jump energetically into the unknown, trusting the formulations of the next generation that by definition defy the logic of the present."[3]

Thanks

We would like to thank our professor, Lutz Kandel, for the trust that, as a professor, he places in us, and for the creative freedom we have enjoyed under his encouraging supervision. This book is being published shortly before his retirement as a university professor – as well as the retirement of his long-term secretary, Christine Neute, to whom we would also like to express our thanks. In addition, we would also like to thank our numerous external lecturers and guest-critics[4] and those colleagues who have, from time to time – either as associate professors or lecturers – contributed to the k_studio, namely: Barbara Böhm, Rudolf Zimmermann, Philipp von Matt, Cornelia Schluricke and Gabor Stark. We would also like to thank our undergraduate assistants, who as a rule worked for two years as members of the team, or are still members and energetically support our teaching work: Katja Barthmuss, Gesa Büttner, Uwe Dahms, Stefan Haas, Marie Harms, Anne Heusmann, Svea Heinemann, Yan Humbert, Christoph Jantos, Philipp Kring, Sven Morhard, Anja Müller, Beate Schmiegel, Johannes Staudt, Dag Thies, Daniel Wahl, and Ariane Wiegner.[5]

NOTES

[1] A list of the lectures appears on p. 296
[2] The specific conditions of studying architecture at the Technical University of Berlin have with the "project-based study" offered students a favourable basis for an all-encompassing, continuous, and integrative study model. All the qualifications in subsidiary subjects should be integrated into the design projects of the main subject area: "Design and Architectural Construction". In autumn 2005 new Bachelor and Masters programmes are launched here. The study programme foresees that because of radically reduced teaching capacity, a simplified foundation will be introduced into the three-year BA course. This will significantly reduce the elements of integrative and experimental tuition concepts, concentrate on basic knowledge of construction in increasingly isolated subject areas, and – in a kind of "retro" development – go back to conservative traditions of education for the BA degree, emphasising "employability" as the study goal for a young BA in architecture, whilst the (subsequent) MA course will offer a wealth of specialisations.
[3] Mark Wigley in *Architectural Design*, Vol 74, No 5, Sept/Oct 2004, pp13ff.
[4] See also "Guest-critics" on p. 297
[5] See also the illustrations on the composition of the team on p.297

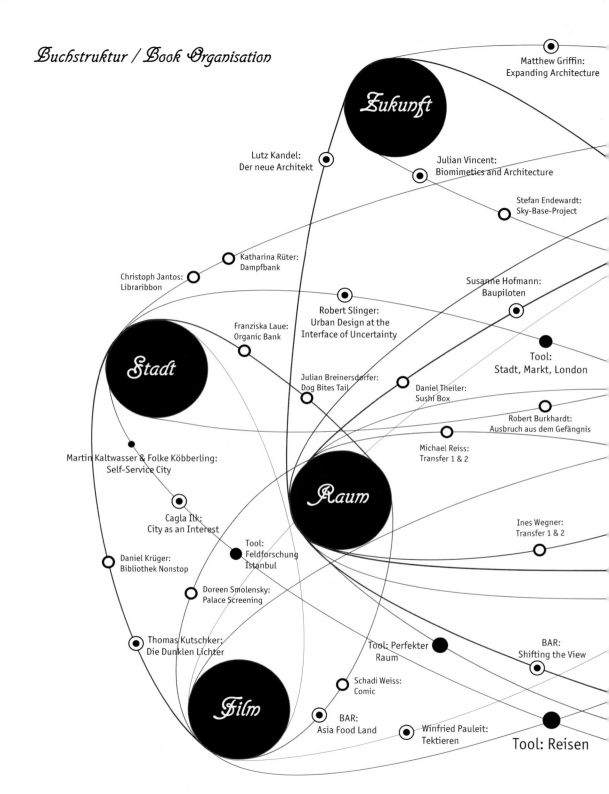

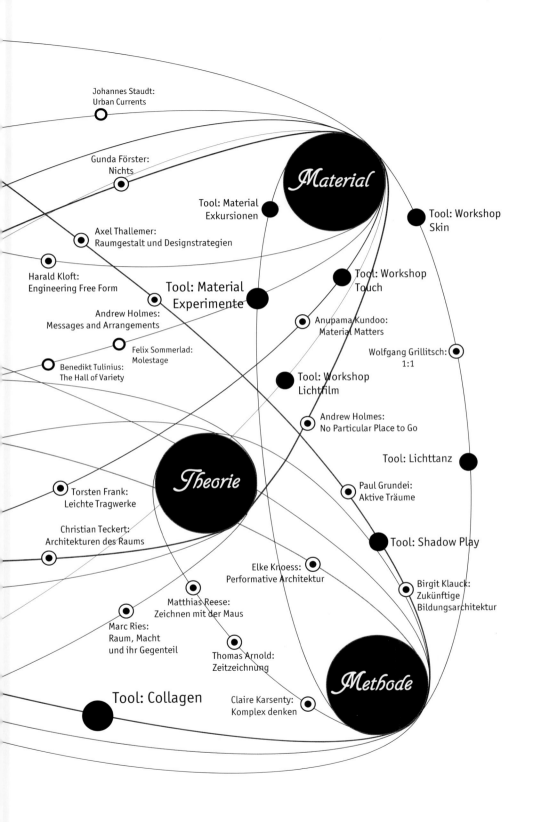

Franziska Laue / Organic Bank 2001/2002

Links: Hybrid Tool: Feuerzeug, entfernt gleichzeitig Teppichbrandlöcher
Rechts: Perfekter Raum: Lichtstudie; Unten: Konzeptmodell, Formstudien

Left: Hybrid Tool: cigarette lighter, which also removes carpet burns
Right: Most Perfect Room: light study
Below: Concept model, scaling and measuring

 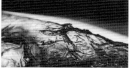  

HYBRID: TEMPTATION   HYBRID: TEMPTATION

Das zweisemestrige Programm bestand in der Entwicklung eines hybriden Gebäudes am Bahnhof Friedrichstraße in Berlin. Über kleine Entwürfe, wie das Hybride Werkzeug, den perfekten Raum (ebenfalls mit einer hybriden Nutzung) und das Templum wurde sich an das Thema und den Ort angenähert. Grundlage des Projektes „Organic Bank" wurde die Beobachtung und Kartierung der Klanglandschaften entlang der Verkehrswege in Berlin. Mit dem Werkzeug des Templums wurden diese Beobachtungen bei einer Ortsbegehung tatsächlich in den Stadtraum eingetragen. Damit manifestierten sich die komplexen Bobachtungen am Ort mit seinen vielen sich überlagernden Verkehrssystemen an einem Punkt und setzten den Ort mit der Klanglandschaft der Stadt in

The two-semester programme consisted of developing a hybrid building at the Friedrichstraße station in Berlin. The subject and location were approached by small designs, such as the hybrid tool, the perfect space (also with hybrid usage) and the templum. The foundation of the project "Organic Bank" was the observation and charting of soundscapes along traffic routes in Berlin. These observations were actually applied to the city space with the templum tool during an on-location visit. In that way, the complex observations of many overlapping traffic systems manifested themselves in one place and connected the location to the city's soundscape. A concept model was developed from the analysis;

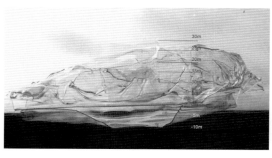 

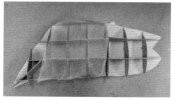

Oben: Konzeptmodell, Skalierung und Vermessung
Oben links: Konzeptmodell am Ort Dreieck Friedrichstraße, die Soundscape des Templums wird räumlich übersetzt
Rechts: Hilfsmodell zur exakten Konstruktion der freien Form

Above: Concept model, scaling and measuring
Above right: Concept model at Friedrichstraße triangle; the soundscape of the templum is spatially translated
Right: Model aid for exact construction of free form

Templum, Bündelung übergeordneter städtischer Klanglandschaften

Links: Markierung des Templums am Kai der Spree
Unten: Richtungsangaben der Klanglandschaft
Rechts: Karte der Klanglandschaft

Templum, aggregation of catalogued urban soundscapes

Left: Drawing of templum on the bank of the river Spree
Below: Collage, direction of soundscape
Right: Map of the soundscape

Beziehung. Aus der Analyse wurde ein Konzeptmodell entwickelt, welches die Beobachtungen in ein räumliches Modell übertrug. Es entstanden dynamische Formen, die sich auf dem Grundstück miteinander verschnitten. Teilweise formten sie sich in den Untergrund ein und hinterließen Öffnungen zu den bestehenden unterirdischen Räumen des Ortes.
Aus Photos des Konzeptmodells wurden Räume collagiert und mit der geplanten Nutzung versehen. Diese Collagen dienten als erster Test für die Tragfähigkeit des Konzeptes. Über mehrere Modellschritte wurde die freie Form rationalisiert und in einen Gebäudemaßstab gebracht.

this transferred the observations to a spatial model. Dynamic forms emerged that intersected with each other on the site. They partially integrated themselves underground and left behind openings to the existing underground spaces at this location.
A collage of spaces was created from photos of the concept model, and the planned usage was added. These collages served as a first test for the concept's feasability. The free form was rationalised by taking several steps in the model phases, and the form was aligned with the scale of a building.

Links: Nutzungsdiagramm
Ganz links: Skizzen zur Gebäudeformentwicklung
Unten: Collagen, Tests zur hybriden Nutzung
1. Badende und S-Bahnhof, im Hintergrund Büroarbeiter beim informellen Gespräch
2. Büroarbeiter und Eingang Bad
3. Wartende Bankkundin und Freizeitaktivitäten

Left: Space use diagram
Far left: Sketches on the building's form development
Below: Collages, tests of hybrid use of bank and bath
1. Bathing woman and S-Bahn station, in the background office workers chatting
2. Office workers and entrance to bathing area
3. Bank customer waiting and leisure activities

Arbeitsmodell Körper/ Haut
Maquette for body/ skin relation

Arbeitsmodell Körper/ Haut mit Ebenen
Maquette for body / skin relation with floor plates

Guckkastenmodell des Interieurs des Bürobereiches
Observation-box model of interior of office area

 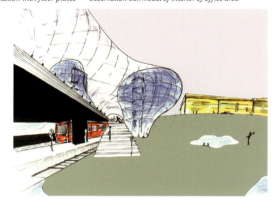

ORGANIC BANK

ORGANIC BANK

Im zweiten Teil des Projektes wurde der Entwurf konstruktiv und atmosphärisch innenräumlich vertieft. Referenzen aus der Natur dienten zur Anregung zum Thema Konstruktion. Der Aufbau der Erdnussschale wurde genau untersucht und in experimentellen Modellen nachgebaut. Die Ergebnisse gingen in die Konstruktion der Decke ein.
 Hier wird auch die Trennung von festen Gebäudeteilen und einer leichten Hülle vorgenommen. Die dadurch entstehenden canyonartigen Räume zwischen den Baukörpern erschließen die verschiedenen Ebenen Bahnhof, Bank und Bad und verknüpfen sie mit den öffentlichen Räumen der Stadt.
Ein Guckkastenmodell zwingt zur genauen Überlegung, was der Gebäudenutzer wahrnimmt. Dabei wird der Blick in eine der Büroebenen

In the second part of the project, the design was extended in construction terms as well as spatial and interior atmosphere. References from nature served as inspiration for the theme of construction. The composition of a peanut shell was precisely studied and reconstructed in experimental models. The results were integrated into the construction of the ceiling. Here, the separation is also performed between solid building elements and a light shell. The canyon-like spaces that are thus created between the building structures give access to the various floors – station, bank and bath – and link them to the city's public spaces. A model observationbox forces precise reflection on what the buildings user perceives.
In this case, the view into one of the office floors is staged.

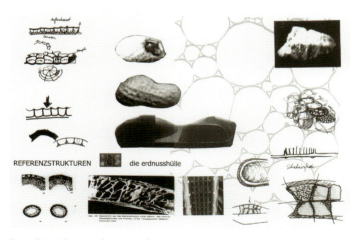

Strukturexperimente aufbauend auf der Naturreferenz
Structural experiments based on nature references

Unterzugplan *Beam layout*

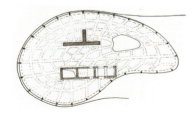

Konstruktive Referenz aus der Natur: Aufbau der Erdnusshülle
Constructive reference from nature: Composition of peanut shell

Links und Mitte: Zeichnungen zur Lokalisierung der Lufträume
Left and center: Drawings to locate air spaces

Rechts: Skizze des Bürobereiches zeigt die Verknüpfung der Geschosse durch Öffnungen
Right: Sketch of office area, showing visual link between floor through openings

 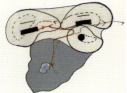 

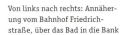
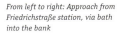

Von links nach rechts: Annäherung vom Bahnhof Friedrichstraße, über das Bad in die Bank

From left to right: Approach from Friedrichstraße station, via bath into the bank

inszeniert. Die Büroebenen sind räumlich durch große Öffnungen miteinander verknüpft, deren Geometrie durch Einschnitte organischer Körper in die Gebäudestruktur entwickelt wurde.
Über einen Comic wird der Weg eines Nutzers von der S-Bahn in die Bank räumlich dargestellt. Direkt vor dem Bahnhof ersteckt sich das abgesenkte Bad. Man kann die S-Bahn fahren sehen und sich dann auf die Haupterschließungsebene des Gebäudes auf Straßenniveau begeben. Dort bewegt man sich zwischen den Baukörpern in einem dynamischen Raum. Im Inneren wird die Verknüpfung der Geschosse deutlich.

The office floors are spatially linked to each other by large openings, whose geometry was developed into the buildings structure by recesses in organic bodies.
A users route from the S-Bahn railway to the bank is spatially illustrated by a comic. The lowered bathing level stretches directly in front of the station. You can see the S-Bahn travelling along and then making its way up to the main access level of the building at street level. There, you pass between the structures into a dynamic space. Inside, The interlinking of the different levels is clearly visible.

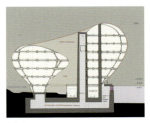

Schnitt
Section

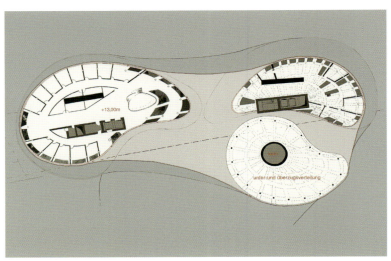

Grundriss der Büroebene
Layout of office level

Julian Breinersdorfer / Dog Bites Tail 2001/2002

01 BADEHAUS / BATH HOUSE

02 RUHEHAUS / RESTING HOUSE

Fingerübung für die zweite Woche: Ein Bad mit 100m³. Hier zählt kein Zustand, vielmehr ein Ablauf. Am Start steht der ermattete Großstädter, am Ziel liegt er und ruht. Dazwischen die benötigten Stationen:

A "finger exercise" for the second week: a bath in an area of 100 sq. m. We are not dealing with a condition, as much as a development. At the beginning we see the exhausted big-city dweller – by the end he is lying down taking a breather. The stations required in-between:

Neues Thema, altes System: Ein Kontemplationsort wird gesucht, ein Wasserkreislauf hilft auch hier. Ob Nizza oder Badewanne: Wasser beruhigt. Der Weg zu innerer Ruhe führt NICHT über die steinigen Pfade von Narkotika, sondern durch DIESEN RAUM.

New subject, old system. A place for meditation is much desired – circulating water will help. Whether in Nice or in a bath – water is always soothing. The path to inner peace does NOT lie over the stony footpaths of narcotics, but through THIS SPACE.

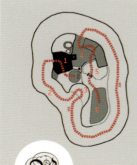

1. Reinigung (Dusche)
2. Arbeit (Gegenstrom)
3. Lockerung (Jakuzzi)
4. Entspannung (Sauna)
5. Abschreckung (Kaltbecken)
6. Schlaf (Ruheliege)

1. Cleaning (Taking a Shower)
2. At Work (Against the Grain)
3. Loosening up (Jacuzzi)
4. Relaxation (Sauna)
5. Aversion Therapy (Cold Bath)
6. Asleep (Lying at Rest)

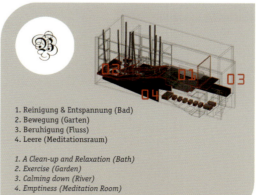

1. Reinigung & Entspannung (Bad)
2. Bewegung (Garten)
3. Beruhigung (Fluss)
4. Leere (Meditationsraum)

1. A Clean-up and Relaxation (Bath)
2. Exercise (Garden)
3. Calming down (River)
4. Emptiness (Meditation Room)

Soweit o.k., nur drängt sich durch das Kreislaufsystem doch deutlich eine vertikale Struktur auf. Wo ein Turm ist, darf kein Flachbau sein. Nur stellt sich jetzt folgende Frage: Wie funktioniert diese begrünte Kommunikationsachse in einem Hochhaus?

So far ok – except that a vertical structure is very obviously working its way through the circulatory system. Where there is a tower, there cannot be any low buildings. It's just that we now have to answer this question: how will this green communication axis work in a high-rise building?

03 MONSTERBANK / MONSTER BANK

Diesmal wird der Kreislauf auf ein Bankgebäude am Bahnhof Friedrichstraße angewandt. Da Banker aber nicht den ganzen Tag schwimmen oder meditieren können, werden andere Stoffwechselprodukte gesucht – Wasser, Klima, Energie. Das kostet alles Geld und wird interessant für den Finanzchef.

This time the notion of circulation is applied to a bank at the Friedrichstraße station. But as bankers cannot spend all day swimming or meditating, different new metabolites are sought – such as water, climate, energy. This all costs money and becomes of interest to the Head of Finance.

RAUMKONZEPT
Ausbildung interdisziplinärer Schnittbereiche
1. Zersetzung des üblichen Ebenensystems
2. Abteilungen wachsen in Bereichen inhaltlicher Überschneidung zusammen
3. Ausbildung einer interdisziplinären Erschließungsachse nach Art eines Straßendorfs
4. Begrünung der Achse durch den Wasserkreislauf

CONCEPT OF SPACE
Development of interdisciplinary transitional areas
1. Breakdown of the usual level-system
2. Divisions grow together in areas of substantive overlaps
3. Formation of an interdisciplinary development axis, on the lines of ribbon housing
4. Greening of the whole axis through water circulation

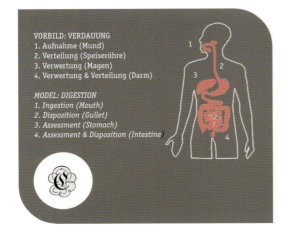

VORBILD: VERDAUUNG
1. Aufnahme (Mund)
2. Verteilung (Speiseröhre)
3. Verwertung (Magen)
4. Verwertung & Verteilung (Darm)

MODEL: DIGESTION
1. Ingestion (Mouth)
2. Disposition (Gullet)
3. Assessment (Stomach)
4. Assessment & Disposition (Intestine)

UMSETZUNG: ENERGIEKREISLAUF
1. Aufnahme & Filter (Zufluss)
2. Energiegewinnung (Turbine)
3. Reinigung (Durchlauferhitzer)
4. Energiegewinnung (Dampfturbine)
5. Klima (Kondensationsklimaanlage)
6. Verwertung (Bewässerung)

TRANSPOSITION: ENERGY CYCLE
1. Ingestion & Filtering (Influx)
2. Energy Acquisition (Turbine)
3. Cleaning (Flow heater)
4. Energy Acquisition (Steam turbine)
5. Climate (Anti-condensation Air-Conditioning)
6. Assessment (Watering)

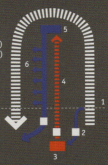

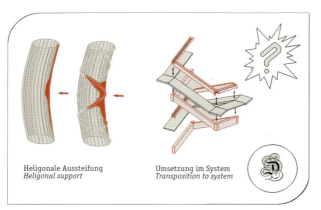

Heligonale Aussteifung
Heligonal support

Umsetzung im System
Transposition to system

04 HOCHHAUSHELIX / HIGH RISE HELIX

Die Suche nach dem Tragwerk bringt die Lösung: Eine Heligonalstruktur steift optimal aus und zeigt die Richtung für die Erschließung.

The search for the load-bearing structure brings its own reward. A heligonal structure gives excellent support and points the way for further development.

Durch die Heligonalerschließung werden die Büroflächen fragmentiert und Arbeitsbereiche nach einem ähnlichen Schema wie in der Monsterbank verbunden. Die Grünflächen sind angenehm für die Mittagspause, der Wasserkreislauf ist gut für die Energiebilanz.

As a result of the heligonal development the office areas are fragmented, and working areas are combined in a scheme similar to that of the monster bank. The green spaces are pleasant for the lunch break; the water-circulation is good for the energy balance.

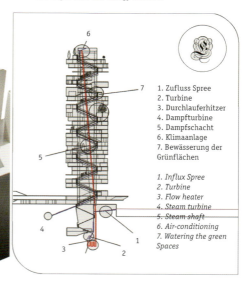

1. Zufluss Spree
2. Turbine
3. Durchlauferhitzer
4. Dampfturbine
5. Dampfschacht
6. Klimaanlage
7. Bewässerung der Grünflächen

1. *Influx Spree*
2. *Turbine*
3. *Flow heater*
4. *Steam turbine*
5. *Steam shaft*
6. *Air-conditioning*
7. *Watering the green Spaces*

04.1 MODULARE ÜBERARBEITUNG / 04.1 MODULAR REVISION

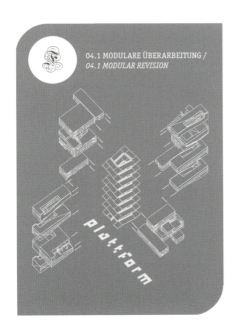

Wenn es diese gewundene Erschließung gibt, warum muss sie sich dann noch kompliziert durch Ebenen fressen? Die Helix trägt und sorgt für Zugang. Die Volumen werden als Module eingehängt, je nach Bedarf.

If this twisting connection exists, why must it also take this complicated course of eating through different planes? The helix carries and guarantees access. The volumes are included as modules, as required.

Zum Energiekonzept: Jalousieartige Solarpaneele beschatten den Innenraum und fangen die Sonne auf. Dazu drehen sie sich nach dem Sonnenstand.

On the energy concept: Solar panels like Venetian blinds make the inner room shadowy and capture any sunlight. What is more, they can swivel towards what sun there is.

04.2 SOLARE ÜBERARBEITUNG / 04.2 SOLAR REVISION

Bewegung der Sonnensegel über 24h / The Solar Awning's 24-hour Swivelling

22h30 16h30 08h30 11h00

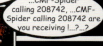

...Of course, time of travel into this legendary part of the world was not to be wasted... The students were encouraged to get used to the many functions and possibilities of the ship... Many daily trips were undertaken in order to fulfill that purpose...

...Onto the control-tower... – the ship´s "brain"!

...The disappointment about the failed lunar excursion vanished soon after "CMF-Spider" had left the harbor of Bremerhaven, Germany, since the ship, a former military aircraftcarrier, had quite a lot to offer...

...Into the ship´s own steel factory...

...The ship-

...And the aircraft yard...

...Just to mention a few...

1_OSN_organic_sensory_navigation
2_OST_organic_sensory_tools
3_OSR_organic_sensory_radar
4_rocketpower_engine
5_IVS_incredibly_variable_space

_cmf-spider I

_momentaufnahme des vollautomatischen raumstations-konstruktions-moduls CMF_SPIDER (construction-material-factory)
_CMF_SPIDER ist in der lage sich durch energieaufwand (rückstossprinzip) im orbit oder unterwasser zu bewegen und mit hilfe organischer tastsensoren OSN (organic_sensory_navigation) als steuereinheit punktgenaue manövriervorgänge zu absolvieren
_CMF SPIDER kann mit hilfe des OSR (organic_sensory_radar) rohstoffe aufspüren und identifizieren
_CMF SPIDER nimmt mit hilfe von greifarmen ausgestattet mit OST (organic_sensory_tools) rohstoffe aus dem orbit, von planeten oder vom meeresgrund auf, je nach programmierung und speist damit riesige rohstofftanks GRT (giant_resource_tanks) in denen vollautomatisch material archiviert wird
_je nach programmierung im CAD-programm können erwünschte rohstoffe he-und verarbeitet werden und mit hilfe der OST punktgenau zu entsprechenden räumlichen konstellationen IVS (incredibly –variable-space) errichtet werden
_OST können die IVS punktgenau platzieren und/oder mit anderen stellen/modulen zusammenfügen

... After days like these at sea...

... We finally safely reached our destination and started our research right away. On land, water and air...

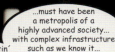

...It keeps gettin´ better still! - A whole city must have vanished here!!!

...must have been a metropolis of a highly advanced society... with complex infrastructure such as we know it...

...How could that happen? What happened to all of the inhabitants?- And when? And what city is this anyway???

...on board of "CMF-Spider"...

...CMF-Spider calling 208742...please reply!...?...!?! - Still no answer !

?

Wow!...

...This is when one gets reminded of the transitoriness of human life...

...philosophize...
...philosophize...

oh!...
I am gettin´ low on oxygen - I better rise to the surface!

  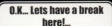 

= People !?!!?

O.K... Lets have a break here!...
Being underway in a submarine in the Bermuda Triangle, somehow getting into some kind of different dimension, discovering an old sunken city on the bottom of the ocean and the many missing ships...
...Which sounds pretty crazy until here already, but it still is imaginable...
But I was definitly thru with it...

...What the hell?! A ship's cemetary!?

...could these be the disappeared ships of the past?

...Gotta get on land and find out !

...14 days later back in Berlin in k_studio, Building of Architecture, Technical University...

...Based on our experiences during the voyage to the Bermudas, everybody was now to work and concentrate on one topic, inherent in their own personal experience...
This topic had to be deepened to a very high degree, so that a self-invented, spatially and temporarily limited stand, built and placed at the location, would represent this topic precisely...
Since my "Shadowplay" with the production designer Udo Kramer, whose main intention of his work is to create the perfect illusion for the movie-camera, I decided on developing a...
...Guess what!? – O.K., I will show you two of my photo works, first...
Maybe you will find an answer more easily afterwards...

...This is where we received our new task... It was about a "public test" in the subway station of Alexanderplatz, one of Berlin's main traffic junctions... They really intended to let us (first semesters) loose on harmless Berlin citizens...

...Well, I produced my own movie in 3-D, that could be viewed with my specially designed portable 3-D-Movie-Cinema... – my BACKPACK FULL OF ILLUSION!!!...

By the way...
The BACKPACK FULL OF ILLUSION could be easily set up within seconds... ...Anywhere... Anytime... ...As you can see below!

...The plot?
A very profane daily situation... You are waiting for the subway train on the platform... Kind of bored, your eyes wander around...

...Impatie[nt]
edge of the p[latform]
still not in si[ght]
scan the sc[ene]
behind, [...]

...BACKPACK FULL OF ILLUSION – Or what would you have developed?...

...When I discovered people – yes, human life – and then realized that these people where part of a film-team involved in a film project...

...I can still remember, that I was strongly impressed by the work of the whole team... But the production designer (Udo) really earned my attention! I kept focussing on him the whole time, and tried to capture every move of this "working machine" on my camera, but I must have somehow lost consciousness at sometime... What then happened? – I got no clue whatsoever...

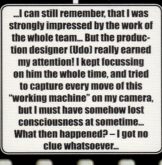

...All I remember is that I woke up in a helicopter on board of "CMF-Spider"... Thank God I took pictures of all of that! – Otherwise probably nobody would believe my story, I guess!... – What a shadowplay!!!

...u move to the very rm but the train is ... gain you dreamily rning your head g the drunks that...

just caused quite some noise, while entering the train on the other track...
– Suddenly the subway train appears out of nowhere and hits you!!!

...Big thanx to Merle Vorwald and Janis for their incredible help...

backpack full of illusion

Birgit Klauck

Zukünftige Bildungsarchitektur

Die Anforderungen an das Leben und das Lernen sind heute andere als noch vor wenigen Jahrzehnten. Einerseits gewinnt das Wissen mehr und mehr an Bedeutung, andererseits relativiert sich dessen Wert aber durch einen enormen Wissenszuwachs und seine immer kürzer werdende Halbwertszeit. Indiz hierfür ist beispielsweise der Bedeutungsverlust der klassischen Vita: Heute in den USA für Bewerbungen zusammengestellte Lebensläufe umfassen meist nur noch die letzten drei Jahre.

Allerorten werden lebenslanges Lernen und kreative Bildung gefordert. Es gibt bislang jedoch keine adäquaten gesellschaftlichen und erst recht keine räumlichen Rahmenbedingungen, die diese Form des Lernens auf eine selbstverständliche Art und Weise fördern. Mit der Bologna-Deklaration[(1)] wurde auf der organisatorischen Ebene ein erster wichtiger Schritt hin zu einem zukunftsweisenden Bildungsmodell mit neuen Studienabschlüssen und offeneren Universitätsstrukturen getan. Details der Deklaration, wie beispielsweise die Erhöhung der Kontaktzeiten von Studierenden mit Lehrenden oder das fachübergreifende Studium, sind wichtig. Sie entfalten ihre volle Wirksamkeit aber nur in einem ganzheitlichen Modell.

Um das Ideal vom lebenslangen Lernen zu verwirklichen, müssten Universitäten nicht nur individuelle Studienpläne ermöglichen, sondern auch ihr traditionell trichterförmiges Karrieremodell zugunsten einer zeitgemäßen Netzwerkstruktur aufgeben. In Deutschland bleiben viele Wissenschaftler während des einzig möglichen und viel zu langen „Königswegs zur Professur" über Studium, Dissertation und Habilitation auf

„Communicator" – Die von Birgit Klauck betreuten 1:1 Installationen der Studierenden des ersten Studienjahrs (WiSe 2004/05) wurden im Rahmen einer finalen Ausstellung der Öffentlichkeit präsentiert.

"Communicator" – The first-year students' 1:1 installations, supervised by Birgit Klauck (WiSe 2004/05), were presented in the context of a final exhibition.

New Educational Architecture

Demands on life and learning are different today than they were twenty years ago. Knowledge has acquired ever more importance, yet its value diminishes in the light of the tremendous expansion of information and its ever-shortening half-life. The loss of meaning in the traditional curriculum vitae is an example of this: in America today a résumé typically covers the last three years of the applicant's work experience and nothing more.

Life-long learning and creative education is demanded everywhere. But so far there have not been adequate societal – not to mention spatial – conditions that naturally promote this form of learning. The Bologna Declaration[1] took the first important administrative step towards establishing an educational model that would pave the way to the future: a model offering new degree qualifications and more open structures. The details of the declaration, such as increased student contact with lecturers and interdisciplinary studies, are important. However, they will only come to fruition in an integrated model.

In order to realise the ideal of life-long learning, universities must offer not only individual degree course schemes, but also give up their traditional pyramidal structures in favour of modern networked structures. In Germany, many academics become stuck on the road from a degree to a doctoral thesis and then to assistant lectureship – the "royal road" to professorship – the only road and one that is far too long. On the way knowledge is hoarded rather than made available

der Strecke. Währenddessen wird Wissen gehortet, anstatt es – unter Berücksichtigung seiner kurzen Halbwertszeit – in modernen Netzwerkstrukturen zur Verfügung zu stellen und die Anwendung zu fördern.

Zudem wurden Defizite in der räumlichen Gestaltung unserer Bildungs- und Forschungsbauten bislang weder benannt noch wurde die Notwendigkeit einer Veränderung erkannt. Dabei belegen Beispiele aus allen Architekturepochen – etwa bei Sakralbauten oder Gebäuden, die politische Macht- oder Repräsentationsansprüche erfüllen –, dass gesellschaftliche Formationskräfte nicht abstrakt sind. Sie finden einen konkreten Ausdruck in gebauter Architektur. Wenn Mensch und Raum sich nicht voneinander trennen lassen, dann ist die Architektur der Universität essentieller Teil eines neu zu definierenden Bildungsmodells.

Die heutigen Universitäten gehen auf das Urmodell der „Schule von Athen" Mittelpunkt. Auch heute, mehr als 2000 Jahre später, fördern Interaktion und „Face to face"-Kommunikation den Austausch von Wissen und die Kreativität. Der direkte Dialog ist gegenseitig befruchtend, und zwar für Studierende und Lehrende.

„Communicator" – Aufgabe war es, ein mobiles Objekt, das seinen Träger oder Nutzer in den geplanten und zufälligen Interaktionen mit der Umgebung unterstützt, zu entwickeln, vor geladenen Gästen vorzuführen und dabei auf seine Tauglichkeit zu testen.

"Communicator" – The task was to develop a mobile object that supports its carrier or user in planned or coincidental interactions with the environment, as well as to introduce it to an invited audience and test its utility value.

Das „Eins zu eins"-Gespräch mit Lehrer und Studienkollege, die zufälligen Treffen und der Austausch mit fachfremden Wissenschaftlern sind nach wie vor unersetzliche Inspirationsquellen. Aber gerade dort, wo eine Kultur des offenen Erfahrungs- und Ideenaustausches, wo Inspiration für kreatives Schaffen zu erwarten wären, findet man vielerorts Raumstrukturen, die diesem Anspruch entgegenwirken. Dort wo man Umgebungen mit hohem kommunikativem Charakter erwarten würde, findet sich das Abbild stereotyper Bürobauten. Die heutigen Gebäude bilden ein undurchlässiges System ab, das vor allem durch sein Streben nach institutioneller Permanenz gekennzeichnet ist, anstatt für Forschung und Lehre angemessene, offene Arbeitsumgebungen zu bilden.

Kommunikation ermöglichen

Wenige realisierte Beispiele belegen die positiven Impulse, die von Architektur auf das Lehren und Lernen ausgehen können. Sie zeigen, dass Gebäude sehr wohl die Fähigkeit besitzen, Kommunikation zu ermöglichen, die anderenorts nicht stattfände. Ein erstaunliches Exempel findet sich im traditionell hermetisch abgeschlos-

as it would be in modern networked structures, where its short half-life can be taken into account and applications encouraged.

Furthermore, the issue of shortcomings in the spatial organization of our educational and research buildings has not been broached, nor has the necessity for change been recognized. However all architectural periods provide examples which prove that the society-shaping forces are not abstract: take the example of church buildings or buildings that express claims to power or political mandates. In finished architecture these forces assume definite form. If man and space cannot be separated, then university architecture is an essential component of the new education model that has yet to be defined.

The contemporary university can be traced back to ancient Greece and the "School of Athens". Socratic dialogue, the one-on-one conversation, was the primary discursive form. Today, more than two thousand years later, interaction and face-to-face communication also require an exchange of knowledge and creativity. Direct dialogue is rewarding for both parties: students and lecturers.

One-to-one conversation between lecturers and students, chance meetings and exchanges with academics from other disciplines are as much irreplaceable sources of inspiration as they have ever been. However, in just those places where one would expect to find an open exchange of experience, ideas and inspiration for creative work, one finds spatial structures that militate against this. Where you might expect surroundings highly conducive to communication, you find generic office buildings. As a result of the desire for institutional permanence, contemporary buildings reproduce an opaque system rather than open surroundings that are conducive to research and learning.

Enabling Communication
There are a few examples which demonstrate the positive impulse that architecture can supply to teaching and learning. They show that buildings do indeed have the capacity to enable communication that would not take place elsewhere. One prodigious example is found in Japan's traditional hermetically sealed building system. In the main building of the Future University of Hakodate, designed by the archi-

senen Bildungssystem Japans. In dem von Riken Yamamoto geplanten Hauptgebäude der „Future University" in Hakodate verbinden sich innovative Lehrinhalte mit einer außergewöhnlichen, auf dieses Lehrangebot abgestimmten räumlichen Struktur. „Complex System Science" und „Information Architecture" werden hier gelehrt. Die beiden Studienfächer vereinen bislang getrennte Fächer (Mathematik, Biologie, Ökonomie sowie Robotik, Network Systems und Design) mit dem Ziel der Erforschung komplexer Systeme und der Ausbildung von Fachkräften für Informationsverarbeitung. Neu ist auch, dass viele der angebotenen Veranstaltungen von der interessierten Öffentlichkeit besucht werden können.

Yamamoto hat alle Forschungs-, Unterrichts- und Verwaltungsräume in einem einzigen Volumen konzentriert. Auf sich zurückstaffelnden Geschossebenen bieten so genannte Studios programmatisch offene Arbeitsflächen, die je nach Bedarf (Einzel- oder Teamarbeit, Gruppenpräsentationen etc.) von den Studierenden neu konfiguriert werden können. Blickbeziehungen zwischen den Ebenen und zu den direkt zugeordneten verglasten Büros und Forschungslaboratorien der Lehrkräfte fördern das „Eins

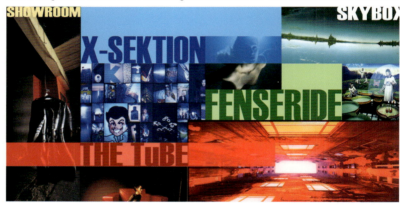

Links: Future University of Hakodate, Riken Yamamoto & Field Shop – Grundriss 3. OG
Rechts: Mathias Bachmann – Entwurfsprojekt im zweiten Studienjahr (SoSe 2004) – Programmstudie für ein Grand Café zeigt die Überlagerung unterschiedlicher, sich widersprechender Funktionen.

Left: Future University of Hakodate, Riken Yamamoto & Field Shop – Layout 3rd upper floor
Right: Mathias Bachmann – Second year design project (SuSe 2004) – programme study for a Grand Café shows the overlapping of different, contradictory functions.

zu eins"-Gespräch mit den Lehrenden und brechen das in Japan sonst übliche, streng hierarchische System auf. Die Zusammenführung und Verdichtung unterschiedlicher Funktionen bei gleichzeitiger Auflösung starrer Grenzen (hier: Präsentations-, Vortrags-, Kommunikations- und Erschließungsflächen, Forschungslabors etc.) generiert Ereignisse. Sie ermöglicht Treffen zwischen Menschen, die sich normalerweise nicht begegnen, und fördert so Kreativität. Dies gilt insbesondere dann, wenn durch die Verknüpfung sich scheinbar widersprechender Programme zwanglose Begegnungen außerhalb der eigenen Arbeitsgruppe und außerhalb des eigenen Arbeitsfeldes entstehen – sich also Menschen begegnen, die nicht das Gleiche tun.

Vor allem dynamische Raumkonfigurationen stiften Interaktion. Dies lässt sich auch bei einem weiteren, in diesem Sinne vorbildlichen Universitätsneubau beobachten, dem „Campus Center" für das Illinois Institute of Technology in Chicago von Rem Koolhaas. Dort erinnert das programmatisch hochkomplexe Raumgefüge mit seinen fließend ineinander übergehenden Nachbarschaften eher an ein urbanes Zentrum, eine „Indoor-Stadt", als an ein Universitätsgebäude. Vorhandene, campusübergreifende Wegebeziehungen wurden aufgenommen und als splitterartige Raumstruktur interpretiert, die sich auf verschiedenen Ebenen ausbreitet. Wände werden durch die

tect Riken Yamamoto, innovative study programmes are combined with an unusual spatial structure attuned to the academic disciplines offered at the university: complex system science and information architecture. These disciplines combine subjects that are traditionally taught separately (mathematics, biology, economics; robotics, network systems and design) with the aim of researching complex systems and training specialists in information processing. Something else that is new is that members of the public can attend many of the lectures on offer.

Yamamoto has concentrated all research, teaching and administrative rooms into a single building. The terraced floors comprise studios, or work areas, that are not designed for a particular purpose but can be reconfigured by students according to need, e.g. private study, team work or group presentations. The line of sight between the floor levels and the glass - fronted offices and research laboratories of the teaching staff promote one-to-one conversation with students and break down the strict hierarchy that is otherwise the norm in Japan. The combination and consolidation of different functions and the simultaneous breakdown of rigid distinc-

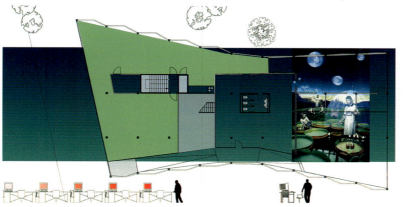

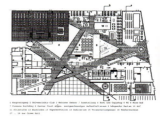

tions between kinds of space (e.g. for presentations, lectures, communication, circulation, research etc.) is creating events. People who would not normally cross paths meet, and their creativity is enhanced. This is especially true when the combination of apparently contradictory programs results in informal encounters between people from different working groups or different fields of research, i.e., meetings between people who do different things.

First and foremost, dynamic configuration of space promotes interaction. An example of this can be seen in another groundbreaking new building: the "Campus Center" for the Illinois Institute of Technology in Chicago, designed by Rem Koolhaas. This highly complex and multipurpose spatial structure, which merges fluidly with its surrounding neighbourhoods (environment), is more reminiscent of an urban centre, an indoor city, than a university building. The existing layout that consisted of pathways throughout the university was interpreted in terms of a splinter-like spatial structure that spreads out on different levels. The height difference between these staggered levels makes the walls largely superfluous, assuring the visual coherence of the internal functions. This is another example of university architecture where events occur through the merging of different programmes of study. The

Links: Mathias Bachmann – Grundrissstudien für ein Grand Café: Die Überlagerung von Arbeit und Freizeit ist wichtiger Bestandteil moderner Arbeitswelten.
Rechts: The McCormick Tribune Campus Center, IIT Chicago, Rem Koolhaas, OMA — Grundriss.

Left: Mathias Bachmann – Layout studies for a Grand Café: the overlapping of work and leisure time is an important part of modern working worlds.
Right: The McCormick Tribune Campus Center, IIT Chicago, Rem Koolhaas, OMA – Layout.

Höhenunterschiede zwischen diesen versetzten Ebenen weitgehend überflüssig, der visuelle Zusammenhalt aller Funktionen ist gesichert. Ereignisse ergeben sich auch hier aus der Überlagerung unterschiedlicher Programme. Das „Campus Center" vereint den Universitäts-Club, das Commons Building, Aufenthaltsräume, Computerarbeitsplätze, ein Auditorium, Veranstaltungs- und Konferenzräume unter einem Dach.

Öffnung nach innen und außen

Umbauter Raum wird auf diese Weise zu einem verdichteten, räumlich temporär belegbaren System, in dem sich Grenzen auflösen oder nach Bedarf auf eine bestimmte Zeit festgesetzt werden können. Starre Raumstrukturen werden durch eine von den Aktivitäten unterschiedlicher Nutzergruppen gesteuerte Umgebung ersetzt. Die bekannte Dichotomie von „privat" und „öffentlich" wird ersetzt durch eine Polarität zwischen Rückzug (Intimität) und Austausch (Offenheit).

Die beschriebenen Gebäude sind nur Anfangspunkte einer möglichen, vielversprechenden Entwicklung. Insbesondere Architekturfakultäten haben das Potential, neben konkreten Gebäudestrukturen sehr viel weitergehende Visionen für kommunikative Raumgefüge aufzuzeigen. Sie können im Rahmen der universitären Vielfalt und im Zusammenwirken mit dem sie umgebenden Know-how nicht nur zur Entwicklung ganzheitlicher Bildungsmodelle beitragen, sondern vor allem dazu passende Universitätsgebäude entwickeln, die der Entfaltung eines durch Ausbildung freien Individuums dienen.

Die genannten Netzwerkstrukturen beinhalten die schon lange eingeforderte Öffnung unseres Bildungswesens – einen engeren Kontakt mit der nichtuniversitären Öffentlichkeit, mehr Kooperationen mit der Wirtschaft und vor allem die Öffnung[2] für Interessenten aller Altersgruppen und verschiedenster Vorbildung. Sie finden ihren Ausdruck in einer adäquaten räumlichen Umgebung, einer transparenten, offenen Bildungs- und Forschungslandschaft. Dabei ist ein Gebäude nicht nur formaler Ausdruck, sondern integraler und inhaltlicher Bestandteil einer solchen Öffnung nach innen und nach außen. Nur ein ganzheitliches Modell, das neue Bildungsformen im Zusammenhang mit den dazugehörigen räumlichen Gefügen denkt, kann auf Dauer erfolgversprechend sein.

ANMERKUNGEN

(1) Am 19. Juni 1999 verabschiedeten 29 europäische Staaten in Bologna eine gemeinsame Erklärung zur grundsätzlichen Reformierung des europäischen Bildungswesens, die so genannte Bologna-Deklaration. Diese Deklaration basiert auf der Sorbonne-Erklärung aus dem Jahr 1998 und greift deren wichtigste Schlagworte erneut auf, darunter lebenslanges Lernen, Wettbewerbsfähigkeit, Steigerung der Mobilität, Qualitätssicherung, vergleichbare Bewertung der Studienleistungen mit Leistungspunkten, zweistufige und vergleichbare Studienabschlüsse.

(2) Öffnung im Sinne von öffentlichen Diskursen, Angeboten für nicht-studentische Gruppen, neuartigen interaktiven Lehrkonzepten etc.

Campus Center combines the university club, common room, lounges, computer workstations, auditorium, and function and conference rooms under one roof.

Openness to the Outside and to the Inside

The above examples show how interior space becomes a concentrated system that can be spatially and temporarily allocated to a given use, a system in which distinctions can be dissolved or fixed for a certain length of time. Rigid spatial structures are replaced by an environment controlled by the activities of different groups of users. The public-private dichotomy is replaced by a contrast between exchange (openness) and retreat (intimacy).

The buildings described here are only points of departure from one possible and very promising line of thought. Architecture departments have the potential to show many more far-reaching visions of communicative spatial structure, in addition to specific examples of building structures. They could not only contribute towards the development of integrated building models, drawing on the academic diversity and the surrounding expertise, but also develop suitable university buildings that allow for the growth of individuals who are, as a result of their education, capable of free thought.

The network structures referred to above imply the opening up of our educational system, something that has been needed for a long time. This means close contact with members of the public from outside the university, more cooperation with industry, and most importantly openness[2] towards all people, regardless of age and prior education. These structures will find expression in a spatial environment entirely adequate to this purpose, a transparent and open educational and research landscape. A building is not only an expression of form, but also an integral and inclusive component of such openness towards the inside and the outside. Only an integrated model that conceives new educational forms in terms of the associated spatial structures can deliver lasting success.

NOTES

(1) In Bologna on June 19, 1999, 29 European states passed a joint declaration on the fundamental reform of the European educational system. This became known as the Bologna Declaration. It was based on the Sorbonne Declaration from the previous year. It reaffirmed the most important phrases, including life-long learning, competition, increased mobility, quality assurance, equal evaluation of qualifications through a point system, two-tiered degrees, and comparable degree qualifications.

(2) Openness in the sense of public discourse, choice for non-students, innovative interactive teaching concepts etc.

Axel Thallemer

Raumgestalt und Designstrategien in der universitären Lehre für das 21. Jahrhundert

Prolog
Bestandsaufnahme zum gegenwärtigen Status von Architektur und Design - zehn Aspekte

Zünfte als Hüter der Zukunft - weiter so?
Verordnete Bereichsabgrenzungen scheitern, da sie nicht intrinsisch motivieren und somit zur Auflösung der Begrifflichkeiten führen, wobei Worthüllen und Worthülsen hinterlassen werden – *blurring boundaries*. Als Folge können „Architekten als Designer, Formgestalter als Baumeister" auftreten.[1] Dies resultiert ebenso in der Auflösung des Designbegriffs: „Im Designerpark – Leben in künstlichen Welten."[2]

Kammern als Bewahrer der Vergangenheit - weiter so?
Rückwärtsgerichtete Besitzstandswahrung und Vereinsmeierei stehen *disembodiment* und Virtualisierung entgegen. Überadministrierte Selbstverwaltung und Vorschriftenauslegung blockieren die Zukunftsausrichtung. Der Bruch mit der Projektrealität bezüglich der Vertrags- und Auftragsumsetzung ist evident.

Projektpräsentationen TU Berlin, Personen von links nach rechts:
Prof. Kandel, Christina Punzel

Project presentations TU Berlin (Technical University, Berlin), people from left to right:
Prof Kandel, Christina Punzel

"Raumgestalt" and Design Strategies in University Teaching for the 21st Century

Prologue
Taking stock of the current status of architecture and design – ten aspects

Guilds as guardians of the future – more of the same?
Ordered area limitations fail because they do not intrinsically motivate people. Instead they lead to the dissolution of conceptualities, whereby word covers and word containers are left behind, blurring boundaries. Consequently, "architects" can appear "as designers, form shapers as master builders".[1] This also results in the dissolution of the concept design: "In the designer park – life in artificial worlds."[2]

Chambers as guardians of the past – ... still?
Retrogressive preservation of the property status quo and society mania stand contrary to "disembodiment" and virtualization. Over-administered autonomy and interpretation of regulations block orientation towards the future. There is an evident break with project reality as regards realizing contracts and orders.

Projektpräsentationen TU Berlin, Personen von links nach rechts: Stefanie Fuhr, Cornelia Schluricke, Elke Knoess, Wolfgang Grillitsch, Thomas Arnold

Project presentations TU Berlin, people from left to right: Stefanie Fuhr, Cornelia Schluricke, Elke Knoess, Wolfgang Grillitsch, Thomas Arnold

Architektur als schöngeistige Behübschung – weiter so?

Die Architekten Schupp & Kremmer haben mit ihrem Buch „Architekten gegen oder und Ingenieur"[3] den Konflikt Künstler vs. Ingenieur genauso thematisiert wie schon Buonarotti und da Vinci. Auch wenn im Bausektor gegenwärtig nicht mehr viel realisiert werden kann, macht es dennoch wenig Sinn, den Designbegriff über „micro-architecture" (Arbeitstitel von R. Horden an der TU München) vereinnahmen zu wollen – obwohl Design an Fakultäten wie Architektur, Forstwirtschaft oder Schiffsbau häufig untergeordnet wird (so zum Beispiel in Houston/Texas (USA), Zagreb/Kroatien oder Australien). Gestaltschaffender oder Ingenieur sind zwei völlig getrennte Denksysteme, die häufig nicht einmal dialogfähig sind, weil verschiedene Sprachen gesprochen werden.[4] Oder es herrschen tradierte Hegemonialbestrebungen ohne Systemverständnis vor. Als Konsequenz prägen Scheitern bei der Umgebungsgestaltung und Hässlichkeit der so genannten, schlecht kopierten „Moderne" unsere Stadtbilder.

Architektur als Formalismus – weiter so?

Wenn Architektur nicht forschend oder wissenschaftlich arbeitend betrieben wird, dann ist sie eine rein „anwendende" Tätigkeit und somit an einer Fachhochschule besser aufgehoben. (Siehe die Ausbildungssituation in Hamburg, wo die „von Dohnanyi-Kommission" 2003/2004 die universitäre Architekturausbildung – im Gegensatz zum Designstudium – an die Fachhochschulen relegiert hat.) Architektur scheitert bei der Markeninszenierung, lässt sie meist vom Design leisten und gibt diese dann als eigene Wertschöpfung aus. Ursache ist häufig die Unfähigkeit der Architekten, die Sprache der Bauherren zu verstehen, und ihr Hang zur Selbstdarstellung gegenüber dem Auftraggeber. Architekten werden durch ökonomisch und technisch geleitete Bauabsichten und das Hinzuziehen von „bloßen" Ingenieuren auf ihr ureigenes Betätigungsfeld reduziert. Prototypisch ist dabei der Gesprächsverlauf über die Qualität von Sichtbetonoberflächen oder Raumwirkungen bei Architektenbeiträgen in Baubesprechungen.

Fachzeitschriften anstelle gesellschaftlicher Relevanz – weiter so?

Die unprofessionelle Gestaltung weiter Teile der Objektwelt zeigt, dass es sich hier um intellektuelle Elitenbildung ohne Masseneffekt handelt. Die Mehrheit der durch Menschen hergestellten Dinge ist nicht bewusst gestaltet. Singuläre Veröffentlichungen fungieren somit als Übersprungsreaktion anstelle allgegenwärtiger, bewusster Gestaltung. Bis vor kurzem gab ein Verlag für Maurer-, Maler- und Lackiererblätter ein Designmagazin heraus.

Handwerk über Design „aufwerten" – weiter so?

Gutes Handwerk bedarf keiner (neu-)„modischen" Repositionierung. Design ist eine rein intellektuelle Tätigkeit des Problemsuchens und -lösens. Beide stehen völlig gleichwertig neben- und in keiner Konkurrenzsituation zueinander, wenn die Kategorien richtig verstanden sind.

Architecture as aesthetic prettification – more of the same?
With their book *Architects against or and Engineers*[3], the architects Schupp & Kremmer have chosen as a central theme the conflict artist vs. engineer, just like Buonarotti and da Vinci. Even if not much more can be realized currently in the construction sector, it still makes little sense to want to occupy the design term via "micro-architecture" (working title of R. Horden at the TU Munich) – although design at faculties like architecture, forestry or shipbuilding engineering is frequently subordinated (for example in Houston, Texas [USA], Zagreb [Croatia] or Australia). Form creators and engineers have two completely separated ways of thinking, which are frequently not even capable of dialogue, because they speak different languages.[4] Or there is a predominance of dated hegemonic efforts without understanding the system. Consequently, our townscapes are characterized by failure in the designing of our surroundings and the ugliness of so-called "modern architecture" (which is also badly copied).

Architecture as formalism – more of the same?
If architecture is not carried out as research or in a scientific way, then it is a purely 'applicable' activity and thus better-off at a university of applied sciences. (See the education situation in Hamburg, where the Von Dohnanyi Commission in 2003/2004 transferred the architecture education courses from the university to the University of Applied Sciences, in contrast to Design Studies.) Architecture fails to orchestrate its brand, mostly borrowing from design and then passing it off as its own added value. Frequently, the cause is architects' inability to understand the language of developers, and their tendency towards self-promotion towards the clients. Architects are led by economic and technical building intentions and reduced to consulting "just" engineers in their very own field of activity. Prototypical in this is the discussion about the quality of exposed concrete surfaces or the spatial effects with architects' contributions at conferences.

Professional journals instead of social relevance – more of the same?
The unprofessional shaping of further parts of the object world shows that here it is a matter of intellectual elite formation without a mass effect. The majority of things created by people are not consciously shaped. Therefore, singular publications function as substitute reaction instead of omnipresent conscious shaping. Until recently, a publishing house for bricklayers', painters' and varnishers' papers published a design magazine.

'Upgrade' crafts above design – more of the same?
Good crafts do not need any (new) "fashionable" repositioning. Design is a purely intellectual activity of searching for a problem and solving it. Both stand alongside each other completely equal and not in competition with each other, if the categories are properly understood.

Design als Tagklinik für Werber – weiter so?
Rein phänomenologische oder formale Entsprechungen, oberflächliches Vorlagewesen statt Innovation und Forschung. Metaphorische oder allegorische Formgebung der Hüllen und Packungen.

Design als Freudenhaus fürs Marketing – weiter so?
Bürokratische Formverwaltung mit dem Ziel der Förderung des Produktabverkaufs ohne Fortschritt. Noch mehr Gegenstände, die keiner wirklich braucht. Verschwendung von Personalressourcen, Energie und Material. Design ohne Innovationen wird als Differenzierungsmerkmal im globalen Verdrängungswettbewerb bei vergleichbaren Funktionalitäten, weltweit harmonisierter Rohstoff- und Dienstleistungsbeschaffung und identischen Produktionsprozessen missbraucht, wenn alternative Preisstellungen nicht möglich oder gewünscht sind.

Design als Frischzellenkur für Entwicklungsabteilungen – weiter so?
Ingenieurausbildung als linear-isotropes Denksystem im Gedankengebäude des 19. Jahrhunderts. Technik vs. Technologie, Schrauber (oder reziprok Schraubenschüttler) vs. (verächtliche) Einschätzung des Designers als „Künstler", der allenfalls noch den Farbton bestimmt. Technikorientierung statt humanistischer Bildung lässt kulturelle Werte zunehmend wichtiger erscheinen. Ein scheidender DaimlerChrysler-Vorstand schlug jüngst – wohl süffisant – in einem Interview ein „Kunststudium" für angehende Vorstände vor.

Wettstreit Architekt vs. Designer, randständige Ingenieure – weiter so?
Geistige Verarmung in der Industrialisierung fördert utilitaristische Verblödung der Gesellschaft, die resultierende, rein teleologische Ausrichtung des Lebens schafft keine kulturellen Werte. Man vergleiche nur die Inhalte privater oder öffentlicher Sendeanstalten mit der zunehmend perfektionierten Bildwiedergabetechnik, die hohlen Markenmythen mit dem essentiellen Kern, den Wissensanwender mit dem Wissenschaffenden. Es besteht ein fachliches und geisteswissenschaftliches Dilemma in der jeweils einschlägigen Ausbildung. Die Kausalkette Abkunft – Bekanntschaft – Vermögen (pekuniäres, nicht fachliches Können!) steht als Hauptlast(er) der Innovierung des Wirtschaftsstandorts Deutschland und der Leistungsfairness entgegen. Kleine und mittelständische Unternehmen vs. persönliche Leistung und individuelle Fähigkeiten polarisieren im Kontext der post-industriellen Gesellschaft. Die Konvention eines konsekutiven Zeitbegriffs wie „Millennium" vs. Parallelität der Stile Bauhaus, International Style, Ulmer Schule lassen geographische Mobilität nur noch sinnvoll erscheinen, wenn lokale kulturelle Werte sichtbar und nachvollziehbar bleiben.

Berufsbild im Wandel
Mit multidisziplinären Wissensansätzen und deren Interdependenzen steht Gestaltung heute am Scheideweg zwischen oberflächlicher Behübschung und technologisch-wissenschaftlicher Innovation. Das Gestaltschaffen, wie es vielleicht zukünftig gelehrt wird, konzentriert sich auf heuristische Inspirationen aus der Natur, virtuelle Modellbildung und iterative Optimierung sowie empirische Verifikation der Gestaltfindungen.

Design as day clinic for canvassers – more of the same?
Emphasis is placed on pure phenomenological or formal equivalents, the surface nature of presentation instead of innovation and research along with metaphorical or allegoric design of covers and packaging.

Design as a house of pleasure for marketing – more of the same?
There is bureaucratic administration of forms with the goal of supporting the sale of the product without progress. Even more objects that no one really needs. Personnel resources, energy and material are wasted. Design without innovations is abused as a characteristic for differentiating in the global competition for markets with comparable functionalities, worldwide harmonized acquisition of raw materials and services and identical production processes, where alternative prices are not possible or desired.

Design as Niehans' therapy for development departments – more of the same?
Engineers are trained in a linear-isotropic system of thought in the edifice of ideas from the 19th Century. It is technique vs. technology, mechanic (or reciprocal "screw shakers") vs. (scornful) assessment of the designer as "artist," who, if need be, still determines the colour shade. Increasingly, orientation towards technique instead of humanistic education lets cultural values seem more important. In an interview, a retiring DaimlerChrysler board member recently proposed – probably smugly – an "arts studies" for prospective board members.

Architect vs. designer competition, marginal engineers – more of the same?
Intellectual impoverishment in industrialization promotes utilitarian stupefaction of society. The resulting purely teleological alignment of life creates no cultural values. Just compare the contents of private or public broadcasting institutions vs. increasingly perfected picture reproduction technology, empty brand myths vs. constitutive core, knowledge user vs. knowledge creator. There is a professional and arts dilemma in the respectively appropriate training. The causal chain origin — acquaintance — wealth (pecuniary, not professional ability!) stands as main load(s) contrary to the innovation of the German economy and performance fairness. The conflict between small and medium-sized companies vs. personal performance and individual skills polarises in the context of the post-industrial society. The convention of a consecutive conception of time, like "millennium", vs. parallelism of the Bauhaus Styles, International Style, Ulm School make geographical mobility just seem sensible if local cultural values remain visible and comprehensible.

Job outline in change
Today, with multidisciplinary scientific approaches and their interdependences, shaping stands at a crossroads between superficial prettification and technological-scientific innovation. Form creation, as it might in future be taught, concentrates on heuristic inspirations from nature, virtual model formation and iterative optimization along with empirical verification of the form finding. Basic

Den Kern der neuen Gestaltungsauffassung bilden Grundlagenforschung und eine (natur-)wissenschaftliche Herangehensweise. In Projekten werden dabei Grundlagen erarbeitet, aus denen reale Anwendungen abgeleitet werden können – aber nicht müssen. In der Berufspraxis kann diese hermeneutische Vorgehensweise zur Entwicklung von industriellen Produkten und deren Programmen bis hin zu ganzen Systemen dienen; gleichermaßen können kleine und mittelständische Betriebe an Gestaltung herangeführt werden, die hier zum Wettbewerbsvorteil bei an sich technisch oder funktional vergleichbaren Produkten und Komponenten im globalen Verdrängungswettbewerb wird. Im Fokus der Tätigkeit steht die schöpferische Intuition – basierend auf Erfahrung, Wissen und Können –, daraus abgeleitet die strategische Konzeption, gefolgt vom Entwurf und dem Training im Neuheitenentwicklungsprozess.

Erst im Zusammenwirken ästhetischer, technologischer, wirtschaftlicher und psychologischer Faktoren formt sich das, was hier unter Gestalt zu verstehen ist. In Abgrenzung dieser Auffassung von den mittlerweile häufig schon negativ besetzten Begriffen „Architektur" oder „Design" wird dafür der Begriff „Gestalt" propagiert. „Gestalt" bezieht sich auf die fundamentale Wissensdatenbank der Natur, auf Erkenntnistheorie und Wahrnehmungspsychologie (vgl. Carl Gustav Jung) ebenso wie auf Zeichen im Sinne von Syntax, Semantik und Semiotik.

Unter Berücksichtigung der vorgenannten Aspekte und Faktoren ist es das Ziel des so verstandenen Gestaltschaffens, im Kontext der gesellschaftlichen Normen und Konventionen „Zeichen" zu kreieren. Diese können zwei- oder dreidimensional sein, virtuell oder real; sie führen Erscheinungsbilder industrieller Produkte, deren Programme und Systeme zu einer eigenständigen, zielgerichteten ästhetischen Gestalt. Drei Wissensbereiche bilden die synergetische Plattform der integrierten Gestaltungsausbildung: Bionik, Computeranwendung und Materialtechnologie.

Die potentiell mögliche Leistung für den jeweiligen Auftraggeber ist eine Produkt- und Unternehmensdifferenzierung gegenüber den Mitbewerbern, die sich nicht allein auf das Styling beschränkt. Somit erfolgt eine charakteristischere, deutlichere Kennzeichnung der Produkteigenschaften und Produktleistungen durch Funktions-, Material- und Fertigungsinnovationen. Das Ergebnis ist eine nicht nur gestalterisch prägnante Positionierung am globalen Markt, sondern eine dementsprechend tiefere Profilierung der Identitäten von Unternehmen sowie deren strategische Planung und Steuerung im Prozess als Innovationsmanagement.

Mögliche Rahmenbedingungen für einen Gestaltstudiengang

Die Absolventen eines Gestaltstudiengangs für Architektur oder Design sind derart trainiert, dass sie das Zusammenwirken der ästhetischen, wissenschaftlichen, technologischen, wirtschaftlichen und psychologischen Aspekte und Faktoren im multidisziplinären, kooperativen Produktneuheiten-Entwicklungsprozess berücksichtigen und innerhalb der geschlossenen, virtuellen Prozesskette auch selbständig umsetzen können. Dabei wird dem angehenden Gestaltschaffenden für die Erfüllung seiner zukünftigen Aufgaben ein Komplex relevanten Wissens verschiedener naturwissenschaftlicher Disziplinen und Fachgebiete angeboten.

Inhalte des ersten Studienabschnitts sind das Erlernen dieses Wissens sowie der theoretischen Grundlagen, die Analyse der möglichen Inspirationen aus

research and a (natural) scientific approach form the core of the new concept of shaping. Fundamentals will be worked out there in projects, from which real applications can be derived — but don't have to be. In professional practice, this hermeneutical approach can help us in developing industrial products and their programmes right up to whole systems. Similarly, small and medium-sized companies can be brought to shaping, which here provides a competitive advantage in the global competition for markets with products and components that are technically or functionally comparable in themselves. Creative intuition, based on experience, knowledge and ability, stands at the focus of the activity. The strategic conception is derived from this, followed by the draft and training in the development process of the novelty.

That which we understand as shaping first forms in the interaction of aesthetic, technological, economic and psychological factors. The term "shaping" is propagated for this in order to differentiate this view from architecture or design, terms that in the meantime are already frequently negatively filled. Shaping refers to the fundamental knowledge database of nature, to epistemology and psychology of perception (cf. Carl Gustav Jung), just as to signs in the sense of syntax, semantics and semiotics.

Considering the aforementioned aspects and factors, it is the target of the thusly understood form-shaping, to create signs in the context of the social norms and conventions. These can be two- or three-dimensional, virtual or real. They lead pheotypes of industrial products, their programmes and systems to an independent, purposeful aesthetic shaping. Three fields of knowledge form the synergetic platforms of the integrated education for shaping: bionics, computer application and material technology.

The potential possible performance for the respective client is a differentiation of product and company compared with the competitors who do not limit themselves to styling alone. A more characteristic, clearer identification of the product properties and product achievements is therefore carried out through innovations in function, materials and manufacturing. The result is a positioning in the global market that is not just structurally concise but an appropriately deeper image of the identities of companies together with their strategic planning and steering in the process as innovation management.

Possible framework conditions/requirements for a new shaping course of studies
The graduates of a course of studies in shaping for architecture or design are trained so that they can consider the interaction of the aesthetic, scientific, technological, economic and psychological aspects and factors in a multidisciplinary, cooperative development process for new products and also to implement it independently within the closed virtual process chain. Here, the prospective form creators are offered a complex relevant knowledge of diverse scientific disciplines and branches for fulfilling their future tasks.

The contents of the first studies section consist of learning this knowledge together with the theoretical basis, the analysis of possible inspirations from nature, constructing strategies for solving morphological problems and knowledge

der Natur, der Aufbau morphologischer Problemlösungsstrategien und ein Wissenserwerb mit den Schwerpunkten Oberflächen-, Material- und Fertigungstechnologien. Die Vermittlung von CAD-Kenntnissen und Rapid-Prototyping-Verfahren ist grundlegend in die Lehre integriert.

Der zweite Studienabschnitt konzentriert sich auf die Anwendung dieser wissenschaftlichen Werkzeuge im forschenden Kontext. Selbstgewählte oder -gestellte Projekte werden mit einem ganzheitlichen Innovationsansatz bearbeitet und für jedes Semester schriftlich aufbereitet. Dadurch erfährt eine zu gründende Material- und Fertigungstechnologie-Datenbank innovativen Input. Die virtuelle Gestaltprozesskette wird für das jeweilige Projekt geschlossen und „meilensteinbezogen" durchlaufen und als Datensatz dokumentiert. Die Forschungsansätze aus der Natur werden in morphologische Kästen strukturiert; ihr Problemlösungspotential wird bezüglich der intendierten Anwendung quantifiziert. Die erzielten Verbesserungen der jeweiligen Produktfunktionen oder Eigenschaften werden im Labor gemessen, so dass sich eine kontinuierliche Optimierung sicherstellen lässt. Auch diese Erkenntnisse werden dokumentiert und in eine spezielle Datenbank eingepflegt, so dass für Veröffentlichungen darauf zugegriffen werden kann.

Ziele des Lehrens und Lernens

Zielsetzung ist, die Studierenden auf die oben beschriebenen Anforderungen künftiger Tätigkeiten bestmöglich vorzubereiten und sie zu befähigen, den Bedarf von Wirtschaft/Industrie und Gesellschaft an Gestalt zu erfüllen. Außerdem gilt es, das ingenieurwissenschaftliche sowie künstlerisch-ästhetische Potential für innovative Entwicklungen und Gestaltungen zu fördern.

Die Ausbildung soll einerseits ästhetisches, wirtschaftliches, technisches und soziales Wissen vermitteln und dieses in seinen Entstehungs- und Wirkungszusammenhängen erkennbar machen. Andererseits soll sie den Studierenden dazu befähigen, mit komplexen Denkansätzen und Arbeitsmethoden umzugehen. Die Ausbildung soll insbesondere bei Entwurfs- und Gestaltungsstudien die Schwerpunktinteressen sowie Begabungen der einzelnen Studierenden individuell berücksichtigen und fördern. Zentraler Ansatz ist ein methoden- und fachintegriertes sowie fächerübergreifendes Lehren und Lernen. Dabei sind Fächerverbindungen und Kooperationen zwischen Lehrenden ausdrücklich erwünscht.

Durch die Vermittlung und Integration von Methoden der eigenständigen Organisationsgestaltung wie auch der Selbststeuerung soll bereits im Studium die Fähigkeit zu klarer Zieldefinition, Zeitplanung sowie Teamarbeit entwickelt werden. Dem Vermitteln und Präzisieren von Arbeitsaufgaben und -methoden sowie der Präsentation von Arbeitsergebnissen und Gestaltkonzepten wird besondere Beachtung beigemessen. Um eine Schwerpunktsetzung der persönlichen Studiengestaltung zu erleichtern, wird die Einbeziehung von Tutoren als ständig begleitende Berater nachhaltig gefördert.

Epilog

Gegenwärtig praktizieren wohl 112.000 Architekten in Deutschland, beinahe ebenso viele wie in sämtlichen Nachbarstaaten Deutschlands zusammen.[5] In China beträgt die

acquisition with the main fields surface technology, materials technology and manufacturing technology. The conveying of CAD knowledge and rapid prototyping procedure is fundamentally integrated into the teaching.

The second studies section concentrates on applying these scientific tools in a research context. Self-chosen or set projects are handled with an integral innovation approach and prepared in writing each term. In the process the experience in underlying materials and manufacturing technology database receives innovative input. The virtual shaping process chain is closed for the respective project and run through in relation to milestones and documented as a database. The research approaches from nature are structured in morphological cases; their problem-solving potential is quantified as regards the intended application. The improvements achieved for the respective product functions or properties are measured in a laboratory, so that continuous optimization can be established. These findings are also documented and worked into a special database, so that it can be accessed for publications.

Targets of teaching and learning

The target is to prepare the students for the requirements of future activities described above in the best possible way and to enable them to fulfil the requirements of business/industry and society for shaping. In addition, it is also necessary to support the engineering-scientific and artistic-aesthetic potential for innovative developments and shaping.

The education should, on the one hand, impart aesthetic, economic, technical and social knowledge and make this recognizable in the connections of its origin and effects. On the other hand, it should enable the students to cope with complex intellectual approaches and methods of working. The education should particularly individually take into account and support the main focus and talents of the individual students with studies of drafts and shaping. The main approach is a form of teaching and learning that is method-integrated, subject-integrated and interdisciplinary. Here, links between subjects and cooperation between teaching staff are expressly welcome.

Already during the studies, the ability to define a clear target and plan time, along with working in a team, should be developed through the imparting and integration of methods of independent organization-shaping along with self-regulation. Special attention is attached to imparting and specifying working tasks and methods along with presenting the results of the work and shaping concepts. Tutors are included as permanent accompanying advisors. This is strongly supported in order to make it easier for students to focus when organizing their personal studies.

Epilogue

Some 112,000 architects currently practise in Germany, almost as many as in all its neighbouring states combined.[5] In China, the annual number of graduates just from state training institutions is at least 21,000 designers. In Taiwan there are around 3,000 each year. The same is true for South Korea.[6] If these graduates have the appropriate foreign-language skills, then they compete with architects in Europe. The glob-

jährliche Absolventenzahl allein von staatlichen Ausbildungsinstitutionen mindestens 21.000 Designer. In Taiwan sind es pro anno etwa 3000; gleiches gilt für Südkorea.[6] Haben diese Studienabgänger entsprechende Fremdsprachenkenntnisse, treten sie in Konkurrenz zu Architekten in Europa. Die global steigenden Designabsolventenzahlen lassen ein neues "studium generale" vermuten, das jedoch stark „modisch" im Sinne von Styling und „hübsch machen" orientiert ist. Die Bundesländer stellen ihre föderalen Bildungskonzepte heute wohl noch nicht ausreichend in Frage – auch in Bezug darauf, ob eine ausgeglichene Relation zwischen betriebswirtschaftlichem Bedarf an Absolventen und tatsächlicher Abgängerzahl vorliegt. Bei sinkenden staatlichen Ressourcen für Ausbildung muss kritisch geprüft werden, ob diese volkswirtschaftlich noch gut investiert sind, und zwar unabhängig davon, welche Güte die Ausbildung hat. Für einen Innovationsstandort ist der Bildungsfortschritt innerhalb der Gesellschaft im internationalen Kontext von zentraler Bedeutung.

Daher soll angeregt werden, mit einer nicht auf Wachstum ausgerichteten Wirtschaftsform zu reüssieren, nachdem auch die Bautätigkeit ohne zerstörerische Einflüsse abnehmen wird und Produkte im ökonomischen Kreislauf einer Überflussgesellschaft immer weniger die Hauptrolle spielen werden. Vielleicht kommt da der Virtualisierung in Form von Wissen eine Schlüsselrolle zu? Nicht mehr der Kaufakt, der zu einem materiellen Objektbesitz führt, wäre dann gesellschaftlich wertbildend, sondern der Status würde sich eher an kommunizierbaren Erfahrungen und am individuell zuzuordnenden Wissen orientieren. Dabei rücken nicht oder nur schwer messbare Qualitätsmerkmale gegenüber rein technischen Daten in den Vordergrund, ebenso wie mangelnder Quantifizierbarkeit von Einflüssen als weichen Faktoren gegenüber der bisherigen „mechanischen" Herangehensweise der Vorzug gegeben wird. Möglicherweise ließe sich der Übergang vom Produktions- zum Know-how-Standort sanfter realisieren, wenn bereits in der einschlägigen Ausbildung – vor allem der Ingenieure – mehr als die Ansätze des frühindustriellen 19. Jahrhunderts gelehrt würde.

ANMERKUNGEN
(1) Vgl. „Wettstreit der Gestalter", Evangelische Akademie Tutzing, 03.–05. Dezember 2004
(2) Vgl. das Buch zur gleichnamigen Ausstellung vom 14.11.2004–20.02.2005, Institut Mathildenhöhe Darmstadt
(3) Berlin, 1929
(4) Vgl. Reese, Jens: *Der Ingenieur und seine Designer*. Berlin/Heidelberg/New York 2005
(5) Laut Aussage des Ordinarius für Architektur, Technische Universität München, am 24. Oktober 2005, anlässlich eines Symposiums über die Zukunft der „Designausbildung" im BMW Forschungszentrum
(6) Äußerungen der jeweiligen Fachreferenten der Außenhandels- und Wirtschaftsministerien der entsprechenden Nationen, jährliche Zahlen seit 1999

ally increasing numbers of design graduates suggest a new general course of studies that is however oriented to being highly 'stylish' in the meaning of styling and 'making oneself pretty'. Today, the federal states in Germany do not yet adequately question their federal educational concepts, particularly regarding a balanced relation between economic need for graduates and the actual number of people completing their education. State resources for education are sinking so they must be critically assessed to see whether these are still being soundly invested economically. This must be independent of the quality the training has. Educational progress within society is vital in an international context for an innovation location.

For this reason, we should advocate succeeding through an economic system not geared towards growth — after building activity without destructive influences also decreases and products in economic circulation decreasingly play the main roles in the affluent society. Maybe virtualization in the form of knowledge will receive a key role here? Maybe the act of buying that leads to a material possession of an object would no longer be socially value-shaping, but the status would orient more towards communicable experiences and to individually attributable knowledge. Here it is quality characteristics that cannot be measured, or which are very difficult, that move into the foreground as opposed to purely technical data, just as the lack of quantifiable influences as soft factors is preferred over the hitherto 'mechanic' approach. Possibly, the transition from production to a know-how location could be more gently realized, if more would already be taught in the appropriate education – above all that of the engineers – than just approaches from the early industrial 19th Century.

NOTES
(1) Cf. "Wettstreit der Gestalter", Evangelische Akademie Tutzing, 3–5 December 2004.
(2) Cf. book to exhibition with the same name, 14 November 2004 - 20 February 2005, Institut Mathildenhöhe Darmstadt.
(3) Berlin, 1929.
(4) Cf. Reese, Jens *Der Ingenieur und seine Designer*, Berlin, Heidelberg, New York, 2005.
(5) According to a statement from the Professor for Architecture, TU Munich on 24 October 2005, on the occasion of a symposium about the future of design training in the BMW Research Centre.
(6) Remarks from the respective experts of the Ministries of Foreign Trade and Trade & Commerce of the corresponding countries, annual figures since 1999.

Andrew Holmes

Nachrichten und Arrangements

"Lauf wie ein Hund. Spüre die Dinge auf. Behalte alles im Auge."
"Visionen entstehen aus dem, was man kennt."

Man wird eine Expedition starten, um nach einer Welt zu suchen, die um uns herum, aber doch unerkannt ist. Alles, was den Teilnehmern zur Verfügung stehen wird, ist die Fähigkeit, konträre Ideen und unterschiedliche Materialien wie Jonglierbälle durch die Luft zu wirbeln, um so jenen schmalen Grat zwischen abgehoben und bodenständig begehen zu lernen. Am Ziel finden sie jene Welt, in der Kunst aus allen Ritzen quillt, aber die Rohrleitungen das Neuste vom Neuen sind.

Der neue Architekturstudent muss nahtlos übergehen können vom Sehen und unmittelbaren Erfahren in Originalgröße zum Vermögen, sich eine neue Realität vorzustellen und diese in einem veränderten Maßstab anderen zu kommunizieren.

„Das Lernen, der Bildungsvorgang ist lange als etwas Verdrießliches betrachtet worden. Wir sprechen vom ‚ernsthaften' Studenten. Unsere Zeit bietet die einmalige Möglichkeit, mittels Humor zu lernen: Ein scharfsinniger Witz kann belangvoller sein als Platitüden zwischen zwei Buchdeckeln." [1]

Neue Studenten kommen an die Architekturschule aus eigenem Antrieb und, weil sie zum ersten Mal in ihrem Leben arbeiten möchten. Englische Architekturschulen sind Teil der Kunstschulen und stehen nicht in der Tradition der Ingenieurausbildung. Im Gegensatz zum Künstler entwirft der Architekt im Allgemeinen ziemlich große, drei-

Studienanfänger Wintersemester 2002 „Kragarm"
Aus Sperrmüll werden im Wettstreit vierer Gruppen Kragarme gebaut, die etwa 6 m überspannen müssen.

Freshmen, WiSe 2002/03 "Cantilever"
In a competition for groups of four, cantilevers are built out of second-hand furniture. They have to span approx. 6 m.

Messages and Arrangements

"Walk like a dog. Sniff things out. Keep on looking."
"Vision is made up of what you know."

An expedition will be mounted to search for a world that is all around but unrecognised. The party will be equipped with little more than an ability to juggle with disparate ideas and different materials, in an attempt to slip into the gap between the sophisticated and the primitive. Beyond is the realm where art seeps through cracks in the walls but where the plumbing is as modern as can be.

The new student of architecture must go from seeing and experiencing directly at full size to being able to imagine a new reality and communicating it at a different scale to someone else.

"Learning, the educational process, has long been associated only with the glum. We speak of the serious student. Our time represents a unique opportunity for learning by means of humour – a perceptive or incisive joke can be more meaningful than platitudes lying between two covers." [1]

First-year students arrive at an architecture school, choosing and wanting of their own accord to work for the first time in their lives. English architecture schools are considered part of the art rather than the engineering tradition. Unlike the artist, the architect generally designs relatively large 3-D objects that are prototypes. Architects tend to use 2-D methods to represent this process to a

dimensionale Objekte, die als Prototypen dienen. Architekten neigen dazu, zweidimensionale Methoden zu verwenden, um diesen Prozess anderen sowie sich selbst darzustellen. Architekten sind beherrscht von der Frage des Maßstabs. Sie nehmen für sich in Anspruch, dass sie alleine dieses System verstehen. Originalgröße versteht jeder.

„Wissen beginnt mit dem Bewusstsein dafür, wie trügerisch unsere normalen Wahrnehmungen sein können." [2]

Mit dem Bewusstsein für Zeit, das von den Naturwissenschaften geschärft wurde, messen die Menschen den Erfolg ihres Lebens an ihrem körperlichen und emotionalen Wohlbefinden. Die letzte Autorität für das universal Gute fand seinen Ausdruck im rechtwinkligen Raster, im stabilen Stahl- oder Betonskelett. In diesem System kam dem Rand größte Bedeutung zu. Das Medium Ingenieurzeichnung, Tuschelinien

Michael Reiß und Torsten Meißner "Lichtmodell" Transfer I, WS 2002/03
Konzeptmodelle werden so gebaut, dass sie mit Licht reagieren oder selbst leuchten. Im Dunkeln photographiert werden sie zu dynamischen Räumen transformiert.

Michael Reiß and Torsten Meißner "Light model", Transfer I, WiSe 2002/03
Concept models are built in such a way that they react with light or are self-illuminating. They are photographed in the dark and transform into dynamic rooms.

auf Papier, war das Ausdrucksmittel schlechthin.

„Wir sind uns heute der Möglichkeit bewußt geworden, die gesamte menschliche Umwelt zum Kunstwerk zu gestalten, zu einer Lernmaschine, deren Zweck es ist, unsere Wahrnehmung auf ein Höchstmaß zu steigern und das alltägliche Lernen in einen Entdeckungsvorgang zu verwandeln. Auf die Praxis angewendet, käme dies einem Thermostaten gleich, der die Raumtemperatur kontrolliert. Es entspräche einem Gebot der Vernunft, Kontrollen solcher Art auf alle Bewußtseinsebenen unseres Sinnendaseins auszuweiten. Wir haben keinen Grund, jenen dankbar zu sein, die um einer zufälligen Erfindung willen mit unseren Bewußtseinsschwellen herumjonglieren." [3]

Die Elemente, die das Denken der Moderne vor die Türe verwiesen haben, könnten wieder eingeführt werden. Die Elemente, die Gefühle hervorrufen: Luft, Wasser, Wärme, Klang, Geruch und Licht würden zu Themen der Architektur, die Elemente, die die Architekten beeinflussen, und nicht die eher nebulösen, abstrakten Ideen von Raum. Die Oberfläche wäre wichtiger als die Rahmenkonstruktion. Die Materialien für die Außenhüllen wären weich, beweglich, transluzent. Es sind immer noch ganz normale Stoffe, die aber neu zusammengefügt werden. Solche Materialien benötigen andere Techniken. Heute zeichnet der Planer mit Licht, nicht mit Tusche, auf einem

variety of people including themselves. Architects are obsessed with scale. They alone claim to understand it. Full size is something everybody understands.

"Knowing begins with the awareness of the deceptiveness of our common sense perceptions." (2)

With the awareness of time created by the sciences people now measure the success of their lives by their emotional and physical well-being. The authority of universal good found expression in the rectilinear grid, in the rigid steel or concrete frame. In this system the edge was all-important. The medium of the engineer's drawing, ink line on paper, was the means of expression.

"We have now become aware of the possibility of arranging the entire human environment into a work of art, as a teaching machine designed to maximize percep-

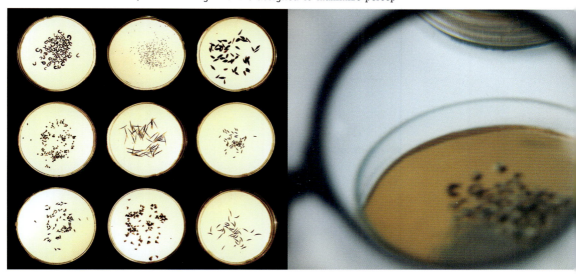

tion and make everyday learning a process of discovery. Application of this knowledge would be the equivalent of a thermostat controlling room temperature. It would seem only reasonable to extend such controls to all the sensory thresholds of our being. We have no reason to be grateful to those who juggle these thresholds in the name of haphazard innovation." (3)

The elements evicted from modernist thinking might be reintroduced. The elements that induce feeling: air, water, heat, sound, smell and light would become the subjects of architecture, the elements that architects control, rather than the more nebulous and abstract idea of space. Emphasis would be placed on the surface rather than the frame. Materials of enclosures would be soft, moving, translucent. It is still ordinary matter put together in new ways. Such materials require different techniques. The designer now draws with light, not ink, on an electronic machine that utilizes time in its programmes.

"All manner of different considerations influence an architect's decisions, the chief of which will always be the probable activities of those people who will enjoy the weather in the space." (4)

Isabell Weiland "Möglicher Blumenstrauß", Transfer I, WiSe 2002/03
Die Schönheit des Blumenstraußes findet sich im Samen wieder. Man kann sich verschiedene Blumensamen zusammenstellen und erhält so einen möglichen Strauß.

Isabell Weiland, "Possible Bunch of Flowers", Transfer I, WiSe 2002/03. The beauty of a bunch of flowers is rediscovered in the seed. You can arrange different flower seeds together, thus creating a possible bunch.

elektronischen Gerät, in dessen Programmen der Faktor Zeit eine Rolle spielt.

„Viele verschiedene Überlegungen beeinflussen die Entscheidungen eines Architekten, die Wichtigste davon dreht sich dabei immer um die möglichen Aktivitäten der Menschen, die das Klima in dem Raum genießen werden." [4]

Ein gängiges Element, das alle diese Dinge, die wir Architektur nennen, verbindet, ist die Verpflichtung zu konstruktiver Logik, zu der häufig Innovation im Bereich der Techniken und/oder Materialien gehört. Die Konstruktion ist das Skelett, das die Grundform des Dings schafft. Die Giraffe sieht nicht aus wie ein Fuchs, aber sie bestehen aus den gleichen Materialien.

Zu jeder Architektur gehört Konstruktion. Ein Großteil der Konstruktionslehre wird verschleiert von Geheimniskrämerei, verdunkelt von langen Kursen, die anschei-

Lisa Theobald "Sounddusche" Transfer I, WS 2002/03
Ein portabler Raum ist mit verschiedenen geschalteten Lautsprechern versehen, die eine mobile Klanglandschaft erzeugen.

Lisa Theobald "Sound Shower", Transfer I, WiSe 2002/03
A portable room is equipped with loud-speakers set at different volumes that create a mobile soundscape.

nend das Verständnis dafür unnötig schwer machen sollen. Als Kommentar zu der Aussage, alles Wissenswerte über Konstruktion könne man in vierzig Minuten lernen, meinte Ron Herron, dass Konrad Wachsmann zehn Minuten dafür für ausreichend hielt.

„Theater ereignet sich allezeit, wo immer man ist. Und die Kunst erleichtert es einfach, uns zu überzeugen, daß dies der Fall ist." [5]

Die Einbindung des Einzelnen in die Gesellschaft hat sich gewandelt, entkolonisiert. Man hält das Leben für kurz. Eine Erfahrungsvielfalt gilt mehr als Konsistenz. Empfindungen, Gefühle hält man für ebenso wichtig wie Gedanken. Bauen sollte ein abenteuerlicher Aufbruch in die gesellschaftlichen Möglichkeiten der Zukunft sein, kein Rückspiegel mit Blick in die Vergangenheit. Alles kann über das Medium Spiel verstanden werden. Jedes Material kann von der Architektur genutzt werden. Alle technischen Probleme sind auch ästhetische Probleme.

Auf der Suche nach dem Erhabenen im alltäglichen Leben muss der Reisende immer in der Gegenwart leben, das Wählen als eine Kunstform einsetzen, die wesentlichen Dinge auf nicht lineare Weise herausfiltern, damit man auftretende Probleme in Möglichkeiten und Chancen wandelt.

A common element, connecting all those things we consider architecture, is a commitment to structural logic, often involving innovation at a level of technique and/or materials. The structure is the skeleton that provides the underlying form of the object. The giraffe does not look like the fox, yet they are made of the same materials.

All architecture involves structure. Much teaching of structure is shrouded in secrecy, obscured by long courses, seemingly devised to make an understanding of it unnecessarily difficult to achieve. When faced with the assertion that all that one needs to know about structures can be taught in forty minutes, Ron Herron replied by citing Konrad Wachsmann's claim that 10 minutes was quite sufficient.

"Theatre takes place all the time; wherever one is, and art simply facilitates persuading one this is the case." [5]

The individual's involvement in society has changed, been decolonised. Life is viewed as short. Variety of experience is valued above consistency. The senses, the feelings are considered as important as thought.

Building should be an adventure into the social possibilities of the future, not a rear-view mirror to the past. Everything can be understood through play. Any material can be the subject of architecture. All technical problems are aesthetic ones. In the search for the sublime in everyday life, the voyager must always exist in the present, deploying choice as an art form, sifting the evidence in a non-linear way, so that the problems encountered are turned into possibilities and capabilities.

"Rearranged working methods. Our time is a time for crossing barriers, for erasing old categories – for probing around. When two seemingly disparate elements are imaginatively poised, put in apposition in new and unique ways, startling discoveries often result" [6]

The young architect needs to communicate ideas and intentions in the most suitable way. To the traditional orthogonal drawing may be added other techniques that use time-based media. The most suitable means of expression are those

Felix Sommerlad "Wobbeling Vibes", Transfer II, SS 2003
Der Raum verändert sein Volumen und seine Form abhängig von der Musik durch expandierende pneumatische Elemente.

Felix Sommerlad, "Wobbling Vibes", Transfer II, SoSe 2003
The space changes its volume and form depending on the music, through expanding pneumatic elements.

"Neu arrangierte Arbeitsmethoden. Unsere Zeit ist eine Zeit, in der es gilt, Schranken niederzureißen, mit alten Kategorien aufzuräumen – nach allen Seiten zu sondieren. Wenn zwei scheinbar unvereinbare Elemente auf phantasievolle Art gegenübergestellt oder auf neue und einzigartige Weise kombiniert werden, ergeben sich oft überraschende Entdeckungen." [6]

Der junge Architekt muss seine Ideen und Ansätze auf die am besten geeignete Weise vermitteln. Zur traditionellen Zeichnung mit ihren geraden Linien könnten andere Techniken hinzukommen, die mit zeitgenössischen Medien erstellt wurden. Die am besten geeigneten Ausdrucksmittel sind die der Filmindustrie, des Modellbaus, der Animationstechniken und der Verbundstoffe, bei denen immer der Übergang wichtig ist und nicht das Feste. Das Wissen ist ein Spezialwissen, das man langsam erwirbt und das am besten auf einen Entwurf angewandt wird, von dem der Student voll und ganz überzeugt ist.

W.: Aller Anfang ist schwer.
E.: Ist doch gleich, womit wir anfangen.
W.: Ja, aber wir müssen uns entscheiden.
E.: Eben. [7]

ANMERKUNGEN
[1] Marshall McLuhan: *The Medium is the Message*, Penguin Books 1967, Seite 10
[2] Ebenda, Seite 36
[3] Ebenda, Seite 68
[4] David Pye: *The Nature of Design*, Studio Vista 1964, Seite 91
[5] John Cage zitiert in: *The Medium is the Message*, Penguin Books 1967, Seite 119
[6] Marshall McLuhan: *The Medium is the Message*, Penguin Books 1967, Seite 87
[7] Samuel Beckett, *Waiting for Godot*, Faber and Faber 1956, Seite 24

of the movie industry; models, animations and composites, in which the stock in trade is transition rather than fixity. The knowledge is specialized, acquired slowly and best applied to a design that the student is committed to.

W.: It's the start that's difficult.
E.: You can start from anything.
W.: Yes, but you have to decide.
E.: True.[7]

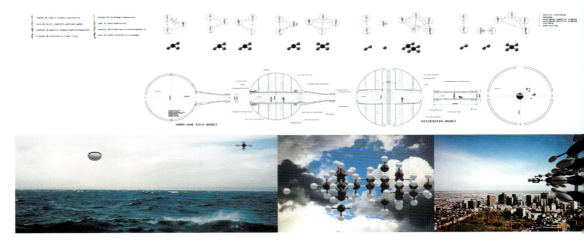

Stefan Endewardt "Sky Base"
Transfer II, SS 2003
Soziale Verhaltensweisen und Probleme des Zusammenlebens werden ins Räumliche übertragen. Mobile Module sprechen vom unmöglichen Traum gleichzeitiger Freiheit und Geborgenheit.

Stefan Endewardt, "Sky Base", Transfer II, SoSe 2003
Social behaviour patterns and problems of living together are transferred to a spatial dimension. Mobile modules speak of the impossible dream of freedom and security at the same time.

NOTES
(1) Marshall McLuhan: *The Medium is the Message*, Penguin Books 1967, Page 10.
(2) Ibidem, Page 36.
(3) Ibidem, Page 68.
(4) David Pye: *The Nature of Design*, Studio Vista 1964, Page 91.
(5) John Cage quoted in: *The Medium is the Message*, Penguin Books 1967, Page 119.
(6) Marshall McLuhan: *The Medium is the Message*, Penguin Books 1967, Page 87.
(7) Samuel Beckett, *Waiting for Godot*, Faber and Faber 1956, Page 24.

Katharina Rüter / Inside Out 2001/2002

INSIDE OUT — UMGESTÜLPT

Berlin, Dreieck Friedrichstraße

Alles fließt hier zusammen. Menschen kommen aus der Erde, ändern ihre Richtung und strömen woanders hin. *Inside out* bedient sich der Menschenströme, nimmt sie auf, verändert ihren Weg und ihre Wahrnehmung, um sie woanders wieder hinauszulassen.

INSIDE OUT — UPENDED

Berlin, Friedrichstraße Triangle

Everything flows together here. People emerge from underground and, changing directions, they stream off elsewhere. *Inside out* makes use of streams of people, taking them in, changing their route and perception, only to let them out again at another place.

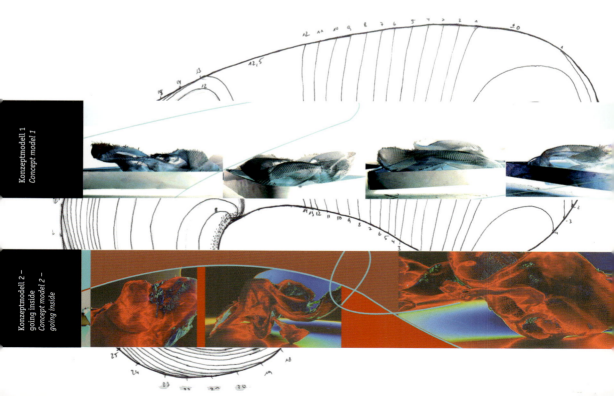

Konzeptmodell 1
Concept model 1

Konzeptmodell 2 – going inside
Concept model 2 – going inside

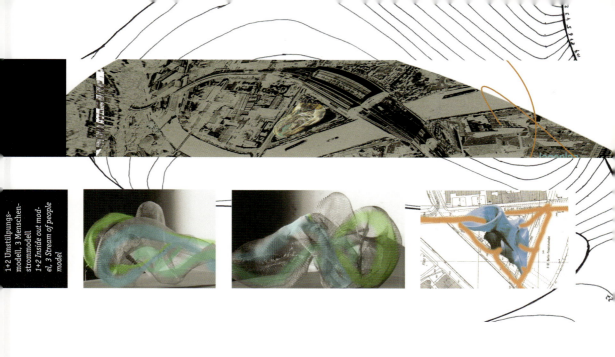

1+2 Umstülpungsmodell, 3 Menschenstrommodell
1+2 Inside out model, 3 Stream of people model

DIE HÜLLE

Die Hülle ist eine einzige Fläche, die, basierend auf drei Hauptmenschenströmen, umgestülpt wurde.

Ein System aus drei Gängen, von denen jeder aus dem Inneren der Hülle, aus der Mitte des Dreieckes, wieder ins Freie hinausführt.

THE SHELL

The shell is a single surface-area that, based on three main streams of people, was turned inside out.

It is a system made of three routes, of which each leads from the shell's interior, from the middle of the triangle out into the open air again.

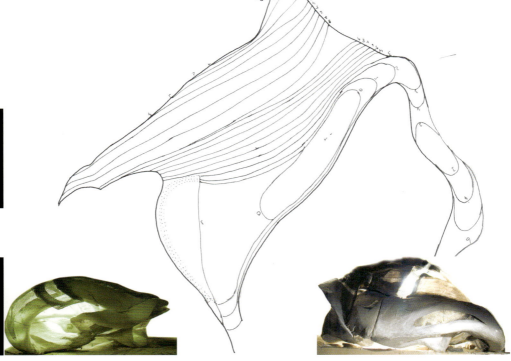

Höhenlinienplan
Upper routes plan

Konzeptmodell 3
Concept model 3

Katharina Rüter / Dampfbank 2001/2002

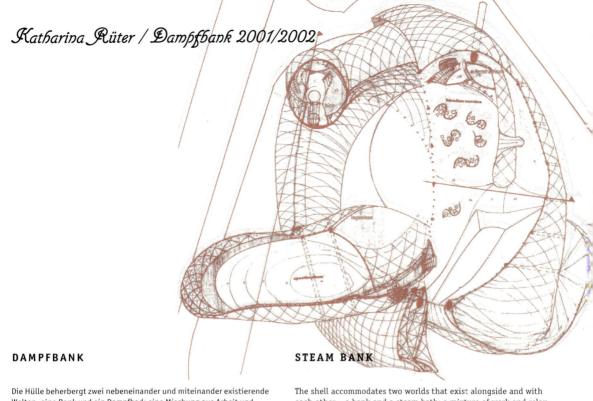

DAMPFBANK

Die Hülle beherbergt zwei nebeneinander und miteinander existierende Welten, eine Bank und ein Dampfbad: eine Mischung aus Arbeit und Erholung, beruhend auf dem Prinzip „Veränderung durch den Weg".

Mittig, fast gänzlich eingeschlossen von den zwei Gebäudekomplexen, liegt ein überdachtes Gewächshaus mit einem Badesee.

STEAM BANK

The shell accommodates two worlds that exist alongside and with each other – a bank and a steam bath: a mixture of work and relaxation, based on the principle of "change by the way".

In the centre, almost totally enclosed by the two building complexes, there is a greenhouse with a bathing lake.

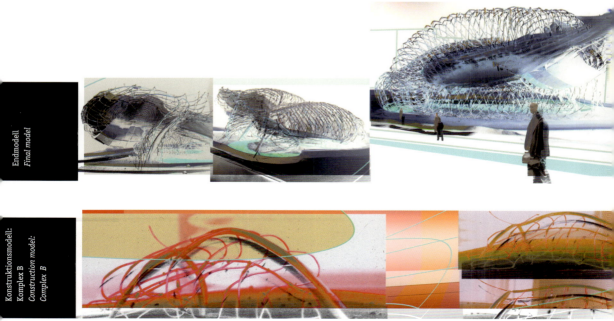

Endmodell
Final model

Konstruktionsmodell: Komplex B
Construction model: Complex B

INTERAKTION

Bank und Dampfbad existieren nebeneinander, miteinander, berühren, spüren und beeinflussen sich: zwei Weggefährten, die ohne den anderen nicht existieren können.

Schnittstellen sind z.B. ein Regengang, dessen Regenfall nur von Besuchern der Bank durch das Betreten bestimmter Regionen ausgelöst wird, und Wasserwände, die je nach Duschtätigkeit der Gäste in Aktion treten.

INTERACTION

Bank and steam bath exist next to each other, with one another, touching, sensing and influencing each other: two companions that cannot exist apart.

Interfaces are, e.g., a rainy walkway, with rainfall only activated by bank customers entering specific zones, and water walls that are activated depending on the shower activities by guests of the steam bath.

Wasserwände
Water walls

Andrew Holmes

Ohne besonderes Ziel

Am liebsten spreche ich so wenig wie möglich und schreibe gar nicht. Mir werden immer zwei Fragen gestellt. Die Antworten lauten: sechs Wochen und Derwent-Farbstift auf Zeichenpapier, auf Karton aufgezogen.

Um neue Aspekte meiner Arbeit aufzudecken, versuche ich, eher meine Materialien als Worte sprechen zu lassen. Ich beobachte die Welt und höre zu. Meine Ideen speisen sich aus dem, was ich sehe, aus Geschichten, die mir zu Ohren kommen, aus Songs, die ich höre. Ich lese Prosa. Andere Leute schreiben besser über meine Arbeit und erklären sie. Die Teile des Hirns, die ich nutze, sind jene weichen Teile an der Vorderseite des Gesichts.

Meinem Thema begegnete ich das erste Mal 1967 auf dem Strip in Las Vegas in Form eines unter Neonleuchten geparkten Deuce Coupé. Eine Oase in der Wüste, sowohl körperlich als auch geistig. Ich reise mit dem Greyhound.

Ich arbeite mit 35-mm-Dias, die ich mit einem Betrachter ans Auge halte. Die Zeichnungen sind annähernd im A1-Format. Eine achtzigfache Vergrößerung. An beiden Enden der Farbtonskala kann ich Informationen abnehmen: Highlights und Schatten, die sich dem bloßen Auge entziehen. Das Ergebnis ist anders als bei einem Photoabzug, der in Ton und Farbe flacher wird. Gesättigte Farben. Warme Farben heben sich intensiv gegen kalte Farben ab.

1972 begann ich, 100 Zeichnungen zu machen. Alle Zeichnungen haben dieselbe Größe und sind in identischen quadratischen Plastikrahmen mit denselben Proportionen wie ein 35-mm-Dia gerahmt. Die Vollendung der Arbeit stelle ich mir als ein flach auf der Wandoberfläche befestigtes Objekt vor. Da sie quadratisch sind, können sie in einem Raster angeordnet werden.

Die Zeichnungen repräsentieren einen Zustand. Es gibt keine Wolken, keine vergänglichen Momente. Es gibt keine Menschen, keine ablenkende Präsenz. Die Zeichnung hängt in der Ewigkeit für tausend Jahre.

Jedes Jahr bereise ich alleine zwei Wochen lang einen Teil der USA. Ich benutze eine 35-mm-Spiegelreflexkamera mit einer 28-80-mm-Linse und vierzig Rollen Ektachromfilm. Ich besuche etwas oder jemanden. Ich photographiere das, was ich auf dem Hin- und Rückweg sehe. Ich kehre mit über tausend Bildern zurück. Zunächst entscheide ich spontan, welche Bilder sich für Zeichnungen eignen. Die endgültigen Entscheidungen brauchen ihre Zeit. Der Titel ist für gewöhnlich in die ausgewählten Bilder geschrieben. Das Bild könnte auf eine vor dreißig Jahren angefertigte Zeichnung Bezug nehmen. Alles, Komposition, Bedeutung, Gefühl, muss stimmen. Sonst kann mit der Zeichnung nicht begonnen werden.

Ich bin ein einfacher Kerl. Ich mag Songs, keine Opern. Die Reise hat mich von New York nach Los Angeles in die Mojave-Wüste geführt. Ich fühle mich heimisch unter den Schattenexistenzen in Slab City, den Speedracern auf dem Salzsee von El Mirage und den Truckern im Miliken Avenue Truckstop.

No Particular Place To Go

I like to talk as little as possible and write not at all. I am always asked two questions. The answers are six weeks and Derwent coloured pencil on cartridge paper dry mounted on card.

Rather than a battle with words, I try work with my materials to uncover new aspects of my work. I observe the world and listen. My ideas come from what I see, stories that I hear, songs that I listen to. I read fiction. Other people write better about my work and explain it. The bits of the brain I use are those soft bits on the front of the face.

I first saw my subject, a Deuce Coupe, parked under neon lights on the Strip in Las Vegas in 1967. An oasis in a desert, both physically and mentally. I was travelling by Greyhound.

I work from a 35-mm transparency that I hold up to my eye with a Lupe. The drawings are close to A1 size. An eighty times increase of size. I am able to see information at both ends of the tonal range, highlights and shadows, unavailable to the naked eye. The result is something unlike a printed photograph, which is flattened in tone and colour. Colour is saturated. Warm colours are intensified against cold colours.

I started in 1972 to make one hundred drawings. All the drawings are the same size, mounted in identical square plastic frames in the same proportion as a 35-mm slide. I think of the finished work as an object mounted flat to the wall surface. Since they are square they can be placed in a grid.

The drawings represent a state. There are no clouds, no fleeting moments. There are no human beings, no distracting presence. The drawing hangs for a thousand years in eternity.

I travel alone for two weeks each year in some part of the USA. I take a 35-mm SLR film camera with a 28-80mm lens and forty rolls of Ektachrome film. I visit something or somebody. I photograph what I see on the way there and back. I return with over a thousand images. The decision to select images that would make drawing is instantaneous. The final decisions are taken over time. The final images usually have their title written in them. The image may respond to a drawing done thirty years ago. Everything, composition, meaning, emotion has to fit or the drawing can't be started.

I'm a low rent kind of guy. I like songs not operas. The journey has taken me from New York, to Los Angeles to the Mojave Desert. I find myself at home among the denizens of the shade in Slab City, the speed racers on the lake bed at El Mirage and the truckers at the Miliken Avenue Truck Stop.

OIL CHANGE, Farbstiftzeichnung auf Karton, 350 x 590 mm   *OIL CHANGE, colored pencil drawing on cartridge paper, 350 x 590 mm*

CT, Farbstiftzeichnung auf Karton, 350 x 590 mm *CT, colored pencil drawing on cartridge paper, 350 x 590 mm*

Werkzeug Collage/ Tool Collage

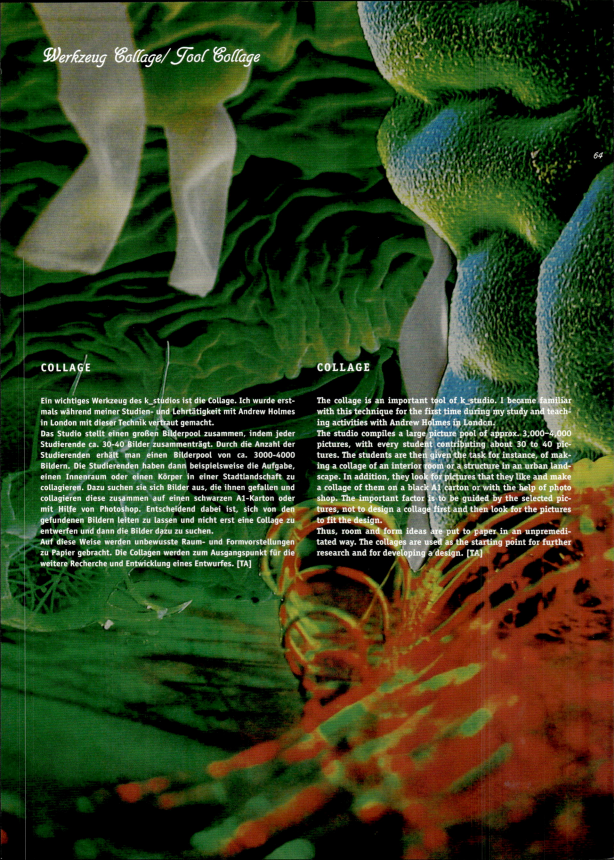

COLLAGE

Ein wichtiges Werkzeug des k_studios ist die Collage. Ich wurde erstmals während meiner Studien- und Lehrtätigkeit mit Andrew Holmes in London mit dieser Technik vertraut gemacht.

Das Studio stellt einen großen Bilderpool zusammen, indem jeder Studierende ca. 30-40 Bilder zusammenträgt. Durch die Anzahl der Studierenden erhält man einen Bilderpool von ca. 3000-4000 Bildern. Die Studierenden haben dann beispielsweise die Aufgabe, einen Innenraum oder einen Körper in einer Stadtlandschaft zu collagieren. Dazu suchen sie sich Bilder aus, die ihnen gefallen und collagieren diese zusammen auf einen schwarzen A1-Karton oder mit Hilfe von Photoshop. Entscheidend dabei ist, sich von den gefundenen Bildern leiten zu lassen und nicht erst eine Collage zu entwerfen und dann die Bilder dazu zu suchen.

Auf diese Weise werden unbewusste Raum- und Formvorstellungen zu Papier gebracht. Die Collagen werden zum Ausgangspunkt für die weitere Recherche und Entwicklung eines Entwurfes. [TA]

COLLAGE

The collage is an important tool of k_studio. I became familiar with this technique for the first time during my study and teaching activities with Andrew Holmes in London.

The studio compiles a large picture pool of approx. 3,000–4,000 pictures, with every student contributing about 30 to 40 pictures. The students are then given the task for instance, of making a collage of an interior room or a structure in an urban landscape. In addition, they look for pictures that they like and make a collage of them on a black A1 carton or with the help of photo shop. The important factor is to be guided by the selected pictures, not to design a collage first and then look for the pictures to fit the design.

Thus, room and form ideas are put to paper in an unpremeditated way. The collages are used as the starting point for further research and for developing a design. [TA]

Michael Kandel, „Struktur" SoSe 03
Michael Kandel, "Structure" SoSe 03

Corinna Fehr „Sky Dive, Aufgang" und „Sky dive, Startplattform" SoSe 01
Corinna Fehr, "Sky Dive, Ascent" and "Sky dive, Starting platform" SoSe 01

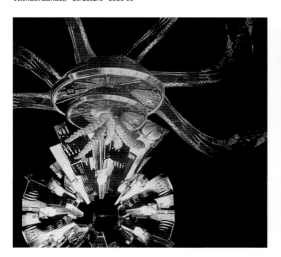

Benedikt Tulinius „Eingang XT 2363" SoSe 03
Benedikt Tulinius, "Entrance XT 2363" SoSe 03

Michael Reiss „Softroom" SoSe 03
Michael Reiss, "Softroom" SoSe 03

Links: Christian Necker, „Grüner Salon" SoSe 03
Left: Christian Necker, "Green Salon" SoSe 03

Matthias Reese

Zeichnen mit der Maus

Im Rahmen von architektonischen Entwurfsprozessen ist der Einfluss der eingesetzten Medien auf Arbeitsprozess und Endprodukt als wesentlicher Faktor in Betracht zu ziehen. Die Beschleunigung der Informationsverarbeitung und -verknüpfung, die uns die neuen Medien ermöglichen, bietet neue Ansätze zur Lösung der anstehenden räumlichen Probleme. Dennoch können diese Mittel die wichtige Rolle des traditionellen Zeichnens nicht ersetzen; beide Darstellungsformen sind in ihren spezifischen Möglichkeiten zu nutzen. Die Erfahrungen mit den neuen Kommunikations- und Darstellungsmitteln üben eine unumkehrbare Wirkung auf unser Rezeptionsverhalten sowie auf die Qualität der Aussage der Darstellung aus. Folglich ist im Entwurfsprozess eine Veränderung der Diskursstruktur zwischen Entwerfer und Werk festzustellen, und diese müssen wir in der Lehre thematisieren.

Das Zeichnen mit dem Stift in der Hand ermöglicht eine unmittelbarere Abfolge von Produktion, Rezeption und Korrektur, das heißt, der beim Zeichnen notwendigerweise auftretende Widerstand kann im Entwurfsprozess durch die Einführung von Korrekturen direkt produktiv gemacht werden. Dieser Widerstand wird über die Körperlichkeit der Hand vermittelt; in den Entwurfsprozess fließen somit auch unmittelbar jene Wissensanteile ein, die wir aufgrund unserer körperlichen Raumerfahrung erworben haben. Im Gegensatz dazu bedingt die Produktion am Bildschirm zunächst ein abstrakteres Arbeiten; das Ergebnis erscheint als Projektion und wird später über den Drucker vermittelt. Durch die verwendete Software werden viele Darstellungsparameter vorab festgelegt und in der Bearbeitung zumeist nicht weiterentwickelt. Entscheidend für die Qualität einer computergestützten Untersuchung ist jedoch die Anpassung dieser Parameter an die Fragestellung. Zu leicht kann die erzeugte Bildoberfläche mit spezifischen inhaltlichen Aussagen verwechselt werden. Dies kann die Ausschöpfung der Möglichkeiten der neuen Medien behindern, insbesondere bezüglich der schnellen Einarbeitung und Visualisierung komplexer Datenmengen. Entscheidend erscheint mir, die Qualität des Rechners in seiner veränderten Ordnungsstruktur zu begreifen, unabhängig von der vermeintlich rasanten Bildoberfläche.

Abgesehen von den eingesetzten Medien lassen sich grundsätzlich zwei Zielsetzungen des Zeichnens unterscheiden. Zunächst geht es natürlich darum, einen Entwurfsgedanken darzustellen und zu vermitteln. Darüber hinaus können aber mittels der Zeichnung bestimmte Sachverhalte untersucht, Annahmen verifiziert oder verworfen werden. Der Aspekt des Darstellens und der des Untersuchens fallen im Zeichenprozess zu einer Arbeit zusammen, die sich in aufeinander aufbauenden Schritten entwickelt. Wir beginnen diese Arbeit mit einer ersten entwurflichen Setzung, mit einer vorläufigen Form. Indem wir diese zu Papier bringen, beginnt eine Interaktion zwischen uns und unserem Objekt. Wir reagieren auf das Produkt unserer Arbeit zunächst intuitiv und bewerten das Ergebnis durch den Filter unserer Vorerfahrung. Entscheidend hierbei ist, dass sich ein Widerstand durch die Materialisierung des Gedankens

Draw with the Mouse

In terms of sketching and design strategies the impact of the media used on the whole process and end product should be considered of vital importance. The speed of information processing and application, which the new media offer, present us with new ways to solve existing problems of space. Even so, these techniques cannot replace the important role of traditional drawing – both methods of representation must be utilised according to their specific attributes. Our experiences with new techniques of communication and depiction have an irreversible impact on our method of reception but also on the quality of the statement the depiction is making. Thus, within the production process we can detect a change in the structure of the discourse between designer and his work, within the immediate sequence of production, reception and correction.

The kind of resistance that inevitably sets in during the sketching process can be rendered highly productive by the introduction of immediate corrections. This resistance is conveyed by the physical agency of the hand; thus, the elements of knowledge we have acquired from our physical sense of space also automatically flow into the sketching process. Unlike drawing with a pencil in your hand, production on the screen initially demands a more abstract way of working – the end-result is a kind of projection, subsequently given concrete form by the printer. The kind of software you use predetermines several parameters of the resulting depiction, which are not – initially at least – generally taken any further. That said, the quality of a PC-supported exploration depends on how closely these parameters relate to the matter in question. The desired picture surface can all too easily be confused with specific "content-statements". This confusion can inhibit the exploitation of new media resources – particularly the swift utilisation and visualisation of complex masses of data. What seems vital to me is to grasp the quality of the structural pattern the calculator is based upon, whatever the ostensibly "untamed" picture-surface.

Irrespective of the media used, we can distinguish in all drawing two different objectives. The first priority, of course, is to depict and communicate a sketch-concept. Over and above this, however, drawing can be a means of investigating certain phenomena and either confirm or reject various assumptions. Within the process of drawing, the elements of depiction and exploration merge into one piece of work, which develops in a series of steps. We start this work with a sketched draft – a preliminary form. Putting this down on paper sparks off an interaction between us and our object. Our initial response to the outcome of our work is intuitive and we assess the end product through the filter of our prior experience. Crucial here is that a resistance develops between the idea's "materialisation" on the surface of the paper or in its visualisation on the screen. We are disconcerted by what we take to be "losses in translation" and realise that, for

auf der Oberfläche des Papiers oder in der Visualisierung auf dem Bildschirm ergibt. Wir stören uns an den vermeintlichen „Übersetzungsverlusten" und erkennen, dass zum Beispiel bestimmte Setzungen nicht in der erhofften Weise aufeinander reagieren. Die Darstellung erlaubt es uns also, die untersuchten Sachverhalte graphisch zu prüfen, und dieser Prozess ist durch eine rein kognitive Evaluierung nicht zu ersetzen.

Der Ort einer Entwurfsaufgabe, genauer die komplexe Überlagerung aller Schichten dieses Ortes, enthält eine zunächst nicht zu verarbeitende Informationsfülle. Um diese im Entwurfsprozess nutzbar zu machen, sind Auswahl und Filterung erforderlich, eine Art selektiver Wahrnehmung. Wesentliche Teilaspekte können durch die Festlegung eines bestimmten Untersuchungsdetektors und zugeordneter auswahlbildender Prozesse des Zeichnens sehr gut aus dem Gesamterscheinungsbild herausgelöst und untersucht werden. In der Beobachtung der Gegenstände eines Raumgefüges lassen sich zwei ihrer Natur nach recht unterschiedliche Annäherungsweisen unterscheiden:

Die erste bezieht sich auf diejenigen Informationen, die sich aus der Untersuchung der Phänomenologie der vorhandenen Oberflächen herleiten lassen. Hier beziehen wir uns im Wesentlichen auf die Summe des intuitiv Erfassten im Umgang mit den uns umgebenden Dingen. Wir haben zum Beispiel genaue Kenntnis über die Textur

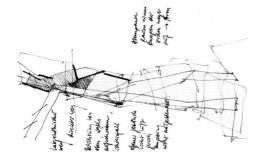
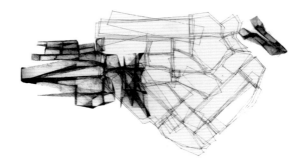

Heike Schneckener: Entwurf für eine „Aussegnungshalle" im Seminar „Statt-Landschaft", KHB Sommersemester 2001
Linke Seite, links: skizzierte Wegeführung
Rechts: Strukturelle Analyse ausgewählter Merkmale einer Feldmark und zweier Siedlungskerne. Hauptaugenmerk wurde auf die Schärfe/Unschärfe der Grenzmarkierungen und -verläufe sowie deren Bezugspunkte gelegt.
Rechte Seite, links: Die Orientierung im Verlauf des Gebäudes sowie Fragen der Grenzausbildung waren zentrale Entwurfsthemen.

Heike Schneckener: Design for a "Consecration Hall" in the seminar, "Instead of a Landscape", KHB Summer Semester 2001
Left page, left: Draft tour d'horizon
Right: Structural analysis of selected features of a landmark and of two estate centres. The focus should be on the sharpness/bluntness of the boundary markings and lines, and on their reference points.
Right page, left: The orientation within the building, as well as issues about how the boundaries were developed were central design themes.

eines bestimmten Stoffes, über seine Funktion und innere Organisation, über den ihm zugeordneten, kulturell tradierten und individuell geprägten emotionalen Gehalt. Diese Kenntnisse können uns helfen, im Entwurfsprozess, bezogen auf die beabsichtigte Wirkung, kohärente Entscheidungen zu treffen. Über den Prozess des Zeichnens wird dieses Wissen aus dem Bereich des Intuitiven herausgehoben und in Dialog mit allen anderen Parametern des Entwurfes gesetzt. Allerdings ist hier kritisch anzumerken, dass es die Wahrnehmungsmuster selber sind, welche die Formen organisieren, die Oberflächen sind also weder unabhängig von dem sie erfassenden Subjekt zu denken, noch unbeeinflusst vom sie umgebenden Feld.

Die zweite Annäherungsweise thematisiert, als Erweiterung der ersten, die Frage nach der in der Realität verborgenen Struktur, dem unsichtbaren Ordnungsmuster eines räumlichen Gefüges. Hierbei geht es nicht darum, die Einzelheiten selber zu zeichnen oder zeichnerisch zu untersuchen, sondern ein Organisationsprinzip zu erfassen, welches in der Realität aufgehoben ist und in der Summe die wesentliche Qualität eines Raumes bestimmt. Entscheidend hierbei ist der Versuch, die Verhältnisse der Dinge zueinander zu ermitteln und zeichnerisch zu bearbeiten. Dies fällt in der Regel zunächst nicht leicht. Wie kann ich etwas zeichnen, was ich nicht sehe?

instance, certain phenomena do not react with each other, as we would have anticipated. Thus, the act of depiction enables us to check graphically the data we have explored, and this process cannot be replaced by a purely cognitive evaluation.

The site where the design is to be located – or, to be more precise, the complex ordering of all this location's various layers – contains a wealth of information, which cannot immediately be fully assessed. To make this useful to the sketching process, some filtering and selection will be required – a kind of selective perception. Distinct properties of the whole can be extracted and duly investigated by determining related and appropriate drawing tools. In observing the objects in a given space, two approaches are evident that are very different in nature.

The first focuses on that information which can be derived from exploring the phenomenology of all available surfaces. Here, we are mainly concerned with the whole of what is intuitively grasped in our contact with our surroundings. For example, we have precise knowledge of the texture of a particular fabric, about its function and internal composition, and about the cultural, traditional and individually characterised emotional input assigned to it. In terms of the intended effect, this knowledge can help us to make coherent design decisions. However, within

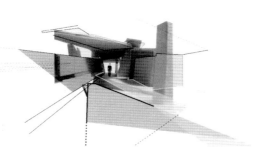 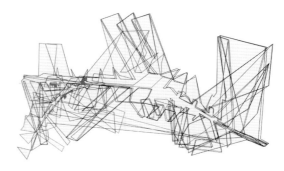

the process of drawing, this knowledge is brought out of the intuitive area and placed in a dialogue with all the other parameters of the design. At any event, a criticism ought to be lodged here – that the patterns of perception themselves organise the forms, which means that the surfaces cannot be perceived independently of the subject who perceives – nor of the influence exerted by the area that surrounds them.

As an extension of the first, the second approach is preliminary to this question: what constitutes the structure latent within reality, what is the invisible organisational pattern underlying a spatial construction? Crucial here is not to draw the details oneself nor to investigate them by drawing at random, but to grasp a principle of organisation that is embedded in reality and that, as a whole, determines the essential qualities of any given space. What matters here is the attempt to convey the relationship that objects have to one another, then to adapt them by drawing. As a rule, this is no easy matter. How can I possibly draw something I cannot see?

It is certainly helpful to put in place the filters and indicators mentioned above – if applied to specific phenomena. These phenomena may include, for

Rechts: Mareille Schlüter, Manuel Oswald: Entwurf im Seminar „Transit", KHB Sommersemester 2002. Räumliches Orientierungsmuster entlang der Bahntrasse zwischen Ostkreuz und Treptower Park, Berlin.

Right: Mareille Schlüter, Manuel Oswald: Design in the seminar: "Transit", KHB Summer Semester, 2002. Spatial Orientation Pattern along the length of the railway line between Ostkreuz and Treptower Park, Berlin.

Hilfreich ist die Setzung der erwähnten Filter und Indikatoren, bezogen auf spezifische Sachverhalte. Diese können sich zum Beispiel auf Massenverteilung, Bewegungsmuster, visuelle Orientierung, auf die Verteilung der infrastrukturellen Einrichtungen usw. beziehen. Wichtig ist, dass der gewählte Detektor präzise bestimmt und mit der Art der Zeichnung kausal verknüpft wird. Eine Strukturzeichnung entwickelt sich letztendlich aus einer sehr genauen, stark gefilterten Untersuchung der Wirklichkeit in Bezug auf zunächst einen ausgewählten Aspekt. Hier kann uns die bereits erwähnte schnelle Visualisierung komplexer Datenmengen durch den Rechner helfen.

Im Ergebnis entwickelt sich eine Darstellung, welche das bekannte Zeichenklischee vermeidet und den Blick für bestimmte Aspekte des Dinglichen neu öffnet. Der Prozess des Zeichnens schließt aufgrund der anfänglich gemachten Festlegung automatisch ablaufende Anteile mit ein und führt so einerseits zu einer gewissen Irritation, andererseits aber auch zu einer Neubewertung des Untersuchungsgegenstandes. Diese Arbeitsweise ist zwischen sehr präzisen, quasi positivistisch determinierten Schritten und intuitiv gesteuerten Anteilen angesiedelt, beide Aspekte werden wirksam gemacht. Die erste Wahl der Studierenden ist in den meisten Fällen intuitiv gesteuert. Wir benötigen diese intuitive Wahl, um das mittels unserer sehr komplex angelegten Sensorik erfasste Wissen über unsere Umwelt im Prozess zu berücksichtigen. Sie dient uns auch dazu, Zusammenhänge zu thematisieren, die wir unbewusst antizipieren, ohne sie eigentlich belegen zu können. In der darauf folgenden Phase wird die Untersuchung den präzisen und objektiv darstellbaren Grundregeln des Detektors folgen und so das „Vorgewusste" im Rahmen der Zeichnung überprüfen und erweitern. Beide Perspektiven werden wechselweise eingenommen und bilden im Sinne einer prozessual entwickelten Collage die Grundlage für den Entwurf.

Zielsetzung dieses Verfahrens ist es nicht, hieraus direkt eine Form abzuleiten. Mit den beschriebenen Arbeitsschritten wird jedoch eine wesentliche Grundlage für den Entwurfsansatz geschaffen, der im Folgenden mit anderen Aspekten, wie programmatischen, infrastrukturellen, technischen und wirtschaftlichen konfrontiert wird. Jeder entwerfende Architekt kennt dies: Keine Arbeit ist jemals linear, vom ursprünglichen Entwurfsgedanken bis zur Realisierung des Gebäudes, und in Gänze rational erklärbar entwickelt worden. Nicht alle Teile eines Gebäudes lassen sich durch einen Bedeutungszusammenhang abschließend erklären, allen anlässlich von Vorträgen und Veröffentlichungen mitgelieferten Deutungen zum Trotz. Der Entwurfsprozess ist durch Brüche und Sprünge gekennzeichnet, durch Verschneidungen mit Themen anderer Diskurse, und dies stellt in meinem Verständnis das Wesentliche des architektonischen Prozesses dar. Die unterschiedlichen Aspekte werden im Werk collagiert und zu einer von den Einzelaspekten unabhängigen Einheit neu verdichtet.

Die Kenntnis und bewusst eingesetzte Führung der impliziten Botschaften des Raumes in Abhängigkeit von den sie umgebenden Feldern stellt eine wesentliche Aufgabe unseres Faches dar. Bei jeder Bauaufgabe werden wir uns fragen müssen: Was ist die eigentliche, grundsätzliche Fragestellung und welchen Beitrag kann der Raum zu ihrer Bewältigung leisten? Welche Mittel setze ich folglich als Architekt ein? Dieses Wesentliche einer Raumgestaltung wird weniger durch die Qualität der Einzelteile als durch die Art der Verknüpfung der gestalteten Artefakte miteinander bestimmt. Der hier beschriebene Zeichenprozess kann uns als ein wichtiges Mittel der Annäherung dienen.

example, distribution en masse, certain patterns of motivation, aspects of visual orientation and the dispersal of "elements of infrastructure". What really matters is that the chosen detector is precisely determined and casually connected to the style of drawing. In due course, a drawing of this structure will then develop from a very precise, strongly filtered investigation of reality on the strength of – initially at least – one selected aspect. Here, as already mentioned, a swift visualisation of complex masses of data by means of a calculator can help.

In this process a representation takes shape that avoids the familiar stereotype of signs and re-opens the individual's eyes for certain aspects of concrete reality. By virtue of the ground-rules we had set at the very outset, the process of drawing also includes elements which automatically occur. These elements might cause some irritation; however, they also result in a re-assessment of the object under scrutiny. This working method lies between very precise, almost positivistically, determined approaches and intuitively driven concerns – each activated by the process itself. In most cases, the relevant students' first choice is intuitive. We need this beginning so that we can go on and utilise our highly complex sensory perception of our environment. It also helps us to identify connections, which we anticipate subconsciously without being able to prove or substantiate them conclusively. In the phase immediately afterwards, our exploration follows the precise and objectively demonstrable ground-rules imposed by the detector – thus assessing and expanding the "pre-known" aspects of the drawing. One by one, both perspectives are included in the drawing process, establishing – in a gradually evolving collage – the basis for the design

This working method is not intended to result directly in a definitive "form". That said, the kind of approach described here constitutes a basic principle for starting the design –– which can than be confronted and merged with other aspects, such as those relating to a programme or infrastructure, as well as technical and economic issues. Every practising architect knows this terrain: no work is ever just linear – from the original design idea to the eventual construction of the building – nor can the whole enterprise be explained in a wholly rational way. Not all parts in a building can be summed up conclusively in a statement of overall significance – in defiance of all the interpretations given by lectures and publications. The sketching process is characterised by interruptions and leaps, by overlaps and subjects from other discourses – and in my view, this is what constitutes the essence of any architectonic process The finished work represents a collage of all the various aspects that go into it, concentrating separate elements into a new whole, independent of them all.

Depending on their surroundings, knowledge about and conscious application of implied messages on space is a key task in our academic and professional field. In any building project we have to ask ourselves: what are the really fundamental issues, and how can space contribute to resolving them? In consequence, what steps should I take as an architect? This essential prerequisite of a "structured space" is determined less by the quality of the component parts than by the way in which the constructed artefacts are connected. The drawing process here described can be a useful method in approaching the problem.

Christian Jeckert

Architekturen des Raums

„Raum" ist ein Begriff, der in der Architektur wie selbstverständlich eine zentrale Stellung einnimmt – ein Begriff, um dessen Entstehungsgeschichte und Bedeutungsverschiebungen in der Architektur und angrenzenden Disziplinen es im Folgenden gehen wird.

Zunächst erscheint es paradox, dass nach dem vermeintlichen Siegeszug einer in den 1990er Jahren viel beschworenen „Visual Culture"[1], die sich mit dem Slogan des „Pictorial Turn"[2] in die Kunstgeschichte eingeschrieben hatte, in der letzten Zeit gerade der Begriff des Raums wieder zu einer Zentralkategorie zahlreicher Diskurse wurde. Stand in der Kunst die Auseinandersetzung mit dem gesellschaftlichen, dem urbanen und dem institutionellen Raum als einem Indikator von Mikropolitiken der Macht[3] im Mittelpunkt des Interesses, so wird in Geographie, Soziologie, Cultural Studies oder Philosophie der Raum in vielfältigen Debatten rund um Postkolonialismus, Migrationsbewegungen und Globalisierung thematisiert. Die Beschäftigung mit dem Raum hat Konjunktur, und etwas verspätet scheint sich damit, zumindest vordergründig, die These Michel Foucaults zu bestätigen, wonach der Raum als gegenwärtiges gesellschaftstheoretisches Ordnungsmodell das vorangegangene Modell der Zeit bzw. der Geschichte als „große Obsession des 19. Jahrhunderts" ablösen würde.[4] Allerdings ist mit der Moderne genau diese Entgegensetzung von Raum und Zeit in die Krise geraten. Durch die Einlagerung von Bildmedien und „virtuellen Räumen" in die materielle Umgebung sieht sich vor allem die Architektur als Disziplin einem Wettbewerb um Aufmerksamkeit mit Fernsehbildschirmen, Mobiltelefonen, Screens usw. ausgesetzt; und die politisch-ökonomische Entwicklung zur gleichzeitigen Globalisierung wie auch zur Regionalisierung von Lebens-, Konsumtions- und Produktionszusammenhängen ließ Autoren wie Fredric Jameson vom „Hyper-Raum"[5] sprechen, der von einer Überlagerung mehrerer räumlicher und zeitlicher Vektoren an einem Ort geprägt ist.[6]

Damit wird auch der Begriff des Raums einer Revision unterzogen, was sich etwa bei Martina Löw in Form einer Kritik am Konzept des „Container-Raums" äußert. Dieser sei aufgrund seiner Limitierung auf die dreidimensionale Geometrie eines homogenen, linearen Weltbilds nicht mehr zeitgemäß, so Löw. Stattdessen wird im Rekurs auf Entwicklungen in der Physik, in den Wahrnehmungstheorien und in den elektronischen Medien ein prozessualer Raumbegriff eingefordert, der Subjekte, soziale Güter und Objekte in einem relationalen, interdependenten Bezugsfeld lokalisiert.[7] Löw geht davon aus, dass Raum etwas ist, das sich als soziales Phänomen in gesellschaftlichen Prozessen konstituiert. Damit verschiebt sich der Fokus vom Modell einer quantifizierbaren, objektivistischen Sichtweise des Raums hin zu einem Raumbegriff, der primär in der Wahrnehmung des Subjekts, in seiner Bewegung durch die Zeit verankert ist. Somit wird die Forderung aufgestellt, den Begriff und die Vorstellung vom Raum zu dynamisieren und den diskursiven wie auch den alltagskulturellen Entwicklungen anzupassen.

Architectures of Space

"Space" is a term that almost naturally takes a central place in architecture. We shall follow, below, the origins and fluctuating meaning of this term in architecture and related disciplines.

Initially, it seems paradoxical that after the supposed rise of "Visual Culture"[1], which was much acclaimed in the 1990s having inscribed itself into art history with the slogan of the "Pictorial Turn"[2], the term "space" recently became a central category again in numerous discourses. Whereas in art, the confrontation with space as a social, urban, or institutional phenomenon was of crucial interest as an indicator of the micro-politics of power[3], the notion of space in areas like geography, sociology, cultural studies, and philosophy, is central to a number of debates focusing on post-colonialism, migratory movements, and globalisation. The preoccupation with space is becoming more popular, and appears to confirm a bit late, at least ostensibly, Michael Foucault's theory in which space as a contemporary model of the social order would replace the preceding model of time, or history as the "great obsession of the 19th century".[4] In any event, contemporaneous with modernism, this opposition of space and time underwent a crisis. Because of the rise of visual media and "virtual spaces" in the material world around us, the discipline of architecture now competed for attention with television screens, mobile telephones, screens, etc. Moreover, the political-economic developments which coincided with globalisation – as well as the regionalisation of patterns of life, consumption and production – caused authors like Frederic Jameson to talk about "hyper space"[5]. "Hyper space" is characterised by several different spatial and temporal vectors stacked one above the other in one place.[6]

In this sense, the concept of space also undergoes a revision, which for instance in Martina Löw's case is expressed as criticism of the concept of "container space". Due to its restriction to the three-dimensional geometry of a homogeneous, linear world view, this was, according to Löw, no longer contemporary. Instead, with recourse to developments in physics, in perception theories, and in the electronic media, a "processual" conception of space is demanded that localises subjects, social goods and objects into a relational, interdependent reference field.[7] Löw's starting-point is that space is something that manifests itself as a social phenomenon in social processes. This shifts the focus away from the model of a quantifiable, objective view of space towards a concept of space which is primarily anchored in its perception of the subject, in its motion through time. This imposes the obligation to dynamise our concept and image of space, and to assimilate the discursive as well as everyday cultural developments.

This shift in the power of defining space – a shift from architect to observing user that is intimately linked to the process of space's constitution – along with the implied demand for a transformed concept of space is only debated in the archi-

Die mit dem Prozess der Raumkonstitution verbundene Verschiebung der Definitionsmacht über den Raum, vom Architekten hin zum wahrnehmenden Benutzer, und die damit einhergehende Forderung nach einem transformierten Raumbegriff werden im Bereich der Architektur nur am Rande diskutiert. Zwar werden permanent neue Begriffsbildungen wie Gefalteter Raum, Fließender Raum, Hyperspace, Eventspace, Cyberspace usw. ins Spiel gebracht; aber dieser inflationäre Umgang mit „Raum" scheint eher dazu angetan, die Auseinandersetzung mit der Bedeutung des Begriffs selbst hintanzuhalten und ihn als quasi neutralen Behälter zu benutzen, der beliebig mit einem Präfix nach dem anderen gefüllt werden kann.

Die Erfindung des Raums

In diesem Zusammenhang erscheint es aufschlussreich, auf eine Debatte des ausgehenden 19. Jahrhunderts zurückzublicken, die zu einem Gründungsmythos der Architekturtheorie wurde.[8] Gemeint ist jener Umbruch in der Kunstgeschichte, im Zuge dessen erstmals der Begriff des Raums überhaupt als Topos der Kunstgeschichte und der Architektur ins Feld geführt wurde. In seiner Antrittsvorlesung an der Universität Leipzig im Jahre 1893 thematisierte August Schmarsow die Architektur nicht mehr, wie es bis zu diesem Zeitpunkt üblich war, rund um Probleme von Stil oder Ornament, sondern über den Raum. Oder, um genauer zu sein, er stellte dar, wie unser Gefühl für den Raum („Raumgefühl") und die Fähigkeit, Raum zu imaginieren („Raumphantasie") zur räumlichen Kreation führen („Raumgestaltung"). Die Architektur ist für Schmarsow primär „Raumgestalterin", sie kann „das geistige Bedürfnis (...) nach Spielraum" befriedigen.[9] Dies stellte im Kontext der Kunst- und Architekturgeschichte einen entscheidenden Perspektivwechsel dar, auf den sich im Weiteren auch Adolf Hildebrand, Paul Frankl oder Heinrich Wölfflin bezogen. Allerdings war „der Rezipient" in diesem Diskurs weniger als spezifischer sozialer Akteur definiert, dem ein bestimmter Raum zugeordnet war, sondern er blieb abstrakt, offen für Projektionen und Einschreibungen. Für die Herausbildung eines veritablen Gründungsmythos der architektonischen Moderne eröffnete dieser Diskurs damit eine doppelte Chance: Einerseits konnte die architektonische Moderne die Beschäftigung mit Stil und Kunstgeschichte ad acta legen und sich als autonome „Raumgestalterin" etablieren, andererseits ließ die Offenheit des Begriffs „Raum" als leerer Signifikant die Interpretationen sprießen. Damit wurde einer bis dato nicht enden wollenden Abfolge der jeweils neuesten zukunftsweisenden Raumdefinitionen Tür und Tor geöffnet. László Moholy-Nagy etwa zählt schon in seinem Bauhaustagebuch von 1929, „Von Material zu Architektur", nicht weniger als 44 Arten von Raum auf[10], thematisiert damit die Heterogenität des Begriffs und betont die synästhetische Qualität der möglichen Raumerfahrungen. Rund um diese Synästhetik der Raumwahrnehmung prägen sich aber auch die mitunter missionarisch anmutenden Versuche aus, den „neuen" Menschen mit entsprechenden Raumeindrücken zu erziehen, seine Bewegung zu antizipieren, zu steuern und zu kontrollieren.[11] Der Begriff des Raums wird dabei im Dienste des Fortschritts und der Utopie durchfunktionalisiert. Die projektive Kraft des Architekten als visionärem Schöpfer entzieht dem raumkonstituierenden Rezipienten Schmarsows rückwirkend wieder seinen Handlungsspielraum.

tectural field in peripheral terms. Admittedly, new conceptual connections like folding space, flowing space, hyperspace, event space, cyberspace, etc. are constantly being introduced. However, this inflationary intercourse with "space" seems more likely to delay discussion of the concept's meaning and to use it as a more or less neutral "container", which can be filled – as required – with one prefix after another.

The Invention of Space

In this context, it seems revealing to recall a late 19th century debate that was to become a "founding myth" of architectural theory. What is meant is the upheaval in the history of art, as a result of which the concept of space first made its appearance as a topos of art history and of architecture.[8] In his inaugural lecture at the University of Leipzig in 1893, August Schmarsow did not refer to architecture – as had been the norm hitherto – in terms of problems of style or ornamentation, but in terms of space. Or, to be more precise, he made it clear how our feeling for space ("sense of space") and our ability to imagine space ("spatial fantasy") can result in spatial creation ("creation of space"). For Schmarsow, architecture is first and foremost "a creator of space" and able to satisfy "the spiritual need (…) for room to manoeuvre".[9] In the context of the history of art and architecture, this represents a decisive change of perspective, one to which Adolf Hildebrand, Paul Frankl and Heinrich Wölfflin have also referred. That said, "the recipient" in this discourse was defined less as a specific social actor, to whom a definite space was assigned; rather, he stayed abstract, open to projections and inscriptions. This discourse thereby opened up two chances for inaugurating a veritable foundation myth of architecture in modernism. On the one hand, architecture in modernism could set aside the obsession with style and art history and establish itself as an autonomous "creator of space"; and on the other hand, the very ambiguity of the term "space" – as an empty signifier – allowed interpretations to take shape. This opened the floodgates to a never-ending sequence of what were then the very latest and most forward-looking definitions of space. In his Bauhaus diary of 1929, "From Material to Architecture", László Moholy-Nagy, for instance, counts no less than 44 different kinds of space.[10] Thus, he thematised the concept's heterogeneity, which emphasises the synaesthetic quality of possible experiences of space. However, around this synaesthesia of space perception, by now, quasi missionary attempts were taking shape to educate the "new" man in appropriate definitions of space, to anticipate, steer and control his movements.[11] With that, the concept of space was recycled into something that served the idea of progress and utopia. The architect's projective power as visionary creator retrospectively deprives Schmarsow's space-constituting recipient yet again of his freedom to manoeuvre.

Modernism's Boundary Delineations

Modernism was obsessed with drawing boundaries and setting up pairs of opposites – if only to celebrate its staged transitions, its thresholds, its masquerades.[12] The separations and combinations between private and public, between inside and outside, between inhabiting and working, and so forth, became a central theme of literature, architecture, urbanism, indeed, of culture as a whole. The matrix, the area

Grenzziehungen der Moderne

Die Moderne war besessen davon, Grenzen zu ziehen und Gegensatzpaare aufzubauen – wenn auch nur, um ihre inszenierten Übergänge, ihre Schweller, ihre Maskeraden zu zelebrieren.[12] Die Trennungen und Verbindungen zwischen Privat und Öffentlich, zwischen Innen und Außen, zwischen Wohnen und Arbeiten usw. wurden zu einem zentralen Thema der Literatur, der Architektur, des Urbanismus, ja der gesamten Kultur. Die Matrix, die Verhandlungsfläche dieses Begehrens, Grenzen zu produzieren, bildet der Raum. Wie Martin Heidegger schon in seinem Vortrag „Bauen Wohnen Denken" im Jahre 1954[13] dargelegt hat, ist der Raum für den Menschen kein a priori bestehendes Gegenüber, sondern er ist Ergebnis einer Grenzziehung zwischen Orten – „Raum ist wesenhaft das Eingeräumte, in seine Grenze Eingelassene." Und weiter: „Die Grenze ist nicht das, wobei etwas aufhört, sondern, wie die Griechen es erkannten, wo etwas beginnt." Der Raum ist hier nicht die Voraussetzung der Möglichkeit, Grenzen zu ziehen, sondern seinerseits erst ein Produkt dieser Grenzziehungen.[14] Man könnte auch sagen, der Raum definiert sich ganz wesentlich durch das, was er ausschließt. Aber wie man spätestens seit Freud weiß, schleichen sich das Ausgeschlossene und das Unterdrückte als Unheimliches, als Wiedergänger durch die letztlich nie ganz verschließbaren Türen des als privat oder individuell bezeichneten „Innen" wieder herein.[15] Anthony Vidler hat diesem „Architectural Uncanny" ein ganzes Buch gewidmet, in dem er die bürgerlichen Ängste und Phobien, die das gerade erst „entdeckte" Individuum befielen, in ihrer Wechselwirkung mit der Architektur beschreibt.[16] Die Vorstellung des Subjekts in der Moderne ist aufs Engste mit der des Raums verbunden.[17] Und wie das als autonomes Individuum idealisierte „Subjekt" der Moderne, so ist auch der „Raum" als diskursiv produzierter Begriff der Kunst- und Architekturgeschichte selbst eine genuin moderne „Erfindung".[18] Man könnte auch sagen, Raum ist das begriffliche Nebenprodukt einer fundamentalen Neuorganisation der Gesellschaft – einer Gesellschaft, die aus familiär bzw. feudal geprägten Strukturen entwachsen war und Ordnungssysteme entwickelte, die der zunehmenden individuellen Mobilität entsprachen und mit der Herstellung neuer Grenzverläufe sowie Differenzierungen, wie etwa „Privatheit" und „Öffentlichkeit", verbunden waren.[19] Das Setzen von Grenzen erscheint als notwendige Vorraussetzung zur Etablierung von Identität[20], wobei die Frage nach dem Raum genauso wie die nach der Identität in dem Moment relevant wird, wo sie kontingent, also grundlos entscheidbar ist.

Rollenspiele und poröse Grenzen

Beatriz Colomina verwies im Zusammenhang mit der Architektur des ausgehenden 19. Jahrhunderts auf den entscheidenden Stellenwert der Maskerade, welche die Identitätskonstitution begleitet: „Architecture fully participates in this pervasive logic of the mask."[21] Und was wäre hinter der Maske? „Nichts", würde Judith Butler sagen, jedenfalls keine Identität, sondern höchstenfalls das Begehren nach einer Identität, eine „Imitation ohne Original"[22]. Dies verbindet das moderne Subjekt mit der modernen Architektur. In „Privacy and Publicity" stellt Beatriz Colomina eindrücklich dar, wie sehr etwa die Räume von Le Corbusier auf ein kinematographisch und die von Loos auf ein theatralisch gefasstes Subjekt hin organisiert waren. Diese Konzeption von Architektur im Hinblick auf die Rollenspiele ihrer Benutzer impliziert nun einerseits die

for negotiating this desire to produce boundaries, is constituted by space. As Martin Heidegger outlined as early as 1954 in his lecture on "Building, Dwelling, Thinking", for human beings space is not some a priori opposite, but the result of a boundary being drawn between different places – "Space is essentially that which is vacated, that which has been left to its own boundary." – And he goes on to say: "The boundary is not the place where something ends, but – as the Greeks realised – where something begins."[13] Here, space is not the prerequisite for the possibility of drawing boundaries, but for its part simply a product of those boundary delineations.[14] One could also say that space defines itself in essence by the very elements it excludes. However, since Freud at the latest, we have known that what is excluded and suppressed has a way of creeping back again – as something sinister or as intrusion – through doors that are never entirely shut and lead to what is privately or individually called "the inside".[15] Anthony Vidler has devoted a whole book to this "architectural uncanny". He describes the rebound effect on architecture of middle-class anxieties and phobias that have assailed the individual, who has only recently been "discovered".[16] In modernism, the idea of the subject is intimately bound up with the notion of space.[17] And just as the autonomous individual is an idealised "subject" of modernism, in the same way "space" – as a discursively produced concept of the history of art and architecture – is itself a genuinely modern "invention".[18] One might even say that space is the cognitive by-product of a fundamental re-organisation of society – a society that had emerged from family, even feudal structures to develop organisational systems which suited society's increasingly individualistic mobility and was linked to the production of new boundary processes as well as differentiations, such as "private" and "public".[19] Setting boundaries appears as a necessary prerequisite for the establishment of identity[20], whereupon the question of space – like that of identity – becomes relevant at the moment when it is contingent, i.e. groundlessly, apparent.

Role Play and Porous Boundaries
In connection with late 19th century architecture, Beatriz Colomina has referred to the vital function of "masquerade", which accompanies the constitution of identity: "Architecture fully participates in this pervasive logic of the mask".[21] And one wonders what lies behind the mask? "Nothing", Judith Butler would say, at least no identity, but at best the yearning for an identity, an "imitation without an original".[22] This connects the modern subject with modern architecture. In "Privacy and Publicity" Beatriz Colomina explicitly demonstrates the degree to which Le Corbusier's spaces were organised in a cinematographic manner, and those of Loos laid out for a theatrically conceived subject. This conception of architecture in respect to its users' role-play implies on the one hand the dramatic enactment of an inner space given by an outer boundary, and equally on the other hand, a questioning or perforation of this boundary line by the actors' theatricality and visuality. Here, perhaps involuntarily, the recipient Schmarsow had in mind again comes into play. That said, he does not so much read and interpret space as use it as a kind of stage set for the role-play for identities, and at the same time is framed by it, placed on a stage.[23] In this context, however, what is of primary interest is the argument in respect to "per-

„Raum für Zwei"
Christoph Jantos kartiert in seinem Zweitsemesterprojekt die Schlussszene aus dem Film *Der Himmel über Berlin* (Wim Wenders, 1987), in der sich Marion und Damiel im Frühstückssaal des ehemaligen Hotel Esplanade, Berlin, treffen. Er beobachtet die räumliche Verschiebung von Raumteilen des ehemaligen Frühstückssaals im Rahmen des Neubaus Sony Center, Berlin, und entwickelt in dem neu entstandenen Raumgefüge einen „Raum für Zwei", für Marion und Damiel.
Er rekonstruiert und interpretiert dafür den Filmraum der Szene: Aus der neuen Cocktail-Bar im Sony Center wird, entsprechend der Kameraeinstellung der Schlussszene des Films, ein Abdruck des Innenraums vom versetzten, ehemaligen Frühstückssaal entnommen, damit wird an der ursprünglicher Stelle des Abdrucks eine räumliche Intervention entwickelt, der Innenraumabdruck wird zum Raumkörper.

"Room for Two"
In his second-semester project, Christoph Jantos charts the final scene from the film Wings of Desire (Wim Wenders, 1987) in which Marion and Damiel meet in the breakfast room of the former Hotel Esplanade in Berlin. He observes the spatial displacement of room elements in the former "Breakfast Room" in the context of the new Sony Center building in Berlin and he develops a "Room for Two", for Marion and Damiel in the newly created space.
For this, he reconstructs and interprets the film space of this scene: out of the new cocktail bar in the Sony Center, in accordance with the camera setting in the film's last scene, a copy is made of the interior of the displaced former breakfast room. Thus, a spatial intervention is developed at the original location of the copy, with the interior spatial copy becoming the body of the room.

Inszenierung eines vom Außen abgegrenzten Innen wie auch andererseits gleichzeitig die Infragestellung, eine Perforation dieser Grenzziehung durch die Theatralik und Visualität der Akteure. Hier kommt, vielleicht ungewollt, wieder der Schmarsow'sche Rezipient ins Spiel. Allerdings liest und interpretiert er weniger den Raum, sondern benutzt ihn als eine Art Bühnenhintergrund zum Rollenspiel der Identitäten und wird gleichzeitig von ihm gerahmt, in Szene gesetzt.[23] In diesem Zusammenhang aber erscheint hier vor allem das Argument der Perforation interessant, der Grenze zwischen Innen und Außen, die an der Neuorganisation des Verhältnisses zwischen Subjekt und Raum entlang eines mobilisierten, von Medien strukturierten Blicks[24] ansetzt. Dazu Colomina: „The inhabitants of Loos' houses are both actors in and spectators of the family scene – involved in, yet detached from, their own space. The classical distinction between inside and outside, private and public, object and subject, becomes convoluted."[25] Die damit antizipierte theatralische Fassung des Subjekts bringt auch noch den nächsten Dualismus ins Wanken, der ebenfalls zu einem Gründungsmythos der Architektur der Moderne gerechnet werden kann: die Korrelation zwischen Form und Funktion. Wenn das Subjekt nun nicht mehr auf seine biologisch-geschlechtliche Hülle hin determinierbar ist – und dahingehend war eine wesentliche Kritik am autonomen Subjektbegriff formuliert –, dann kann auch der Raum nicht über eine spezifische Form bestimmt werden, sondern bestenfalls über die Bedeutungen, die man ihm, diskursiv produziert, zuschreibt. Allerspätestens mit der Hochblüte der schon verlassen geglaubten, dann aber gentrifizierten und nobilitierten ehemaligen Industriebauten in Städten rund um den Globus wurde deutlich, wie fragil die Beziehungen zwischen geplanter Funktion und realer Nutzung sind. Dazu Jeffrey Kipnis: „Solange sie bestehen, sind die Beziehungen zwischen Form und Programm weitaus eher affiliativ als angleichend, eine Tatsache, die die endlose Anzahl von Umprogrammierungen (...) mehr als bezeugt. Das soll nicht heißen, es gäbe keine Beziehung zwischen Form und Funktion, sondern nur, dass diese Beziehung im Kern schwach ist."[26] Schon 1963 argumentierte der Urbanismus-Theoretiker Melvin Webber: „ (...) people gather in spatial settings for non-spatial reasons."[27] Mittlerweile erscheint jeder Versuch, eine organische Verbindung zwischen Form und Funktion herzustellen, als hoffnungslos idealistisch oder hoffnungslos autoritär.

Damit wird aber auch ein substantieller Kontrollverlust der Architektur über den Raum und infolgedessen über den imaginären Nutzer evident. So, wie das Subjekt ideengeschichtlich einer positivistischen, rationalistischen Vorstellung von Autonomie entzogen wird, entzieht sich auch der Raum zusehends der Kontrolle, Planbarkeit und Determinierbarkeit seitens der Architektur. Und wie das Subjekt nur noch als Hybrid von kontingent gefügten Identitäten zu denken ist, so ist auch der Raum nur noch als komplexes Gefüge von Vorstellungen, Bildern, Machtverhältnissen denkbar.[28] Damit verändert sich der Raumbegriff der Moderne, gemäß dem der Raum etwas architektonisch zu Beherrschendes, mit physischen Mitteln zu Gestaltendes sei, hin zu einer Vorstellung von Raum als Beziehungsgefüge, als Matrix, in sich Machtverhältnisse, Ideologien, Akteure und Projektionen einschreiben und zu analysieren sind. Architektur ist nur noch eine Einflussgröße unter vielen in diesem Spiel der Kräfte.

foration", the boundary between interior and exterior, which starts at the re-organisation of the relationship between subject and space along a mobilised, media-structured view.[24] Colomina says of this: "The inhabitants of Loos' houses are both actors in and spectators of the family scene – involved in, yet detached from, their own space. The classical distinction between inside and outside, private and public, object and subject, becomes convoluted."[25] The theatrical version of the subject that is thus anticipated also destabilises the next dualism, which can be considered, too, as a founding myth of architecture in modernism: the correlation between form and function. If the subject can no longer be defined by his or her biological-gender envelope – and an essential criticism of the autonomous concept of subject was formulated in this sense – then even space can no longer be determined by means of a specific form, but at best through the meanings which – discursively produced as they are – one attributes to them. At the very latest, at the height of interest in old industrial buildings in cities around the globe – which were first seen as ruins, and then were ennobled through gentrification – it became evident how delicate relations really are between planned function and actual use. Jeffrey Kipnis commented as follows: "For as long as they exist, the relationships between form and programme are much more affiliating than imitative – a fact amply demonstrated by the endless sequence of re-programming (...) that goes on. This is not to say that form and func-

Von links nach rechts:
Collage, Bildsequenz der Schlussszene;
Konzeptmodell, Schlussszene, Marions Weg, Plexiglas und Farbfolien;
Kartierung der Wegverläufe von Marion und Damiel in der Schlussszene, Grundrisse von „Palmenhof" und Frühstückssaal im ehemaligen Hotel Esplanade, Berlin;
Gegenüberstellung der räumlichen Anordnung von „Kaisersaal" und „Frühstückssaal" im ehemaligen Hotel Esplanade, Berlin, vor und nach der Verschiebung im Zuge des Neubaus des Sony Center, Berlin, mit Kartierung des Wegverlaufs von Damiel

  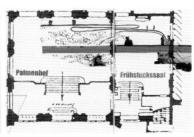 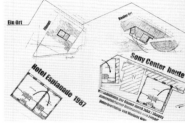

tion are not related, but simply that this relationship has a weak core".[26] Already in 1963, Melvin Webber, the urbanism-theoretician, argued that: "(...) people gather in spatial settings for non-spatial reasons."[27] More recently, every attempt to create an organic connection between form and function has shown itself to be either hopelessly idealistic or hopelessly authoritarian.

However, this also manifests a substantial loss of control on the part of architecture over space – and, in consequence, over the imaginary user. Accordingly, just as the subject is historically deprived of a positivist, rationalistic view of autonomy, so too, space more and more defies control and determinability through architecture. And just as the subject can only be conceived as a hybrid entity by contingently composed identities, so too, space can only be imagined as a complex composition of ideas, images, and power-relationships.[28] In that sense, modernism's whole concept of space changes, according to which space becomes something to be dominated architectonically, to be structured by physical means – all the way to a notion of space as a network of relationships, as a matrix, in which power relationships, ideologies, actors and projections are brought into play. Architecture is but one more highly influential dimension among many in this interplay of forces.

From left to right:
Collage, Picture sequence of the last scene;
Concept model, last scene, Marion's way, perspex and colour sheets;
Charting the routes of Marion and Damiel in the final scene, layouts of the "Palm Courtyard" and "Breakfast Room" in the former Hotel Esplanade, Berlin;
Comparison of spatial arrangement in the "Emperor's Room" and "Breakfast Room" in the former Hotel Esplanade, Berlin, before and after their displacement for the new building of the Sony Center, Berlin, with charting of Damiel's route

Raum jenseits der Dualismen

Angesichts der zunehmenden Auflösung dualistischer Grenz- und Differenzvorstellungen ist auch der Versuch von Seiten der Sozialwissenschaften, der Cultural Studies wie der Philosophie zu verstehen, Raumkonzepte zu entwickeln, die den in die Krise geratenen Dualismen entgehen, um stattdessen Hybridbildungen differenter Identitäts- und Raumvorstellungen zu thematisieren. Autoren wie Edward Soja[29] oder Homi K. Bhabha[30] verwendeten dazu den Begriff „Third Space", der in der Nachfolge von Henri Lefebvre primär als soziale Konstruktion gemeint ist, „das heißt auch als Verräumlichung im Sinn von Performativität sozialer Beziehungen."[31] Der Fokus liegt hier auf der Verhandelbarkeit sozialer und kultureller Identität, wobei dieser Verhandlungsspielraum nicht nur räumlich, sondern auch zeitlich gemeint ist – ein Zwischenzeitraum[32], in dem sprachliche, soziale, symbolische Verhandlungen zwischen unterschiedlichen kulturellen Subjektivitäten Hybridbildungen produzieren, die angesichts der realpolitischen Allgegenwart von translozierten, migrierten oder temporär dislozierten Identitäten mehr zur Regel denn zur Ausnahme werden.[33] Und nicht zufällig entspringt dieser Diskurs um den „dritten Raum" der Postkolonialismus-Debatte, also einem Diskurs, der die sozialen und ästhetischen Effekte von Raumpolitik und ihren materiellen Äußerungen untersucht.[34]

Die Architektur steht angesichts dieser Entwicklungen vor einem Dilemma: Zwar erfährt Schmarsows Konzeption des vom Betrachter-Subjekt konstituierten Raums ein „revival", aber die Architektur ist darin nur noch eine marginalisierte Größe in der Gemengelage von an- und abwesenden Räumen an einem Ort. Sie darf folglich weniger unter Gesichtspunkten der Repräsentation denn als „Parergon"[35], als Rahmenwerk, als Supplement betrachtet werden[36], das einen – wenn auch unverzichtbaren – Hintergrund für die (Ver-)Handlungen des Raums bietet. Martin Prinzhorn hat in Bezug auf die funktional unterdeterminierten Räume bei Kazuo Sejima (SANAA) einmal von „deflationistischer Architektur" gesprochen[37] – von einer Art elaboriertem Rückzug im Gefecht um die Kontrolle über den Raum und um seine antizipierte Nutzung. Diese Entkopplung von Signifikant und Signifikat produziert allerdings immer auch eine eklatante, immanente Widersprüchlichkeit: Wenn nämlich das Unvorhergesehene schon mit eingeplant ist, dann verkommt es zur vorhersehbaren Größe, wie unbestimmt diese auch sein mag. Das Benutzer-Subjekt verhält sich dann in jedem Fall erwartungsgemäß und „programmatisch anarchistisch", es konsumiert seinen eigenen Freiheitsanspruch. Entscheidend wird also für die Architektur in der Auseinandersetzung mit dem Raum sein, inwieweit es gelingen kann, die Kontingenz und Komplexität ihrer eigenen Verfahrensweisen sichtbar zu machen, die Mechanismen der Institutionalisierung und Naturalisierung als produktiven Widerspruch darzustellen und vor allem: den Raum nicht zu „kontrollieren", sondern Mechanismen zur Sichtbarmachung seines Zustandekommens zu entwickeln.

Sony Center, Berlin, Lageplanausschnitt, mit Außenaufnahmen der im Rahmen des Neubaus vom Sony Center versetzten, ehemals zusammengehörigen Raumteile des Frühstückssaals" im ehemaligen Hotel Esplanade, Berlin, 2002

Sony Center, Berlin, excerpt of floor plan, with external photographs taken during the new building of the Sony Center of the displaced and previously adjoining room elements of the "Breakfast Room" in the former Hotel Esplanade, Berlin, 2002

Space Beyond Dualisms

Taking into account increasing dissolution of dualistic boundaries and differences in outlook, it is easy to understand attempts on the part of social sciences, cultural studies and philosophy to develop notions of space that avoid crisis-ridden dualisms in favour of thematising hybrid formations of different concepts of identity and space. Authors like Edward Soja[29] and Homi K. Bhabha[30] use the term "third space" to describe this state of affairs that in the wake of Henri Lefebvre is primarily conceived as a social construct, "in other words, as spatialization in the sense of the performativity of social relationships".[31] Here the focus is on the negotiability of social and cultural identity. In this case, the freedom to negotiate is not merely intended as spatial, but also temporal – an "interstitial future"[32], in which linguistic, social and symbolic negotiations between different cultural subjectivities lead to hybrid forms. In turn, in the light of the omnipresent Realpolitik of translocated, migrated, or temporarily dislocated identities, these hybrid forms become more the rule than the exception.[33] It is no coincidence that this discourse revolves around the "third space" of the post-colonialism debate, in other words, it explores the social and aesthetic effects of "spatial politics" and its material manifestations.[34]

Taking into account these developments, architecture is presented with a dilemma: whilst Schmarsow's idea of space as constituted by the observer-subject

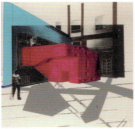
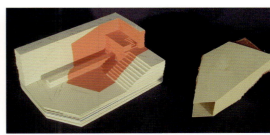

undergoes a "revival", in this paradigm architecture is only a marginalised entity within the mix of present and absent spaces in any given location. Hence, rather than considering it in the categories of representation, it should be regarded as a "parergon"[35], as a framework, as something supplementary[36] offering a backdrop, albeit an indispensable one, for spatial actions and negotiations. In relation to the functionally indeterminate spaces at work by Kazuo Sejima (SANAA), Martin Prinzhorn once spoke about "deflationary architecture"[37] – a kind of elaborate retreat in the battle for control over space and its anticipated use. This decoupling of significance and signifier certainly always produces a striking, if immanent contradictory quality. If for instance unpredictable elements are pre-planned, the anticipated final shape will inevitably materialise no matter how uncertain its form may be. The "user-subject" then behaves in each case just as expected and it consumes – "programmatically anarchic" – its own claim to freedom. Thus, what will prove to be crucial for architecture in its confrontation with space is how far it can succeed in making visible the contingency and complexity of its own procedures, in depicting the mechanisms of institutionalisation and naturalisation as a productive contradiction; and – above all – in not "controlling" space, but developing mechanisms to render its production visible.

Links: Collage, Cocktail-Bar im ehemaligen Frühstückssaal, Markierung der Kameraeinstellung für die Schlussszene des Films;
Mitte: „Raum für Zwei", räumliche Intervention, Außenansicht des erneut verschobenen Raumabdruckmodells aus der heutigen Cocktail-Bar vor die restlichen Innenfassaden des ehemaligen Frühstückssaals;
Rechts: Modell, Raumabdruck und räumliche Intervention „Raum für Zwei", Pappe und Silikon

Left: Collage, cocktail bar in the former "Breakfast Room", marking of the camera setting for the film's final scene;
Center: Collage, "Room for Two". spatial intervention, external view of newly displaced model of the room copy from today's cocktail bar in front of remaining inner façades of the former "Breakfast Room";
Right: Model, room copy and spatial intervention "Room for Two", cardboard and silicon.

ANMERKUNGEN

(1) Siehe dazu z.B.: Mirzoeff, Nicholas: *An Introduction to Visual Culture*. London u.a. 1999
(2) Mitchell, William J. T.: „The Pictorial Turn". In: Kravagna, Christian (Hg.): *Privileg Blick. Kritik der visuellen Kultur*. Berlin 1997, 15-40
(3) Siehe dazu u.a.: Rakatansky, Mark: „Spatial Narratives". Nachgedruckt in: Steiner, Dietmar M. (Hg.): *Sturm der Ruhe. What is Architecture?* Salzburg 2001, S. 82-128
(4) Foucault, Michel: „Andere Räume". In: Barck, Karlheinz u.a. (Hg.): *Aisthesis. Wahrnehmung heute oder Perspektiven einer anderen Ästhetik*. Leipzig 1990, S. 34-46
(5) Siehe dazu: Jameson, Fredric: *Postmodernism, or, The Cultural Logic of Late Capitalism*. Durham, NC, 1991
(6) Eine detaillierte Diskussion der Raumkonzepte von Jameson ist zu finden in: Smith, Michael Peter: *Transnational Urbanism. Locating Globalization*. Oxford u.a. 2001.
(7) Löw, Martina: *Raumsoziologie*. Frankfurt am Main 2001
(8) Siehe dazu auch den Vortrag: Jöchner, Cornelia: „Wie kommt ‚Bewegung' in die Architekturtheorie? Zur Raum-Debatte am Beginn der Moderne",
unter: http://www.tu-cottbus.de/BTU/Fak2/TheoArch/Wolke/deu/Themen/041/Joechner/joechner.htm
(9) Schmarsow, August: „Das Wesen der architektonischen Schöpfung. Antrittsvorlesung an der K. Universität Leipzig 1894". Auszugsweise in: Moravánszky, Ákos (Hg.): *Architekturtheorie im 20. Jahrhundert. Eine kritische Anthologie*. Wien u.a. 2003, S. 153-158.
(10) Moholy-Nagy, László: *Von Material zu Architektur*. Mainz u.a. 1968 (Orig. 1929), S. 194f.
(11) Hier sei neben den Texten Moholy-Nagys auf die „promenade architecturale" Le Corbusiers hingewiesen oder auf die Versuche von Gropius, den Betrachter durch Raumeffekte zu überwältigen, wie etwa in dem mit Piscator konzipierten Totaltheater.
(12) Siehe: Colomina, Beatriz: *Privacy and Publicity. Modern Architecture as Mass Media*. Cambridge, 1994, S. 21f.
(13) Heidegger, Martin: „Bauen Wohnen Denken". Auszugsweise in: Moravánszky, Ákos (Hg.): *Architekturtheorie im 20.Jahrhundert. Eine kritische Anthologie*. Wien u.a. 2003, S. 510-514
(14) Siehe dazu: Baecker, Dirk: „Die Dekonstruktion der Schachtel. Innen und Außen in der Architektur". In: Luhmann, Niklas u.a. (Hg.): *Unbeobachtbare Welt. Über Kunst und Architektur*. Bielefeld 1990, S. 67-104
(15) Freud, Sigmund: „Das Unheimliche". In: Ders.: *Studienausgabe. Band IV, Psychologische Schriften*. Hg. v. Alexander Mitscherlich. Frankfurt am Main 1970, S. 241-274
(16) Vidler, Anthony: *The Architectural Uncanny. Essays in the Modern Unhomely*. Cambridge, MA 1992
(17) Siehe dazu das Interview mit Anthony Vidler von Juliane Rebentisch und Beate Söntgen: „Bauen Wohnen Fürchten". In: *Texte zur Kunst. Nr. 47*. Berlin 2002, S. 53-61
(18) Siehe dazu: Vidler, Anthony: *Warped Space. Art, Architecture, and Anxiety in Modern Culture*. Cambridge, MA u.a. 2000, S. 1-14
(19) Zur Differenzierung des Wohnhauses in getrennte, separat zugängliche „Appartements" siehe: Teyssot, Georges: *Die Krankheit des Domizils. Wohnen und Wohnbau 1800-1930*. Braunschweig u.a.1989, S. 80f.
(20) Siehe: Burgin, Victor: *In/Different Spaces. Place and Memory in Visual Culture*. Berkeley u.a. 1996, S. 146f.
(21) Colomina, Beatriz: *Privacy and Publicity. Modern Architecture as Mass Media*. Cambridge, MA, 1994, S. 26
(22) Butler, Judith: *Das Unbehagen der Geschlechter*. Frankfurt am Main 1991, S. 203
(23) Zur räumlichen Logik von Maskerade und Theatralität in der Architektur siehe: „Dislocated". In: Spiegl, Andreas/Teckert, Christian (Hg.): *Prospekt. Büro für kognitiven Urbanismus*. Köln 2003, S. 156-157
(24) Siehe dazu: Friedberg, Anne: *Window Shopping. Cinema and the Postmodern*. Berkeley 1993, S. 20f.
(25) Colomina, Beatriz: *Privacy and Publicity. Modern Architecture as Mass Media*. Cambridge, MA, 1994, S. 244
(26) Kipnis, Jeffrey: „InFormation / DeFormation". In: *Arch+. Nr. 131*, Aachen 1996, S. 31
(27) So zusammengefasst bei Wigley, Mark: „Resisting the City". In: Brouwer, Joke u.a. (Hg.): *TransUrbanism*. Rotterdam 2002, S. 106
(28) Oder wie Victor Burgin die Beziehung zwischen Stadt und Subjekt einmal auf den Punkt brachte: „The city in our actual experience is at the same time an actually existing physical environment, and a city in a novel, a film, a photograph, a city seen on television, a city in a comic strip, a city in a pie chart, and so on." In: Burgin, Victor: *In/Different Spaces. Place and Memory in Visual Culture*. Berkeley u.a.1996, S. 28
(29) Soja, Edward W.: *Thirdspace. Journeys to Los Angeles and other real-and-imagined Places*. Cambridge, MA, u.a. 1996
(30) Bhabha, Homi K.: *The Location of Culture*. London u.a. 1994
(31) Nierhaus, Irene: „Positionen". In: Dies. u.a. (Hg.): *Räumen. Baupläne zwischen Raum, Visualität, Geschlecht und Architektur*. Wien 2002, S. 16
(32) Bhabha, Homi K.: *The Location of Culture*. London u.a. 1994, S. 219
(33) Siehe: Appadurai, Arjun: *Modernity at Large. Cultural Dimensions of Globalization*. Minneapolis u.a. 1996
(34) Eine höchst empfehlenswerte Zusammenstellung aktueller Positionen zum Raum in den sozialwissenschaftlichen Diskussionen findet sich in: Bormann, Regina: *Raum, Zeit, Identität. Sozialtheoretische Verortungen kultureller Prozesse*. Opladen 2001, S. 233-306
(35) Siehe dazu: Derrida, Jacques: *Die Wahrheit in der Malerei*. Wien 1992
(36) Siehe dazu auch: Gleiter, Jörg H.: *Rückkehr des Verdrängten. Zur kritischen Theorie des Ornaments in der architektonischen Moderne*. Weimar 2002, S. 264-275
(37) Prinzhorn, Martin: „Raum und Bedeutung. Die deflationistische Architektur von Kazuyo Sejima". *In: Texte zur Kunst. Nr. 47*. Berlin 2002, S. 63-69

NOTES

(1) Cf e.g. Mirzoeff, Nicholas: *An Introduction to Visual Culture*. London ia, 1999.
(2) Mitchell, William J.T.: "The Pictorial Turn". In: Kravagna, Christian (Ed.): *Privileg Blick. Kritik der visuellen Kultur*. Berlin, 1997, pp. 15–40.
(3) Cf among others: Rakatansky, Mark: "Spatial Narratives". Reprinted in: Steiner, Dietmar, M (Ed.): *Sturm der Ruhe. What is Architecture?* Salzburg, 2001, pp. 82–128.
(4) Foucault, Michel: "Andere Räume". In: Barck, Karlheinz et al. (Ed.) *Wahrnehmung heute oder Perspektiven einer anderen Ästhetik*. Leipzig, 1990, pp. 34–46.
(5) Cf: Jameson, Frederic: *Postmodernism, or, The Cultural Logic of Late Capitalism*. Durham, NC, 1991.
(6) A detailed discussion of Jameson's Concepts of Space is to be found in: Smith, Michael Peter: *Transnational Urbanism. Locating Globalization*. Oxford ia, 2001.
(7) Löw, Martina: *Raumsoziologie*. Frankfurt am Main, 2001.
(8) Cf: the lecture by Jöchner, Cornelia: "Wie kommt Bewegung in die Architekturtheorie. Zur Raum-Debatte am Beginn der Moderne."
At: http://www.tu-cottbus.de/BTU/Fak2/TheoArch/Wolke/deu/Themen/041/Joechner/joechner.htm
(9) Schmarsow, August: "Das Wesen der architektonischen Schöpfung. Antrittsvorlesung an der K. Universität Leipzig 1894". Extracts in: Moravánszky, Ákos (Ed.): *Architekturtheorie im 20. Jahrhundert. Eine kritische Anthologie*. Vienna ia, 2003, pp. 153–158.
(10) Moholy-Nagy, László: *Von Material zu Architektur*. Mainz ia, 1968 (Orig. 1929), pp. 194f.
(11) Here, along with the Moholy-Nagy texts, we should also mention the "promenade architecturale" by Le Corbusier or the attempts by Gropius to overwhelm the observer by spatial effects, as in the "total theatre", which he devised with Piscator.
(12) Colomina, Beatrix: *Privacy and Publicity. Modern Architecture as Mass Media*. Cambridge, M 1994, pp. 21f.
(13) Heidegger, Martin: "Bauen Wohnen Denken". Extracts in: Moravánszky, Ákos (Ed.): *Architekturtheorie im 20. Jahrhundert. Eine kritische Anthologie*. Vienna ia, 2003, pp. 510–514.
(14) Cf: Baecker, Dirk: "Die Dekonstruktion der Schachtel. Innen und Außen in der Architektur". In: Luhmann, Niklas, et al.(Eds.): *Unbeobachtbare Welt. Über Kunst und Architektur*. Bielefeld, 1990, pp. 67–104.
(15) Freud, Sigmund: "Das Unheimliche". In: Freud: *Study Edition, Vol. IV, Psychological Writings*. ed. by Alexander Mitscherlich, Frankfurt am Main, 1970, pp. 241–274.
(16) Vidler, Anthony: *The Architectural Uncanny. Essays in the Modern Unhomely*. Cambridge, MA, 1992.
(17) Cf the interview with Anthony Vidler by Juliane Rebentisch and Beate Söntgen: "Bauen Wohnen Fürchten". In: *Texte zur Kunst, No. 47*. Berlin, 2002, pp. 53–61.
(18) See also: Vidler, Anthony: *Warped Space. Art, Architecture, and Anxiety in Modern Culture*. Cambridge, MA, etc., 2000, pp. 1–14.
(19) On the difference to the dwelling house in freestanding, separately accessible "apartments", see: Teyssot, Georges: *Die Krankheit des Domizils. Wohnen und Wohnbau 1800-1930*. Brunswick etc., 1989, pp. 80f.
(20) Cf: Burgin, Victor: *In/Different Spaces. Place and Memory in Visual Culture*. Berkeley ia, 1996, pp.146f.
(21) Colomina, Beatriz: *Privacy and Publicity. Modern Architecture as Mass Media*. Cambridge, 1994, p. 26.
(22) Butler, Judith: *Das Unbehagen der Geschlechter*. Frankfurt am Main, 1991, p. 203.
(23) On the spatial logic of masquerade and theatricality in architecture, see: "Dislocated". In: Spiegl, Andreas / Teckert, Christian (Eds.): *Prospect. Büro für kognitiven Urbanismus*. Cologne, 2003, pp. 156–167.
(24) Cf: Friedberg, Anne: *Window Shopping. Cinema and the Postmodern*. Berkeley, 1993, pp. 20f.
(25) Colomina, Beatriz: *Privacy and Publicity. Modern Architecture as Mass Media*. Cambridge, MA, 1994, p. 244.
(26) Kipnis, Jeffrey: "InFormation/DeFormation". In: *Arch+. No.131*. Aachen, 1996, p. 81.
(27) Summarised like this in Wigley, Mark: "Resisting the City". In: Brouwer, Joke et al. (Eds.) *TransUrbanism*. Rotterdam, 2002, pp. 106f.
(28) Or else as Victor Burgin once cogently expressed the relationship between city and subject: "The city in our actual experience is at the same time an actually existing physical environment, and a city in a novel, a film, a photograph, a city seen on television, a city in a comic strip, a city in a pie chart, and so on." In: Burgin, Victor: *In/Different Spaces. Place and Memory in Visual Culture*. Berkeley ia, 1996, p. 28.
(29) Soja, Edward W.: *Thirdspace. Journeys to Los Angeles and other real-and-imagined Places*. Cambridge, MA, ia, 1996.
(30) Bhabha, Homi K: *The Location of Culture*. London, etc., 1994
(31) Nierhaus, Irene: "Positionen". In: Dies et al.(Eds.): *Räumen. Baupläne zwischen Raum, Visualität, Geschlecht und Architektur*. Vienna, 2002, p. 16.
(32) Bhabha, Homi K: *The Location of Culture*. London ia, 1994, p. 219.
(33) See e.g.: Appadurai, Arjun: *Modernity at Large. Cultural Dimensions of Globalization*. Mineapolis ia, 1996.
(34) A highly recommended compilation of current positions on space in social-science discussions is to be found in: Bormann, Regina: *Raum, Zeit, Identität. Sozialtheoretische Verortungen kultureller Prozesse*. Opladen, 2001, pp. 233–306.
(35) Cf: Derrida, Jacques: *Die Wahrheit in der Malerei*. Vienna, 1992.
(36) See also: Gleiter, Jörg H: *Rückkehr des Verdrängten. Zur kritischen Theorie des Ornaments in der architektonischen Moderne*. Weimar, 2002, pp. 264–275.
(37) Prinzhorn, Martin: "Raum und Bedeutung. Die deflationistische Architektur von Kazuyo Sejima". In: *Texte zur Kunst, No. 47*. Berlin, 2002, pp. 63–69.

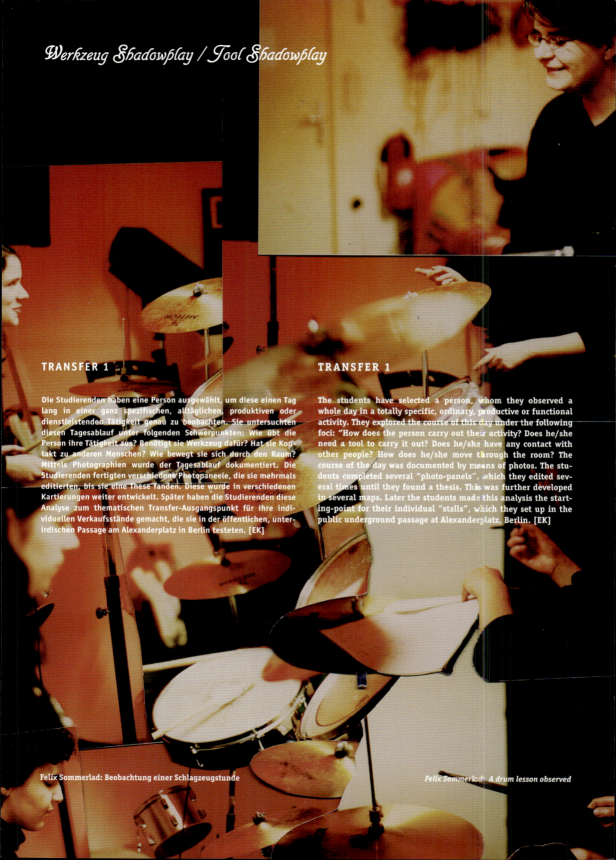

Werkzeug Shadowplay / Tool Shadowplay

TRANSFER 1

Die Studierenden haben eine Person ausgewählt, um diese einen Tag lang in einer ganz spezifischen, alltäglichen, produktiven oder dienstleistenden Tätigkeit genau zu beobachten. Sie untersuchten diesen Tagesablauf unter folgenden Schwerpunkten: Wie übt die Person ihre Tätigkeit aus? Benötigt sie Werkzeug dafür? Hat sie Kontakt zu anderen Menschen? Wie bewegt sie sich durch den Raum? Mittels Photographien wurde der Tagesablauf dokumentiert. Die Studierenden fertigten verschiedene Photopaneele, die sie mehrmals editierten, bis sie eine These fanden. Diese wurde in verschiedenen Kartierungen weiter entwickelt. Später haben die Studierenden diese Analyse zum thematischen Transfer-Ausgangspunkt für ihre individuellen Verkaufsstände gemacht, die sie in der öffentlichen, unterirdischen Passage am Alexanderplatz in Berlin testeten. [EK]

TRANSFER 1

The students have selected a person, whom they observed a whole day in a totally specific, ordinary, productive or functional activity. They explored the course of this day under the following foci: "How does the person carry out their activity? Does he/she need a tool to carry it out? Does he/she have any contact with other people? How does he/she move through the room? The course of the day was documented by means of photos. The students completed several "photo-panels", which they edited several times until they found a thesis. This was further developed in several maps. Later the students made this analysis the starting-point for their individual "stalls", which they set up in the public underground passage at Alexanderplatz, Berlin. [EK]

Felix Sommerlad: Beobachtung einer Schlagzeugstunde

Felix Sommerlad: A drum lesson observed

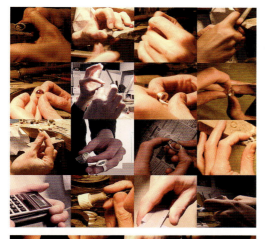

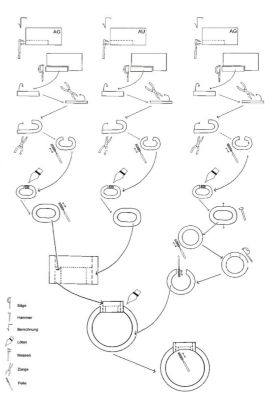

Anne Röhl: Photopaneele und Kartierung zur Entstehung eines Ringes

Anne Röhl: Photo-panel and chart for the creation of a ring

Nina Hosni: Kartierung der Kommunikation in einer Druckerei

Nina Hosni: Map of communication in a printing works

Michael Reiss / Transfer 1 & 2   2002/2003

  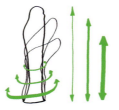 

Schnitte Sections

Funktionsdiagramm und Testsituation Function-diagram and test-situation

GET WRAPPED

Jörg verkauft Wein, Oliven, Wurst und Käse. Die Waren werden morgens ausgepackt und dekorativ in der Auslage zur Schau gestellt. Abends wird alles in Frischhaltefolie verpackt und für den nächsten Tag geschützt gelagert. Jörg und seine Kolleginnen entwickelten im Lauf der Zeit eine Technik, um diesen sich mehrmals wiederholenden Arbeitsschritt schnell und effizient abzuwickeln. Nach genauer Beobachtung war es möglich, mit Hilfe von Photopaneelen und Kartierungen das Prinzip exakt darzustellen. Diese Analyse stellt die Grundlage für die Entwicklung eines Marktstandes und dessen Test im Untergeschoss des Bahnhofs Alexanderplatz dar. Ähnlich den Produkten Jörgs, die jeden Abend in eine zweite Haut gepackt werden, bietet das Objekt Get

GET WRAPPED

Jörg sells wine, olives, sausage and cheese. The items are bought in the morning and decoratively put on display. In the evening, everything is packed in plastic foil and preserved for the next day. In due course, Jörg and his female colleagues developed a technique for performing this frequently repeated task swiftly and efficiently. After exact observation it proved possible – with the help of photo-panels and card-indices – to give a precise depiction of this principle. This analysis establishes the basis for developing a market stall and its test-run in the underpass of Alexanderplatz Station. Like Jörg's products, which are packed into a second skin every evening, the object Get Wrapped offers one the chance to package

Jörgs Tagesablauf Jörg's typical day

Genauere Betrachtung der Verpackungstechnik in ihren wesentlichen Schritten A more precise observation of the packing technique in its essential phases

Hineinschlüpfen in die Latexhaut Slipping into the latex skin

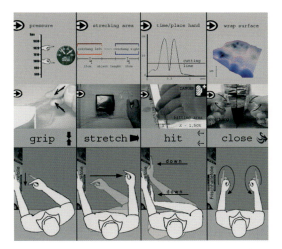 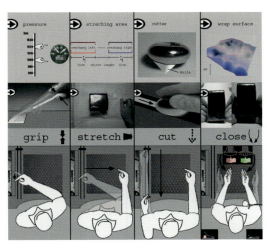

Kartierung und Optimierung des Verpackungsautomatismus   Card-index and optimalization for the packing automat

Wrapped die Möglichkeit, sich selbst zu verpacken. Es besteht aus einer Latexhülle, in die man durch eine enge Öffnung einsteigt und sie dann entlang des Körpers bis über den Kopf zieht. Je weiter man sich aufrichtet, desto stärker spannt sich die Latexhaut und schränkt die Bewegung ein. Vollständig verpackt und der Umgebung entzogen, befindet man sich in einem engen, vollkommen dunklen Raum. Durch die Hülle dringen nur noch gedämpft Geräusche. Um den räumlichen Effekt zu verstärken, sind in das Kopfteil der Hülle Lautsprecher eingearbeitet, die abwechselnd monotone Musik wiedergeben. Nach der Überwindung, sich vor aller Augen der eigenen Sicht zu berauben, beschrieben die Testpersonen die Erfahrung als durchaus angenehm.

oneself. This consists of latex wrapping, into which one clambers through a narrow aperture and tugs down over the whole body, including the head. The harder one tries to stand upright, the more the latex skin pulls tight, severely restricting movement. Completely packed up and removed from your surroundings, you find yourself in a small, totally dark room. Only muffled sounds come to you through this wrapping. To increase the effect of space, loudspeakers have been built into the top of the wrapper; and they take turns to broadcast monotonous music. After feeling strong enough to deprive oneself of one's own sight in front of everyone, the people in the test described the whole experience as very pleasant.

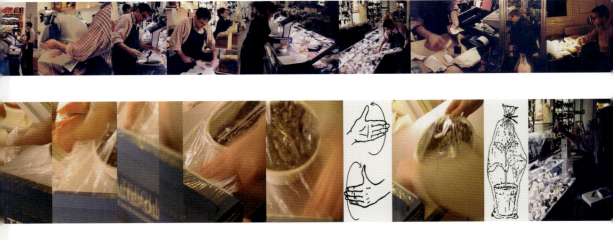

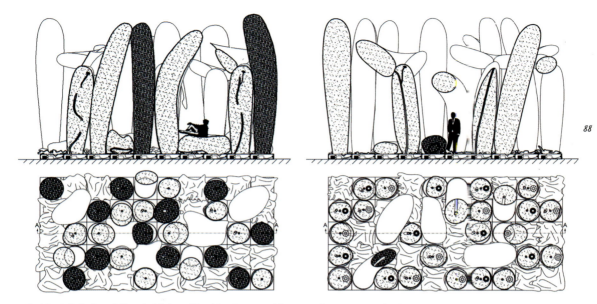

Zwei Zustände des *Space Inflators* in Schnitt und Grundriss   Two states of the Space Inflator *in section and outline*

THE SPACE INFLATOR

„In der Berliner Innenstadt wird für zwei Jahre ein Ort für Dienstleistungen zur Verfügung gestellt. Auf einer Fläche von vier Parkplätzen gilt es einen Transferort zu planen." Ausgehend von Innenraumcollagen und deren Übersetzung in mehrere Modelle entstand das Projekt *Space Inflator*. Der *Space Inflator* ist ein Objekt, das Raum durch aufblasbare Elemente erzeugt und sich fließend einer passiven oder aktiven Nutzung anpasst. Zwei unterschiedliche Formen und vier verschiedene Oberflächenbeschaffenheiten ergeben acht Pneu-Varianten, die sich je nach Bedarf miteinander kombinieren lassen. Diese werden über eine Bodenstation mit Luft gefüllt und zu einem Objekt miteinander verbunden. Die Gestaltung des Raumes lässt sich stetig durch Aufblasen und Entleeren

THE SPACE INFLATOR

"In Berlin city centre a space has been set aside for 2 years for services. It was agreed to plan a 'transfer area' on a site encompassing four parking spaces." Starting from interior space collages and their translation into a number of models, the *Space Inflator* Project was created. The *Space Inflator* is an object, which creates space by its inflatable elements, and which can be used in either a passive or active role. Two different formations and four different surface-configurations offer a total of eight "pneumatic variations", which can be combined as needed. These are filled with air by means of a "ground-station" tied to a certain object. The space's size and shape can constantly be altered by inflating and emptying the air-bags.

Verschiedene Szenerien in Abhängigkeit von Tageszeit und Nutzern   Various scenarios depending on the time of day and the users

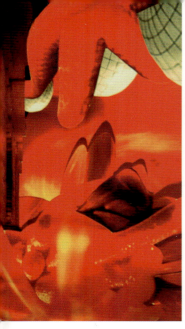 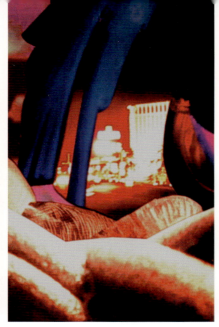  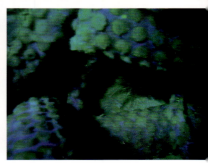

Innenraumcollagen: angeregt/entspannt   *Interior space collages: activated/relaxed*   Modellstudien   *Model studies*

der Pneus verändern. Halbaufgeblasen dienen die Elemente als Sitz- oder Liegemöbel. Zusätzlich zum haptischen Erleben der Pneuoberflächen ist in jedes Element eine weitere Funktion integriert. So gibt es Pneus aus glatter Folie, die von innen beleuchtet werden, andere mit einer wabenartigen Oberfläche, aus der warmer Dampf tritt. Besetzt mit Noppen, die jeweils eine LED-Leuchte einschließen, erzeugen diese Pneus ein flirrendes Licht und aus Pneus mit rissiger, schroffer Haut dringt Musik. Die technische Ausrüstung hierfür befindet sich ebenfalls in der Bodenstation. Somit lassen sich verschiedene Szenerien erschaffen, die auf wechselnde Tageszeiten, Lichtverhältnisse und Nutzer reagieren können.

When half inflated, the air-bag elements can be used as furniture to sit or lie on. As well as the haptic experience of the pneumatic surfaces, every element has another function built into it. Thus, some air-bags, made of clear foil, can be lit up from inside; others, with a surface like a honey-comb, emit warm steam. Provided with naps, each of which include an LED display, these air-bags give off a flickering light; and from air-bags with fissured, jagged skin music can be heard. The technical equipment for all these facilities is also to be found in the ground station. All in all, then, a number of different scenarios can be brought into play, which can react to different times of the day, as well as light conditions and users.

Der *Space Inflator* auf der Karl-Marx-Allee in Berlin   *The* Space Inflator *at the Karl-Marx-Allee in Berlin*

Daniel Theiler / Sushibox 2004/2005

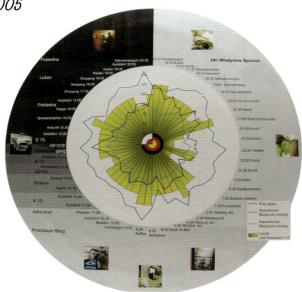

SCHATTENSPIEL

Ich habe einen Koch 24 Stunden lang bei seiner Arbeit in einem Berliner Restaurant und in seiner polnischen Heimat begleitet. Meinen Focus setzte ich auf die Korrelation von körperlichem Befinden und äußeren Einflüssen. Diese erfasste ich mit Hilfe eines Pulsmessgerätes und legte die Daten tabellarisch an.

SHADOWPLAY

I accompanied a chef for 24 hours during his work at a Berlin restaurant and at his home in Poland. I concentrated my attention on the correlation of physical well-being and external influences. I assessed this with the help of a gadget to measure your pulse and compiled a table of the data.

Knotendiagramm der Ergebnisse des Shadowplays
Knot diagram of results from the shadowing game

Ausschnitt aus dem Lehrvideo
Excerpt from the instructional video

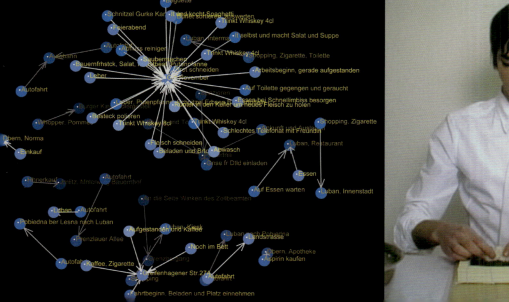

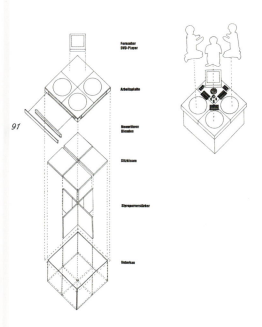
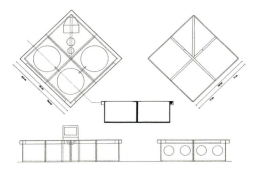

Links: Aufbauanleitung   *Left: assembly instructions*
Oben: Grundrisse   *Above: layouts*

SUSHIBOX

Auf der Grundlage der Beschattung eines Kochs, den ich einen Tag lang begleitete, entwickelte ich einen mobilen Stand. Diese Mikroarchitektur sollte neben guter Mobilität ein interaktives Element beinhalten. Die entstandene SUSHIBOX wurde am Alexanderplatz in Berlin präsentiert. Dort wurde auch ihre Tauglichkeit unter Beweis gestellt. Sie bietet ihren Teilnehmern die Möglichkeit, anhand eines Lehrfilms innerhalb von 4 Minuten die Zubereitung von Sushi zu erlernen und vor Ort durchzuführen.

SUSHIBOX

Building on the results of my "shadowing", I developed a mobile stand. This micro-architecture was to represent an interactive element as well as good mobility. The SUSHI BOX that was created as a result was presented at Berlin's Alexanderplatz. There, its suitability was also put to the test: with the assistance of an instructional film, it offered users the opportunity to learn how to prepare sushi in four minutes and to taste it on the spot.

Public Test am Alexanderplatz
Public test-run at Alexanderplatz

Elke Knoess

Performative Architektur

Handeln im öffentlichen Raum

Die unterirdische Passage zwischen dem U- und dem S-Bahnhof Alexanderplatz in Berlin verwandelte sich am Nachmittag des 31. Januar 2003 in einen bunten Bazar. Innerhalb kurzer Zeit strömten 120 Architekturstudierende des k_studios der TU Berlin mit ihren mobilen Verkaufsständen in den nüchternen Verbindungsraum und bauten in nur einer Stunde einen lebendigen Markt auf.

Das Spektrum reichte von klassischen Ständen mit ausgefeilten Geschäftsideen, an denen es Praktisches zu erwerben gab, über körperbezogene, figurative Objekte, die zum Teil zur Maskerade einluden, bis hin zu kleinen begehbaren Räumen mit unterhaltsamen und informativen Angeboten. Die Passanten konnten sich zum Beispiel am Informationsstand einen Überblick verschaffen oder zu einer Führung anmelden, sie konnten ihre Schuhe putzen lassen, Cocktails trinken, Delikatessen kosten, am Karaoke-Stand singen, sich aus der Hand lesen lassen, eine Sounddusche nehmen, sich einer Lichttherapie unterziehen, ein Theaterstück besuchen, sich in eine Operndiva verwandeln, mit dem rosaroten Minifahrrad fahren, in eine Latexhaut schlüpfen, Raum aus einer ganz anderen Perspektive erleben und vieles mehr.

Am späten Abend wurden die bewusst mobil konzipierten Verkaufsstände innerhalb einer Stunde wieder abgebaut. Die Studierenden und Lehrenden waren vom Erfolg der urbanen Intervention überzeugt. Die Passanten zeigten sich durchweg interessiert und bereit, am Marktgeschehen teilzunehmen. Auch der Gemüsehändler, der ein Ladenlokal in der Passage betreibt, wünschte sich, dass dieser Markt öfter

Nina Hosni: „Kommunikator"

Nina Hosni: "Communicator"

Performative Architecture

Action in Public Space

On the afternoon of 31 January 2003, the underground passage linking the subway and train stations at Alexanderplatz in Berlin was transformed into a colourful bazaar. One hundred and twenty architecture students from k_studio of the Technical University Berlin poured into the utilitarian connecting passage and, in just one hour, set up their lively market. The spectrum was vast. It ranged from traditional stalls with sophisticated business ideas where practical items could be bought, to figurative objects through to small rooms, which could be entered, offering various forms of entertainment and information. Passers-by could get an overview at an information stand or register for a tour, they could have their shoes polished, drink cocktails, eat at a deli, sing at a karaoke stand, have their palm read, take a sonic-shower, undergo a light therapy session, see a play, be transformed into an opera diva, ride a pink mini-cycle, slide into a latex skin, experience space from a completely different perspective, and much more.

Late in the evening, the stalls, which were intentionally designed to be mobile, were taken down within one hour. The students and lecturers were convinced of the success of their urban intervention. The passers-by had been consistently interested and willing to participate in the market. Even the greengrocer who runs a shop in the passage said he wished the market could take place more often. The representative of the Berlin transport company, who had kept a watchful eye over the entire event, was relieved when the group left the passage

Aufbau des Marktes in der Passage unterhalb des Alexanderplatzes

Assembling the market in the passage at Alexanderplatz

stattfände. Doch ein Angestellter der Berliner Verkehrsgesellschaft, der das ganze Ereignis freundlich und streng überwacht hatte, war erleichtert, dass die Gruppe nun endlich die Passage verließ und dieser öffentliche Raum wieder genauso nüchtern, sauber und leer war wie zuvor. Sichtlich enttäuscht über die Intervention, weil er sich unter einer „Ausstellung" etwas anderes vorgestellt hatte, fragte er zum Schluss: „Und was hat das alles mit Architektur zu tun?"

Transfer Architektur im Wandel

Die beteiligten 120 Studierenden realisierten die urbane Intervention in der Passage unterhalb des Alexanderplatzes als ersten öffentlichen Test zu Beginn ihres viersemestrigen Grundstudiums. Das Programm dieser beiden Jahre gestaltete sich unter dem Titel „Transfer" im Sinn einer sich aktuell verändernden Relation von Strukturen,

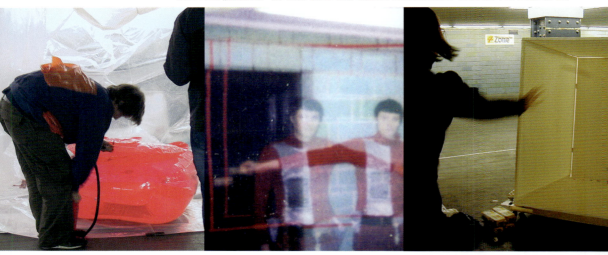

Links: Sönke Hartmann: „Rough 'n' Ready"
Mitte: Robert Burghardt: „Raumanzug"
Rechts: Lisa Seibert: „Frustomat"

Left: Sönke Hartmann: "Rough 'n' Ready"
Center: Robert Burghardt: "Space Suit"
Right: Lisa Seibert: "Frustomat"

Medien, Technologien, Handlungsmustern und Kulturen. Im ersten Semester wurde der Schwerpunkt bewusst auf das Thema Arbeitswelten und Dienstleistung gelegt, auch wegen der damals so aktuellen „Ich-AG"-Debatte rund um erstarrte Beschäftigungsstrukturen, mehr Eigenverantwortung und Mikro-Ökonomien.

Mit diesem zweijährigen Grundstudiums-Programm wurde gleichzeitig der Transfer vom „klassischen" Berufsbild des Architekten, der ausschließlich funktionale Gebäude baut und hierzulande zunehmend unter Auftragsarmut leidet, hin zu einem zeitgemäßen Berufsbild thematisiert, in dem Architekten auch private und öffentliche Ereignisse konstruieren, soziale und informelle Situationen im Zwischenraum entwerfen, Strategien zur temporären räumlichen Aneignung planen und sich zunehmend als Initiatoren oder Manager von Prozessen sehen.

Die schlechte Auftragslage für Architekten und die derzeitige Diskussion um schrumpfende Regionen und temporäre Nutzungen machen eine Neuorientierung in der Lehre, der Praxis und im öffentlichen Diskurs notwendig. Trotz allem oder vielleicht gerade deswegen ist Berlin ein einzigartiges Experimentierfeld, das den Freiraum und die Möglichkeit bietet, neue Strategien zu testen.

as clean, empty and utilitarian as we had found it. He was visibly disappointed with the intervention because he thought the word "exhibition" suggested something else. At the end he asked, "And what did that have to do with architecture?"

Transfer, Architecture in Flux

The 120 students carried out the urban intervention scheme in the passage beneath Alexanderplatz as the first public test to mark the beginning of their four semesters of introductory studies. The program of studies during their first two years is organised under the title "transfer", in the sense of a changing relationship between structures, media and technology and patterns of action and cultures. In the first semester, the topic was consciously emphasised on work environments and the service industry. One reason for this was the debate that

was going on in Germany at the time, which centred around entrepreneurship and the problem of moribund business structures and the need for more individual responsibility and micro-economies.

Another theme of this two-year course of introductory studies is the transfer of the architect's traditional role from designing purely functional buildings (such work has become scarce in Germany) to the contemporary role of organizing public and private events, creating informal and social situations in connecting spaces, planning strategies for the temporary conversion of space and, increasingly, adopting a role as an initiator or manager.

The dire shortage of work for architects and the current discussion about shrinking regions and temporary use has necessitated a reorientation in teaching, practice and public discourse. Nevertheless – or perhaps just because of this – Berlin is a unique test bed, which offers the space and the opportunity for testing new strategies.

Links: Jürgen Missfeld: „Schuhputzstand"
Mitte: Christin Freier: „Fingerabdruck-analyse im Zelt"
Rechts: Kristin Wehner: „Postkarten drucken"

Left: Jürgen Missfeld: "Shoe-Shine Stand"
Center: Christin Freier: "Fingerprint Analysis in the Tent"
Right: Kristin Wehner: "Printing Postcards"

Laborartige Situation

Die Konzipierung und Umsetzung ihres Verkaufsstandes mit einer eigenen Geschäftsidee entwickelten die Studierenden auf der Grundlage einer analytischen Untersuchung und Beobachtung einer Person ihrer Wahl (Shadowplay), die eine Dienstleistung ausführt.

Die unterirdische öffentliche Passage diente als Experimentierfeld, um die von den Studierenden im Maßstab 1:1 realisierten Projekte zu erproben. Dieser öffentliche Test war mehr als eine bloße Zurschaustellung von Studentenarbeiten. Es wurde eine laborartige Situation konstruiert, in der die Studierenden performative Handlungen ausführten und über ihre aufgebauten Verkaufsstände, Objekte und Räume verschiedene Dienstleistungen für reale Kunden anboten. Performativ bedeutet, dass etwas durch Handlung entsteht. Mit einer performativen Arbeitsweise werden wirklichkeitsgenerierende Prozesse und Aufführungssituationen erzeugt.

„Wo Kulturen sich ereignen, wird Performativität zum Signum ihrer Konstitution, Organisation und Reflexion. Mit der Fokussierung von Performativität rücken die

Von links nach rechts:
Alireza Shalviri: „Infostand"
Mari Pape: „Plattenbau"
Melanie Fessel: „Die Verwandlung"
Anna Kasper: „Privatsitz"
Ines Wegner: „Slawamobil"

From left to right:
Alireza Shalviri: "Information Stand"
Mari Pape: "Plattenbau"
Melanie Fessel: "The Transformation"
Anna Kasper: "Private Seat"
Ines Wegner: "Slavamobile"

Austauschprozesse, Veränderungen und Dynamiken, die Akteure und kulturelle Ereignisse ausmachen, in den Blickpunkt des kulturwissenschaftlichen Interesses. Kunst und Kultur werden nicht mehr auf materielle Artefakte (Monumente, Bilder usw.) bzw. Texte reduziert. Die bis in die achtziger Jahre dominierende Erklärungsmetapher 'Kultur als Text' wird so wesentlich erweitert zur 'Kultur als Performance bzw. Aufführung'. Dieses Konzept ermöglicht einen veränderten Blick auf bekannte Themenkomplexe wie Inszenierung, Spiel, Maskerade, Spektakuläres, und lenkt das Augenmerk auf die Materialität, Medialität und interaktive Relation kultureller Handlungen." [1]

Ursprünglich entstand der Begriff des Performativen in der Sprachphilosophie mit der Ausarbeitung der Sprechakttheorie und der sich verbreitenden Überzeugung von Sprechen als Handeln. Im Gegensatz zum Theater, wo performative Aufführungen den Zuschauer zum Akteur werden lassen, entstand im öffentlichen Test der Studienprojekte eine reale Verkaufssituation mit angebotenen Dienstleistungen und Kunden.

Die performative Herangehensweise ist eine Möglichkeit, sich als Architekt neue Tätigkeitsfelder zu erschließen und diese gleichzeitig zu kommunizieren. Architekten und Studierende handeln, sie schaffen sich selbst einen Markt und warten

The Test Bed

The students based the planning and realisation of their market stalls and business ideas on the analysis and observation of a person of their choice: a person who provides some kind of service.

"The underground public passage served as a test bed for assessing the students' project on a 1:1 scale. This public test involved more than a display of students' work. This was a laboratory in which the students carried out performative acts and, via their stalls, objects and spaces, offered different services to real clients. Performative means something that arises through action. A performative work style produces reality-generating processes and staged situations.

"Where cultures happen, performativity becomes emblematic of their constitution, organisation and reflection. When cultural studies focuses on performativity, its gaze can shift to the processes of exchange, the changes and the dynamics that make up actors and cultural events. Art and culture are no longer

reduced to material artefacts (such as monuments or pictures) or texts. In this way, the explanatory metaphor that predominated into the 1980s – 'culture as text' – is significantly expanded to 'culture as performance'. This framework offers an altered perspective on familiar thematic complexes, such as mise en scène, play/game, masquerade, or the spectacular, and redirects attention to the materiality, mediality, and interactive relations of cultural acts." *(1)*

The concept of the performative arose originally from linguistic philosophy and speech-act theory as well as the widespread conviction that speech was action. In contrast to theatre, where performative staging turns the spectator into an actor, the students were placed in a real sales situation during the public test of their projects.

The performative approach is an opportunity for the architect to enter into new fields of activity and articulate them at the same time. Architects and students took action; they created a market by themselves and did not wait for the client to come to them. The reaction of passers-by who became clients gave students and architects a fuller picture of users and their specific needs.

"The new city and its spatial structures require a new human being who, rather than being primarily understood as Homo Faber, would be described as

Links: Mari Pape: „Plattenbau"
Mitte: Martin Mohelnicki: „Sind sie ein Familenmensch?"
Rechts: Sönke Hartmann: „Rough 'n' Ready"

Left: Mari Pape: "Plattenbau"
Center: Martin Mohelnicki: "Are You a Family Person?"
Right: Sönke Hartmann: "Rough 'n' Ready"

nicht, bis ein Auftraggeber zu ihnen kommt. Die Reaktion der Passanten, die zu Kunden werden, verschafft den Studierenden und Architekten ein erweitertes Bild von Nutzern und deren Bedürfnissen.

„Die neue Stadt und ihr Raumgefüge rechnen mit einem neuen Menschen, der nicht mehr primär als Homo Faber zu verstehen wäre, sondern der zutreffender als Homo Ludens beschrieben würde. Johan Huizinga, der das Spiel als Grundkonstante menschlicher Existenz reklamierte, legte den Gedanken nahe, dass sich am Ende des industriellen Zeitalters die Prägung des Homo Faber als eine bloße Überkrustung erweisen würde." (2,3)

Robert Burghardt: Public Test des „Raumanzuges" am Alexanderplatz, Berlin

Robert Burghardt: Public test of the "Space Suit" at Alexanderplatz, Berlin

Die Verwandlung der unterirdischen, nüchternen Verbindungshalle in einen bunten Bazar, der die sonst zielstrebig und zügig vorbei schreitenden Passanten verführte und zu Flaneuren und Kunden machte, konstruierte einen sozialen Raum. Dieses Ereignis, ganz im Sinne des situationistischen Erbes, ist ein öffentlicher Test für den spielerischen Umbruch des Alltagslebens und die Aneignung von Stadt. „Für uns ist sozialer Raum tatsächlich der konkrete Raum, wo Menschen Kontakte miteinander pflegen." (4)

ANMERKUNGEN
(1) Fischer-Lichte, Erika: *Kulturen des Performativen - Performative Turns im Mittelalter, in der Frühen Neuzeit und in der Moderne*. Berlin 2003, aus der Programmbeschreibung des SFB 447, Institut für Theaterwissenschaft der Freien Universität Berlin
(2) Costa, Xavier: *Le grand jeu à venir: Situationistischer Städtebau*. Daidalos 67, März 1998, S. 78—81.
(3) Huizinga, Johan: *Homo Ludens. A Study of the Play Element in Culture*. Boston 1950
(4) Constant: *Le grand jeu à venir*, in: *Potlatch. Informations intérieures de l'Internationale situationniste*. nouv. série, no. 1, 15 July 1959, S.3-5

Homo Ludens. Johan Huizinga, who identified play as the fundamental constant of human existence, suggested that at the end of the industrial age the designation Homo Faber would be proven to be a mere anachronism." [2,3].

The transformation of the utilitarian underground connecting passage into a colourful bazaar created a new social space. Passers-by who would otherwise have walked quickly through the area were tempted to browse and buy. This event, entirely in keeping with the situationist legacy, was a public test of the playful upheaval of everyday life and the appropriation of the city. "For us, social space is actually the concrete space where people maintain contact." [4]

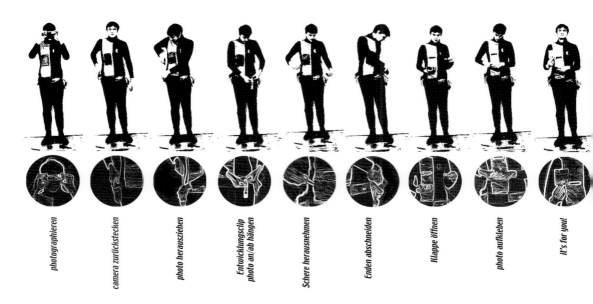

Robert Burghardt: Kartierung des „Raumanzuges"

Robert Burghardt: Mapping of the "Space Suit"

NOTES

(1) Fischer-Lichte, Erika: *Kulturen des Performativen - Performative Turns im Mittelalter, in der Frühen Neuzeit und in der Moderne*. Berlin 2003, excerpt of the programme summary of SFB 447, Theater Studies, Freie Universität Berlin
(2) Costa, Xavier: *Le grand jeu à venir: Situationistischer Städtebau*. Daidalos 67, March 1998, p. 74—81.Cf.
(3) Huizinga, Johan: Homo Ludens. *A Study of the Play Element in Culture*. Boston 1950
(4) Constant: *Le grand jeu à venir*, in: *Potlatch. Informations intérieures de l'Internationale situationniste*. nouv. série, no. 1, 15 July 1959, P.3-5

BAR

Shifting the View
Documentation of the Commonplace

In den letzten Jahren hat die Erforschung der Alltagserfahrung zunehmend an Bedeutung für die Architekturausbildung gewonnen. Dieser Text fasst eine Veröffentlichung der Architektengruppe BAR (*Base for Architecture and Research*) zusammen, die unter dem Titel: *Shifting the View – Documentation of the Commonplace* [1] erschienen ist. Darin stellt BAR eigene Dokumentationstechniken vor, deren Zweck es ist, ein tieferes Verständnis und umfassendere Kenntnisse über menschliche Handlungs-weisen zu entwickeln.

Der Antrieb für diese Untersuchungen und Aufzeichnungen entspringt der Lust, alltägliche Räume zu erkunden. Um einen Einblick in die Komplexität und Gebrauchsvielfalt der Alltagswelt zu bekommen, war es wichtig, längere Zeiträume an einem Ort zu verbringen, „sich einzugraben". Dies führte dazu, dass die zeitliche Dimension, die aufgrund des vordringlichen Interesses von Architekten am dreidimensionalen Raum häufig nur wenig Beachtung findet, immer wichtiger für uns wurde. Das machte das Experimentieren mit Techniken wie Film und Video notwendig, um den Gebrauch von Orten oder Gebäuden über einen gewissen Zeitraum hinweg zu dokumentieren. Die Frage danach, ob ein dokumentierter Ort alt oder neu ist, war für uns von geringer Bedeutung; weitaus wichtiger erschien die Frage nach der innewohnenden Modernität eines Ortes, die sich in den Möglichkeiten zeigt, zeitgenössische Nutzungsmuster aufzunehmen. Die Dokumentation ist ein Weg, dies zu entdecken.

Der Regisseur Robert Bresson schreibt dazu: „Ideen, die aus dem Lesen von Büchern gezogen werden, werden immer Bücherideen sein. Gehe direkt zu den Personen

k_studio, Studentenprojekt von Lisa Theobald: „Vintage Store", Camden Market, London, 2003

k_studio, student project by Lisa Theobald: "Vintage Store", Camden Market, London, 2003

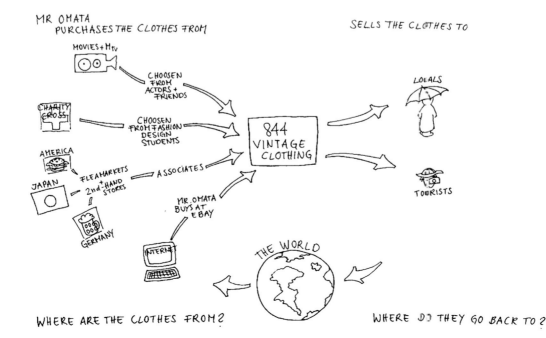

Shifting the View
Documentation of the Commonplace

During the last years, research into the everyday has developed an increasing importance for architectural education. This text presents a summary of a publication by the group of architects, *BAR (Base for Architecture and Research)*, titled: *Shifting the View – Documentation of the Commonplace* [1]. This publication addresses techniques of documentation practised by the *BAR*, whose purposes are to acquire an understanding and knowledge of ordinary human experiences.

The driving force for this process of investigation and mapping is a desire to expose oneself to ordinary spaces. To understand the full complexity of everyday life and use, it was important to spend great lengths of time in one place, "to dig oneself in." As a result, the temporal dimension, often given scant attention due to the architect's overriding interest in three-dimensional space, became increasingly significant to us, and called for experimentation with techniques such as film to document how a place or building is used over time. Of little importance is whether the documented places are old or new; much more important is the question of an inherent modernity, found in the ability of a place to accommodate a contemporary pattern of use. Documentation is a way of identifying this.

The director Robert Bresson writes: "Ideas gathered from reading will always be bookish ideas. Go to the persons and objects directly." [2] We have done just that: gone to places and people directly, and documented what we have found – both the personal world we inhabit and the observed habits of others. We have called this the

k_studio, Studentenprojekt von Lisa Theobald: „Vintage Store", Camden Market, London, 2003

k_studio, student project by Lisa Theobald: "Vintage Store", Camden Market, London, 2003

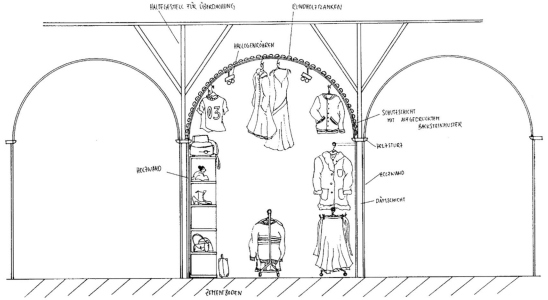

und Gegenständen."[2] Genau das haben wir getan: Wir sind direkt zu den Orten und Menschen gegangen und haben dokumentiert, was wir gefunden haben – sowohl die ganz persönliche Welt, in der wir leben, als auch die Gewohnheiten, die wir bei anderen beobachteten. Wir nannten dies ‚Documentation of the Commonplace' und meinten damit die Möglichkeit, sich Tatsachen und Zusammenhänge des Alltags vor Augen zu führen. Vor diesem Hintergrund wollen wir über den Alltag nicht nur als Theorie sprechen, sondern mit einem Einblick, der die Art und Weise unseres Entwerfens verändert.

Dieser Ansatz begründet sich in den Erfahrungen aus dem Leben in Berlin in der einzigartigen Zeit nach dem Fall der Mauer, Erfahrungen, die dazu führten, die Rolle von Architekten und Planern weiter zu hinterfragen, so wie wir es in unserer Studienzeit begonnen hatten. Auf der einen Seite gab es die Erfahrung des Alltagslebens in Ostberlin; auf der anderen Seite gab es eine Flut von neuen Architektur- und Stadtplanungen – bald vom Spektakel ihrer Umsetzung gefolgt – die dem Stadtzentrum eine neue urbane Vision aufoktroyierte. Die Größe und das Ausmaß dieses Wandels zwang uns zur Auseinandersetzung mit dem Planungs- und Gestaltungsprozess, der sich zu einer parallelen Welt, losgelöst von allen persönlichen Erfahrungen in der Stadt, entwickelte. Welchen Sinn hatten die Zerstörungen und Baumaßnahmen, die überall in der Stadt stattfanden? Ging es bei den Planungsmaßnahmen nur um die logistische Meisterleistung, es zu schaffen, anstatt um die Stadt, die daraus entstehen sollte? Wie viel der vorhandenen Struktur der Stadt musste zerstört werden, um das zu bewerkstelligen? Die Diskrepanz zwischen diesen Planungen und unserer Alltagserfahrung ermutigte uns, die Suche nach einer alternativen Arbeitsmethode fortzusetzen. Uns interessierte, das Potential für einen Wandel innerhalb der bestehenden Stadt zu finden; eine Methode, die neben der Komplexität des Alltags, „der konkreten Vielfalt einer wahren Ordnung", [3] existieren konnte.

Die Begegnung mit dem Nicht-Vertrauten war vielleicht ein notwendiger Bestandteil dieses Prozesses. Für uns war sicherlich die Beschäftigung mit Ostberlin nach der Öffnung der Mauer entscheidend; wichtig waren auch Besuche in England, Italien und Russland, die einen Teil unserer Arbeiten inspirierten. Dennoch ist die überzeugendste Arbeit des Architekten für uns letztlich die Arbeit eines Insiders: desjenigen, der aus einer gewissen Vertrautheit mit dem Kontext heraus arbeitet, die anderen fehlt. Das eigene Umfeld mit der Offenheit und Neugierde eines Fremden erfassen zu lernen, die Fülle im Vertrauten zu entdecken und einen Weg zu finden, als Architekt wirksam in dieser Alltagswelt zu handeln: Dies war die Herausforderung und das Potential, das uns die Dokumentationsarbeit bot.

Der Wert des Dokumentierens liegt sowohl im Sammeln von ortsbezogenem Wissen als auch, auf abstrakterer Ebene, in den Themen und Ideen, die sich beim Erstellen der Dokumentationen herauskristallisieren. Unsere Absicht ist es nicht, eine Entwurfsmethode zu definieren, sondern wir möchten aufzeigen, wie Dokumentation mehr sein kann als nur das Zusammensuchen von Informationen. Durch den Wechsel der Perspektive ergibt sich die Möglichkeit, unserer Architekturpraxis eine neue Richtung zu geben.

ANMERKUNGEN
(1) Shifting the View - Documentation of the Commonplace, Public Access Press, SCI-Arc (Los Angeles, 1999)
(2) Robert Bresson, *Noten zum Kinematographen*, Hanser Verlag, München 1980, dt. von Andrea Spingler, S. 76
(3) Claude Lévi-Strauss, „Pionierzone" in: *Traurige Tropen*, Suhrkamp, Frankfurt am Main 1978, dt. von Eva Moldenhauer, S. 114

'documentation of the commonplace'. It is a way of putting the facts of the particular onto the table. With these facts, we can talk about the everyday not as theory, but with an insight that can actually change how we create architecture.

This interest had much to do with the experience of living in Berlin in the unique period after the fall of the Wall, an experience that led us to continue the questioning of the roles of architect and planner that had begun during our studies. On the one hand there was the day-to-day experience of living in East Berlin; on the other hand there was the flood of urban and architectural planning – soon to be followed by the spectacle of its construction – which grafted a new urban vision to the centre of the city. The scale and thoroughness of the transformation forced us to confront the extent to which the planning and design process occupied a parallel world, detached from any personal experience of the city. What was the point of the demolition and the construction that was taking place all over the city? Had the real focus of the planning become the logistical feat of getting it done, rather than the city that resulted? How much of the existing city structure had to be destroyed to get it done? The lack of common ground between this planning and our experience encouraged us to continue the search for an alternative way of working. We were interested in finding the potential for change within the existing city; a method that could coexist with the complexity of the everyday – "the concrete diversity of a realistic order of things." [3]

Encountering the unfamiliar was perhaps a necessary part of this process. Certainly for us the initial encounter with East Berlin after the opening of the Wall was decisive; also important were the visits to England, Italy, and Russia that inspired several of our works. Yet for us the most powerful work of the architect is, in the end, the work of the insider: the one who works with a degree of familiarity with the context, which others lack. To learn to approach one's own surroundings with the openness and curiosity of a stranger, to detect richness within the familiar, and to find a way to act effectively as an architect within this everyday world: this was the challenge and the potential offered by what we call documentation of the commonplace.

The value of documentation lies in both the collection of local knowledge and, at a more abstract level, in the themes and ideas that have emerged in the course of making the documents. We are not trying to define a design method but rather to indicate how documentation can be much more than just the gathering of information. The shifting of perspective has the potential to shift the way that we practice architecture.

NOTES
(1) *Shifting the View - Documentation of the Commonplace*, Public Access Press, SCI-Arc (Los Angeles, 1999)
(2) Robert Bresson, *Notes on the Cinematographer*, trans. Jonathan Griffin (London, 1986), p. 120
(3) Claude Levi-Strauss, "Pioneer Zone" in *Tristes Tropiques*, trans. John and Doreen Weightman (London, 1974)

Werkzeug Reisen 1 / Tool Travel 1

LONDON IM KOFFER

Auf einer Exkursion nach London, im Oktober 2003 untersuchten die Studierenden Märkte. Es wurden zahlreiche Besichtigungen, vom Wochenmarkt über Flohmarkt, Großmarkt für Obst und Gemüse, Fischmarkt bis hin zur Börse der London Metal Exchange unternommen. Grundlage der Forschung war auch hier ein „Shadowplay". Die Studierenden sprachen eine Person ihrer Wahl an und beobachteten ihren Tagesablauf. Wenn möglich, erforschten sie auch ihr Wohnumfeld. Neben der photographischen Dokumentation sollten die Studierenden auch genaue Schnitte und Grundrisse der Marktsituation anfertigen. Ein Koffer diente Ihnen als Container für ihre Forschung. Zurück in Berlin übertrugen sie ihre Forschungsergebnisse auf eines von fünf verschiedenen Grundstücken in der Nähe des Moritzplatzes in Kreuzberg. Dort planten sie ein hybrides Gebäude zum Arbeiten und Wohnen. [EK]

LONDON IN A SUITCASE

During an excursion to London, in October 2003, the students explored various markets. They looked around many different ones – a weekly market, flea-market, a wholesale market for fruit and vegetables, as well as a fish market, and the trading market of the London Metal Exchange. The basis of this exploration was again a "Shadow play". The students addressed a person of their choice and observed their typical day. If possible, they also explored the environment around where they lived. Apart from the photographic documentation they completed, the students were also expected to prepare sections and ground plans of the markets. A suitcase provided a receptacle for their research findings. Once back in Berlin, they took the fruits of their research to one of five different locations near Moritzplatz in Kreuzberg. There they designed a hybrid building to work and live in. [EK]

Mari Pape: Aufmaß eines „any-item-50p" Standes, Brixton Market

Mari Pape: Survey of a 50p-stall, Brixton Market

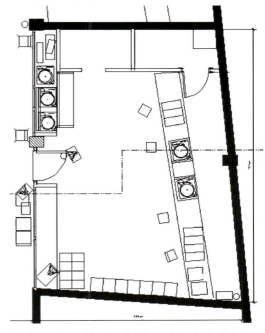

Schadi Weiss: Aufmaß von Alton Ellis Juniors Plattenladen, Brixton Market

Schadi Weiss: Survey of Alton Ellis Junior's record shop, Brixton Market

Hannah Bönninger: Aus der Untersuchung eines Seifenstandes entstand dieser Seifenkoffer mit Geruchsschläuchen. Die Ideen von Geruch und Licht wurden in einer Parfümfabrik umgesetzt.

Hannah Bönninger: This soap-case developed out of an investigation of a soap stall with "smelling tubes". The ideas of smell and light were transferred to a perfume factory.

Benedikt Julinius / The Hall of Variety 2003/2004

TRANSFER LONDON – BERLIN

Die Menschen, auf die man in London trifft, haben häufig ihren sehr persönlichen Lebensstil und entstammen einem multikulturellen Kontext. Die Unterschiedlichkeit der Menschen, ihre Hautfarbe und ihre Persönlichkeit, fällt sofort auf, wenn man einen Markt in London besucht. So verschieden die Menschen sind, so unterschiedlich sind auch die Waren und das gesamte Angebot. Durch Beobachten der Menschen, ihres Umfelds und der jeweiligen Beziehungen kann man wichtige Erkenntnisse gewinnen über die Dinge, die wichtig für die Entwicklung eines geeigneten Raumes sind. Daher basiert das Bauprogramm für das Gebäude, das in Berlin entstehen soll, auf den Grundsätzen – „Integration der bestehenden Strukturen der Umgebung" – „Vielfalt ist die Grundlage für Entwicklung" – „wahres Leben bedeutet Begegnung".

TRANSFER LONDON – BERLIN

The people who you can meet in London often have their own unique way of living and a multi-cultural background. The variety of the people, their colours and styles, is the thing that immediately strikes you when you are visiting a London market. The goods and activities on offer are as colourful as the people. By observing these subjects and objects and relations between them lessons are learned, which are essential for the development of a suitable space. Thus, the program of the building to be located in Berlin is based on principles – "integration of existing structures of the area" – "variety is the basis of evolution" – "real living is meeting".

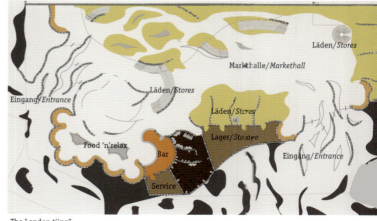

"The London t'ing"

Links: Stromlinien aus Menschen an der Liverpool Street Station
Oben: Grundriss, basierend auf den Stromlinien

Left: Flows of people in streamline at Liverpool Street Station
Above: Ground plan, based on the streamline

...wicklung 2003: Evolution der "fließenden" Form. Jedes Modell fügt dem Raum ...enschaften hinzu.

Development 2003: evolution of the "flowing" form. Every model adds qualities to the space.

  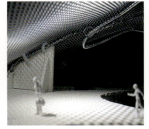 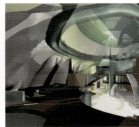

... *Clay*   Kupfer *Copper*   Metall *Metal*   Drei-D *Three-D (CAD)*

DIE HALLE DER VIELFALT

Die Beobachtung, dass Menschen feststehenden Objekten immer ausweichen, führte zur Form des Gebäudes. Die Menschen „durchströmen" das Gebäude, sie bilden Inseln zum Handeln, sie werden langsamer oder ruhen sich ein wenig aus. Auf diese Weise wird der Raum in der Halle der Vielfalt strukturiert. Die Eigenschaften des Gebäudes werden mit einer Reihe von Modellen überprüft. Jedes besteht aus einem bestimmten Material und besitzt seine eigene Sprache. Beim Tonmodell kommen die fließenden und höhlenartigen Eigenschaften hinzu, beim Kupfermodell die Hügel und der Glanz, beim Metallmodell die Konstruktion und lichtdurchflutete Atmosphäre, beim CAD-Modell das Glas als Material, so dass dieses alle Aspekte der anderen Modelle hinsichtlich Form und Funktion vereint. Aus dieser Addition von Eigenschaften entsteht jener einzigartige Mix, der sich auch in dem Endentwurf findet.

THE HALL OF VARIETY

The fact that a group of people moves around fixed objects led to the form of the building. People "flow" through it, they form islands of trade, they slow down, or rest for a while. In this way, the space in the hall of variety is organized. The qualities of the building are tested in a row of models. Each has its own material and style. The clay model adds the flow and caves, the copper model adds the hills and the glimmer, the metal model adds the structure and the atmosphere of light, the computer-assisted model adds glass as a material and unites the aspects of all other models in form and function. This addition of qualities forms the unique mix, which is to be found in the final design.

...D-Zeichnungen zur Entwicklung der Form ...)/3D).
...D-drawings for the development of form ...i/3d)

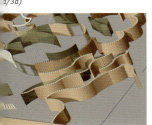  

Entwicklung 2004: Reorganisation des Raumes – von CAD zum Modell, Drahtgitter mit Texturen verschiedener Materialien

Development 2004: reorganisation of Space – from CAD to model, texturing the with materials

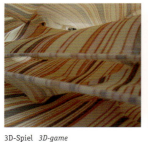   

3D-Spiel *3D-game* Landschaft *Landscape* Gitter *Grid* Drahtgitter mit Texturen *Textured g*

DIE HALLE DER VIELFALT

THE HALL OF VARIETY

Die Halle der Vielfalt in Berlin, Moritzplatz/Prinzenstraße 34 besteht aus einer multifunktionalen Markthalle mit einem Club und Erholungsbereichen, acht Leben-und-Arbeiten-Modulen für individuelles Wohnen und mit Präsentationsflächen (Größe für 1-2 Personen) sowie einer neuartigen Struktur und Neuorganisation des bestehenden Flohmarkts. Sie vereint Möglichkeiten für Wohnen, Handel, Arbeiten und Freizeitaktivitäten unter einem Dach. Das gesamte Projekt bietet sowohl öffentliche Räume als auch Räume für Einzelpersonen und unabhängige Händler. Diese Menschen können sich oder ihre Produkte präsentieren, und es bietet sich ihnen darüber hinaus auch die Möglichkeit, mit anderen in Kontakt zu treten und Erfahrungen auszutauschen.

The Hall of Variety at Berlin, Moritzplatz/Prinzenstrasse 34, consists of a multi-functional market hall with club and relaxation areas, eight live-and-trade-modules for individual living and presentation (size for 1-2 persons) and a new structure and reorganisation for the existing flea market. It includes functions like living, trading, working, and free-time activities under one roof. The whole project offers space for the public as well as space for individuals and independent traders. These persons can present themselves or their products on the one hand. On the other hand, they can come into contact and communicate with others.

3D-Spiel und Liegelandschaft *3D-game and chill-out-scape*

ck von der Straße *View from street*

e 'n' trade Areal *Live 'n' trade area*

Texturmodell *Textured model*

Die Halle der Vielfalt ist sowohl ein öffentlicher als auch ein privater Raum. Das Konzept sieht eine 24-Stunden-Nutzung vor und jeder ist eingeladen, den offenen Raum zu nutzen, teilzunehmen und zu genießen. Sehr wichtig für die Produktvielfalt ist, dass nur kleine Firmen oder unabhängige Teams und Personen einen Laden und eine Wohnung mieten dürfen. In dieser Vielfalt liegt die Hauptattraktion der Halle für die Besucher. Indem der Moritzplatz zu einem Ort der Kommunikation und des Handels wird, kommt es zu einer Reaktivierung dieses Stadtteils, und es können neue kommerzielle, soziale und informelle Strukturen entstehen. Das Netzwerk aus Individualität und Einzigartigkeit beginnt sich zu etablieren – denn Vielfalt schafft Einzigartigkeit.

The Hall of Variety is dedicated to the public as well as to the individual. As a 24-hour usable concept it invites everybody to use its open space, to take part or to enjoy. The fact that only small companies or independent teams and persons should be allowed to rent the stores and flats is important for the grade of the variety of the products. This variety is the core of the hall's attraction to the public. By activating the Moritzplatz as a place for communication and trade, it will be stimulated again, and new commercial, social, and informal structures can arise. The network of uniqueness starts to work – because variety creates uniqueness.

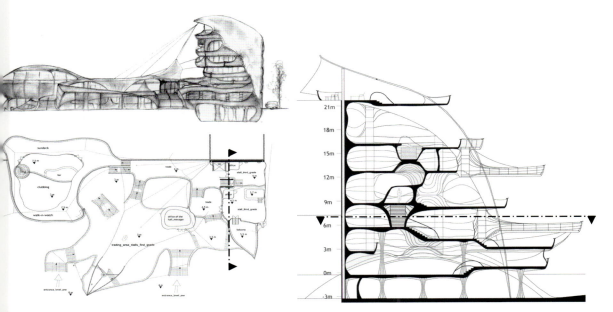

Antje Buchholz

Asia Food Land Berlin

Asia Food Land Berlin (S-VHS, Berlin 1999, Antje Buchholz/Kilian Schmitz-Hübsch) ist eine 12,5-minütige Dokumentation von über einen asiatischen Laden im ersten Stock eines Mietshauses in der Wilmersdorfer Straße in Berlin, dessen Eingang durch einen Zeitungsladen führt und der neben dem Lebensmittelverkauf diverse andere Angebote hat, wie beispielsweise einen Stehimbiss zur Mittagszeit, ein Reisebüro und eine Videothek. In Interviews beschreiben Kunden ihre Wahrnehmung und die räumliche Eigenheit des Ladens. Daran schließt sich ein kurzes Porträt des Ladenbetreibers an, das seine räumliche Konzeption deutlich macht:

„Erstaunlich, man glaubt es nicht. Man kommt da in so'r Zeitungsladen rein und man hat mir das zwar beschrieben, das ist nun mal so mysteriös, Treppe hoch und dann geht das los, es war ungewohnt, völlig fremd, fast wie so Chinatown (Schinataun), oder wie Chinatown (Scheinataun) oder wie das heißt, ja aber wenn man hier dann ist, dann ist das alles verständlich."

„Aufjefallen? Naja, zig mal aufjefallen, wenn ich mal sonnabends auf'm Markt war oder wat, aber sonst man achtet ja nicht drauf, man geht ja immer dran vorbei und fertig weil keene große Reklame, kleener Eingang kaum zu sehen, wa. Wissen se, anders so wie der in der Kantstraße, der Asiashop oder wat mit seene Vasen und Buddhas in de Schaufenster, der wirkt natürlich anders als wie det kleene Ding hier, also janz klar."

„Ist irgendwie merkwürdig, weil man ist es ja nicht gewohnt durch'n Kiosk zu gehen und gleichzeitig in einen anderen Laden hineinzukommen. Am Anfang habe ich das schon komisch gefunden, aber jetzt ist es ganz normal für mich."

Eingang zu Asia Food Land,
Wilmersdorferstraße, Berlin

*Entrance to Asia Food Land,
Wilmersdorferstraße, Berlin*

Asia Food Land Berlin

Asia Food Land Berlin (S-VHS, Berlin 1999, Antje Buchholz/Kilian Schmitz-Hübsch) is a 12.5 minute documentary about an Asian shop on the first floor of a tenement house in Wilmersdorferstraße, Berlin, which is entered through a newspaper shop and, beside groceries, also offers a stand-up snack bar at lunchtime, a travel agency and a video rental store. In a series of interviews customers describe their impressions and the spatial characteristics of the shop space. Attached to these is a brief portrait of the shop owner, who clarifies his own concept of the space:

"Amazing, – you just wouldn't believe it. You walk into this newspaper shop and, though it was described to me, right, it still seems really weird, know what I mean. You go up these stairs and there you are, okay, it was totally strange to me, like something out of Chinesetown, I mean: Chinatown, or whatever it's called, but once you're there it all sort of makes sense, right?"

"Noticed it? Well, yeah, sure I noticed it loads of times – I mean, when I was at the market on Sat'day, right, I didn't notice it – just went straight past it, because there's no big deal sign up, you see, and no spectacular way in, nothing. Totally different to that shop on Kantstraße, ain't it? That Asian shop they got with vases and Buddhas and stuff in its shop windows, know what I mean? Obvious, ain't it? That has a totally different feel to it than this poky little place – different league!"

"Though it's really amazing. In its way. I mean, you don't normally just walk in through some kiosk, like, and find yourself in another shop, right? That was first off, – first off it seemed sort of funny, though now it seems pretty normal,

Interviews mit Kunden und dem Inhaber des Asia Food Land. Film-Stills aus *Asia Food Land Berlin* 12.30 min., S-VHS, Berlin 1999

Interviews with customers and the owner of Asia Food Land, film-stills from Asia Food Land Berlin, 12.30 min., S-VHS, Berlin 1999

Ich find's auch sehr praktisch, also weil man kommt hier rein, man wird zwar schon vom Laden unten her so hingewiesen, dass hier oben noch ein Asiashop ist, aber dass das hier dann so groß ist und dass man hier so essen kann, also ist schon was Spezielles und ist auch interessant, wenn man einmal hier war, dann denkt man daran."

„Also, ich hab's als sehr verwinkelt empfunden. Ich hoffe, dass ich auch wieder rauskomme hier, aber ich glaub schon. Ja, es is so'n bisschen so ne Mischung aus offiziell und inoffiziell, das hat irgendwie auch so, macht auch so den Ort hier aus."

„My sister has show me this place, my sister she live in Frankfurt and she come to Berlin often and then she buying food here and I know this shop because of my sister."

„In Thailand so'n Laden? Ja, ich kenn das so, weil meine Tante hat auch ein Geschäft in Thailand, ein, sagt man hier, Krämerladen oder so, wo alles mögliche verkauft wird und ja also es ist ziemlich üblich in Thailand, dass alles in einem vereint ist, also einkaufen vielleicht auch noch'n bisschen was essen, manchmal war sogar 'ne Tankstelle gleich in einem drin, also Tankstelle und so, ist ganz normal."

„Eigentlich, jede Ecke ja, hat ihre Bedeutung. Also, wenn ich zum Beispiel vorne an der Kasse stehe, da liegen so tausende von Kassette, die so viel wie in Thailand ein Geschäft hat. Wir haben so jede Ecke ausgenutzt, dass es so fast keine leeren Räume gibt und darauf sind wir sehr stolz, dass wir jede Ecke so nutzbar machen.

Aber wir haben so bei diese Laden sehr schwer, zum Beispiel unten in der Zeitungsabteilung. Früher wussten wir auch nicht wie wir das machen. Das wurde einmal so leer gemacht, also gar keine Ausstellung da unten und dann haben wir Idee gehabt, da müssen wir was ausstellen, damit die Kunde kommen. Dann einmal war ich in Hermersdorf und da war ich in einem Zeitungsladen mit Lotto. Da habe ich gedacht, mein lieber Gott, das ist ganz weit weg, also so abgelegene so Ecke, aber trotzdem können die Zeitungen verkaufen. Dann habe ich gedacht, warum sollte nicht in der Wilmersdorfer Straße diese unten irgendwie nutzbar sein. Und gerade bei Fußgängerzone wie Wilmersdorfer Straße. Dann bin ich auf Idee gekommen von diese Zeitung und das hat gut getroffen. Dann können wir unsere Thaizeitungen, deutsche Zeitungen, Zigarette, also Süßigkeit was man so braucht, dieser Helikopter vor dem Laden auch noch ausstellen, also das hat diese Ecke später, nach zwei drei Jahren auch wieder richtig nutzbar gemacht und auch geschäftlich richtig passiert."

know what I mean? Pretty good, really – in you come, okay? – then you're directed up here by the shop down below, to this Asian shop up here, okay, but the sheer size of the place, and the fact that you can eat here, too. I mean, that's really special, and dead interesting, like – okay? I mean, once you've been here you think of it."

"Well, anyway, to me it seemed full of nooks and crannies, like. Hope I can find my way out again – daresay I can. Anyway, it's a bit of a mixture, – know what I mean? – official and unofficial. But that's what it's like, okay, that's what makes the place what it is."

"My sister has show me this place, my sister she live in Frankfurt and she come to Berlin often and then she buying food here and I know this shop because of my sister."

"A shop like this in Thailand? Oh yeah, sure, because my auntie's got a shop like this in Thailand, a – grocery shop, I suppose – which sells all sort of things, see. In Thailand it's pretty common for everything to be all in one place, know what I mean? You can buy stuff and eat it both in the same place – sometimes, you can even get petrol, too, I mean, it's quite normal – to get your petrol tank filled, too."

"In fact, every corner's important in its way. Know what I mean? If I'm standing out front by the cash till, see, I see thousands of cassettes lying around – like lots of shops in Thailand have got, okay? We've used every nook and cranny, see, so there's hardly any empty space – and we're really proud of using every last bit of room.

But we have had problems with shops like this – I mean, down below in the newspaper section, for instance. At one time, we didn't have a clue how to manage. The whole place had been stripped bare, see, there was nothing to see down there – and then we got this idea: let's display something or other, to attract customers. I found myself in Hermersdorf, see, and I went into this paper shop, which did lottery tickets. Jesus Christ, I thought to myself: it's miles from anywhere, I mean the back of beyond, but they sell newspapers like there was no tomorrow. So I thought to myself: back in Wilmersdorferstraße why shouldn't the lower floor be put to good use – know what I mean? Specially in a pedestrian precinct, like Wilmersdorferstraße is. So then I got this idea about selling the papers, see, and they went like a bomb – Thai papers, German papers, cigarettes and – why not throw in sweets, too – anything that takes people's fancy – and display this helicopter outside the shop, see, and in time – two or three years, say – this corner will have really made its mark again and be a real commercial hit, too."

Werkzeug Reisen 2 / Tool Travel 2

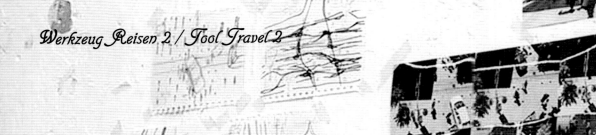

FELDFORSCHUNG IN ISTANBUL 2002

„Die Kraft der Landstraße ist eine andere, ob einer sie geht oder im Aeroplan darüber hinfliegt. So ist auch die Kraft eines Textes eine andere, ob einer ihn liest oder abschreibt. Wer fliegt sieht nur, wie sich die Straße durch die Landschaft schiebt, ihm rollt sie nach den gleichen Gesetzen ab wie das Terrain, das herum liegt. Nur wer die Straße geht, erfährt von ihrer Herrschaft und wie aus eben jenem Gelände, das für den Flieger nur die aufgerollte Ebene ist, sie Fernen, Belvederes, Lichtungen, Prospekte mit jeder ihrer Wendungen so herauskommandiert, wie der Ruf des Befehlshabers Soldaten einer Front. So kommandiert allein der abgeschriebene Text die Seele dessen, der mit ihm beschäftigt ist, während der bloße Leser die neuen Ansichten seines Innern nie kennen lernt, wie der Text, jene Straße durch den immer wieder sich verdichtenden inneren Urwald, sie bahnt: weil der Leser der Bewegung seines Ich im freien Luftbereich der Träumerei gehorcht, der Abschreiber aber sie kommandieren lässt. Das chinesische Bücherkopieren war daher die unvergleichliche Bürgschaft literarischer Kultur und die Abschrift ein Schlüssel zu Chinas Rätseln." (Walter Benjamin: *Einbahnstraße*)

In Istanbul suchten die Studierenden nach einer bestimmten Situation, die thematisch zu ihrem vorangegangenen hybriden Entwurf in Berlin-Friedrichstraße passte. Neben der Dokumentation mit Photographien, Filmen und Skizzen, lag der Schwerpunkt darauf, ein genaues Aufmaß anzufertigen. Sie sollten wie ein Anthropologe vorgehen, ohne voreingenommen zu sein, mit dem Blick von außen. Wichtig war es, dass die Studierenden nicht nur photographierten, denn das käme dem „Überfliegen einer Landstraße" gleich. Das Aufmaß mit genauen Zeichnungen ist im Sinne von Benjamin wie das Begehen einer Straße, das Abschreiben von Texten und Strukturen, um diese fremde Situation wirklich kennen zu lernen. Diese Untersuchung wurde öffentlich an der Mimar Sinan Universität in Istanbul präsentiert. [EK]

FIELD RESEARCH IN ISTANBUL 2002

"The power of a main road is different depending on whether you walk along it or fly over it in an aeroplane. In the same way, the power of a text is different, whether you read it or copy it out. Anyone who flies sees only how the road pushes through the landscape – it rolls away according to the same rules as the terrain that lies all around. Only the person who walks along the road can experience its hegemony and how to order this terrain – which for the pilot is nothing but a rolled-up plain – and all the distances, belvederes, clearings, and distant views, with all their winding pathways, curling away in front, like a sergeant-major bawling commands at front-line soldiers. In a similar fashion, the copied text only rules the soul of whoever is involved with it, whilst the mere reader never gets to know his soul's new insights, just like the text moves forward along that route through the inner jungle, which is constantly growing denser: because the reader is obeying the movement of his or her ego in the free air of dreams, whereas the copyist allows it to control. Accordingly, Chinese book copying was an incomparable testimony of literary culture, and writing out a book was a key to China's riddles." (Walter Benjamin: *Einbahnstraße*)

In Istanbul, the students looked for a specific situation, which would connect thematically to their previous hybrid sketch in Berlin-Friedrichstraße. Apart from documentary evidence, including photographs, films and sketches, the emphasis was on producing an exact offset. They were to proceed like an anthropologist, without prejudging anything and looking from the outside. It was vital that the students did more than simply take photos, as that would have been much the same as "flying over a main road". Measuring up with precise drawings is the "Benjaminesque" equivalent to walking along a street, or writing out texts and structures, in order to get to know this strange situation really well. The resulting investigation was presented at the Mimar Sinan University in Istanbul. [EK]

Show and Tell in der Mimar Sinan Universität, Istanbul 2002

Show and tell in the Mimar Sinan University, Istanbul 2002

Johannes Staudt: Analyse von Menschenströmen, Istanbul 2002   Johannes Staudt: Analysis of streams of people, Istanbul 2002

Johannes Staudt: Die Auflösung der Kurven in ihre Tangenten zeigt Ereignisse, die Menschen von ihrer Laufrichtung abgebracht haben, Istanbul 2002.
Johannes Staudt: The tangents of curves identify events, which have diverted people from the direction in which they are walking, Istanbul 2002.

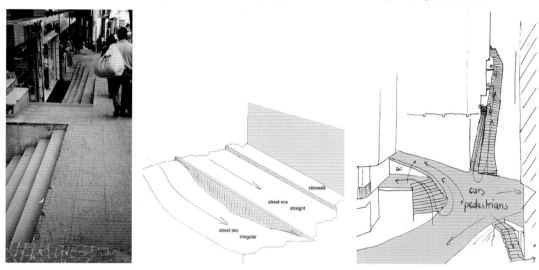

Franziska Laue: Untersuchung bestimmter Höhenniveaus, Istanbul 2002   Franziska Laue: Investigation of certain height levels, Istanbul 2002

Studierende des k_studio der TU Berlin fertigen in sieben Schritten eine Döner-Mahlzeit, Istanbul 2002   In seven steps students from the k_studio of the TU Berlin prepared a doner kebab meal, Istanbul 2002.

Elke Knoess

Istanbul, Konstantinopel, Byzanz:

„Nun machen wir die phantastische Annahme, die Stadt sei nicht eine menschliche Wohnstätte, sondern ein physisches Wesen von ähnlich langer und reichhaltiger Vergangenheit, in dem also nichts was einmal zustande gekommen war, untergegangen ist, in dem neben der letzten Entwicklungsphase auch alle anderen noch fortbestehen." [1]

Im Mai 2002 reisten Lehrende und 85 Studierende des k_studios der TU Berlin zu einer Exkursion nach Istanbul. Mit einem dicken „Reader" im Gepäck und einem vollen, ausgearbeiteten Programm versuchte das k_studio innerhalb einer Woche einen Ausschnitt dieser komplexen Stadt zu erfahren. Neben Chora-kloster, den Kuppelkonstruktionen von Sinan und zahlreichen Besuchen in Badehäusern lag ein besonderer Schwerpunkt in der Erforschung informeller Stadtplanung. Unter der Leitung von Çagla Ilk wurde das k_studio durch verschiedene Gecekondu-Viertel geführt und erhielt somit einen wesentlichen Eindruck. [2] Die Reisenden erforschten, welche informellen Strategien sie von der 13-Millionen-Metropole Istanbul, der *Self-Service-City* [3], auf ihre Heimatstadt Berlin übertragen konnten.

Mit der freundlichen Unterstützung der Architekturfakultät der Mimar Sinan Universität war es möglich, die gefertigten Untersuchungen vor Ort zu präsentieren.

Präsentation des k_studio der TU Berlin an der Mimar Sinan Universität, Istanbul, während der Exkursion im Mai 2002

Presentation by the k_studio of the TU-Berlin at Mimar Sinan University, Istanbul, during the excursion in May 2002

ANMERKUNGEN
(1) Freud, Sigmund: *Das Unbehagen in der Kultur.* Wien 1930, Psychologie Fischer S. 27
(2) Vgl. dazu in diesem Buch: Çagla Ilk: *City as an Interest.* S. 130ff.
(3) Vgl. dazu in diesem Buch: Martin Kaltwasser / Folke Köbberling: *Istanbul: Self-Service-City.* Seite 118ff; die Autoren begleiteten die Exkursion des k_studios als Gäste.

Hybrid City

"Now we make the fantastic assumption that this city is not somewhere that houses people, but a physical being with a past that is as long as it is rich, in which nothing that ever existed has ever perished, in which alongside the latest phase of development all the previous ones are still present." [1]

In May 2002, tutors and 85 students from the k_studio of the TU Berlin went on an excursion to Istanbul. With a full programme, they attempted, within a week, to experience a section of this complex city. As well as Chora monasteries, the domed structures of Sinan, and numerous visits to bath-houses, a particular focus in the whole investigation was informal urban planning. Under the direction of Çagla Ilk the k_studio was taken through various Gecekondu districts, and thereby gained a lasting impression of the city. [2]

The travellers investigated how they could apply certain informal strategies of Istanbul, the metropolis of 13 million people and *Self-Service-City* [3], to their hometown Berlin.

The kind support of the Faculty of Architecture at Mimar Sinan University made it possible to present the completed investigations then and there.

NOTES
[1] Freud, Sigmund: *Das Unbehagen in der Kultur*. Vienna 1930, Psychologie Fischer, p. 37
[2] See also in this book: Çagla Ilk: *City as an Interest*. pp. 130ff.
[3] See also in this book: Martin Kaltwasser/Folke Köbberling: *Istanbul: Self-Service-City*. Pp. 118ff.; the authors took part in the exkursion of the k_studio

Das k_studio der TU Berlin im Chora-Kloster, Istanbul, während der Exkursion im Mai 2002

The k_studio of the TU Berlin in the monastery of Chora, Istanbul, during the excursion in May 2002

Martin Kaltwasser / Folke Köbberling

Istanbul: Self-Service-City

Istanbul, die größte Stadt in der Türkei, ist von einer Vielzahl informeller Überlebensstrategien ihrer Bewohner geprägt. Der Begriff „informell" bezieht sich vor allem auf Do-It-Yourself-Praktiken der Stadtbewohner, die illegal Häuser und Infrastrukturen errichten oder Handel und Gewerbe jenseits administrativer Kontrolle selbst organisieren.

Ökonomische und politische Umwälzungen haben Istanbul von 1950 bis 1995 von einer auf 13 Millionen Einwohner anwachsen lassen. Dieses Stadtwachstum vollzog sich zu 60 Prozent in Gecekondus (Gecekondu = Haus, über Nacht gebaut), den informellen Neuansiedlungen. Ohne die Selbstbedienung der Zugezogenen am kommunalen Boden wäre dieser Prozess niemals so zügig und erfolgreich abgelaufen. Die Gecekondus sind somit Ergebnis eines selbstorganisierten Wohnungsbeschaffungsprogramms, bei dem einerseits soziale Netze geknüpft und Sicherheiten für Neuankömmlinge geschaffen werden, das jedoch andererseits mit Zersiedlung, Umweltzerstörung und mafiös organisierter Bodenverteilung verbunden ist.

Es gibt drei Gecekondu-Generationen: Zunächst entsteht (über Nacht) ein eingeschossiger Ziegelbau, der in den ersten Jahren als Behausung dient. Sobald sich die darin wohnende Familie finanziell konsolidiert hat, wird er durch ein geräumigeres Haus ersetzt. Schließlich, wenn das Gecekonduviertel etabliert ist, wird mit Hilfe eines Bauunternehmers ein drei- bis fünfgeschossiges Haus gebaut. Unternehmer und Eigentümer teilen sich den Hausbesitz: eine Hälfte für den Bauunternehmer zur Spekulation, die andere für die Bewohner.

Blick vom Istanbuler Stadtviertel
Alibeyköy in Richtung Levent 4

*View from the Istanbul district of
Alibeyköy towards Levent 4*

Istanbul: Self-Service-City

Istanbul, the largest city in Turkey, is marked by the variety of informal survival strategies adopted by its residents. The term 'informal' refers primarily to the do-it-yourself methods of the city dwellers, who build illegal houses and infrastructure or organize trade and industry beyond administrative control.

Radical economic and political changes between 1950 and 1995 have allowed Istanbul to grow to a city of 13 million residents . Sixty percent of this urban growth occurred in Gecekondus (Gecekondu = house, built over night), the informal new settlements. Without the autonomy of the newcomers on the communal land, this process would never have run so speedily and so successfully. The Gecekondus are therefore the result of a self-organized programme for the provision of dwellings, which, on the one hand, connects social networks and creates security for new arrivals, and on the other hand is linked to uncontrolled urban sprawl, environmental destruction and mafia-organized land distribution.

There are three stages of Gecekondu development. Initially, a single-storey brick building is built overnight to serve as accommodation, intended for the first few years. A more spacious house replaces it as soon as the family living there has consolidated its financial position. Finally, a three- to five-storey house is constructed with the help of a building contractor once the Gecekondu quarter is established. Entrepreneur and inhabitant share ownership of the house: one half for the building contractor for speculation – the other for the residents.

Modegeschäfte in Laleli

Fashion shops in Laleli

Den historischen Innenstadtvierteln Istanbuls und den modernen, westlich geprägten Vierteln stehen die chaotisch anmutenden Gecekondus gegenüber, die einer permanenten Umformung unterworfen sind. Bürgerliche Kreise sehen sich durch die teilweise hochpolitisierten Gecekondus bedroht und streben ein bereinigtes Istanbul an. Die Stadtverwaltung hat bereits Komplexe von Sozialbauten auf freiem Bauland errichten lassen, um Gecekondu-Bewohner dorthin zu übersiedeln. Dafür gibt es jedoch noch einen weiteren Grund: das jederzeit drohende Erdbeben. Da Istanbul an der Grenze zweier Kontinentalplatten liegt, stürzten hier beispielsweise beim Erdbeben 1999 Hunderte Häuser ein. Viele Gecekondus, aber auch Innenstadtgebiete gelten seitdem als besonders gefährdet. Angehörige der Oberschicht lassen sich derweil unter Duldung der städtischen Verwaltung inmitten von Naherholungsgebieten iLegale *gated communities* errichten und sichern sich so die allerbesten Plätze in erdbebensicheren Lagen.

Informelle Lebenswelten

Für die Ausstellung *Learning from**, die wir 2003 in der *Neuen Gesellschaft für Bildende Kunst in Berlin* realisiert haben, hatten wir ein Jahr zuvor Istanbul bereist. Wir erkundeten die dortigen informellen Lebenswelten und führten Interviews.

Laleli

Im Istanbuler Innenstadtviertel Laleli dreht sich alles um Mode. Wir gehen in eine der unzähligen Souterrainpassagen, darüber befinden sich labyrinthisch mäandernde oder opulente Galerien, Leuchtreklamen, sorgfältig gestaltete Auslagen und unendlich viele Schaufenster mit aktueller westlicher Mode. Türkisch und russisch sprechende Männer sitzen vor den Geschäften, junge Männer tragen schwere Bündel umher.

    Nach Aussage der Künstlerin Gülsün Karamustafa hat sich Laleli in den letzten Jahren drastisch verändert. Mitte der 1990er Jahre war das heruntergekommene Viertel Schauplatz eines völlig unorganisierten Textilhandels. Russische Frauen flogen nach Istanbul und kauften dort Textilien ein, um sie daheim teurer zu verkaufen. Das Geld zum Einkauf verdienten sie sich in Istanbul durch Prostitution sowie durch den Verkauf von russischen Waren. Man nannte dies *Kofferökonomie*, weil die Russinnen alles, was sie zum Handel brauchten, in Koffern transportierten. Inzwischen ist dieser Handel völlig durchorganisiert, Laleli ist ein zentraler Umschlagplatz der türkischen Bekleidungsindustrie geworden. Als Handelsplatz zwischen Süd- und Westeuropa sowie den ehemaligen Sowjetrepubliken hat die gesamte Stadt eine enorme Bedeutung, aber gerade Laleli wurde in kürzester Zeit mit Textilgeschäften, Großhandelszentren, Lagerhäusern und Großhotels umgebaut und umfunktioniert. Heute fliegen russische Geschäftsfrauen nach Istanbul und erstehen in Laleli in kürzester Zeit große Mengen Textilien. Diese werden vor Ort verpackt und auf dem Rückflug mitgenommen.

    Wir führen ein Interview mit jungen Männern, die Pakete mit Textilien flugfertig machen. Sie erzählen uns, dass sie Arbeitspendler aus Montenegro sind. Sie packen und wiegen die Stoffe direkt auf der Straße, beschriften und kontrollieren sie für den Abtransport zum Flughafen. Die Textilhändler lassen die Ware auch zu den Hotels der russischen Geschäftsfrauen bringen. Die Bürgersteige sind voll von Paketen.[2]

    Der türkische Schuhfabrikant Cuma Küsüni betreibt in Laleli einen Factory-Outlet-Store. Wir können ihn spontan für ein Interview gewinnen, anschließend lädt er

The historic inner-city quarters of Istanbul and the modern, western-influenced quarters contrast with the chaotic Gecekondus, which are subject to constant remodelling. Middle-class residents see themselves threatened by the Gecekondus, which are often highly politicised, and strive for a cleaner Istanbul. The city administration has already had community-housing complexes constructed on free building land, in order to relocate residents of the Gecekondus. However, there is another reason for this: the constant threat of earthquakes. As Istanbul lies on the boundary between two continental plates, hundreds of houses collapsed in the earthquake of 1999. Since then, Gecekondus are often seen as particularly vulnerable, as well as inner-city areas. Meanwhile, members of the upper class build themselves illegal fenced-off communities in the midst of recreational areas, a move which is tolerated by the municipal administration, and thus safeguard for themselves the very best locations in earthquake-proof areas.

Informal Life World

We organised the exhibition *Learning from** in 2003 in the *Neue Gesellschaft für Bildende Kunst in Berlin*. We travelled through Istanbul a year earlier for the purpose of finding out about the informal life worlds that existed there and to hold interviews.

Laleli

In the inner-city Istanbul district Laleli, everything revolves around fashion. We walked through one of the countless basement passages, above which meandered labyrinthine and opulent galleries decked out with neon signs, carefully arranged displays and infinite rows of shop windows flaunting the latest western fashions. Men talking in Turkish and Russian sit in front of the shops; younger men carry heavy bundles around.

The female artist Gülsün Karamustafa says that Laleli has changed drastically in recent years. In the mid-90's, the shabby quarter was the scene of a completely disorganized textile trade. Russian women flew to Istanbul and bought textiles there in order to sell them back home for a profit. They earned the money for their purchases through prostitution in Istanbul along with selling Russian goods. It was called the 'suitcase economy', because the Russian women transported everything they needed for trading in suitcases. In the meantime, this trade has become completely well organized. Laleli has become a central trade centre of the Turkish clothing industry. The whole city has an enormous importance as a trading centre between South and Western Europe along with the former Soviet Republics, but precisely Laleli was rapidly rebuilt and transformed with clothes shops, wholesale centres, warehouses and large hotels. Today, Russian businesswomen fly to Istanbul and purchase large amounts of textiles in Laleli. These are packed on the spot and taken on the return flight.

We interview young men who make the parcels with textiles ready for the flight. They tell us that they are migrant workers from Montenegro. They pack and weigh the parcels directly on the road, address and check them for the dispatch to the airport. The textile traders also allow the parcels to be brought to the hotels of the Russian businesswomen. The pavements are full of parcels.[2]

uns in seine Schuhfabrik in der *Tuzla Leather City* ein, einer riesigen Sonderproduktionszone östlich von Istanbul. Die Fabrik steht nach seiner Aussage in den Startlöchern für die anstehende EU-Erweiterung. Die Produktion läuft derzeit weit unterhalb der möglichen Kapazität: Nur ein Drittel der Arbeitsplätze ist besetzt. Cuma Küsüni lässt Kopien bekannter Marken wie beispielsweise Prada herstellen. Er erklärt: „Die russischen Leute kommen hierher und kaufen Schuhe wie beim ‚Kofferhandel'. Sie kommen meistens montags und sagen, dass sie die Ware bis Mittwoch brauchen. Seit einigen Monaten hat sich das aber verändert. Ich glaube, die russische Regierung will den Handel legalisieren. Sie wollen Steuern haben. Die Leute kommen jetzt nicht mehr hierher, wie im letzten Jahr. Deswegen ist der Markt ruhiger geworden." *(3)*

Zeytinburnu
Im zentrumsnahen Viertel Zeytinburnu interviewen wir einen arbeitslosen Dolmetscher, der jetzt in einem der vielen Sweatshops dieses Viertels arbeitet. Sweatshops (sweat, engl. = Schweiß) sind informelle Textilproduktions- und Verarbeitungsunternehmen in engen räumlichen Verhältnissen mit primitiver Produktionstechnik und unterbezahlten Arbeitskräften. Alle Markenkonzerne lassen ihre überteuerte Kleidung weltweit in Sweatshops produzieren. In diesem Sweatshop, einem nahezu unbelüfteten, überhitzten Erdgeschossraum, werden von acht Angestellter Berge an Kleidungsstücken jeglicher Art im Akkord von Hand gebügelt, gefaltet und verpackt. *(4)*

Pendik
Wir fahren im Vorortzug nach Pendik, 50 km östlich des Stadtzentrums. Während die Gegend um den Bahnhof von dichter Geschäfts- und Mietshausbebauung geprägt ist, beginnt jenseits der Bahnanlagen eine unübersichtliche, pittoreske Mischung aus Wohnen, Gewerbe, Fabriken, Berggassen und Gärten. Dort lernen wir die Familie Aksu kennen, ein älteres Ehepaar, das mit Kindern und Enkelkindern in einem Gecekondu der zweiten Generation lebt: einem mehrgeschossigen Stahlbetonskeletthaus mit Ziegelausfachung, wunderschön am Berghang gelegen. Der Mann kann ein wenig Deutsch, weil er als Gastarbeiter in Rüsselsheim gearbeitet hat. Auf dem Dach sieht man Armiereisen herausragen. Sie wollen aufstocken, es fehlt aber die behördliche Erlaubnis.

Beylikdüzü
Beylikdüzü erblicken wir nach einstündiger Autofahrt ca. 60 km westlich des Zentrums. Am Rand eines unbebauten Sumpfgebiets erstreckt sich eine kilometerlange Wand von Hochhausrohbauten. Die Parkplätze der fast komplett leer stehenden Hochhaus-Satellitenstadt für 400.000 Einwohner, durch deren Schlammpisten wir fahren, sind mit Plastik-Wachschutzkabinen gesäumt, die den Aufdruck „Güvenlik" (türk.: Sicherheit) tragen. Sicherheitspersonal bewacht die Bauruinenstadt, die vor 1999 spekulativ in der erdbebengefährdetsten Zone Istanbuls unweit des Marmarameers errichtet wurde und nun keine Interessenten mehr findet.

Gazimahallesi
Gazimahallesi ist ein hochpolitisiertes Gecekondu, errichtet in den 1980er Jahren. Wir besuchen das alevitische Ehepaar Sarigöl: „Wir hatten gar nicht vor, ein eigenes Haus

The Turkish shoe manufacturer Cuma Küsüni runs a factory outlet Store in Laleli. We are able spontaneously to win him over to an interview, and then he invites us into his shoe factory in the Tuzla Leather City, an enormous special production zone east of Istanbul. According to what he says, the factory is on its marks for the upcoming EU expansion. The production currently runs far below possible capacity: only one third of the jobs are taken. Cuma Küsüni lets copies of well-known brands, such as Prada, be produced. He explains, "The Russian people come here and buy shoes like with the 'suitcase trade'. They come mostly on Mondays and say, that they need the goods by Wednesday. However, this has been different for a few months. I believe the Russian government wants to legalize the trade. They want to have the taxes. The people now no longer come here like they did last year. That is why the market has gotten quieter." (3)

Zeytinburnu
In the quarter of Zeytinburnu close to the centre, we interview an unemployed interpreter, who now works in one of the many sweatshops off this quarter. Sweatshops are informal textile production and processing companies in cramped spatial conditions with primitive production technique and underpaid labour force. All brand companies let their over-expensive clothing be produced worldwide in sweatshops. In this sweatshop, an almost unvented overheated ground floor room, eight employees iron, fold and pack mountains of garments of all kinds in piecework. (4)

Pendik
We travel down with the commuter train to Pendik, 30 km east of the city centre. Whereas the area around the station is marked by commercial properties and rented flats, beyond the railway starts a confused, picturesque mixture of living, industry, factories, mountain lanes and gardens. There we get to know the Aksu Family, an older married couple, who live with children and grandchildren in a Gecekondu of the second generation: a multi-storeyed reinforced concrete framed house with brick filler wall, lying wonderfully on the mountain slope. The man can speak a little German because he worked as a foreign worker in Rüsselsheim. On the roof you can see steel reinforcement sticking out. They want to build another storey, but they lack official permission.

Beylikdüzü
We see Beylikdüzü after one hour's car drive approximately 40 miles west of the centre. On the edge of an undeveloped swamp there extends a half-mile-long wall of high-rise shells. The car parks of the almost completely empty high-rise satellite town for 400,000 residents, through whose muddy tracks we travel, are lined with plastic cabins for the security guards carrying the imprint 'Güvenlik' (Turk.: safety). Security personnel guard the unfinished building city, which was constructed before 1999 speculatively in the zone of Istanbul most vulnerable to seismic shock close to the Sea of Marmara and that now no longer finds prospective buyers.

zu besitzen. Es war eigentlich nicht unser Lebensentwurf, sondern ein von der Türkei auferlegter Zwang. (...) Die türkische Ökonomie zwingt einen, ein Haus zu besitzen, weil man in einem Mietshaus in der Türkei keine Rechte hat. Außerdem steigen die Betriebskosten in solchen Wohnungen stetig an. Wir hatten also keine andere Alternative (...)."
[5] Ein anderer Gecekondu-Bewohner erzählt, dass er Stromzähler bei einer privaten Elektrizitätsgesellschaft war. Den überteuerten Strom konnte sich niemand leisten. Er half als Ableser den Leuten dabei, Zähler zu manipulieren und falsche Angaben einzutragen. Dafür bekam er Schmiergeld von den Kunden. So konnte er existieren. Ismail und Türkan Gölsam führen uns auf den Friedhof von Gazimahallesi. In Sichtbeziehung zur Polizeikaserne betrachten wir die geschmückten Märtyrergräber politischer Gefangener.

Alibeyköy

Der Onkel von Herrn Sarigöl wohnt mit seiner Frau in einem Haus der ersten Gecekondu-Generation im benachbarten Viertel Alibeyköy. Sie kamen schon in den 1960er Jahren her, als hier

Links: Gececondu der 1. Generation in Baulücke Levent
Mitte: Alibeyköy: Die Mulde
Rechts: Bewohner eines Gecekonduhauses der 2. Generation

Left: First generation in gecekondu in a building gap in Levent
Center: Alibeyköy: the Trough
Right: Second generation inhabitants of house in Gecekondu

noch hügeliges Weideland war. Mittlerweile ist ihr schlichtes Haus von fünfgeschossigen Wohnblocks umgeben. Die einstmals wunderschöne Aussicht endet jetzt nach 15 Metern an einer Wand. Sie hatten jahrelang anderen beim Hausbau geholfen, aber versäumt, ihr eigenes Haus weiterzuentwickeln. Welchen spekulativen Wert Alibeyköy heute hat, zeigen Apartmentblocks, die unweit des Hauses an den oberen Rand eines Abhangs gebaut wurden, neben eine Talmulde, in die man jahrzehntelang den Schlamm des Goldenen Horns pumpte. Solange die Gegend unbewohnt war, sahen die Verantwortlichen darin kein Problem. Durch das unablässige Schlammpumpen bildete sich ein richtiger See von übelriechender, giftiger Substanz. Allmählich rückte die Bebauung aber immer näher heran. Die Wohnblocks stehen nun als Rohbauten oberhalb des Schlammsees auf extra aufgeschüttetem Terrain. Sie dürfen nicht bewohnt werden, da der Boden nachgelassen hat und sie jederzeit drohen, in die Mulde zu kippen.

Fazit

Gecekondus und *gated communities* bedrängen die verbliebenen Wald- und Trinkwassergebiete Istanbuls. Die Stadt zerstört ihre Lebensgrundlagen und produziert extremes Verkehrsaufkommen, schlechte Luft, Wasserverschmutzung, die Gefahr von

Gazimahallesi

Gazimahallesi is a highly politicized Gecekondu, built in the 80s. We visit the Sarigöls from Alevite: "We didn't intend at all to own an own house. It wasn't really our life plan, but a compulsion imposed by Turkey. (...) The Turkish economy forces you to own a house, because anyone in a block of rented flats in Turkey has no rights. In addition, the operating costs in such flats are continuously rising. We had no other alternative (...)." [5]

One other Gecekondu resident explained that he was an electricity reader with a private electricity company. Nobody could afford the over expensive electricity. As reader he helped manipulate the counter and enter false information. He received bribes from the customers for this. In that way he was able to survive. Ismail and Türkan Gölsam lead us to the cemetery of Gazimahallesi. We view the decorated martyrs' graves of the political prisoners, within sight of the police barracks.

Alibeyköy

The uncle of Mr. Sarigöl lives with his wife in a house of the first Gecekondu generation in the neighbouring quarter of Alibeyköy. They came here back in the 60's, when it was still hilly grazing land. In the meantime, five-storied blocks of flats surround their simple house. The once lovely view now ends after 15 meters at a wall. For years, they had helped others with their house building, but neglected to further develop their own house. What speculative value Alibeyköy has today is shown by two apartment blocks, which were constructed close to the house at the upper edge of a slope next to a basin, in which the sludge of the Golden Horn was pumped for decades. Those responsible saw no problem in this, as long as the area was uninhabited. Through continual sludge pumping, a proper lake of foul-smelling poisonous substance formed. However, the building gradually moved ever closer. The blocks of flats now stand as empty shells on the built-up ground above the sludge lake. It cannot be inhabited as the ground has subsided and the building threatens to tip over into the cavity.

Links: leerstehende Häuser in Beylikdüzü
Rechts: Straße in Gazimahallesi

Left: empty houses in Beylikdz
Right: street in Gazimahallesi

Umweltkatastrophen und massenhaft Herz- und Kreislaufkranke, weil sich die Bewohner kaum noch unmotorisiert bewegen. Es fehlt an Raum zum Gehen, Laufen, Fahrrad fahren, Sport treiben, kurz: zur Erholung. Wer es sich leisten kann, verlässt die innere Stadt. Dadurch wird die besiedelte Fläche immer größer. Die Stadtverwaltung versucht verzweifelt einzugreifen. Was aber allein zu funktionieren scheint, ist der Markt: Seit dem Erdbeben 1999 stagnieren wirtschaftliche Entwicklung und Stadtwachstum.

Lernen von Istanbul?

Wäre es also dennoch erstrebenswert, die informellen Praktiken einer explosiv wachsenden Stadt auf eine schrumpfende Stadt wie Berlin zu übertragen?

Selbstbedienungszentrale

Im finanziell zugrunde gerichteten Berlin – von dessen Administration keinerlei Impuls für eine selbstbewusste, ausdifferenzierte städtische Kultur mehr zu erwarten ist, die stattdessen das gesamte urbane Leben den monetären Interessen privater Investoren

Die „Selbstbedienungszentrale" in der Ausstellung „Fast umsonst" in der Galerie NGBK, Berlin 2004

The "Self-Service Center" in the exhibition "Next to Nothing" in the NGBK Gallery, Berlin 2004

zu überlassen gewillt ist – bleibt gar nichts anderes übrig, als von der Self-Service-City zu lernen und informelle Überlebensstrategien zu erfinden. Wir haben dies verinnerlicht und im Frühjahr 2003 eine beispielhafte Einrichtung ins Leben gerufen: Im Glaspavillon am Rosa-Luxemburg-Platz errichteten wir ein öffentliches Auskunftsbüro, die Selbstbedienungszentrale. Hier sammelten wir Anfragen und Meldungen über alles, was es in der Stadt umsonst gibt. Wir riefen die Bevölkerung zur massenhaften Teilnahme auf. Alle Fundorte und Meldungen, Gesuche und Angebote veröffentlichten wir auf einer großen Zettelwand und markierten den Stadtplan entsprechend. Die Selbstbedienungszentrale existiert weiter, um Selbstorganisation und Vernetzung im No-Budget-Bereich als moderne Überlebensstrategie in unserer Stadt zu verankern.

Hausbau in der Gropiusstadt

Unsere Gecekondu-Erfahrungen mündeten in ein kleines temporäres Bauprojekt: In einer Augustnacht des Jahres 2004 errichteten wir am Rande der Berliner Gropiusstadt ein illegales Einfamilienhaus. Als Baumaterialien verwendeten wir Abfallholz von Berliner Baustellen. Mit unseren Kindern bewohnten wir das Haus eine Woche lang und arbeiteten kontinuierlich daran weiter. Wir eigneten uns so im Schatten der einstmals

Conclusion

Gecekondus und gated communities exert pressure on Istanbul's remaining forest and drinking water areas. The city is destroying its basic living conditions and producing extreme volume of traffic, poor air, water pollution, the danger of environmental catastrophes and cardiovascular diseases on a mass scale because the residents hardly move around other than in cars. There is no room to walk, bicycle, to do sport, in short: for relaxation. Anyone who can afford it leaves the inner city. Through this, the settled area expands ever more. The municipal authority attempts in despair to intervene. The only thing that appears to function is the market. Since the earthquake of 1999, economic development and urban growth have stagnated.

Learning from Istanbul?

Would it still therefore be desirable to transmit the informal practices of an explosively growing city to a shrinking city like Berlin?

Self-Service Centre

Berlin is financially ruined. No impetus can be expected from its administration for a self-conscious, differentiated urban culture. It is instead willing to leave the whole urban life to the monetary interests of private investors – there is no other option than to learn from the Self-Service-City and invent informal survival strategies. We have internalized this, and in spring 2003 instituted an exemplary service: in the glass pavilion on Rosa-Luxemburg-Platz in Berlin, we set up a public information office, the self-service centre. Here, we collected enquiries and announcements about everything that was to be had for free in the city. We called upon the population to participate on a massive scale. We published all locations, announcements, petitions and offers on a file-card wall and marked the map of the city accordingly. The self-service centre continues to exist in order to anchor self-organization and networking in the no-budget sector as modern survival strategies in our city.

Die „Selbstbedienungszentrale" in der Ausstellung „Fast umsonst in der" Galerie NGBK, Berlin 2004

The "Self-Service Center" in the exhibition "Next to Nothing" in the NGBK Gallery, Berlin 2004

House Construction in the Gropiusstadt

Our Gecekondu experience led to a small temporary construction project: during an August night in 2004 we constructed an illegal one-family house on the edge of

als „gebaute Utopie" entstandenen Gropiusstadt und des zukürftgen Großflughafens Schönefeld ein Stück Land an. Mit leichter Ironie demonstrierten wir weithin sichtbar für die Bewohner der Gropiusstadt die Potentiale zur informellen Aneignung dieser Gegend. Die Bevölkerung reagierte neugierig und freundlich auf uns und unser Leben im kleinen, stetig wachsenden Haus, das wir aber nach einer Woche wieder abbauten; die Teile nahmen wir mit. Was blieb, ist ein von uns gedrehter Film, der zeigt, dass unser Bau bei vielen, die uns in dem Haus besuchten, den eigenen Wunsch nach einer derartigen Behausung weckte.

Gropiusstadt-Gecekondu, verschiedene Ansichten mit Wohnhochhäusern der Gropiusstadt, Berlin 2004

Gropiusstadt-Gecekondu: various views with high-rise apartment blocks in Gropiusstadt, Berlin 2004

ANMERKUNGEN
(1) Den Titel *Self-Service-City* erfanden wir für zwei Istanbul-Themenabende, die wir 2003 in der Volksbühne am Rosa-Luxemburg-Platz in Berlin veranstalteten. Ein 2004 im b_books-Verlag erschienenes Buch über Istanbul trägt denselben Titel.
(2) Esen, Orhan/Lanz, Stephan (Hg.): *Self Service City: Istanbul*. Berlin 2004
Burbaum, Claudia/Köbberling, Folke/Kaltwasser, Martin/Reichard, Katja/Becker, Jochen/Lanz, Stephan (Hg.): *Learning from – Städte von Welt, Phantasmen der Zivilgesellschaft, Informelle Organisation*. Berlin 2003. S.58
(3) Ebd. S. 60
(4) Ebd. S. 62
(5) Ebd. S. 71

QUELLEN
Stadtbauwelt Nr. 139 *Istanbul*. Berlin 1998
Altvater, Elmar/Mahnkopf, Birgit: *Globalisierung der Unsicherheit. Arbeit im Schatten, schmutziges Geld und informelle Politik*. Münster 2002
Trialog Themenheft Istanbul. 2/1996, Berlin
Kortun, Vasif (Hg.): *Becoming a Place Yerleşmek*. Projekt 4L, Istanbul Museum of Contemporary Art, Istanbul 2001

the Berlin Gropiusstadt. We used waste wood from Berlin construction sites for construction materials. We lived in the house together with our children for a week, while we continued working on it. Thus we appropriated a piece of land in the shadow of the Gropiusstadt – once a 'constructed utopia' – and the future major airport Schönefeld. With light irony, we visibly demonstrated to residents of the Gropiusstadt the potential for informal appropriation of the area. The population reacted curiously and amicably to us and our life in the small, continuously growing house that we did however take down again after a week, taking the parts away with us. What remains is a film we made that shows how our house woke the desire for similar accommodation in many of those who visited us.

Gropiusstadt-Gecekondu, Innen- und Außenansicht, Berlin 2004

Gropiusstadt-Gecekondu: interior and exterior views, Berlin 2004

NOTES

(1) We invented the title *Self-Service-City* for two Istanbul theme evenings, which we organized in 2003 at the Volksbühne at Rosa-Luxemburg-Platz in Berlin. A book which appeared in 2004 in the b_books publishing company about Istanbul carried the same title.
(2) Orhan Esen, Stephan Lanz (Ed.): *Self Service City: Istanbul*. Berlin 2004
Claudia Burbaum, Folke Köbberling, Martin Kaltwasser, Katja Reichard, Jochen Becker, Stephan Lanz,(Ed.): *Learning from*- Städte von Welt, Phantasmen der Zivilgesellschaft, Informelle Organization*. Berlin 2003 p. 58
(3) Ibid. p. 60
(4) Ibid. p. 62
(5) Ibid. p. 71

SOURCES

Stadtbauwelt Nr. 139, Istanbul. Berlin 1998
Altvater, Elmar / Mahnkopf, Birgit: *Globalisierung der Unsicherheit. Arbeit im Schatten, schmutziges Geld und informelle Politik*. Münster, 2002
Trialog 2 / 1996 Themenheft Istanbul. Berlin 1996
Kortun, Vasif (Ed.): *Becoming a Place Yerlesmek*. Project 4L Istanbul Museum of Contemporary Art. Istanbul 2001

Çagla Ilk

Stadt als Profit

In den frühen fünfziger Jahren kamen viele Menschen aus den ländlichen Gebieten der Türkei nach Istanbul und siedelten auf staatseigenem Land in und um die Stadt. Sie erbauten Häuser, die man als Gecekondus[1] kennt; später – nach Einführung des Grundbesitzes – wurden daraus legale Wohngebäude. YAP-SAT, das übliche Programm zur Umwandlung der ersten Gecekondus in drei- bis viergeschossige Häuser, baute später die Gecekondus zu mehrgeschossigen Häusern um.

Das folgende Interview wurde während einer Exkursion des k_studios der Architekturfakultät der TU Berlin im Jahre 2002 geführt. Aufgezeichnet wurde es in Zeytinburnu, einem der ältesten noch existierenden Gecekondubezirke. Die Frau, die interviewt wird, ist fünfundfünfzig Jahre alt, lebt seit dreißig Jahren in ihrem eigenen, einstöckigen Gecekondu und besitzt zudem noch ein fünfstöckiges Haus auf der anderen Straßenseite (in der Abschrift wird dieses zweite Gebäude als D.A.H. – das andere Haus – bezeichnet). Sie lebt seit fast einem halben Jahrhundert in Istanbul, sie hat mit zwanzig geheiratet und ihr Mann, der vom Land kam, ist vor fünf Jahren gestorben. Durch ihren Mann erhält sie eine regelmäßige Pension und nimmt außerdem noch die Miete für die Wohnungen D.A.H. ein.

Çagla: Wie lange leben Sie schon in Istanbul? Frau: Seit zweiundvierzig Jahren. Meine Eltern haben sich 1960 hier in Zeytinburnu angesiedelt. Sie kamen aus Konya (einer Stadt mitten in Anatolien).

C.: Sie haben mir erzählt, dass Sie ein Haus auf der anderen Straßenseite besitzen und dass es früher genau so ein Gecekondu war wie dieses. Könnten Sie erklären, wie Sie Ihr Gecekondu zu einem fünfgeschossigen Haus umgebaut haben?
F.: Das ursprüngliche Gecekondu baute mein Vater fünf Jahre nach unserer Ankunft in Istanbul. Zu dieser Zeit baute jeder Gecekondu. Meine Mutter und mein Vater lebten dort bis 1992. Nach ihrem Tod erbten mein Bruder und ich das Gecekondu. Da mein Bruder vor vierzig Jahren nach Deutschland emigrierte, um zu arbeiten, musste ich den Umbau selbst organisieren. Ich beauftragte einen angesehenen YAP-SAT-Bauunternehmer aus diesem Stadtteil, der viele Wohnungen in dieser Gegend gebaut hat, auch die auf der anderen Straßenseite. In weniger als zwei Jahren führte er den ersten Umbau des Gecekondus zum mehrgeschossigen Wohnhaus aus und meine Kinder leben jetzt dort seit acht Jahren.

C.: Welche Geschichte verbirgt sich hinter dem Gecekondu, in dem Sie jetzt leben? Warum leben Sie lieber in diesem Haus? F.: Dieses Gecekondu wurde gebaut, als ich heiratete – fünf oder sechs Jahre nach dem ersten. Mein Vater und mein Mann haben es zusammen gebaut. Ich lebe noch immer lieber hier, weil es mein eigenes Haus ist.

C.: Warum ziehen Sie nicht in D.A.H.? F.: Weil ich dort Miete einnehme und es hier einfach besser für mich ist, weil ich lieber allein lebe als mit vielen Nachbarn. Da alle meine Kinder, außer meiner Tochter, gegenüber wohnen, verbringe ich mehr als die Hälfte des Tages dort, aber eigentlich lebe ich hier in diesem kleinen Gecekondu. Durch

City as an Interest

During the early 50's many people from rural areas in Turkey moved to and settled on state-owned land in and around Istanbul. They constructed houses, known as Gecekondus[1] that later became legal residences once land ownership was established. Gecekondus were subsequently converted into multi-story buildings by YAP-SATs, the common model for converting a first generation Gecekondu into a three- to four-storey house.

The following interview was conducted during a trip in 2002 to Istanbul by the k_studio, TU Berlin, Faculty of Architecture. It was recorded in Zeytinburnu, one of the oldest remaining Gecekondu areas. The woman being interviewed is fifty-five years old, has lived in her own one-storey Gecekondu for thirty years, and also owns a five-storey house just across the street (in the transcript this second structure will be referred to as T.O.H.: the other house). She has lived in Istanbul for almost half a century, she married when she was twenty, and her husband, who came from a rural area, died five years ago. She receives a regular pension from her husband and also earns the rents of the apartments in T.O.H..

Çagla: How long have you been living in Istanbul? Woman: For forty two years. My parents settled here in Zeytinburnu in 1960. They migrated from Konya (a city in the middle of Anatolia).

C: You told me that you own the house across the street and that it was previously a Gecekondu like this. Could you talk about how you converted your Gecekondu into a five-storey house? W: Originally, my father built the old Gecekondu five years after we arrived in Istanbul. At that time everybody was building Gecekondus. My mother and father lived there until 1992, and when they died, my brother and I inherited the Gecekondu. Since my brother emigrated forty years ago to work in Germany, I had to manage the conversion myself. I hired a well-known YAP-SAT contractor from this area who has built many homes around here, including the ones across the street. He finished the first multi-storey apartment conversion of the Gecekondu in under two years and my children have been living there now for eight.

C: What's the history behind the Gecekondu that you are living in now? Why do you prefer to live in this house? W: This Gecekondu was built when I got married, five to six years after the first one. My father and husband built it together. I still prefer living here, because it's my own house.

C: Why don't you move to T.O.H.? W: Because I'm earning rent from it and it's just better for me to be here since I prefer to live by myself than to living with a lot of neighbours. All my children, except one daughter, live across the street so I do spend more than half of the day there, but I really live here in this small Gecekondu. We're also now making 250 million Lira a month renting out the shop downstairs to a small textile manufacturer that preps and irons the finished products.

die Vermietung des Ladens im Erdgeschoss an einen kleinen Textilhersteller, der fertige Produkte bearbeitet und bügelt, verdienen wir jetzt auch 250 Mill. Lira im Monat.

C.: Hatten Sie teil am Planungsprozess D.A.H.? F.: Ja, natürlich, wir fanden es besser, zwei Zimmer auf der Rückseite zu haben, Küche und Wohnzimmer aber zur Vorderseite, da die Frauen und Kinder meiner Söhne den größten Teil ihrer Zeit dort verbringen. Der Bauunternehmer war auch der Ansicht, dass der Platz nur für den Bau einer Zweizimmerwohnung reichte. Da aber meine Söhne viele Kinder haben, musste ich mich mit ihm auseinandersetzen und darauf bestehen, dass er eine Dreizimmerwohnung daraus macht. Ich wollte auch einen Balkon, aber den habe ich nicht bekommen.

C.: Wird ein anderes YAP-SAT-Bauunternehmen dieses Haus auch irgendwann umbauen? F.: Letzten Monat hätten wir fast einen Bauunternehmer beauftragt. Bei dem Geschäft wurden uns drei Wohnungen in Aussicht gestellt, da ich aber vier Kinder habe und möchte, dass jedes eine Wohnung bekommt, wurde der Plan vorerst aufgegeben.

Studierende des k_studios, TU Berlin in Alibeyköy, Istanbul, 2002

Students of the k_studio TU Berlin in Alibeyköy, Istanbul, 2002

C.: Sind Sie der Meinung, dass die staatlichen Leistungen ausreichen? F.: Nein, die Politiker zeigen sich nur zu den Wahlen und hinterher verschwinden sie wieder.

C.: Beziehen Sie legalen Strom? F.: Nein, hier zahlt niemand für den Strom.

C.: Zahlen Sie irgendwelche Steuern? F.: Da ich kein Geld einnehme, kann ich keine Steuern zahlen (Türkische Hausbesitzer müssen jährlich Steuern zahlen).

C.: Wenn Sie in einem anderen Haus leben könnten, wie sähe das aus? F.: Es hätte eine größere Küche und einen Garten. Aber ich bin glücklich in diesem Haus. Da ich älter werde, ist die Heizung das einzige wirkliche Problem. Nach dem Erdbeben fühle ich mich sogar sicherer in diesem Gecekondu.

C.: Haben Sie für den Fall eines Erdbebens irgendwelche Sicherheitsmaßnahmen für D.A.H. vorgenommen? F.: Eigentlich nicht. Aber ich glaube, dass das Haus sicher ist, weil der Bauunternehmer dort auch für seine Tochter eine Wohnung haben wollte.

ANMERKUNGEN

(1) Gecekondu ist eine Art von Ansiedlung, die illegal auf staatseigenem Land gebaut wird. Auf Türkisch bedeutet es wörtlich „über Nacht erbaut".

C: Did you participate in the planning process of T.O.H.? W: Yes of course, we thought it would be better to design it with two rooms in the back and have the kitchen and living room up front since both of my sons' wives and children spend most of their time in these rooms. The contractor also thought there was only enough space to build a two-room flat, but because my sons have many children I had to argue with him and insist that he make it a three-room flat. I also wanted a balcony but I did not get it.

C: Will another YAP-SAT contractor eventually convert this house as well? W: We almost hired a contractor last month. We were promised three apartments in the deal, but since I have four children and I want each one to have an apartment, the plan was cancelled for now.

C: Do you think the state services are sufficient? W: No, the politicians only show up for the elections and then they disappear again afterwards.

C: Do you get your electricity legally? W: No, nobody pays for electricity here.

Studierende des k_studios, TU Berlin in Gültepe, Istanbul, 2002

Students of the k_studio TU Berlin in Gültepe, Istanbul, 2002

C: Do you pay any taxes? W: Since I don't make any money, I can't pay any taxes. (Homeowners in Turkey must pay yearly taxes).

C: If you had a chance to live in another house what would it be like? W: It would have a bigger kitchen and a garden. But I'm happy with this house, the only real problem is heating it since I am getting older. Even after the earthquake, I feel safer in this Gecekondu.

C: Have you taken any safety precautions for T.O.H., in case of an eartquake? W: Actually no. But I think the house is safe, because the contractor also wanted to have an apartment for his daughter there.

NOTES

(1) Gecekondu is the type of squat unit that is built illegally on state land, meaning exactly "landed in one night" in Turkish.

Robert Slinger

Städtebauliches Entwerfen an der Schnittstelle der Unschärfe

„Denn die Messanordnung verdient diesen Namen ja nur, wenn sie in enger Berührung steht mit der übrigen Welt, wenn es eine physikalische Wechselwirkung zwischen der Messanordnung und dem Beobachter gibt."[1]

Im ersten Studienjahr dämmen konventionelle Ansichten zur Entwurfslehre städtebauliche Entwurfsprojekte maßgeblich ein. Folglich wird das Thema erst später im Studium aufgegriffen, sodass architektonische Projekte lediglich in ihrem unmittelbaren Kontext wurzeln – oder ganz ungerührt hermetisch bleiben. Oder man bezieht sich auf Urbanität durch Vereinfachungstaktiken, indem man vereinfachte grundlegende „Wahrheiten" vermittelt, die später ausgearbeitet und/oder hinterfragt werden können. Die Gleichsetzung der Unerfahrenheit im Entwurf von Städten mit der Unerfahrenheit bezüglich ihrer Beschaffenheit bildet die Basis für diesen Ansatz. Die Studenten werden als „leere Gefäße" betrachtet, denen man ein methodisches Regelwerk an die Hand geben muss, das sie zum Handeln befähigt.

Wenngleich „Anfänger" im städtebaulichen Entwurf, so doch erfahrene Großstadtbewohner, halte ich die Studenten der ersten Semester [2], die ich im städtebaulichen Entwerfen unterrichte, für befähigt, sowohl synthetisch als auch kreativ mit der urbanen Struktur in all ihrer Komplexität umgehen zu können, da sie ein Kontext ist, an dem sie täglich teilhaben.

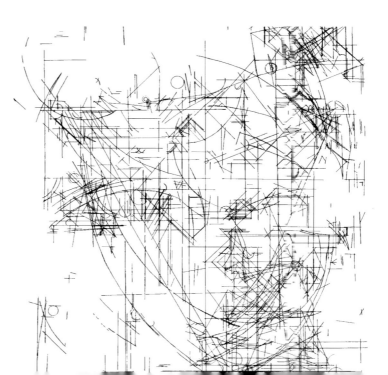

Rissboden der Kathedrale von Wells.
Zeichnung von John Harvey

Wells Cathedral tracing-floor.
Drawing by John Harvey

Urban Design at the Interface of Uncertainty

"The measuring device deserves this name only if it is in close contact with the rest of the world, if there is an interaction between the device and the observer."[1]

Much conventional wisdom about architectural design teaching mitigates decisively against urban design projects in the first year of study. As a result, the subject is often left until later in a course, with the result that the architectural projects can take root only in their immediate context, or remain unapologetically hermetic. Alternatively, urbanism is addressed early on via tactics of simplification, communicating simplified, basic truths, which can later be fleshed out and/or questioned. At the basis of this lies the equation of inexperience in designing the city with inexperience of its nature. Students are considered as *empty vessels*, who need to be handed a methodological corpus in order to act.

In teaching Urban Design to first-year students[2], I consider the participants, "beginners" all to urban design as experienced inhabitants of the metropolitan condition, able to deal synthetically and creatively with the urban fabric in all its complexity, since it is a context with which they participate on a daily basis.

My teaching is based on the conviction that the metropolitan condition is defined by the heterogeneity and complexity of its exchanges. My own teaching incorporates an uncertainty principle via the introduction of two parameters which question simplified urban *readings*.

Stanley Cursiter:
„The Sensation of Crossing the Street", 1913, Öl auf Leinwand, 51x61cm

Stanley Cursiter: "The Sensation of Crossing the Street", 1913, oil on canvas, 51x61 cm

Mein Lehransatz fußt auf der Überzeugung, dass der Zustand des Urbanen durch seine Heterogenität und die Komplexität seines Austausches definiert ist. Mein Ansatz bezieht eine Art Unschärfenprinzip ein durch Einführung zweier Parameter, die vereinfachte urbane „Lesarten" hinterfragen.

    1. Man nutzt persönliche Erfahrungen, um unbewusste Annahmen bewusst artikulieren zu können und erforscht die Städte unserer Träume, die in ungewöhnlichen Zusammenhängen oder parallelen Realitäten existieren, um Werturteile und Voraussetzungen formulieren zu können.

    2. Man beurteilt von einem bestimmten Standpunkt aus die vielfältigen Lesarten, die die grundlegende Polyvalenz von Städten ausdrücken, ohne sich in Objektivierungen oder Vereinfachungen zu flüchten.

Generell gesagt, basiert diese pädagogische Methode eher auf einem dialogischen Prinzip (wobei auf einen intensiven Meinungsaustausch ohne Vorurteile vertraut wird) als auf einem didaktischen (in dem der Einzelne dazu aufgerufen ist, seinen Diskurs mit einer begrenzten Zahl von präzise beschriebenen Präzedenzfällen abzugleichen).[3]

Positionierung – Formen der Beteiligung
„(...) wir müssen uns daran erinnern, dass das, was wir beobachten, nicht die Natur selbst ist, sondern Natur, die unserer Art der Fragestellung ausgesetzt ist."[4]

Wir gehen niemals unbeteiligt in die Stadt, sondern erfahren sie stets durch unsere Teilhabe, sei es als neugierige Entwerfer auf der Suche nach Inspiration, sei es als engagierte Bürger, die sich mit bestimmten Orten identifizieren, sei es als Reisende zwischen zwei Punkten oder als Handelnde vor Ort. Diese und andere Formen „der Beteiligung" die sich von Ort zu Ort, von Minute zu Minute, von Vorhaben zu Vorhaben ändern, bestimmen und transformieren die Bedeutung der Stadt, ihre strukturelle Hierarchie, ihre programmatische Ordnung, ihre Grenzen, Ränder und Schwellen vehement. Verständnis und Identifikation mit urbanen Zusammenhängen werden durch die Beschaffenheit dieser Formen definiert. Dies betrifft uns sowohl als Bewohner dieser Zusammenhänge als auch als auf mögliche zukünftige Entwicklungslinien Spekulierende. Tatsächlich könnte man, Heisenbergs oben genannte These als allgemein anwendbar vorausgesetzt, folgern, dass Stadt nicht außerhalb solch partizipierender Realitäten beschrieben werden kann. Die Formen der Beteiligung sind ein Weg, den nebulösen, allumfassenden Begriff des „Kollektivs" (jenes vagen und widersprüchlichen „Kunden" des Urbanen) beschreibbar zu machen. Denn wir alle sind im Wechsel Reisende im Verkehrsnetz der Stadt, Akteure auf ihrer Bühne, Konsumenten ihrer Waren oder sich unter ihren Schutz Stellende.

Abstrahierung: Diagramme / Embleme
„(...) dass die Begriffe der gewöhnlichen Sprache, so ungenau sie auch definiert sein mögen, bei der Erweiterung des Wissens stabiler zu sein scheinen als die exakten Begriffe der wissenschaftlichen Sprache, die als eine Idealisierung aus einer nur begrenzten Gruppe von Erscheinungen abgeleitet sind." [5]

Die Stadt stellt sich uns als ein Kontinuum von Realitäts- und Partizipationsebenen dar, von äußerst intimen bis zu analytisch-kartographischen. Sie bietet den

1. Using personal experience to bring unconscious assumptions to conscious articulation - exploring the cities of our dreams, which exist in extraordinary contexts or parallel realities, to help articulate value judgements and assumptions.

2. Measuring a singular position against the plural readings embodied in the fundamental polyvalency of the city, without resort to objectivities or simplifications.

Put generally, the pedagogic method is based on a dialogic principle of development (wherein faith is placed in the vigorous exchange of opinions without prejudice), rather than a didactic one (wherein the individual is called upon to position their discourse in respect of a limited number of rigorously described precedents).[3]

Positioning - Modes of Engagement

"(...) we have to remember that what we observe is not nature in itself, but nature exposed to our method of questioning."[4]

We never go innocently into the city, but always experience it through our participation; by turns as curious designers searching for inspiration, as engaged citizens identifying with its places, as passengers suspended between destinations, or as performers on location. The meaning of the city, its structural hierarchy, programmatic order, limits, edges and thresholds are all profoundly dependent upon and transformed by these and other modes of engagement. These modes of engagement change from place to place, minute to minute, and intention to intention. Both as inhabitants of the urban environment and as speculators upon its possible future trajectory, our understanding of and identification with the environment are largely defined by the nature of these modes. Indeed, it could be argued, if one accepts Heisenberg's hypothesis above as generally applicable, that the city cannot be described from outside such engaged realities. Modes of engagement are a means through which that nebulous, all-inclusive term "the collective" (that vague and always contradictory "client" of urbanism) can become describable. For we are all by turns passengers in the city's networks, actors on its stage, consumers of its wares, or shelterers under its protection.

Abstracting: Diagrams / Emblems

"(...) the concepts of natural language, vaguely defined as they are, seem to be more stable in the expansion of knowledge than the precise terms of scientific language, derived as an idealization from only limited groups of phenomena."[5]

The city reveals itself to us as a continuum of scales of reality and engagement, from the painfully intimate to the analytically cartographic. It provides the settings for our immediate encounters and, at the same time, the markings for our mental maps. Taken together with our ever-changing modes of engagement, the city's chimerical manifestation presents us with a Gordian Knot of possible relationships, questioning any overarching conceptual framework applied to it, whilst at the same time evading summary through dissection. The simplifications and abstractions of traditional urban design method are responses to this difficult reality. But rather than generating simplified figures which are then taken for

Rahmen für unsere unmittelbaren Begegnungen und gleichzeitig die Markierungen für unsere geistige Karte. Betrachtet man dies im Zusammenhang mit unseren stets sich wandelnden Modi der Partizipation, so beschert uns die chimärische Erscheinungsform der Stadt einen Gordischen Knoten von möglichen Beziehungen, der sowohl jegliches umfassende konzeptuelle Gerüst als auch die Analyse durch Sezierung in Frage stellt. Die Vereinfachungen und Abstraktionen der traditionellen Methode städtebaulichen Entwerfens sind Reaktionen auf diesen Widerspruch. Abstraktion kann aber – neben der Generierung vereinfachter Größen, die dann für die Realität gehalten werden – einen Raum der Unschärfe erzeugen, der den Einsatz der Interpretationsfähigkeit erfordert, um Bedeutungen und Zusammenhänge zu postulieren. Daraus können Darstellungen von eher potenter als latenter Bedeutung entstehen[6], wie in einem Tarotkartenspiel, dessen Diagramme/Embleme Bedeutungskonstellationen implizieren, deren Sinn sich jedoch erst durch den Wahrsager erschließt.

Der Rissboden der Kathedrale von Wells[7]

Im Kapitelsaal der hochgotischen Kathedrale von Wells in Somerset findet sich ein komplexes Muster aus feinen, kaum sichtbaren Linien, die in weichen Gips geritzt wurden. Während des Baus der Kathedrale war dieser Raum fest verschlossen und tabu für alle außer den Steinmetzmeistern. Nach Vollendung des Baus wurde der Rissboden für gewöhnlich zerstört oder überdeckt. Es war dies der Ort für geheime Diskussionen und das Reißbrett, an dem geometrische Konstruktionen entworfen wurden.[8] Diese Verbindung von Diskurs und Handwerk ließ eine Geometrie entstehen, die den Grundriss der Kathedrale in die Ansicht projizieren und so Raum entstehen ließ.

An Hand der die ad triangulum-Methode untermauernden Euklidischen Mathematik ließ sich die Übersetzung in eine an Schönheitsideal und Transzendenz orientierte Architektur verwirklichen. Fragen der strukturellen Geschlossenheit, der Logik der Konstruktion und der Umsetzung der Symbolik verschmolzen miteinander.

Die eingeritzten Linien beschreiben eine Suche nach Antworten sowohl auf praktische als auch auf spirituelle Fragen (angemessene Proportionen für ein Haus Gottes). Dieser Ort wird durch einen zweifachen Glaubensakt bestimmt, der sich in den Einritzungen gleichzeitig als Projektionsfläche, Skizzenbuch und derer Überreste darstellt.

Der Rissboden ist hier nicht als Bild relevant, sondern als Verkörperung analytisch-symbolischer Handlungen. Sowohl als Ort der Diskussion als auch der Entscheidung ist er eine Stelle, an der Wissenschaft und Mythos, Analyse und Handwerk aufeinander treffen und verschmelzen. Für die Steinmetze war jede Linie und jeder Schnittpunkt, die sie zeichneten, nicht etwa abstrakt, sondern vielmehr in höchstem Maße determinativ und spezifisch. Die Abstraktion stellt sich daher nur dem Nichteingeweihten dar. Als Nichtmitglieder werden wir durch unsere Unwissenheit bezüglich der verlorenen Geheimnisse der mündlichen Überlieferung ausgeschlossen. Wir wissen, womit die Linien zu tun haben, können aber der Logik ihrer Bahnen und Beziehungen nicht folgen. Die generative Geometrie des uns umgebenden Gebäudes ist auf dem Boden durchstrichen – das Versprechen der Enthüllung von Geheimnissen durch ein unverständliches, unleserliches Palimpsest. Als eine erläuternde Ausführungszeichnung frustriert und verwirrt der Boden den Betrachter eher als dass er ihn aufklärt. Diese „Unschärfe" ist der Ursprung einer Abstraktion, die auf eine unsichtbare Logik ver-

reality, abstraction can also produce a space of uncertainty, provoking the engagement of the interpretative faculty in order to postulate meaning and synthesis. It can generate representations whose meaning is "potent rather than latent"[6], not unlike the figures in a pack of tarot cards, whose implied significance can only be gauged when a soothsayer makes sense of them.

Wells Cathedral Tracing-Floor[7]

A complex pattern of fine, barely visible lines is inscribed in soft plaster in the chapter house of the high gothic cathedral at Wells in Somerset. During the construction of the cathedral, the room was closed under lock and key and declared out of bounds to all but the master masons. On completion of the building, the tracing-floor would usually be destroyed or covered up. It was the site of secret discussions and the drawing board upon which geometrical constructions were executed.[8] Through this combination of discourse and craft, a geometry was determined, that allowed the plan of the cathedral to be projected into elevation, thereby generating space.

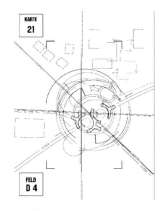

Robert Slinger:
Tarotkarte Nr. 21 „Der Sturm"

Robert Slinger:
Tarot card no. 21 "The storm"

Through the Euclidian mathematics that underpin the ad triangulum method, the translation into architecture of ideals of beauty and transcendence was drawn out, questions of structural integrity, constructional logic and symbolic embodiment melted together.

The inscribed lines describe a search for answers to both pragmatic and spiritual questions (the appropriate proportions for the "House of God"). It is, therefore, the site of a two-fold act of faith, represented simultaneously as projection-screen, sketchbook and residue in the inscribed markings.

The tracing-floor is relevant here not as an image but because of the analytical-symbolic activities that it embodied. As both site of discussion and determinant field, it is a place where science and myth, analysis and craft meet and fuse with each other. For the masons who drew it, each line and crossing point was always highly determinant and specific, never abstract. Abstraction is, therefore, only present here for the uninitiated. We, the non-members, are separated by our ignorance of the oral tradition's lost secrets. We know what the lines are about, but cannot follow the logic of their trajectories and relations. The generative geometry of the building around us is scored out in the floor, a promise of secrets revealed articulated in an inaccessible, illegible palimpsest. As an explanatory execution drawing, the floor frustrates and confuses the observer much more than it reveals. This "Unschärfe" (blurring) is the source of an abstraction hinting at an invisible logic, provoking and challenging us to search out the building's hidden meaning. Its role becomes heuristic rather than didactic. Returning to the nave after observing the tracing-floor, we search out in the enormous empty volume the dynamic connections hinted at in its striations, grids, diagonals, clusters, and arcs. We search in vain, we think we can discern possible alignments and we leave having thrown imaginary lines through the space, never knowing how many of them we discovered and how many were just imagined.

weist, die uns provoziert und dazu herausfordert, den verborgenen Sinn des Gebäudes ausfindig zu machen. Ihre Rolle ist eher heuristisch als didaktisch. Zurück im Längsschiff, machen wir in dem enormen leeren Raum die dynamischen Verbindungen ausfindig, auf die uns die Riefungen des Rissbodens verwiesen haben: die Raster, die Diagonalen, die Bündelungen, die Bögen, die Ecken und deren Schnittpunkte verbinden. Wir suchen vergeblich, wir denken, dass wir mögliche Übereinstimmungen ausmachen, und im Nachhinein stellen wir fest, dass wir imaginäre Linien in den Raum projiziert haben, ohne zu wissen, wie viele von ihnen wir tatsächlich entdeckt und welche wir uns nur vorgestellt haben.

Das konzentrierte Studieren der Karte einer Stadt, die einem zwar historisch vertraut ist, die man jedoch noch nie besucht hat, kann einen ähnlich schwindelerregenden Gedankengang auslösen.

Die Karte – als spezifisches Diagramm – nimmt einen heuristischen Charakter an durch die Abstraktion, die teilweise aus der Diskrepanz zwischen Karte und beschriebener Stadt, teilweise aus der Diskrepanz zwischen dem was wir wissen und was wir uns aus Unwissenheit vorstellen, entsteht. Es entsteht, vermittelt durch das Medium, eine Reziprozitätszone zwischen der Stadt (als Ursprung und Ergebnis) und ihrer Abstraktion. Die hier beschriebene Reziprozität stellt ein Analogon zu dem Rissboden dar, der aus einer glatten Fläche (dem weichen, formbaren Gipsfeld) und der geritzten Fläche (den darauf befindlichen Spuren) besteht.[9]

Stanley Cursiter: The Sensation of Crossing the Street

Cursiters 1918 entstandenes Gemälde illustriert die kulminierenden Konsequenzen der Expansion der Metropolen des 19. Jahrhunderts, die Intensivierung zufälliger Begegnungen und indifferenter Bewegungsbahnen. Die hektische Menge wird überlagert durch neue Formen des motorisierten Verkehrs, der den öffentlichen Raum zu Cursiters Zeit in zunehmendem Maße bestimmte. Diese Überlagerung steht für den Konflikt von Beteiligung und Bedeutung, den wir heutzutage für die Definition der Straße als solche halten. Dies manifestiert sich im Moment ihrer Überquerung. Verschiedene Formen der Beteiligung" am Bild der Straße und ihrer Bauweise, menschliche und mechanische Elemente werden in figurativer Klarheit repräsentiert: eine historische Skyline, deren Architektur sich ambivalent zum zentralen Thema verhält; die Menge, die sich in Strömen nach rechts und links parallel zur Bildebene bewegt; bedrohliche Maschinen, die perspektivisch aus dem Bild ragen; eine zentrale Figur, die sich wie Baudelaires Flaneur gegen den Hintergrund der Masse abhebt; Kontrollinstanzen – eine Uhr, ein Polizist. Über diesen Realismus hinaus wird künstlerische Abstraktion eingesetzt, um die verschiedenen Elemente in einer Synthese zusammenzubringen und ein Verschmelzen von Räumen und Zielrichtungen zu bewirken. Geometrische Felder aus Farben, Raster und Rahmungen strukturieren das Bild. Diese überlagern jedoch die figurativen Formen nicht, vielmehr sollen jene transformiert und irritiert werden. Die so entstandenen Transparenzen hinterfragen sowohl die Solidität von Farben und Oberflächen als auch die Integrität von Formen, Räumen und Protagonisten. Durch Schraffur diagonal miteinander verwobene Bildteile implizieren eine Schicht von Bewegung und Geschwindigkeit.

Durch Abstraktion werden zwischen den Protagonisten, die ursprünglich gegeneinander gesetzt waren, Beziehungen hergestellt und Geschichten impliziert.

Intently studying the map of a city you have never visited but are nonetheless familiar with through its history, can sometimes set up similar, vertiginous trains of thought.

The map, drawn as an explicit diagram, takes on a heuristic character through an abstraction created partly out of the distance between it and the city it describes, and partly out of that which is between what we know and what we can imagine because we do not. A zone of reciprocity is established between the city (both as source and result) and its abstraction, mediated by the interlocutor. This reciprocity described is analogous to the tracing-floor, comprising a smooth space (the field of soft, pliable plaster) and a striated one (the markings upon it).[9]

Stanley Cursiter: The Sensation of Crossing the Street

Painted in 1918, Cursiter's The Sensation of Crossing the Street illustrates the climactic consequences of the metropolitan enlargement of the 19th Century, the intensification of accidental encounter and indifferent transit. New forms of mechanized transport which were increasingly inhabiting the public realm in Cursiter's time are overlaid upon the hectic bustle of the crowd. This overlay defines the conflict of interest and meaning that we take today for the definition of the street made manifest in the moment of its crossing. Different modes of engagement with the streetscape and its built, human and mechanical elements are represented with figurative clarity: a historical city skyline, its architecture detached from the central theme; the crowd, moving to the left and to the right in planar flows parallel to the picture plane; threatening machines looming out of the picture in perspective; a central figure, like Baudelaire's flaneur against the backdrop of the masses; controlling instances – a clock, a policeman. In addition to this realism, painterly abstraction is employed to synthetically bring together the disparate elements and effect a melting into each other of spaces and intentions. Geometric fields of colour, grids and frames structure the image. These are not, however, overlaid onto the figurative forms but rather employed to transform and disturb them. Transparencies appear, questioning the solidity of colours and surfaces, as well as the integrity of forms, spaces and characters. Images are diagonally hatched into each other, implying movement and velocity in the overlay.

Through abstraction, relationships are established between characters initially set against each other and narratives are implied. Passengers in the tram become pedestrians on the street and vice versa; the geometry of the crowd becomes that of the tram, body becoming vehicle. The central figure is pushed along by the velocity of the overlaid and abstracted crowd. We become uncertain as to where she is on the street, she is forced off the pavement. The crowd disembodiesthe head and the *Faneur* begins to melt into the crowd, losing the detached specificity which her sideways glance implies, rendered anonymous by the dynamic of the metropolis. The force of the city in motion undermines the rigidity of policeman and clock, the mechanisms attempting to bring control and order to the city.

It is through the uncertainty introduced by the abstraction of the image that possible narratives are set in motion, whereby Modes of Engagement become manifest as relational networks and not as hermetic conditions. The elements making up this particular atmosphere in the city are clearly described, whilst the com-

Straßenbahnpassagiere werden Fußgänger auf der Straße und umgekehrt; die Geometrie der Menge wird die der Straßenbahn, der Körper wird Verkehrsmittel. Die zentrale Figur wird von der Geschwindigkeit der sie überlagernden, abstrahierten Menge vorangetrieben. Wir sind nicht sicher, wo in der Straße sie sich befindet – sie wird vom Gehsteig gedrängt. Die Menge lässt den Kopf körperlos erscheinen und den Flaneur mit der Menge verschmelzen. Dabei verliert er seine, durch den seitwärts gerichteten Blick angedeutete, losgelöste Individualität. Die Dynamik der Stadt lässt ihn anonym werden. Die Härte des Polizisten und der Uhr, jener Mechanismen, die die Stadt zu kontrollieren und zu ordnen versuchen, werden durch die Kraft der sich bewegenden Stadt aufgelöst.

Die durch die Abstraktion des Bildes entstehende Unschärfe löst mögliche Geschichten aus, wobei die „Formen der Beteiligung" sich als Netzwerk von Beziehungen und nicht als hermetische Bedingungen manifestieren. Die Elemente, die die besondere Atmosphäre der Stadt ausmachen, sind deutlich dargestellt. Der komplexe Hintergrund von widersprüchlichen Beziehungen innerhalb derer sie sich bewegen, wird an keiner Stelle negiert oder vereinfacht.

Die obigen zwei Beispiele sollen einige der Eigenschaften, die solchen Abstraktionen innewohnen, verdeutlichen. Sie beschreiben die Suche nach einer urbanen „potentia", einer gedachten Topographie, die geträumte und existierende Städte in einem Raum zwischen Realität und Ideal aufeinander treffen und interagieren lässt, der Schöpfung einer „strange kind of physical reality just in the middle between possibility and reality".[10]

ANMERKUNGEN

(1) Heisenberg, Werner: *Physics and Philosophy*, Penguin, London 1990
Deutsche Zitate nach: Werner Heisenberg: *Physik und Philosophie*, S. Hirzel Verlag, Stuttgart 2000, S. 84 Die Definition des Begriffs „Stadt" und seine Artikulation scheinen mir eng an die Grundthese, die die Kopenhagener Deutung untermauert, angelehnt. Bohrs erste Experimente, die zeigten, dass sich Licht entweder als Welle oder als Teilchen verhält – je nachdem, wie es untersucht wird – entsprechen der präzise beschreibbaren jedoch, grundlegend ungewissen Beschaffenheit, die ich urbanen Bedingungen zuschreiben würde.

(2) Siehe: Luise King (Hrsg.): *Die Stadt, das Schiff und das Kamel*, Technische Universität Berlin 2000, und R. Slinger, S. Rivière (Hrsg.): *The Matrix : An Urban Design Project*, Technische Universität Berlin 2004

(3) Jean-Francois Lyotard: *La condition postmoderne* Paris: Editions de Minuit, Paris 1979 – dtsch.: *Das Postmoderne Wissen*, Passagen, Wien 1994

(4) Heisenberg, ebd. S. 85

(5) Heisenberg, ebd. S. 279/280

(6) Siehe: Robin Evans: *In Front of Lines That Leave Nothing Behind*, AA Files 6 (Mai 1984)

(7) Siehe: John Harvey: *The medieval Architect*, London, 1978, S. 114

(8) Zum freimaurerischen Geheimgebot siehe: Joseph Rykwert: *On the Oral Transmission of Architectural Theory*, AA Files 6, Mai 1984, S. 14–27

(9) Zur Reziprozität von glatten und gekerbten Flächen siehe: Gilles Deleuze und Felix Guattari: *Mille Plateaux*, Band 2 von *Capitalisme et Schizophrénie*, Editions de Minuit, Paris 1980, S. 474–500 – dtsch.: *1000 Plateaus*, Merve Verlag, Berlin 1992, S. 657–693

(10) Heisenberg, ebd. S. 61

plex matrix of contradictory relationships within which they exist is at no point denied or simplified.

With the above two examples I have attempted to illustrate some of the properties found in the kind of abstract devices I sought for in my own pedagogy of urbanism. They describe a search for Urban Potentia, a mental topography allowing dreamt-of and found cities to meet and interact in the space between the actual and the ideal, the creation of "a strange kind of physical reality just in the middle between possibility and reality".[10]

NOTES

(1) Werner Heisenberg: *Physics and Philosophy*, Penguin, London 1990, p. 45
 The question of what the term "City" means and how it can be articulated strikes me as closely analogous to the fundamental hypotheses underpinning the Copenhagen Interpretation. Bohr's first experiments, demonstrating how light behaves either as wave or particle, depending on how it is observed, parallel closely the precisely describable but fundamentally uncertain nature, which I would ascribe to the urban condition.
(2) See: Luise King (ed.): *Die Stadt, das Schiff und das Kamel*, Technische Universität Berlin 2000, and R. Slinger, S. Rivière (ed.): *The Matrix: An Urban Design Project*, Technische Universität Berlin 2004
(3) Jean-Francois Lyotard: *La condition postmoderne*, Editions de Minuit, Paris 1979, translated by G. Bennington and Brian Massumi as *The Postmodern Condition: A Report on Knowledge*, Manchester University Press, Manchester 1984
(4) Heisenberg, op.cit., p. 46
(5) Heisenberg, op.cit., p. 188
(6) See Robin Evans: *In Front of Lines That Leave Nothing Behind*, AA Files 6 (May 1984)
(7) See John Harvey: *The Medieval Architect*, London, 1978, p. 114
(8) On the Masonic imperative to secrecy, see Joseph Rykwert: *On the Oral Transmission of Architectural Theory*, AA Files 6 (May 1984), pp. 14–27
(9) On the reciprocity of smooth and striated space, see Gilles Deleuze and Felix Guattari: *Mille Plateaux*, Volume 2 of *Capitalisme et Schizophrénie*, Les Editions de Minuit, Paris 1980, translated by Brian Massumi as: *A Thousand Plateaus*, Athlone Press, London 1988, pp. 474–500
(10) Heisenberg, op.cit., p. 29

Claire Karsenty

Komplex Denken

Wer Architektur und Gestaltung unterrichten möchte, muss sich unter anderem fragen, welcher Grad an Komplexität zu Beginn der Architekturausbildung angemessen ist. Bei der Entwicklung einer Methodik für die Lehre von Gestaltung muss man sich von linearen gedanklichen Mustern befreien und assoziatives Denken zulassen, durch das die Synthese unterschiedlicher konzeptioneller und pragmatischer Ansätze möglich ist.

   In den ersten beiden Studienjahren müssen die Studenten die konzeptionellen, theoretischen und praktischen Aspekte lernen, anhand derer mögliche Gestaltungsmethoden, die zu untersuchen und zu bewerten sind, eingeordnet werden können. Im Lauf der vergangenen fünf Jahre wurde in unserem Büro ein Übungskatalog erstellt, bei dem nicht so sehr das Erlernen bestimmter Techniken oder Methoden im Vordergrund steht, sondern der die Studenten in die Lage versetzen soll, Gestaltung als Ausdrucksmittel für drei wesentliche Elemente zu verstehen: Beobachtung, Experimentieren und die Synthese von unterschiedlichen Anforderungen. Mit der Vorstellung von zwei dieser Übungen lässt sich dieser Ansatz für die Lehre von Gestaltung vielleicht am besten aufzeigen:

Kragarm

Diese erste Übung für die Studenten wurde inspiriert von einer Aufgabenstellung von Andrew Holmes. Im Laufe einer Woche muss jeder Student so viel Ausgangsmaterial wie möglich im Büro sammeln, um einen Kragarm von 4 m Länge für eine vorgegebene Belastung zu bauen. Die gesammelten Objekte sollen Fundstücke von Müllhalden, Schrottplätzen oder von der Straße sein. Für den Bau des Kragarms steht nur eine begrenzte Zeit zur Verfügung, jede Gruppe erhält fünfzehn Minuten, um aus dem Fundmaterial die für den Bau einzusetzenden Teile auszusuchen, und weitere fünfzehn Minuten für die Konzeption und den Zusammenbau ihrer Konstruktion. Jeder Student muss dann in weiteren dreißig Minuten drei Zeichnungen der Konstruktion in drei unterschiedlichen, frei zu wählenden Medien anfertigen.

Hybrid

Dieses Projekt ist ein Kurs im zweiten Ausbildungsjahr und erstreckt sich über ein gesamtes Semester. Lernziel dabei ist das Erkennen der programmatischen Dimension von Architektur. Das Projekt gliedert sich im Wesentlichen in drei Phasen:

   - Eine Phase der Betrachtung der besonderen Bedingungen, die typisch für den Begriff Hybrid sind. Untergliedert wird diese Phase in eine Reihe von Übungen, in denen das Aufzeichnen und die Analyse von Situationen, die Überlagerung von Funktionen sowie das Ausformulieren eines Bauprogramms abgestimmt auf die Interessenslage jedes Studenten erlernt werden soll.

   - Eine Phase der experimentellen Gestaltung, in der die Studenten Vorstudien nach den Vorgaben eines speziellen Rahmenprogramms anfertigen (eine Übung hatte

Complex Thinking

In teaching architectural design, one is faced, among other things, with the question of the degree of complexity appropriate at the beginning of an architect's education. In developing a design methodology, one must be able to liberate oneself from linear patterns of thought, in favour of associative ones enabling the synthesis of different conceptual and pragmatic parameters.

In the first two years of study, a student must learn to deal with the conceptual, theoretical and practical factors that enable reflection on possible methods of design to be investigated and assessed. Over the course of the last 5 years, a framework of exercises has been established in our studio, which attempts not so much to articulate particular techniques or methodologies as to act as enablers for the students to comprehend design as a means to articulate three main aspects: observation, experimentation and the synthesis of different requirements. Two of our exercises perhaps best illustrate this approach to teaching design:

The "Kragarm" (Cantilever)

This first exercise undertaken by students is inspired by a brief devised by Andrew Holmes. Over the course of a week, each student has to collect as much raw material as possible in the studio, in order to construct a 4 m long cantilever, capable of carrying a given load. The elements collected are found objects, salvaged from rubbish dumps, junk yards or the street. The execution of the cantilevers is organised as a race against the clock, each group being given just 15 minutes to select elements to be used from the assembled materials, and 15 minutes for the conception and assembly of their structure. Each student is then given 30 minutes to produce three drawings of the structure using three media of their choice.

The Hybrid

This project has been carried out as a second-year course lasting one full semester. It is designed to provoke reflection about the programmatic dimension of architecture. The project is articulated in three principle phases:

- A period of observation of particular conditions characteristic of the notion of the hybrid. This phase is structured by a series of exercises enabling the cartography and analysis of situations, the superposition of function and the formulation of an agenda particular to each student's interests.

- A period of design experiment where students produce preliminary studies responding to a particular programmatic frame (for example, one exercise was based on the hybrid association of the themes exchange/inhabitation). The exercises are framed so as to avoid purely typological responses, in favour of a tactical understanding of observed practices.

zum Beispiel als Grundlage die Hybridassoziation der Themen Wechsel/Bewohnen). Durch die Anlage der Übungen werden nach Möglichkeit rein typologische Lösungen vermieden und statt dessen taktisches Verstehen beobachteter Praktiken gefördert.

- Eine Phase der Entwicklung von einer der Strategien für hybride Räume, die während der vorangegangenen Phasen geprüft wurden. Die unterschiedlichen programmatischen Elemente werden definiert, sie erhalten eine Form und werden von jedem Studenten in einen bestimmten Kontext gestellt. So entwickelt jeder Student ein Gebäude an Hand anderer programmatischer Vorgaben und spiegelt damit wieder, wie nach seinem speziellen Verständnis miteinander zusammenhängenden Funktionen nahe beieinander liegen, sich ergänzen oder im Widerspruch zueinander stehen können.

Diese beiden Übungen zwingen – jede auf ihre Weise – die Studenten dazu, reflektiert zu arbeiten, ohne dabei auf stereotype Antworten zurückzugreifen. Da die Aufgabenstellung recht unkonventionell ist, lernen die Studenten, die jeweiligen Einschränkungen bei einer Gestaltung zu erkennen, indem sie intuitiv ohne Verwendung von Standardlösungen reagieren müssen. In beiden Projekten bildet eigenes Experimentieren den Auftakt zur Untersuchung von vorhandenen Beispielen. Analyse wird nicht zur Vorbedingung für Aktion, sondern ist ein deskriptives Mittel zur Erläuterung des experimentellen Prozesses. Da die Studenten nach einem Spiegel suchen, der es ihnen ermöglicht, das, was sie bereits geschaffen haben, besser zu verstehen, wird die zentrale Absicht von Analyse wesentlich intensiver und dauerhafter herausgearbeitet.

Beim Hybrid-Projekt war es interessant zu beobachten, dass die programmatische Komplexität – die Verbindung von zwei gegensätzlichen Funktionen, die a priori nichts miteinander zu tun haben – die Studenten weder überrascht hat noch ihnen anachronistisch erschien. Diese Situation findet sich in der Aufgabenstellung und dem Handlungsumfeld von Architektur heute beständig. Indem der Student die innere Sprache der Komplexität lernt, gewinnt er ein Verständnis für Raum im Kontext einer zeitgenössischen Realität, die von Vielfalt und der Konfrontation kultureller, politischer und gesellschaftlicher Systeme beherrscht ist. Zwar erzählen Funktionen wie Wohnen, Arbeiten, Schlafen, Kochen, Verkaufen noch von profanen Traditionen, aber sie tun dies abgeschwächt und sind vermischt mit Praktiken, die so unterschiedlich sind, dass sie kaum mehr festzumachen sind.

Komplexität muss mit einem gewissen didaktischen Hintergrund in die Lehre der Architektur eingeführt werden, aber die Konfrontation mit Problemen, die aus unterschiedlichen Blickwinkeln untersucht werden müssen, kann durchaus auch als Einstieg in das Gestalten dienen. Einerseits wird der Student in die Lage versetzt, einen persönlichen Ansatz zu dem untersuchten Thema zu formulieren, aber andererseits wird auch die Diskussion in der Gruppe gefördert. Die vielfältigen Ansätze zur Bearbeitung des gleichen Themas tragen zum theoretischen Austausch über allgemeinere Fragestellungen bei. Auf Quellen und Vorbilder wird nicht zurückgegriffen um zu imitieren, sondern um in Worte (oder Bilder) zu fassen, was geschaffen oder gedacht wurde.

Der Vergleich und die Unterschiedlichkeit individueller Strategien ermöglichen es den Studenten in den ersten Jahren ihrer Ausbildung, für sich einen kollektiven Rahmen mit Referenzmaterial zu schaffen, der für die analytische Kritik der Experimentalmethode notwendig ist. In den folgenden Jahren kann jeder diese persönlichen Ansätze durch einen Prozess des Dialogs und der Suche nach Affinitäten weiterentwickeln.

— A period of development of one of the hybrid space strategies tested during the previous phases. The different programmatic components are defined, given form, and placed in a particular context by each student. As a result, each student develops a building around different programmatic parameters, reflecting a specific understanding of the proximity, complementarity or contradiction of the related functions.

These two exercises, each in their own way, oblige the students to reflect for themselves without resort to stereotypical responses. The unconventional nature of the brief enables students to understand specific design constraints by obliging them to react intuitively without recourse to standard solutions. In both projects, direct experimentation is the prelude to the study of examples. Analysis becomes not a precondition for action, but a descriptive means of clarifying the experimental process. Because the students search for a mirror permitting them to understand better what they have already produced, the focus of the analysis is rendered all the more intense and durable.

With the hybrid project, it has been interesting to observe that the programmatic complexity — the combination of two disparate functions lacking any a priori relationship to each other — does not in any way surprise or appear anachronistic to the students. It is a concept inherent in the contemporary practice and experience of architecture. As the student learns a language from the complexity out of which it is constituted, the comprehension of space is apprehended in the context of a contemporary reality characterised by diversity and the confrontation of varied cultural, political and social systems. If functions like inhabitation, work, sleep, cooking, and selling still recount secular traditions, then they do so in a manner which has become diluted and mixed with practices so varied as to be no longer locatable.

Whilst complexity must be introduced into architectural education with a certain didactic reflection, it appears that confrontation with such problems, which have to be examined from different angles, also functions as an instigating parameter in design. On the one hand, it enables the student to define a personal approach to the studied theme, whilst on the other stimulating a collective discussion. This diversity of approach to the same subject matter contributes to the theoretical exchange on the general topic. Research into specific references is not motivated by a will to imitation, but rather by the need to put in words (or images) what has been produced or thought.

The comparison and contrast of individual strategies enables students during the first years of their studies to establish the collective frame of reference necessary for analytical critique of experimental method. During the following years, each of them is empowered to develop these personal approaches through a process of dialogue and affinity.

Christoph Jantos / Hybrid: Temptations 2001/2002

Lageplan *Site plan*

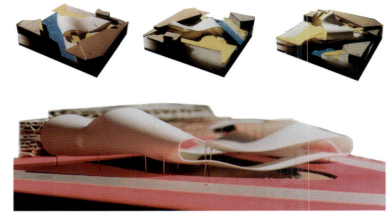

Konzeptmodelle *Concept models*

„WOW LOOK!! CONCRETE NEVER SEEMED SO INVITING!"

Zwischen S-Bahnhof, Spree und Friedrichstraße bettet sich das neue Gebäude der Staatsbibliothek zu Berlin mit der Abteilung für Film- und Theaterwissenschaften in Form einer überdimensionalen Schleife ein.
Die leicht und weich wirkende Gebäudehülle aus Sichtbeton ist äußerer Ausdruck der geistigen Tätigkeit im Inneren des Gebäudes.
Die geschwungenen Schlaufen des Gebäudes schaffen einerseits die notwendige Abgrenzung zur belebten und lauten Straße und erzeugen andererseits eine Sogwirkung ins Innere des Gebäudes.

"WOW LOOK!! CONCRETE NEVER SEEMED SO INVITING!"

The new building of the Staatsbibliothek zu Berlin (Berlin State Library) is embedded in the form of a gigantic loop between the S-bahn stations of Spree and Friedrichstraße. The building has a section devoted to film and theatre studies. Its outer layer of exposed concrete appears both light and soft and is the external expression of the intellectual effort going on inside the building. On the one hand, the building's curving loops create the necessary distance from the very busy and noisy road, while on the other hand they act as a kind of "suction mechanism" to attract people inside the building.

Bauschild *Construction sign*

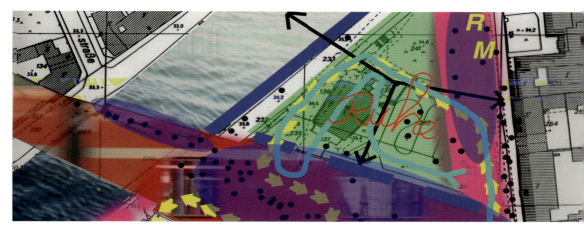

Ortsbewegungsanalyse *Analysis of movement on-site*

„I JUST POPPED IN ON MY WAY HOME!"

""Vorhandene Bewegungsströme wie Straße, Fußgängerverkehr, Wasserverlauf und Transportmittel wie S- und U-Bahn umfließen, durchdringen und durchstoßen Bereiche des Gebäudes und unterstreichen die Idee der Verschmelzung zwischen öffentlichem Platz und halböffentlicher Bibliothek.
Das Gebäude verfügt über mehrere Ein- und Ausgänge, welche die vorhandenen Bewegungsströme anzapfen und eine leichte, schnelle und unkomplizierte Durchwegung ermöglichen.
Das Dach des Gebäudes dient als Ort des öffentlichen Lebens, das Gebäudeinnere als Ort des Ruhens.

"I JUST POPPED IN ON MY WAY HOME!"

Existing avenues of movement, such as the road, pedestrian traffic, waterway and transport facilities like the S-Bahn (city railway) and the U-Bahn (underground) penetrate and punctuate some areas of the building, underlining the idea of blurring the distinction between public square and semi-public library. The building boasts several entrances and exits, which tap into the existing streams of movement and make possible a straightforward, swift and uncomplicated "through-passage". The building's roof acts as a focal point of public life, and the interior as a place of peacefulness.

Längsschnitt *Section*

Arbeitsregal *Workshelf* Straßenmobiliar in Inneren *Street "furniture" in the interior* Wasserraum *Water space*

„YOU CAN FIND KUBRICK NEXT TO THE STOP-SIGN!"

Die Straße mit ihrer zugehörigen „Möblierung" (geplante Baumbepflanzung, Straßenbeschilderung, Bodenbelag, Mülleimer, Bänke, ...) und das Wasser der Spree dringen in das Gebäudeinnere hinein und vermischen sich mit ihm. Die Grenze zwischen Innen und Außen ist fließend.
An mehreren Stellen wird die Gebäudehülle von Märkischen Kiefern durchstoßen, die sich mit dem statisch notwendigen Stützenwald vermengen.
Im Innenraum befinden sich spezielle Bücherregale, welche auch als multimediale Arbeitsplätze dienen und auf unkonventionelle Weise gemeinsam mit dem Stützenwald als Raumteiler fungieren.

"YOU CAN FIND KUBRICK NEXT TO THE STOP-SIGN!"

The road, with its accompanying "furniture" – planned tree-planting, street-signs, surfacing, refuse bins, benches, etc) and the water of the River Spree, intrude into the building's interior and merge with it. The boundary between interior and exterior is fluid. At several points the building's shell is penetrated by "pines from the Marches", which blend in with the load-bearing forest-trees. In the interior there are special bookshelves, which also act as multi-media workplaces, and – in an unconventional way – fulfil the function of a room-divider along with the load-bearing forest-trees.

Längsschnitt mit Märkischen Kiefern *Longitudinal section with regional pines*

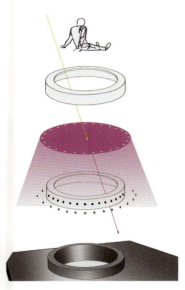  

Explosionszeichnung einer Pondbrane   *Explosion sketch of a pondbrane*   Licht-Liege-Membrane = Pondbranes   *light-couch-membrane = Pondbranes*

„MY PONDBRANE IS MY CASTLE – AND THE MOST RELAXING I'VE EVER CONQUERED!!"

Von außen wahrnehmbar und nach innen verführend sind die sogenannten „pondbranes" (textile Membranen), die das Licht in verschiedenen Farben nach innen und außen filtern.
Im Gebäudeinneren dienen sie durch die Möglichkeit, sich hineinzulegen, als Lese- wie auch als Entspannungsort und lassen den nahen Bezug zum Wasser, hier die Spree, erkennen.
Geistiges Arbeiten und Entspannen wird durch die „pondbranes" geschickt verknüpft.

"MY PONDBRANE IS MY CASTLE – AND THE MOST RELAXING I'VE EVER CONQUERED!!"

Visible from the outside and seductive on the inside, the so-called pondbranes (textile membranes) filter light inside and outwards in a variety of colours. Inside the building, they serve as a place for reading and relaxation because they offer an opportunity for a lie-down and they evoke the presence of water – here the River Spree. The pondbranes skilfully combine the functions of intellectual work and relaxation.

Querschnitt durch Bibliothek und Bahnhof   *Cross section through library and railway station*

Robert Burghardt / [Ausbruch aus dem] Gefängnis für Intellektuelle 2003/2004

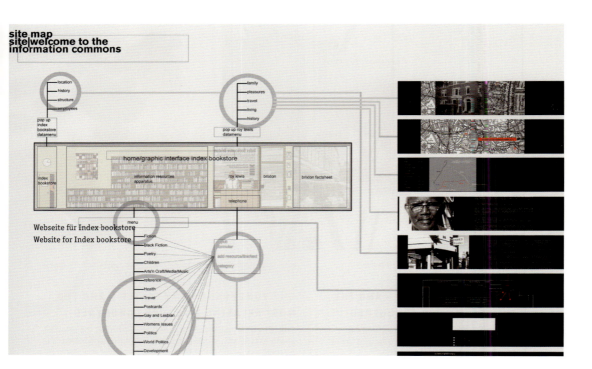

Webseite für Index bookstore
Website for Index bookstore

Startpunkt für das Entwurfsprojekt war der Besuch des Index Bookstore auf dem Brixton Market in Süd-London, der Teil einer mit einer sozialistischen Partei assoziierten Kette war. Heute ist der Laden auf verschiedene politische Titel und Lernbücher spezialisiert. Von Überlegungen zu der Bedeutung von Wissen und Wissensproduktion ausgehend, entwickelte sich das Programm des Gebäudes.

The starting point for the design project was a visit to the Index bookstore at Brixton market in south London, the branch of a chain of shops that is associated with a socialist party. Today, the shop specialises in various political and educational books. The programme of the building developed from reflections on the significance and production of knowledge.

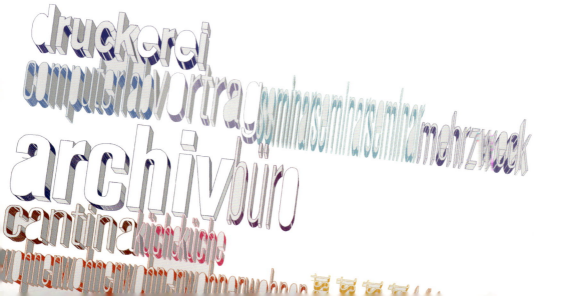

Willkommen in der Deutschen Oper zu Berlin

Rückseite der Deutschen Oper, Berlin *Back side at the Deutsche Oper, Berlin*

BLICKEN SIE HINTER DIE KULISSEN!

Hintereingang: Das Gebäude ist der Versuch, die Offenheit von Handlung zunächst von ihrem Gegenteil her zu denken: also nicht das verglaste, vermeintlich transparent und offene Gebäude, sondern ein geschlossenes, sich verweigerndes Gebäude. Die Fassade, die erst mal nichts verspricht. Dabei habe ich mich mit der Situation des Hintereingangs im Theater beschäftigt, wo der Gegensatz zwischen der repräsentativen Fassade und der funktionalistischen Rückseite besonders deutlich wird.
Backstage is stage: Der Hintereingang stellt die Verbindung zu den Räumen hinter der Bühne her. Dort wird geprobt, diskutiert und kritisiert. Es handelt sich um Räume der Produktion, ständig im Prozess der alltäglichen Performativität.

TAKE A LOOK BEHIND THE SCENES!

The backstage entrance: the building is an attempt first to consider the openness of action from the opposite viewpoint – so, it's not the glass façade and seemingly transparent and open building, but a closed building that refuses entry and a façade that initially promises nothing. In this case, I was working with the idea of the backstage entrance of a theatre, where the contrast between a representative façade and a functional rear entrance becomes especially visible.
Backstage is stage: the backstage entrance creates the connection to spaces behind the stage. Here people rehearse, discuss, and criticise. The spaces are for production that continues without a break and with daily performance culture.

Sequenz: Zustände der Kommunikation *Sequence: states of communication*

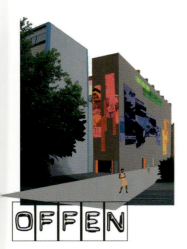

OFFEN

geschlossen

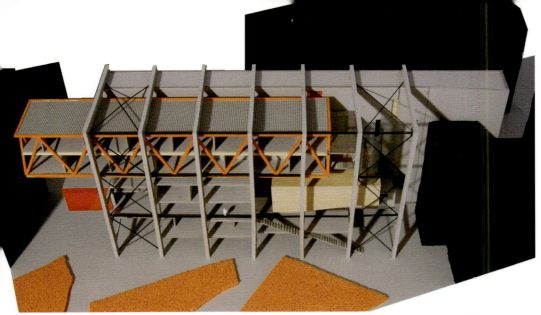

Modell *Model*

UNIVERSITÄT

Intellektuelle: Wir entwerfen Modelle, um komplexe Zusammenhänge zu verstehen, wir konstruieren unsere Realität mit Hilfe von Theorien, die wir als Werkzeuge für Handlung verstehen, um an einen Punkt zu kommen, an dem ein anderes Handeln denkbar wird und wir verinnerlichtes Handeln verlernen können.
In unseren Diskussionen, in unserer Kommunikation entwickeln wir eigene Sprachen. Dabei schaffen wir Grenzen und definieren gemeinsame soziale Räume, Die Fragen die sich stellen: Wie werden Grenzen überschritten, wie werden sie verwischt oder unlesbar gemacht, oder können Sie durch Sichtbarmachung angegriffen werden?

UNIVERSITY

Intellectuals: We develop models in order to understand complex systems, we construct our reality with the help of theories that we understand as tools for acting, in order to reach a point where we can imagine a different kind of acting, and "unlearn" our normative behaviour.
In our discussions, in our modes of communication, we develop different languages. By doing so, we create borders and define common social spaces. The questions that arise: how are borders crossed, how are they blurred or made illegible? Alternatively, can making borders visible expose them to attack?

Längsschnitt durch das Gebäude   *Longitudinal section of the building*

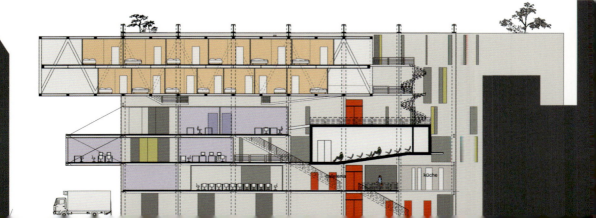

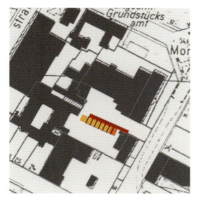

Lageplan *Site-plan*

Blick in die Bibliothek *View into the library*

Querschnitt *Cross-section*

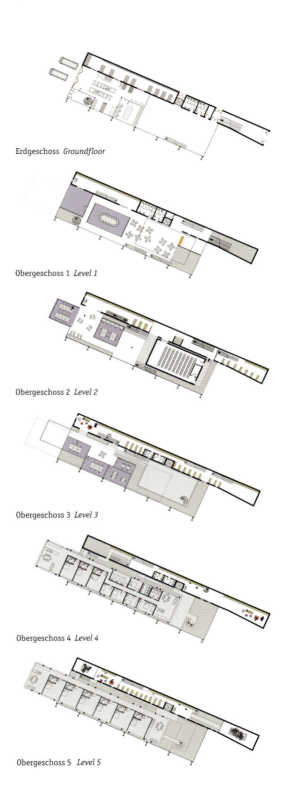

Erdgeschoss *Groundfloor*

Obergeschoss 1 *Level 1*

Obergeschoss 2 *Level 2*

Obergeschoss 3 *Level 3*

Obergeschoss 4 *Level 4*

Obergeschoss 5 *Level 5*

Zeitzeichnung

Architektur erschließt sich über die sinnliche Wahrnehmung. Dabei ist Raumwahrnehmung an die Zeit gebunden und ständiger Veränderung unterworfen. Die wichtigsten Parameter sind Licht, Schatten, Materialität, Proportionen, Klanglandschaft[1] und die Menschen im Raum.

Trotzdem kommen die beiden unverzichtbaren Werkzeuge des Architekten, Grundriss und Schnitt, ohne die Zeit aus. Sie ermöglichen das Schreiben und Lesen eines zeitlosen, dreidimensionalen Raums. Dieser in unserer Vorstellung entstehende Raum ist somit eine Momentaufnahme unter Ausschluss der Veränderungen jener Parameter (Licht, Schatten, Klanglandschaft und Menschen), die wichtig für die sinnliche Wahrnehmung sind. Doch durch das Einbringen der Zeit in Grundriss und Schnitt lassen sich Raum und Nutzer bereits im Entwurf miteinander verknüpfen. Es entsteht eine „Zeitzeichnung" [2]. Unter den verschiedenen Ansätzen zu Zeitzeichnungen findet sich einer der interessantesten im Werk der Architekten Diller und Scofidio – Architekten, die seit langem ihre Projekte konkret auf die Wahrnehmung der Nutzer hin aufbauen und entsprechend eine eigene Art der Zeitzeichnung entwickelt haben. Sie verknüpfen über unterschiedlichste 2D-Darstellungsarten, wie Linienzeichnung, Photographie, Diagramm, akustisches Profil und Text, die Parameter ihres Entwurfs in der Zeichnung und weben auf diese Weise eine dichte räumliche Geschichte [3].

    Ein erfahrener und bauender Architekt kann durch Grundriss und Schnitt die Zeit mit entwerfen: Je mehr Erfahrung er hat, desto präziser treffen seine Vermutungen ein. Was aber macht ein Studienanfänger? Wie kann bereits im Entwurf die Beziehung zwischen Mensch und Raum, Wahrnehmung und Atmosphäre mitgedacht und mitgezeichnet werden? Gerade beim „Architektur lesen und schreiben"-Lernen ist es wichtig, von Anfang an die Zeit mitzuzeichnen; also nicht nur dreidimensional zu zeichnen, sondern vierdimensional.

    Zu den Werkzeugen des k_studios gehörte es, die vierte Dimension über die Analyse von Spielfilmen in den Rahmen des Entwurfs einzubinden. Grundidee war dabei, von der im Film vorhandenen intensiven Verschneidung von Bild, Ton und Zeit zu lernen. Im Film müssen komplexe Handlungen extrem abstrahiert werden; dabei werden Bild und Ton während des gegebenen Zeitablaufs miteinander verwoben und es wird eine Dramaturgie geschaffen. Dies ist vergleichbar mit dem Raum, da auch hier die wichtigsten Parameter visuell und akustisch wahrgenommen werden. Der Unterschied liegt in der Dramaturgie: Während sie im Film auf der Zeitachse linear abläuft, erfolgt sie im Raum durch die Bewegung des Nutzers selbst.

Die Studierenden hatten zwei Filme, die in Berlin spielen, zur Auswahl: *Lola rennt* von Tom Tykwer und *Der Himmel über Berlin* von Wim Wenders. Aus einem der Filme haben die Studierenden eine Schlüsselszene ausgewählt und analysiert. Dabei wurde die Sequenz in ihre Einzelbilder zerlegt und zusammen mit den Tonspuren in einer Zeichnung entlang der Zeitachse dargestellt.[4] Eine weitere Zeichnung entstand aus dem inhaltlichen Thema der

Time Drawing

Architecture is revealed by sensory perception. In this process, perception of space is time-bound and subject to constant change. The most important parameters are light, shade, materiality, proportions, soundscape[1], and human beings in space.

That said, the architect's two indispensable tools, ground plan and cross-section, can manage independently of time. They make it possible to write and read a kind of space that is timeless and three-dimensional. Accordingly, this space – created in our imagination – is a momentary phenomenon, which excludes the changes effected by those parameters (of light, shade, soundscape and human beings) that are vital to sensory perception. Yet bringing time into ground plan and cross section is a way to bring together the concepts of space and user as early as the sketching stage. This results in what one might call a "time drawing".[2] Among the various stimuli to time-drawings, one of the most productive is in the work of the architects Diller and Scofodio – architects who for a long time now have based their projects on the user´s perceptions, and have – in the process – developed their own specific form of time-drawing. Through a wide range of 2D imaging techniques – such as line drawing, photography, the use of diagram, acoustic profile and text – the parameters of their design weave together a dense spatial story in the drawing.[3]

An experienced, constructing architect can also sketch in time within his or her ground plan or cross-section – the more experience they have, the more precise their assumptions. What, on the other hand, can a beginner achieve? How can they "think in" as well as draw in – as early as the sketching stage – the relationship between human being and space, perception and atmosphere? Especially in the early stages of learning the language of architecture it is vital, from the very beginning to include time in one's drawing – in other words, to draw not merely in a three-dimensional but in a four-dimensional way.

Among the k_studio's tools was the notion of including the fourth dimension in the process of sketching, by analysing feature films. The underlying notion was to learn about film's intensive merging of image with sound and time. In film, complex plots must be taken to abstract extremes; in the process, image and sound are woven together during the allotted time – which results in a form of dramaturgy. This is comparable to space, since here, too, the most important parameters are perceived both visually and acoustically. The distinction lies in the dramaturgy. Whilst in the film they proceed in a linear way along the "time axis", in space they proceed by the movement the user makes.

The students could choose from two different films playing in Berlin. They were: *Run Lola run* (Lola rennt) or Wim Wenders's *Wings of Desire* (Der Himmel über Berlin). The students selected and analysed a key scene from one of these films. In the process, the sequence was broken down into its constituent images and depicted – along with the

Sequenz. Die Studierenden haben letztendlich die Sequenz neu zusammengefasst, um sie für den Entwurf nutzbar zu machen. Aus diesen Zeitzeichnungen heraus wurden dann architektonische Räume an einem der Filmschauplätze entworfen.

Ein weiteres Werkzeug war die Erweiterung des „Schattenspiels".[5] Beim Schattenspiel wurden Dienstleister über einen Zeitraum von 24 Stunden „beschattet" und mit ihrem Einverständnis bei ihren Tätigkeiten photographiert. Diese Photos wurden dann editiert, in verschiedenen Paneelen zusammengefasst und im Hinblick auf die Tätigkeiten im Raum verdichtet.[6] Ausgehend von den editierten Photopaneelen fertigten die Studierenden Zeichnungen an, die in Grundriss und Schnitt die Ereignisse und Handlungen des Schattenspiels zeigten. Dazu war es nötig, eigene Symbole für bestimmte Vorgänge zu entwickeln. Es entstanden Zeitzeichnungen, die als eine der Grundlagen für den Entwurf eines mobilen Dienstleistungsstandes dienten.[7] Im Anschluss an den Test wurden die Objekte gezeichnet und die tatsächlich erfolgte Nutzung wieder in einer Zeitzeichnung kartiert.

Ergänzend zu den Zeitzeichnungen wurden die Werkzeuge „Schnappschusscollage" und Comic eingeführt. Schnappschusscollagen sind sorgfältig inszenierte „Raum-Blicke" des Projekts aus der Sicht des Nutzers, die wie Schnappschüsse wirken. Dabei ist der Entwerfende gezwungen, die zukünftige Wahrnehmung der Räume zu zeigen.[8] Das Werkzeug des Comics schließt wiederum die Zeit mit ein, denn zukünftige Abläufe werden wie in einem Storyboard gezeigt.[9] Auch hier bringt die Darstellung von agierenden Figuren im entworfenen Raum zusammen mit den Dialogen und Geräuschen der Sprechblasen Raum und Nutzer zusammen. Der Studierende kann spielerisch überprüfen, ob seine Vorstellung vom Raum zutrifft.

Die Entwicklung der Zeitzeichnung steht beispielhaft für unsere Haltung des Experimentierens und Testens von Positionen zum Entwerfen, ganz im Sinne von Mark Wigley: „Auch wenn Architekten tausende von Jahren über Architektur diskutiert und ihre Expertise entwickelt haben, gibt es keinen allgemeingültigen Kern der Weisheit, kein Grundwissen, dem alle Entwerfenden zustimmen. Dieses endlose Nicht-Einverständnis, das Spüren, dass die Aussage eines Gebäudes immer vielfältig und unklar ist, beschreibt präzise die Magie der Disziplin. (...) Die Vielfältigkeit der Meinungen und die Vielfältigkeit der Schulen ist deshalb lebenswichtig für die andauernde Debatte und zentral für das Überleben der Architekten als Art."[10]

ANMERKUNGEN

(1) Der Begriff Klanglandschaft, engl. Soundscape, wurde von R. Murray Schafer geprägt und beschreibt meiner Meinung nach am besten die Wahrnehmung und Aufzeichnung vielfältiger akustischer Reize im Raum. Murray Schafer *The Soundscape: Our Sonic Environment and the Tuning of the World*, Rochester 1977

(2) Ich möchte mich hiermit ausdrücklich auf die 2D-Zeichnung beziehen und experimentelle Entwurfsmethoden durch Filme oder 3D-Software außerhalb der Betrachtung lassen. Letztlich müssen auch mit solchen Methoden entwickelte Entwürfe durch maßstäbliche Grundrisse und Schnitte überprüft werden.

(3) Vergleiche auch Diller and Scofidio, *Case # 00-17163* in Jonathan Crary und Sanford Kwinter (Ed.), *Incorporations*, New York 1992, Seite 345f.

(4) Siehe auch Doreen Smolensky, *Palace Screening*, Seite 160f.

(5) Das Schattenspiel wurde von Andrew Holmes im Rahmen der Lehre an der University of Westminster für das erste Studienjahr entwickelt.

(6) Siehe auch Werkzeug *Shadowplay* Seite 84, Michael Reiß, *Transfer 1 und 2*, Seite 86f.

(7) Siehe auch Elke Knoess, *Performative Architektur*, Seite 92f.

(8) Siehe auch Felix Sommerlad, *Mole stage*, Seite 196f.

(9) Siehe auch Schadi Weiss, *Backpack full of Illusion*, Seite 24f., Daniel Krüger, *Missing*, Seite 254f.

(10) Mark Wigley in *Architectural Design*, Volume 74, No 5, Sept/ Oct 2004, Seite 13f.

relevant sounds – in a drawing along the time-axis.[4] A further drawing emerged from the sequence's substantive theme. Finally, the students put the sequence together once again, to make it useful for the sketch. Out of these "time drawings", architectonic spaces were then sketched out at one of the film's locations.

Another tool was the extension of the "shadowplay"[5], whereby service-providers are "shadowed" for a period of 24 hours, and – with their agreement – photographed going about their business. These photos were then edited, mounted on a number of panels, and condensed in space.[6] With the edited photo-panels as their starting-point, the students completed drawings, whose ground plan and cross section recorded the shadow play's events and actions. To achieve this, the students needed to work out certain symbols of their own for certain incidents. This resulted in time-drawings, which acted as one of the bases for the design of a mobile service-stand.[7] As a supplement to the text, the objects were drawn and the actually resulting use "filed" once again in a time-drawing.

As an extension to the time-drawings the tools "snapshot collage" and "comics" were introduced. Snapshot collages are carefully arranged "space views" within the project from the standpoint of the user – with the effect of snapshots. In the process, the person making the sketch is compelled to show the future perception of the spaces concerned.[8] The comics tool again includes the element of time, as future developments are shown as if on a story-board.(9) Here, too, the depiction brings characters involved in the sketched space together with the speech bubble dialogue and ambient sounds – thus combining space and utiliser. The students can playfully check whether their notion of space applies.

The development of time-drawing is a kind of yardstick for our maintenance and testing of positions related to sketching – exactly following Mark Wigley's view: "Even if architects have been discussing architecture for thousands of years and have developed their own expertise, there is no universally valid core of wisdom, no basic knowledge, with which all those who do the sketching can concur. This infinite lack of understanding, the feeling that a building's "statement" must always be ambivalent and indistinct, exactly describes the discipline's real magic ... Thus, the very variety of opinions and the wealth of different schools are a vital contribution to the continuing debate, and crucial for the survival of architects as a species."[10]

NOTES

(1) The term: "Soundscape" was coined by R. Murray Schafer and – in my opinion – best describes the perception and noting down of several different acoustic stimuli in a given space. Cf: Murray Shafer: *The soundscape: Our Sonic Environment and the Tuning of the World*, Rochester, 1977.
(2) Here, I am specifically ignoring 2D work and experimental sketching methods through films or 3D software. In the final analysis, sketches developed by such methods must be checked against ground plans and cross sections drawn to scale.
(3) Cf also: Diller and Scofodio, *Case # 00-17163* in: Jonathan Crary and Sanford Kwinter (Ed.), *Incorporations*, New York, 1992, pp. 345ff.
(4) See also: Doreen Smolensky, *Palace Screening*, pp. 160ff.
(5) The shadowplay was developed by Andrew Holmes for the first year of study in the context of his teaching work at the University of Westminster.
(6) See also: *Shadowplay Tool*, pp. 84f., Michael Reiß: *Transfer 1 and 2*, pp. 86ff.
(7) See also Elke Knoess, *Performative Architecture*, pp.92 ff.
(8) See also Felix Sommerlad, *Mole Stage*, pp.196 ff.
(9) See also Schadi Weiss, *Backpack full of Illusions*, pp. 24 ff., and Daniel Krüger, *Missing*, pp. 254ff.
(10) Mark Wigley, in: *Architectural Design*, Vol 74, No 5, Sept/Oct 2004, pp. 13ff.

Doreen Smolensky / Palace Screening SoSe 2001

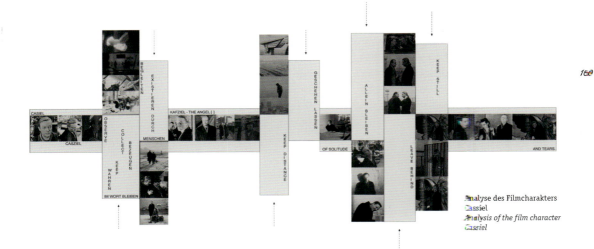

Analyse des Filmcharakters Cassiel
Analysis of the film character Cassiel

DER HIMMEL ÜBER BERLIN

Palace Screening resultiert aus einer konzeptuellen Analyse des Spielfilms *Der Himmel über Berlin* von Wim Wenders. Die engere Recherche zu einem der Hauptprotagonisten ermöglicht dem Projekt erste thematische Bezüge.
Cassiel, ein Engel, beobachtet die Stadt an der Seite seines Freundes Damiel, begleitet das Dasein der von der Großstadt durchfluteten Menschen die offenen Szenen ihrer Entwicklung. Besucht die Orte ihres Wirkens mit der Anteilnahme, durch sie zu leben. Seine notierende Anwesenheit durchzieht den gesamten Film. Einzig die Sequenz "paranoid" bezeugt seine innere Zerissenheit, das Dasein des gefallenen, nie menschwerdenden Engels.

WINGS OF DESIRE

Palace Screening is the result of a conceptual analysis of Wim Wender's film *Wings of Desire*. More focused research on one of the main protagonists facilitates the project's first thematic references. Cassiel, an angel, observes the city at his friend Damiel's side, accompanying life as such in the big city overflowing with people – and the open scenes of their development. He visits their places of influence and empathises so as to live through them. His note-taking presence continues through the entire film. Only the "paranoid" sequence shows his inner conflict – the existence of the fallen angel that never attains human form.

Mind map der "paranoid" Sequenz
Mind map of the sequence "paranoid"

Zoomsequenz
Zoom sequence

Bildverzerrung
Picture distortion

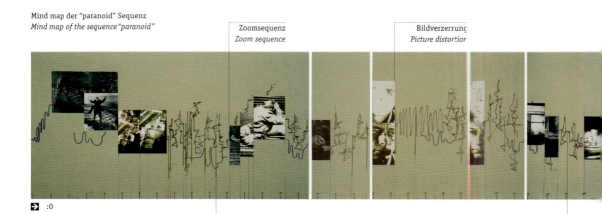

▶ :0
0:00:00

Cuts

Cello

Konzeptmodell für die "paranoid" Sequenz
Concept model for the "paranoid" sequence

PARANOID — DIE SCHNITTSEQUENZ

"Paranoid" ist die Schlüsselsequenz für Palace Screening. Die Analyse erfolgt über eine präzise Zählung der einzelnen Sequenzschnitte, die einer Differenzierung in der Art ihrer Bildqualitäten unterliegen (siehe unten). Daneben veranschaulicht die mind map eine assoziative Notation der Klangkulisse, welche die Sequenzatmosphäre maßgeblich definiert. Die Überlagerung beider Kartierungen beinhaltet zudem ihre Klimaxkurve. Das Konzeptmodell leitet sich als Bewegungsmodell von der „paranoid" Analyse ab. Es übernimmt die Reihung der einzelnen Schnittlängen, abstrahiert die Bildparameter durch Farb- und Schwarzweißnegative und ersetzt verzerrte Bilder über reflektierende, komprimierbare Metallsegmente.

PARANOID — THE CUT SEQUENCE

"Paranoid" is the key sequence for the Palace Screening. The analysis is made by a precise count of the individual sequence cuts, which are subject to differentiation in the type of their image qualities (see below). In addition, the mind-map illustrates an associative notation of the sound scenery, which considerably defines the sequence atmosphere. The overlay of the two chartings also includes their climactic curve. As a dynamic model, the concept model derives from the "paranoid" analysis. It takes control of ordering the lengths of individual cuts, abstracting the picture parameters by colour and black-and-white negatives and replacing distorted pictures by reflecting compressible metal segments.

Lichtspalten — Der Jetztort — Der Sozialpalast in Berlin
Light columns the "Now" location — the Social Palace in Berlin

Der Nichtort — Ein Parkhaus in Amsterdam
The "None"-place — a car park in Amsterdam

DER SCHAUPLATZ

Die Transformation des Bewegungsmodells findet ihren Ort der Intervention am Sozialpalast in Berlin, jener der unzähligen Stationen, die Cassiel in der „paranoid" Sequenz passiert. Wiederauffindbar werden formale Lichtsituationen. Die lichtdurchlässigen Negativspalten stehen analog zu der vor Ort entdeckten Lichtkluft zwischen einem Bunker des Zweiten Weltkriegs und dem Sozialpalast, der ihn umschließt. Der soziale Wohnungsbau aus den späten 70er Jahren erstreckt sich, das Gebiet aus dem sozialen Hintergrund trennend, inmitten Berlin-Schönebergs, mit einer Länge von 210 m brückenartig über die Pallasstraße.

THE SETTING

The transformation of the dynamic model finds its place of intervention at the Social Palace in Berlin, that is one of the countless stations that Cassiel passes in the "paranoid" sequence. Formal light situations are rediscovered. The translucent negative columns stand analogous to the light gap that was discovered on location between a Second World War bunker and the Social Palace surrounding it. The late 1970s social housing stretches out right in the centre of Berlin-Schöneberg, regardless of the social context; and it spans Pallasstraße like a bridge measuring 210 meters in length.

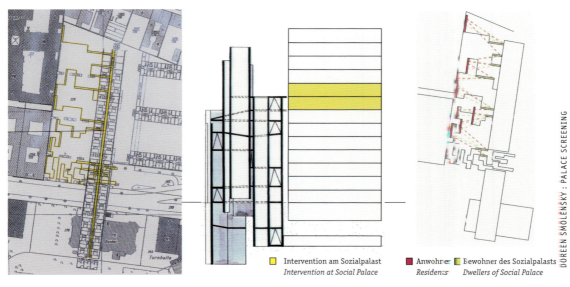

■ Intervention am Sozialpalast   ■ Anwohner   ■ Bewohner des Sozialpalasts
Intervention at Social Palace   *Residents*   *Dwellers of Social Palace*

Palace Screening Ansichtscollage mit Intervention
Palace Screening – Collage view with intervention

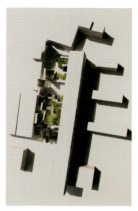

Modell 1: 500 aus der Vogelperspektive
Model 1:500, a bird's eye view

Querschnittscollage der Intervention
Cross-section collage of the intervention

PALACE SCREENING

Die segmentartige Struktur des Konzeptmodells gliedert sich in die Freifläche neben dem Sozialpalast ein und durchbricht die Seine. Dabei provoziert der komprimierte, zur Straße ausgerichtete Teil eine Durchgangssituation, die mit partiellen Lichtdurchflutungen und der Enge aneinander und z.T. tief in die Erde ragenden Metallsegmente an Cassiels beklemmenden Lauf durch Berlin anlehnt. Unterirdisch lassen sich Räume erschließen, welche alternativ von der sozialen Szene genutzt werden können. Die über Rampen erfolgende Entwindung der Segmente bewirkt durch die weite Tageslichtausbreitung eine Entspannung der vorherigen Situationen und öffnet sich natürlichen Freiräumen und Zugängen zum Sozialpalast, die miteinander kommunizierend bespielt werden.

PALACE SCREENING

The segment-like structure of the concept model is integrated into the open space beside the Social Palace and breaks through its structure. The compressed element aligned to the road provokes a passage situation to support Cassiel's oppressive walk through Berlin by means of partial illuminations and metal segments tightly packed and driven deep into the earth. Underground spaces become accessible and can be used alternatively by the social scene. The tearing away of the segments by use of ramps causes a relaxation of previous situations by the far-reaching influx of daylight. Natural free spaces open up as well as entrances to the Social Palace, which are used by the settlers and residents of the Social Palace who are communicating with one another.

Collagen *Collages*   Schwelle *Threshold*   Einblicke *Insights*   Ausblicke *Outlooks*

Eine Bedrohung schwingt mit in dem Titel, der sich zunächst der Logik entzieht. Lichter, die dunkel sind? Licht und Dunkel sind traditionell Antagonisten: Der Gegensatz „Tag – Nacht" wird gleichgesetzt mit „Gut – Böse". Dunkelheit verunsichert. Helligkeit verspricht Sicherheit.

Vor 300 Jahren gab es in Paris und London Fackelträger, die man mieten konnte, um sich den Weg nach Hause leuchten zu lassen. Die Londoner Fackelträger waren für ihre guten Kontakte zur Unterwelt bekannt.

Streben nach Helligkeit im Stadtraum entspricht der Entwicklung der technischen Möglichkeiten, diese zu erzeugen. Im Titel des Films klingt die Sehnsucht nach einer überschaubaren, gestalteten Dunkelheit an, die Raum für Träume bietet.

Ein deutscher Medizinalrat behauptete, Gaslicht sei zu rein für das menschliche Auge und unsere Enkel würden blind werden.

Stadtansichten. Ein Umherschauen in einer menschenleeren Stadt. Ein Flanieren, ohne sich wirklich fortzubewegen. Nur wenige Kamerabewegungen durchbrechen die bühnenhaften Bildkompositionen. Die Stadt ist aus Fragmenten vieler Orte zusammengesetzt, aus Details und Perspektiven, die in ihren nächtlichen Schatten und Reflexionen mehr Geschichten preisgeben als am Tage.

Vor 206 Jahren stand in einem Lehrbuch für Staats- und Polizeiwesen: Jeder, der zu ungewöhnlicher Zeit, an einem ungewöhnlichen Ort ohne Licht angetroffen wird, muss sich der strengsten Untersuchung unterwerfen.

In zwei dramaturgischen Bögen nähert sich der Film dem Zentrum der fiktiven Stadt. Der Stadtraum wird in Loops durchschritten. Klar abgegrenzte Szenen repräsentieren die verschiedenen Epochen der Entwicklung des künstlichen Lichts: von der Peripherie über Wohngebiete und Industrie hin zu Einkaufskomplexen, Unterführungen und Verwaltungsgebäuden.

Vor 110 Jahren wurde das elektrische Bogenlicht auf Großbaustellen eingesetzt und im Kolonialkampf im Sudan, um die einheimischen Kämpfer zu blenden.

Obscure Lights

The title resonates with a threat that initially escapes logic. Lights that are dark? Traditionally, light and dark are antagonists: the opposite "day – night" is equated with "good – bad". Dark makes uncertain. Brightness promises security.

There were torch bearers in Paris and London 300 years ago. You could hire them to light your way home. London torch bearers were known for their good contacts with the underworld.

The striving for brightness in urban areas corresponds with the development of technical possibilities for generating this. The film's title touches on the longing for a clear, arranged darkness, one offering room for dreams.

A German senior medical officer claimed that gas light was too pure for the human eye and that our grandchildren would go blind.

City images. Taking a look around in a deserted city. A stroll, without really moving. Just a few camera movements break through the stage-like picture compositions. The city is composed of fragments of many places combined, of details and perspectives, which reveal more stories in their nightly shadows and reflections than during the day.

A manual for state administration and police wrote some 206 years ago: anyone found at an unusual time, in an unusual place that is not carrying a light source will be subjected to strictest investigation.

The film approaches the centre of the fictitious town in two dramaturgical arches. The city area is stridden through in loops. Clearly delimited scenes represent the diverse epochs of the development of artificial light: from the periphery via residential areas and industry towards shopping complexes, underpasses and administrative buildings.

The electrical arc light was deployed 110 years ago on building sites and in the colonial fight in Sudan in order to dazzle local fighters.

Die Immaterialität des Lichts wird auf Film gebannt. 25 Bilder pro Sekunde. Aufgenommen mit einer Sekunde Belichtungszeit pro Bild. 12.000 Einzelbilder, die die Reflexionen des nächtlichen Lichts einfangen. Die geringen Unterschiede in der Belichtung der einzelnen Filmbilder durch die manuelle Auslösung ergeben Unregelmäßigkeiten, die den Film für unsere Augen flackern lassen.

Der Reiz der Dunkelheit stieg mit ihrem Verschwinden.

Dieses „Atmen" der Filmeinstellungen verstärkt zum einen den altmodischen, filmischen Eindruck der Szenen, entspricht zugleich aber auch dem pulsierenden Wesen des Lichts. Die Makroaufnahmen der Lichtquellen, die die einzelnen Stadtsequenzen trennen, sind in Zeitlupe mit 75 Bildern in der Sekunde gedreht. Die nicht wahrnehmbare Dehnung des Zeitkontinuums unterstreicht das Ätherische, Ungreifbare der profan sichtbaren Lichtquellen wie Glühdraht und Neonröhre.

Vor 176 Jahren stand in einer deutschen Zeitung: Jede Straßenbeleuchtung erscheint als Eingriff in die göttliche Ordnung. Gegen sie dürfen wir uns nicht auflehnen – die Nacht nicht zum Tage verkehren wollen. Die künstliche Helle verscheucht das Grauen vor der Finsternis, das schwache Seelen von mancher Sünde abhält.

Die folgenden Textauszüge sind Zitate aus den letzten 300 Jahren. Anekdoten, Gedanken und politische Statements reflektieren die unterschiedlichen Haltungen zu den jeweils gerade aufkommenden Licht-Erfindungen.

Helligkeit ist relativ. Offenes Feuer, Öllampe, Gaslicht, Bogenlampe, elektrische Glühbirne, Neonlicht, Kaltlichtlampen: Die „neuen" Lichtquellen waren jeweils heller als ihre Vorgänger.

Ein neuer Stern leuchtet über den Städten. Schrecklich, dem Auge unerträglich. In diesem Licht lassen sich nur Morde und öffentliche Verbrechen vorstellen oder die Korridore von Irrenanstalten.

Die erzählte historische Zeit läuft chronologisch ab, parallel zu den Stadtszenen. Die Wiederholungen der Reaktionen, der freudigen Erwartung sowie der Ängste, werden zum Spiegel der unterschiedlichen Grundhaltungen zur Welt und ihren Veränderungen und sind zugleich Variationen des ewig gleichen vergeblichen Kampfes um technischen Fortschritt oder Bewahrung des Bestehenden. Die Stimme hat etwas Lakonisches. Sie erzählt die Ereignisse unaufgeregt, beiläufig.

Des Nachts wird jeder beleuchtete Bereich als Innenraum erlebt. Die seitlichen Begrenzungen sind die illuminierten Häuserfronten, Schaufenster, Restaurants. Die Decke ist dort, wo die kommerzielle Beleuchtung endet.

Die Soundebene klingt computergeneriert, besteht jedoch ausschließlich aus analogen Originalklängen und -geräuschen der Lichtquellen und der Orte, die man sieht. Die Komposition entwickelt für jede Szene eine Dramaturgie, die dann vom musikalischen Thema der Lichtquellen unterbrochen wird. Die Sichtbarmachung des Lichts

The immateriality of light is captivated on film. Twenty-five images per second. Recorded with a one second exposure time per image. Twelve thousand individual images that capture the reflections of light at night. The small differences in the exposure of the individual film images thanks to the manual releasing produce irregularities, making the film flicker before our eyes.

The allure of darkness increased with its disappearance.

This 'breathing' of film settings strengthens, on the one hand, the old-fashioned cinematic impression of the scenes, but at the same time corresponds with the pulsating nature of light. The macro filming of light sources, separating the individual city sequences, were recorded in slow motion with 75 images per second. The non-perceptible stretching of the time continuum underlines the ethereal, out of reach, of the profane visible light sources like filaments and neon tubes.

A German newspaper wrote the following some 176 years ago: street lighting is regarded as an infringement on the divine order. Artificial lighting banishes the fear of darkness, which keeps many weak souls from committing sin.

The text excerpts are quotes from the last 300 years. Anecdotes, thoughts and political statements reflecting the different attitudes towards the respective light inventions just emerging. Brightness is relative.

 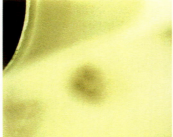 

Open fire; oil lamp, gaslight, arc lamp, light bulb, neon light, and cold light lamps. Each of the 'new' light sources was in turn brighter than their predecessors.

A new star is rising above the cities. Unbearable to the eye, like something from another world. In this light you see only murders, public crimes or the corridors of asylums.

The historical time talked about runs chronologically, parallel to the town scenes. The repetitions of the reactions, of the happy expectation as well as the fears, become a mirror of the different basic positions to the world and its change and are variations of the eternally same supposed fight for technical advance, or protecting the existing. The voice has something laconic. It narrates the events unexcitedly, casually.

At night every illuminated area is experienced as an interior space. Lit walls, shop windows and restaurants form its edges. Its ceilings appear where the commercial illumination ends.

The sound level sounds computer-generated, exists however exclusively from analogue original sounds and noises of the light sources and the places you see. For every scene, the composition develops a dramaturgy, which is then interrupted from the musical theme of light sources. The redisplaying of the light corresponds with the

entspricht dem akustischem Aufzeichnen der Emissionen, die bei der Interaktion von Energie und Materie entstehen und dann den Widerstand der Energie im Material hörbar machen.

Die Glühbirne werde uns niemals die Träumereien ermöglichen, die jene lebendige Öllampe mit ihrem Licht entstehen ließ. Wir leben im Zeitalter verwalteten Lichts.

Geloopt und digital bearbeitet, beschreiben diese *ambient sounds* die Atmosphäre der Orte und lassen sie zugleich entrückt und unwirklich erscheinen, da die unseren Ohren vertrauten Geräusche völlig fehlen

Man könne Elektrizität ohne die geringste Gefahr einatmen. Außerdem steige sie gleich nach oben unter die Decke, und so habe man nichts zu befürchten.

Die Bild-, Ton- und Textebenen sind jeweils für sich schlüssig aufgebaut, entwickeln sich aber unabhängig voneinander. Sie haben Berührungspunkte, momentane Übereinstimmungen, sind aber ansonsten autark. Dies deckt sich mit unserer Wahrnehmung von Licht.

Augenspezialisten in England behaupteten: Das elektrische Licht werde letztendlich die gesamte Bevölkerung erblinden lassen.

Es ist unsichtbar – nicht Teil dieser Welt - und wir können es nur anhand seines Aufpralls auf die Materie erkennen. Die fortschreitende Aufhellung der nächtlichen Lebensumwelt in Großstädten ging mit der Aufklärung, der Erforschung und Verbreitung wissenschaftlicher Erkenntnisse unter den Menschen einher – oder umgekehrt.

Vor 97 Jahren stand in einer „Zeitschrift für Elektrizität": Nicht einmal ein enthusiastischer Anhänger der Elektrizität stiere unbegrenzt in eine Glühlampe.

Kann man sich eine mögliche Zukunft vorstellen, wenn man den Film weiter denkt? Die Stadt als Experimentierfeld.

Wenn Licht ist, ist Tag.

Illustration: Film-Stills aus dem Film
DIE DUNKLEN LICHTER
Kurzfilm, 16mm, 13:35 Minuten, Farbe
© 1996, Thomas Kutschker – filmisches Berlin

acoustic recording of the emissions arising from the interaction of energy and material, which makes audible the resistance of the energy in the material.

The light from an electric bulb will never provoke the same fantasies, as did the shine from those lively oil lamps. We live in the age of administered light.

Looped and digitally processed, these ambient sounds describe the atmosphere of the places and simultaneously allow them to appear otherworldly and visionary, since they lack the noises which our ears are used to.

Electricity can be inhaled without the slightest danger. Furthermore, it immediately rises to the ceiling, so there is nothing to be feared.

The image, sound and text levels are respectively built up in a manner conclusive for themselves. However, they develop independently of each other. They have contact points, short-term agreements, but are otherwise self-sufficient. This corresponds with our perception of light.

Eye specialists in Great Britain predicted that the electric light would cause blindness in the entire population.

It is invisible - not part of this world -, and we can only recognize it with its impact on material. The progressive brightening of the nightly living environment in cities accompanied the Enlightenment, the research and spreading of scientific knowledge among people - or the other way round.

A "Magazine for Electricity" wrote some 97 years ago that not even an enthusiastic fan would stare forever at a light bulb.

Can we conceive of a possible future, if we think the film further? The town as a field for experiments.

When there is light, it is daytime.

Illustration: film-stills from the Film
OBSCURE LIGHTS
Short-film, 16 mm, 13.35 minutes, Colour
© 1996, Thomas Kutschker – filmisches Berlin

Marc Ries

Raum, Macht und ihr Gegenteil in Stanley Kubricks „Full Metal Jacket"

I.

Die erste Szene des Films *Full Metal Jacket* (GB 1987)[1] zeigt eine Reihe von kurzen Einstellungen, in denen Rekruten die Haare wegrasiert werden. Der Film schafft gleich zu Beginn exemplarische Situationen und Figuren. Vermittels des einfachen, doch sehr sinnlichen Akts des Kahlrasierens – der Verwandlung behaarter, normaler, unterschiedlicher Köpfe in kahle, genormte, entindividuierte Schädel – wird ein erster großer Raum etabliert: ein Raum oder – mit Foucault gesprochen – das „Diagramm einer

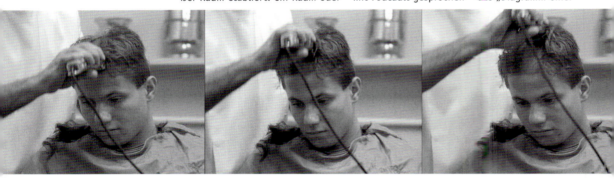

Bildfolge aus Stanley Kubricks
Full Metal Jacket

Frames from Stanley Kubrick's
Full Metal Jacket

Macht", einer Ordnung, einer Institution, die es sich zum Ziel setzt, aus normalen jungen Männern „Tötungsmaschinen" zu machen. Das Rasieren selbst stellt für den Zuschauer eine Koinzidenz her, da jeder diesen Eingriff kennt und sich auch das Gefühl eines komplett rasierten Kopfes vorstellen kann; somit wird Nachvollziehbarkeit möglich. Der Akt selbst ist innerhalb der filmischen Repräsentation die einzige „performative Äußerung" des ersten Teils – der Eintritt in die Armee ist gleichbedeutend mit Kahlkopfrasur. Auf die Köpfe selbst wirkt also bereits in diesen ersten Einstellungen die Koinzidenz, das Zusammenfallen mit der – jetzt noch anonymen – Macht, als zwanghaftes Befolgenmüssen von Akten der Entindividuierung, der Disziplinierung.

Soweit eine erste Beschreibung. Michel Foucaults *Überwachen und Strafen* kann man, auch wenn Foucault das selbst nur an wenigen Stellen tut, gleichfalls als eine dichte Analyse militärischer Disziplinar- und Zuchtgewalt lesen: „In der zweiten Hälfte des 18. Jh. ist der Soldat etwas geworden, was man fabriziert. Aus einem formlosen Teig, aus einem untauglichen Körper macht man die Maschine, derer man bedarf; Schritt für Schritt hat man die Haltungen zurechtgerichtet, bis ein kalkulierter Zwang jeden Körperteil durchzieht und bemeistert, den gesamten Körper zusammenhält und verfügbar macht und sich insgeheim bis in die Automatik der Gewohnheiten durch-

Space, Power, and its Opposite in Stanley Kubrick's "Full Metal Jacket"

I.

The first scene of the film *Full Metal Jacket*[1] shows a series of short takes, in which recruits have their hair shaved off. Right at the start, the film creates exemplary situations and figures. A first large space is established with the help of the simple, yet very sensory act of shaving someone's head. Hairy, normal, varying heads are transformed into bald, standardized, de-individualised skulls. This space or 'the diagram of a power' is an order, an institution, which sets as its

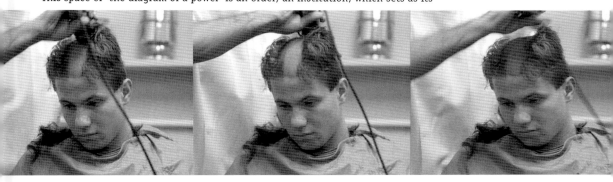

goal the creation of 'killing machines' from normal young men, to quote Foucault. The shaving itself represents a coincidence for the viewer since everyone knows this infringement and can also imagine the feeling of having a completely shaved head. It helps us to put us in the men's place. The act itself is the only 'performative expression' of the first part within the cinematic representation. Entry into the army is synonymous with a bald-headed haircut. In these first takes, therefore, the coincidence with the power, now still anonymous, as compulsive and having to comply with acts of de-individualisation, of disciplining, already works on the heads themselves.

That is just a first description. We can similarly read Michel Foucault's *Discipline and Punish* as a proper analysis of military, disciplinary violence and disciplinary authority, even if Foucault himself only does this at a few points: "In the second half of the 18th Century the soldier became something that was fabricated. Shapeless dough, an unsuitable body was made into a machine that was needed. Step-by-step the posture was dressed until a calculated constraint ran through and mastered every body part, holding together the whole body and making it available, and asserted itself secretly up to automising its habits." [2] According to Foucault,

setzt."[(2)] Innerhalb dieser „Mikrophysik der Macht" gilt, so Foucault, „die Aufmerksamkeit dem Körper, den man manipuliert, formiert und dressiert, der gehorcht, antwortet, gewandt wird und dessen Kräfte sich mehren." Vier große Techniken von Disziplinargewalt werden angewandt, um dieses Ziel zu erreichen: Sie konstruiert Tableaus; sie schreibt Manöver vor; sie setzt Übungen an; und um das Zusammenspiel der Kräfte zu gewährleisten, ordnet sie „Taktiken" an.

Der Herrschaftsraum bildet sich zunächst über Tableaus aus, die ein Wahrnehmungsdispositiv begleiten. Über dieses verfügt ausschließlich der Sergeant des Korps, das sich ihm zu unterwerfen hat. Die autoritäre, disziplinierende und demütigende Sichtbarkeit soll genormte Körper, genormtes Wahrnehmen und Reagieren produzieren. Die Marines sehen sich selbst in diesen Akten der Disziplinierung untereinander nicht (exemplarisch der formierte Block beim Laufen), einzig der Sergeant hat die Übersicht und damit die Kontrolle. Jeder ist mit sich und seiner „Militarisierung"

Storyboard – eine Film-Sequenz, Sommersemester 2001: Christoph Jantos, Sequenzkarte der Trapez-Szene mit Marion und Damiel aus *Der Himmel über Berlin*

Storyboard of a film sequence, summer semester 2001: Christoph Jantos, Sequence card of the Trapeze Scene with Marion and Damiel from *Wings of Desire*.

beschäftigt, das Befehlen führt die notwendige Transformation des individuellen Körpers in einen seriellen Körper an. Abseits der Befehle ist jedoch auch Bestrafung möglich, die vor allem Leonard zu spüren bekommt. Gerade die Bestrafung vermag jedoch auf Dauer Kontingenz auszulösen. So wird er der einzige sein, bei dem die Transformation nicht gelingt und sich ein Verhalten ausbildet, das so niemand erwartet hat.

Wichtig erscheint mir an dieser Stelle auch, auf eine andere Definition der Individualisierung Bezug zu nehmen, die Foucault vorgeschlagen hat und die den oben skizzierten Praktiken der Entindividualisierung entgegensteht: „In einem Disziplinarregime ist die Individualisierung ‚absteigend': Je anonymer und funktioneller die Macht wird, um so mehr werden die dieser Macht Unterworfenen individualisiert: durch Überwachungen, durch vergleichende Messungen, durch Abstände (...)". Und besonders folgendes Zitat scheint auf die Zucht des Sergeanten anwendbar: „(...) auch wenn man den gesunden, normalen, gesetzestreuen Erwachsenen individualisieren will, so befragt man ihn immer danach, was er noch vom Kind in sich hat, welcher gemeine Irrsinn in ihm steckt, welches tiefe Verbrechen er eigentlich begehen wollte."

what is valid within this "microphysics of power" is "the attention to the body which has been manipulated, formed and trained, which obeys, replies and is utilised and whose strengths are increasing." Four main techniques of disciplinary power are applied in order to attain this goal. It constructs tableaux, prescribes manoeuvres, organises exercises, and arranges "tactics" in order to guarantee the interplay of forces.

Initially, the area of control develops via tableaux, which accompany a perceptional dispositive. This is at the exclusive disposal of the sergeant of the corps. They must submit to him. The authoritarian, disciplining and humiliating visibility should produce standardized bodies, standardized perception and reaction. The marines do not see each other in these acts of disciplining (exemplary here the formed block whilst running); the sergeant alone has the overview and thus the control. Everyone is busy with themselves and their 'militarization'. The

ordering leads to the required transformation of the individual body into a serial body. However, beyond the orders, punishment is also possible. This is something that Leonard above all gets to experience. However, the punishment can trigger contingency over a short period. In this way, he will be the only one for whom the transformation has not succeeded and he develops behaviour nobody expected.

It seems to me that what is also important, at this point, is to refer to a different definition of individualization. Foucault suggested this and it stands contrary to the practices of de-individualization outlined above: "Individualization is 'declining' in a disciplinary regime: the more anonymous and functional the power becomes, all the greater will those subjugated by this power be individualized: through supervision, through comparative measurements, through distances (...)". The following quote in particular seems to apply to the discipline of the sergeant: "(...) even if you do want to individualize the healthy, normal, law-abiding adult, so he is always asked afterwards what he still has of a child remaining in him, which cruel insanity is in him, which low crime he actually wanted to commit."

Aufgabe war, einen Charakter im Film Der Himmel über Berlin zu beobachten und in einer selbst ausgewählten Szene detailliert zu kartieren. Dabei diente der Film als Laborsituation für die Analyse von Bild/Ton/Zeitverknüpfung zur Herstellung einer dramaturgisch-räumlichen Situation.

The task was to observe a character in the film, Wings of Desire, and to make a detailed file on a scene one chose oneself. This made the film fulfil a laboratory function to analyse picture/sound/timing in order to create a dramatic/spatial situation.

II.

Wenn es das Ziel des ersten Teils des Films ist, einen großen Ordnungsraum und eine Logik der disziplinierenden Sichtbarkeit zu entwerfen, so ist das des zweiten Teils das Umkippen dieser Ordnung und Sichtbarkeit in ihr Gegenteil. Während die erste Hälfte des Films die Ausbildung zum Großen Krieg, der „Etappe und Front, Erholungsphasen und Schlacht" (Münkler) kennt, als eine Transformation des „natürlichen Körpers" in eine Kampfmaschine minutiös verfolgt, zeigt die zweite Hälfte den tatsächlich sich ereignenden Kleinen Krieg in dem bereits verwüsteten Vietnam. Der Kleine Krieg bringt alle Begrenzungen, Regeln, Ordnungen, die einer militärischen Logik folgen, zum Verschwinden: „Er ist", so Herfried Münkler, „ubiquitär und permanent. Während der Große Krieg gemäß dem Prinzip der Konzentration der Kräfte bestrebt ist, den Raum, in dem gekämpft wird, auf die Front einzuschränken und die Dauer eines bewaffneten Konflikts auf einen möglichst kurzen Feldzug zu begrenzen (...), entfaltet sich der Partisanenkrieg in der Tiefe des Raumes und der Dauer der Zeit, um so die auf der Begrenzung von Raum und Zeit beruhende Überlegenheit der regulären Armee zu unterlaufen. (...) Der Partisanenkrieg ist, so gesehen, ein Krieg der Schwachen, die ihre waffentechnische und materielle Unterlegenheit dadurch auszugleichen versuchen, daß sie Raum und Zeit in Ressourcen der Kriegführung verwandeln. Dabei geht es zunächst weniger um die physische Vernichtung des Gegners als vielmehr um seine Demoralisierung. Die räumliche Orientierung der Soldaten wird verwirrt, weil die Unterscheidung von „vorn und hinten" obsolet wird und ihre physische und psychische Belastung wächst durch das Erfordernis ständiger Kampfbereitschaft."[3]

  Zunächst will ich jedoch noch auf jenen ominösen Schnitt zurückkommen, der den ersten vom zweiten Teil trennt. Dieser Schnitt ist ein epistemologischer. Er trennt zwei Räume sauber voneinander, den Raum der Macht von dem Raum der Ohnmacht, den Raum, der vor allem auf Koexistenz aufbaut, von dem, der Koinzidenz bewirkt. Der „gekerbte Raum" der Militärausbildung wird gleich zu Beginn in einen „glatten Raum" der Intensitäten überführt: Eine Prostituierte nähert sich den Marines und bietet ihre Dienste an, akustisch überhöht von einem schwungvollen Schlager der Zeit.[4] Das also ist Krieg. Krieg ist Entgrenzung: Entgrenzung der Körper, Entgrenzung des Raums.

  Es lässt sich sagen, dass im zweiten Teil eine „Enthegung" des Kriegs vor sich geht, er platzt aus der vorgesehenen symmetrischen Logik eines geordneten, gelernten Kämpfens und wirft jeden Einzelnen auf sich selbst zurück. Das ist nun nicht mehr der Rahmen, in dem man lernte, Soldat zu sein. In der partiell ausgesetzten Koexistenz droht Koinzidenz mit dem Feind, und zwar als Erfahrung der Kontingenz: Alles ist möglich, alles kann jederzeit anders sein. Diese Erfahrung ist kennzeichnend für alle nachfolgenden Kriege, die gleichfalls bürgerkriegsähnlichen Status haben und mit Enzensberger auch als „molekulare Kriege" beschreibbar sind: Bosnien, Tschetschenien, Afghanistan, Irak.

  In der letzten Phase des Films wird dieses Umschlagen exemplarisch ausgeführt. Der Trupp hat die Orientierung verloren. Ruinen schauen nun einmal überall gleich aus. Dann tritt ein Sniper – uneinsehbar – in Aktion. Im Gegensatz zu den amerikanischen Soldaten kennt der Scharfschütze – eine „tellurische Existenzform" – sein Territorium: Das Unübersichtliche, Ungeordnete, Unwegsame ermöglicht seine territo-

II.

If the goal of the first part of the film is to design a great disciplining space and a logic of disciplining visibility, then that of the second is to turn this order and visibility into its opposite. The first half meticulously followed training for the great war, which knows "stages and fronts, recovery phases and battle" (Münkler), as a transformation of the "natural body" into a fighting machine. By contrast, the second half shows the real small war that occurred in a Vietnam that was already devastated. The small war makes all limitations, rules and orders that follow a military logic disappear: "It is," according to Herfried Münkler, "ubiquitous and permanent. Whereas the great war endeavours to limit the area in which the fighting occurs to the front and the length of an armed conflict to a possible short campaign, according to the principle of concentrating the strength on powers, (...), the partisan war develops in the depth of the area and the length of time, in order to so avoid the superiority of the regular army that relies on the limitation of space and time. (...) Seen in this way, the partisan war is a war of the weak, attempting to compensate for their inferior arms technology and material by changing space and time into resources of warfare. Here it is initially less a matter of physically destroying the opponents as demoralizing them. The soldiers' spatial orientation is confused, because the distinction between "front and behind" becomes obsolete and their physical and psychological burden increases through the requirement of being continuously ready to fight."[3]

However, I still want to return to that ominous scene separating the first part from the second. This scene is epistemological. It cleanly separates two areas from each other, the area of power from the area of powerlessness, the area that is primarily based on coexistence from that which causes coincidence. Right at the start, the "notched space" of the military training is converted to a "smooth space" of intensities: a prostitute approaches the marines and offers her services, acoustically dramatized by a lively musical hit from the time.[4] That then is war. War is liberation: liberation of bodies, liberation of space.

We can say that in the second part war is unleashed. It bursts out of the envisaged symmetrical logic of ordered, learned fighting and makes us all dependent on our own selves. That is no longer the framework in which we learned to be soldiers. In the partially interrupted coexistence, coincidence with the enemy threatens, and equally the experience of contingency. Everything is possible. Everything can be different at any time. This experience is characteristic for all subsequent wars, which likewise virtually have civil war status and can also be described as "molecular war": Bosnia, Chechnya, Afghanistan, Iraq, according to Enzensberger.

In the last phase of the film, this change is carried out in an exemplary manner. The troop has lost its orientation. Ruins now seem the same all over. Then an invisible sniper enters the action. In contrast to the American soldiers, the sniper knows his territory. His is a "terrestrial" form of existence. The confused and unordered, the pathless enables his territorial power. It is simultaneously the snare for his enemies. The contingency with this divergent form of war created by

riale Macht, es ist zugleich der Fallstrick für seine Feinde. Die mit dieser abweichenden Kriegsform von Nordvietnam selbst erzeugte Kontingenz verlegt alle Vorteile möglicher Aggressionen auf die Seite des Vietnamesen – der Vietnamesin, wie sich zum Schluss herausstellt, denn Kontingenzmacht ist geschlechterindifferent. Strukturell gesehen, ist sie eine Reaktion auf die militärisch-technische Übermacht der Amerikaner. Partisanen, heute Terroristen, müssen ihre Gewalttaktiken wie -mittel in einer Weise konzeptualisieren, die sich strikt den Logiken und Logistiken des überlegenen Gegners entzieht. Contingere, das ursprünglich ein Berühren meint, passiert nun in zweierlei Maß. Einmal werden die Soldaten buchstäblich in die Knie gezwungen, müssen kriechend und sich versteckend, die Erde „berührend", das Ausweglose der Situation wahrnehmen. Zum anderen im Ausgeliefertsein gegenüber den Geschossen des Scharfschützen,

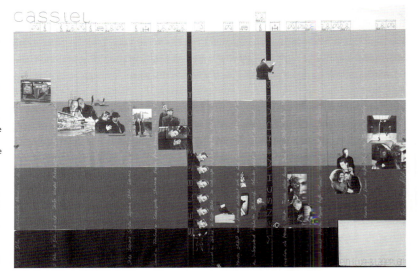

Storyboard – ein Film-Charakter, Sommersemester 2001: Anne Dose, Kartierung der Bewegungen von Cassiel im Film *Der Himmel über Berlin*. Die Studierenden haben einen Filmcharakter verfolgt und seine Bewegungen mit den Orten verknüpft. Dabei konzentrierten sie sich auf Ereignisse, die ihnen von Bedeutung waren, wie zum Beispiel Anne Dose auf Selbstmord und Menschwerdung oder Daniel Wahl auf die Verwandlung von Damiel auf der Treppe der Staatsbibliothek (nächste Seite).

Storyboard for a film character, summer semester 2001: Anne Dose, card-indexing of the movements of Cassiel in the film Wings of Desire. *The students have followed a film character and connected his or her movements to various places. In so doing, they focus on events that were important to them, as for instance Anne Dose on suicide and becoming human, or Daniel Wahl on Damiel's transformation on the staircase of the State Library (see next page).*

der die gefallenen Körper mit bewusst platzierten Schüssen quasi foltert. Koinzidenz und Kontingenz fallen zusammen. Für den Zuschauer, die Zuschauerin, die gleichermaßen weder Aussicht noch Ausflucht erfahren, dürfte diese Sequenz, dieses Ausgeliefertsein an eine fremde Kontingenz, an eine lebensvernichtende Koinzidenz kaum noch Argumente für die Berechtigung von Krieg produzieren.

ANMERKUNGEN
(1) Stanley Kubrick: *Full Metal Jacket*. GB 1987
(2) Michel Foucault: *Überwachen und Strafen*. Frankfurt am Main 1976, S.173
(3) Siehe Herfried Münkler: *Über den Krieg*. Weilerswirst, Velbrück 2002
(4) Zum Begriff des "gekerbten" und des "glatten Raumes" siehe Gilles Deleuze, Félix Guattari: *Tausend Plateaux*. Berlin 1992, Kapitel "1440 - Das Glatte und das Gekerbte, S. 657–694

North Vietnam itself transfers all advantages of possible aggressions to the side of the Vietnamese man, or woman, as it turns out in the end. This is because contingency power is indifferent to sex. Seen structurally, it is a reaction to the military-technical superior strength of the Americans. Partisans, today terrorists, must conceptualize their violent attacks and means in a way that strictly escapes the logic and logistics of the superior opponent. *Contingere*, originally meant a touch, but now it occurs in a twofold manner. First, the soldiers are forced literally to their knees. They must be aware how hopeless their situation is, whilst creeping and hiding themselves, and "touching" the earth. Second, the fact that they are at the mercy of the sniper's bullets. He practically tortures the fallen bodies with consciously placed shots. Coincidence and contingency coincide. Similarly, this

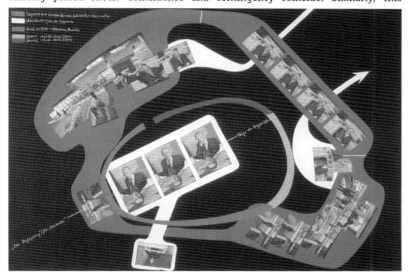

Storyboard – ein Film-Charakter, Sommersemester 2001: Daniel Wahl, Wandlung des Damiel aus dem Film *Der Himmel über Berlin*

Storyboard for a film character, summer semester 2001: Daniel Wahl, Damiel's Transformation from the film Wings of Desire.

sequence, this helplessness with a strange contingency, with a life-destroying coincidence hardly offers the viewers, male or female, a chance or an excuse to produce any more arguments for the legitimacy of war.

NOTES

(1) Stanley Kubrick: *Full Metal Jacket*. GB 1987
(2) Michel Foucault: *Discipline and Punish*. London 1991, p.171
(3) See Herfried Münkler: *Über den Krieg*. Weilerswirst, Velbrück 2002
(4) On the term of "notched" and "smooth space" see Gilles Deleuze, Félix Guattari: *Tausend Plateaux*. Berlin 1992, Chapter "1440 - Das Glatte und das Gekerbte, p. 657—694

Winfried Pauleit

Tektieren

Notizen für ein performatives Verständnis von Raum- und Zeitkünsten

„Filme sind imaginäre Architekturen in der Zeit" (Heinz Emigholz)

Historisch betrachtet ist die Architektur – neben der Malerei und der Skulptur – eine Kunst des Raums, die sich an bestimmten Gesetzmäßigkeiten und ästhetischen Regeln orientiert. In ihrem Anspruch auf Gestaltung größerer Zusammenhänge wie Gebäudekomplexe, Plätze, Städte und so weiter ordnet sich die Architektur den anderen Künsten (Malerei und Skulptur) unter und wird gewissermaßen zur „Archi-Kunst", zum Leitmedium. Ein entscheidendes Kriterium für den Aufstieg der Architektur zur Kunst ist dabei ihre Theoretisierung und Verschriftlichung in der Architekturtheorie. Sie fällt zusammen mit einer Verschiebung in der Auffassung des Begriffs Architektur: Architekt, gr. architekton, Erzkünstler, Baumeister (archi., arch. gr. Präfix mit der Bedeutung erster, oberster, Ober-, Haupt-, Ur-, Erz- und tekton, gr. Baumeister, Zimmermann). Das Altgriechische bezieht sich noch ganz auf den Handwerker mit seinen Fähigkeiten, auch wenn mit der Kennzeichnung „archi"- seine Stellung herausgehoben wird.

Architectura ist eine griechisch-lateinische Hybridbildung; erst im Lateinischen entsteht ein allgemeinerer Begriff der Baukunst, der über das Handwerkliche hinausgeht. Vitruvs zehnbändige Schrift (1. Jh. v. Chr.) *De architectura* ist der Markstein, der den allgemeinen Begriff der Architektur nicht nur im Titel trägt, sondern ihn auch in seiner Fülle über das Handwerk hinaus mit seinen zahlreichen Nebenbezirken als grundlegende Wissenschaft beschreibt. Vitruv war Ausgangspunkt für die Architekturtheorien des Mittelalters und seine Schriften avancierten schließlich zur Bibel der Renaissancearchitekten (auch Alberti bezieht sich auf Vitruv in seiner Schrift *De re aedificatori*).

In der griechischen Wurzel architekton auf der einen Seite und ihrer Ableitung, der lateinischen Hybridbildung architectura, auf der anderen stehen sich – grammatisch betrachtet – handelndes Subjekt und gefertigtes Objekt gegenüber. Sucht man nach einem Prädikat, das als performatives Element das Subjekt (den architekton) und das Objekt (die architectura) in Beziehung setzt, so denkt man im Deutschen ans Bauen oder Zeichnen. Beide Praktiken beschreiben handwerkliche Tätigkeiten und schließen die Zusammenhänge von Schrift und Theoriebildung der architectura nicht unbedingt ein. Sie lösen auch nicht die Wünsche ein, die von Architekten immer wieder genannt werden, man denke an Corbusiers: „Man müsste so bauen, wie Josephine Baker tanzt".

Ein älterer Begriff stellt das Performative zwischen architekton und architectura in einem umfassenden Sinn heraus: das „Tektieren", was soviel bedeutet wie „eine fehlerhafte Stelle in einem Buch überkleben". Auch wenn sich das Tektieren auf eine

"Tektieren"

Notes for a Performative Understanding of Spatial and Temporal Arts

"Films are imaginary architectures in time" (Heinz Emigholz)

Seen historically, architecture is an art of space, alongside painting and sculpture. It is one aligned towards specific orders and aesthetic rules. Architecture is subordinate to the other arts (painting and sculpture) with their claim to style larger connections such as building complexes, squares, cities, etc., becoming a sort of "archi-art", the underlying medium. One decisive criterion in architecture's rise to art is the theorization and writing down of architecture theory. It corresponds with a shift in the interpretation of the term architecture:

Architect, Greek architekton, arch-artist, master builder (archi., arch. Greek prefix meaning first, top, over, chief, primeval, arch and tekton, Greek for master builder, carpenter). The ancient Greek term still completely refers to the craftsman with his skills, even if the label "archi" is used to highlight his position.

Architectura is a Greek-Latin hybrid word form. It is in Latin that the concept first becomes a more general one of architecture extending beyond just the technical. Vitruvius' ten-volume work (1st century B.C.) *De architectura* is the milestone. Architecture is not just contained as a general term in the title, but is also described in its richness as a basic science with numerous subdivisions beyond just the technical. Vitruvius was the starting point for the architecture theories of the Middle Ages with his writings finally advancing to become the Bible of Renaissance architects (Alberti also referred to Vitruvius in his work *De re aedificatori*).

From a grammatical standpoint, the active subject and the finished object stand opposed to each other with the Greek root architekton on one the one side and its derivation, the Latin hybrid formation architectura on the other. If we search for a predicate, one connecting the subject (the architekton) and the object (the architectura) as a performative element, we would think of building or drawing in English. Both practices describe technical activities and do not necessarily include the connections between writing and forming theory of the architectura. They also don't solve the wishes that architects identify again and again. You only have to think of Corbusier's: "We have to be able to build like Josephine Baker dances."

There is an older term in German emphasizing the performative between architekton and architectura: "Tektieren". It means "pasting an amendment over an erroneous place in a book". This, however, refers to working on texts and books so it doesn't work with a semiotic concept of textuality (i.e. a concept that comprehends architecture as text alone). The term means much

Arbeit an Texten und Büchern bezieht, so geht es nicht auf in einer semiotischen Vorstellung von Textualität (einer Vorstellung also, die Architektur nur als Text begreift). Das Tektieren meint vielmehr das handwerkliche Überkleben und die konkrete Arbeit am Text. Übertragen auf Städtebau und Architektur, ließe sich nun folgern, dass es beim Tektieren sowohl um den verändernden Eingriff, zum Beispiel in eine Stadt durch konkretes Bauen, als auch um textliche Veränderungen geht, die ein Lesen zur Voraussetzung haben. Das Charakteristikum des Tektierens ist dabei ein Setzen, das gleichzeitig etwas anderes verschwinden lässt. Es umfasst also nicht nur das performative Element und den Bezug zu Schriftlichkeit und Architekturtheorie, sondern deutet zudem neben dem Raumbezug auch eine grundlegende Beziehung zu Zeit und Zeitlichkeit an. Ähnlich wie überklebte Stellen in einem Buch lassen sich auch in einer Stadt Bruch- und Nahtstellen der Architektur aufspüren. Die eigentliche Performanz des Tektierens entgeht dem Leser eines Textes ebenso wie dem städtischen Flaneur. Nur ihre Spuren sind zugänglich. Die Zeitlichkeit der Architektur zeigt sich vor allem in sozialen, gesellschaftlichen Prozessen oder in eigens zur Bewegung vorgesehener Verkehrsmitteln wie Eisenbahnen, Aufzügen, Hebebrücken und Automobilen.

Dem Film gelingt es – als neue „Archi-Kunst" –, die Performanz der Architektur nicht nur nachzuzeichnen, sondern diese zu integrieren und spielerisch, rhythmisch neu zu gestalten. Der Film spielt mit der Architektur, kann sie tanzen lassen, auf den Kopf stellen und schon in den ersten Filmen der Brüder Lumière zum Beispiel Einstürze rückgängig machen. Dies beruht auf einer spezifischen Medialität, die es ermöglicht, die Raumkünste zeitlich noch einmal zu formen und zu verformen. Erst der Film – so könnte man behaupten – erschließt uns im 20. Jahrhundert das Performative der Architektur als Tektieren und damit als spezifische raum-zeitliche Kunstform.

Dieses Erschließen gelingt dem Film durch seine mediale zeitliche Anordnung und seine räumliche Begrenzung des Bildkaders. Dort, wo die Architektur ihre Grenzen als Raumkunst in der Zeit erfährt, zeigt uns der Film als Zeitkunst einen jeweils eingegrenzten Raum. Im Film fügt sich dabei eine Folge von unterschiedlichen Einstellungen zu einer Gesamtheit der Filmerfahrung zusammen. Eine Einstellung verweist immer auf ein zunächst nicht sichtbares Anderes, das sich außerhalb des Bildfeldes befindet: das „Off". Wird dieses „Draußen" durch eine zweite Einstellung sichtbar, so entsteht ein neues unsichtbares Bildfeld. Deshalb erscheint das „Off" des Films belebt in dem Sinne, dass Figuren das Bildfeld verlassen und somit verschwinden können und dennoch (in der Wahrnehmung) anwesend bleiben. Sie können ebenso gut die Bildgrenze wieder überschreiten und ins „On", das heißt ins sichtbare Bildfeld zurückkehren. Jedes Bildfeld des Films verweist daher mehr oder weniger auf einen weiteren Raum, so wie die Architektur auf andere Zeitdimensionen verweist.

Der Film ist aber nicht nur die „Archi-Kunst" des 20. Jahrhunderts, die sich die Architektur spielerisch einverleibt. Der Film bleibt auch ihr verhaftet. Das Kino als Lichtspielhaus ist gleichsam Teil der städtischen Architektur und Kreuzungspunkt unterschiedlicher Dispositive der ästhetischen Wahrnehmung. Auf der Schwelle von Stadtraum und Kinosaal, dort wo der Blick auf die Fassade des Kinos verloren geht, der Kinosaal aber noch nicht erreicht ist, überlagern sich Raum- und Zeitkünste. In diesem Zwischenraum findet eine spezifische Bildform ihren Platz: Filmstarbilder.

more than manually sticking over and concretely working on the text. Transferred to urban development and architecture, we could conclude that it is a matter of both the altering intervention, for example through actually building in a town, as well as of textual changes, which have reading as a prerequisite. In this, the characteristic of the action is a setting, one that simultaneously allows something else to disappear. That means it does not just incorporate the performative element and the relation to writing and architectural theory, but also indicates a fundamental relation to time and temporality alongside the spatial relationship. The breaks and joints in the architecture of a town can be traced, just like the covered-over parts of a book. The actual performance of pasting over escapes the reader of a text just like the urban stroller. Only their traces are accessible. The temporality of architecture reveals itself above all in social processes in the service of the community or in means of transport specifically provided for movement like railways, lifts, liftbridges and motorcars.

As a new "Archi-art", the film succeeds not just in copying the performance of architecture, but also in integrating these and reordering them playfully and rhythmically. Films play with the architecture, allowing it to dance and then standing it on its head. Collapses were already being reversed back in the first films of the Lumière Brothers, for example. This was based on a specific mediality, one enabling the spatial arts to be formed once again in time and to distort them. We could claim that, thanks to film, the performative of architecture as "tektieren", and so as a specific space-time art form, first became accessible to us in the 20th century.

Films succeed with this opening up through their medially temporal order and their spatial limitation of the image cadre. There, where architecture experiences its limits as spatial art in time, films show us a respectively limited area as temporal art. In the films, a succession of different settings join together in the process to a totality of film experience. One setting always refers to an initially non-visible something else that is outside the frame: the "off". A new invisible frame arises when this "outside" becomes visible through a second setting. For this reason, the "off" of the film enlivens in the sense that the figures can leave the frame and so disappear and still remain present (in the perception). They can equally transgress the edge of the image again and return to the "on", i.e. to the visible frame. For this reason, every frame of the film refers more or less to a further space, just like architecture to other time dimensions.

However, film is not just the "Archi-art" of the 20th century playfully incorporating architecture. Film also remains committed to it. The cinema as a picture theatre is simultaneously part of the urban architecture and crossing point of differing dispositives of aesthetic perception. Spatial and temporal arts overlap at the threshold of urban space and cinema hall, where the view of the façade of the cinema becomes lost, but the cinema hall is not yet reached. A specific picture form finds its space in this gap: film stills.
Film stills belong to the spatial arts as photography, on the one hand. However, they are simultaneously part of the film and, so to speak, a fragment of the tem-

Filmstandbilder gehören auf der einen Seite als Photographie den Raumkünsten an, auf der anderen Seite sind sie gleichzeitig Teil des Films und damit sozusagen ein Fragment der Zeitkünste. In dieser Doppelbesetzung kommt ihnen eine besondere Funktion zu. Sie sollen das Laufpublikum, die Kinogänger, verführen und ins Kino locken. Filmstandbilder sind also Teil einer Passage und vermitteln zwischen zwei Orten. Und so wie jede Vermittlung nicht ohne Ansprache des Begehrens auskommt, arbeiten auch Filmstandbilder mit einem Versprechen. Sie führen dabei nicht einfach nur von der Straße ins Kino wie Jahrmarktschreier oder Animiercamen. Sie begleiten vielmehr die Filmaufführung: Sie bereiten sie vor und trauern ihr nach. Vor dem Film kann man auf die Filmstandbilder noch einen prüfenden Blick werfen. Man betrachtet die Bilder und vergewissert sich dabei seiner selbst, bevor man einen Teil dieser Selbstverfassung vorübergehend im Kino aufgibt. Nach dem Film begegnet man den Filmstandbildern von neuem. Dann zeigen sie sich in einem anderen Licht: Es sind jetzt Erinnerungsbilder, die ein Wind aus Melancholie umweht, vergleichbar mit den Photos vom letzten Urlaub. Gleichzeitig ist ihre Präsentation von Anfang an als vorübergehend gekennzeichnet. Sie werden in Schaukästen mit Nadeln oder Reißnägeln angesteckt und bilden ein Provisorium, solange wie der Film im Kino gezeigt wird. Danach verschwinden sie entweder in einem Archiv, bei Sammlern, Fans oder im Abfall.

Bildtheoretisch markieren Filmstandbilder also eine Differenz zwischen zwei unterschiedlichen Bildauffassungen. Die gängige Auffassung, die auch die Photographie und alle Raumkünste einschließt, begreift das Bild als ein Standbild. Mit der Erfindung des Films wurde diese Position zu einem theoretischen Problem: Zum einen erscheint der Film als ein Bewegungsbild, das den Betrachter aufgrund seiner zeitlichen Struktur in einen anderen Wahrnehmungsmodus versetzt. Zum anderen besteht der Film in seiner Materialität als ein Filmstreifen weiterhin aus einzelnen statischen Bildern. Dieses bildtheoretische Paradoxon zeigt sich bis heute. Filmstandbilder verkörpern es. Sie verweisen damit gleichzeitig auf eine Bruchstelle, die das Denken der Künste mit seiner Kategorisierung in Raum- und Zeitkünste bisher nicht gemeistert hat.

Der Begriff des Tektierens kann hier vermitteln. So wie das Filmstandbild als Schwellenphänomen des Films die Zuordnungen zu Raum- und Zeitkünsten überlagert, so erlaubt das Tektieren die Wahrnehmung der Architektur in ihrer Zeitlichkeit. Im Tektieren sind nicht nur das Zeichnen, Planen und die anschließende Ausführung aufgehoben, sondern auch jene forschenden und intervenierenden Tätigkeiten, die man mit Hilfe von Photographie und Film an und mit spezifischen Orten, Architekturen und Stadträumen vornehmen kann.

poral arts. In this double role they are allocated a special function. They should lure the occasional public, the cinema visitors, into the cinema. In this way, film stills are part of a passage and mediate between two locations. Just as every mediation cannot get by without addressing desire, film stills also work with a promise. In doing so, they don't just lead from the street into the cinema like fair barkers or hostesses. Much more, they accompany the screening: they prepare for them and mourn them. Before the film you can still take another testing glance at the film stills. You look at the pictures and make sure of yourself in the process, before you temporarily surrender one part of this state of self in the cinema. After the film you meet the film stills once more. Now they reveal themselves in a different light. They are now memories, surrounded by a breeze of melancholy, comparable with photos from your last holiday. Simultaneously, right from the start their presentation is marked as temporary. They are pinned up in showcases with needles or thumbtacks and remain provisional as long as the film is being shown in the cinema. Afterwards they disappear either in an archive, with collectors, fans, or in the garbage.

That means that in terms of image theory, film stills mark a difference between two differing concepts of images. The common opinion, which also incorporates photography and all spatial arts, sees the picture as a still. This position became a theoretical problem with the discovery of film: on the one hand, the film appears as a moving image, one putting the viewer in a different mode of perception thanks to its temporal structure. On the other, in its materiality the film still consists of filmstrips from individual static images. This picture-theoretical paradox can still be seen today. Film stills embody it. They simultaneously refer to a break, which artistic thinking with its categorizing in spatial and temporal arts has not yet mastered.

The concept of "tektieren" can mediate here. Just as the film-still, as threshold phenomena of the film, superimposes the assignments to spatial and temporal arts, so this act allows the perception of architecture in its temporality. It doesn't just cover the drawing, planning and the following execution, but also those inquiring and intervening activities, which you can carry out with the aid of photography and film and with specific places, architectures and urban spaces.

Gunda Förster

Nichts

Abends, wenn die Sonne untergeht, ist das Licht sehr sanft. Der Himmel spannt sich transparent über die Stadt. Verwandelt sich von Knallorange in Zartrosa. Bis der Horizont fast völlig verschwunden ist. Graue Häuser schieben sich zu Mauern zusammen. Die Konturen lösen sich auf. Nur noch ein paar Lichtpunkte. Die Stadt ist unsichtbar. Die Dunkelheit verschlingt alles. Eine undurchsichtige tiefe Fläche. Was ist das, dieses undurchdringliche Schwarz? Wenn ich nichts hören würde, wäre da Nichts. Ist das Nichts schwarz? Ein Lichtstrahl durchdringt die Finsternis. Alles wird hell. Von Licht überflutet und dann plötzlich wieder ins Dunkel getaucht. Grau die Luft, die sich in feinen undurchlässigen Schichten kaum dunklerer Tönung um mich herum ausbreitet. Früher dachte ich, ich könne die Luft sehen, abends, wenn es dunkel war im Zimmer, das Krisseln vor meinen Augen. Aber ich kann die Luft nicht sehen. Genauso wie ich auch das Licht nicht sehen kann. Immateriell. Nichts. Ist das Nichts weiß? Licht breitet sich aus, verdrängt die Finsternis. Die schwarze Fläche, zunächst düster, beginnt zu strahlen. Flirren. Flimmern. Sich unaufhörlich wandelnde Strukturen, kein Stillstand, immer wieder anders. Ständige, stetige Veränderung. Heute bin ich schon wieder jemand anders als ich gestern noch war. Alles befindet sich im Fluss. Ich muss auf die Verlagerungen und Verschiebungen achten, auf Bewegungen und Zerstreuungen, um das Spiel des Sinns erkennen und mitspielen zu können. Das leuchtende Wabern spiegelt sich im Fenster. Ein Bild und sein Gegenbild. Wahrheit und Täuschung. Gibt es zwischen dem Wirklichen und unserem Bild von ihm überhaupt eine Entsprechung? Was ist wirklich? Was ist real? Wo ist die Grenze zwischen Realität und Schein? Alles ist miteinander verbunden, vermischt, verwoben. Verweise und Bezüge verlagern sich mit zunehmender Geschwindigkeit. Ich muss mich beeilen. Immer schneller. Immer weiter. Immer will ich woanders sein, als ich gerade bin.

    Die Sonne brennt. Der Mund wird trocken. Die Augen können das grelle, blendende Licht kaum ertragen. Ich fahre. Der Motor brummt. Eine an Unendlichkeit grenzende Weite. Glitzerndes Weiß. Nichts, woran sich das Auge festhalten kann. Durch die Geschwindigkeit stirbt der Raum. Es bleibt nur noch die Zeit. Sie vergeht und scheint doch stillzustehen. Zähflüssiges Dahinrasen. Die Gedanken lösen sich auf. Ich verwische meine Grenzen und scheine in diesem grenzenlosen Verwischen selbst zu verschwinden. Nichts mehr. Ist das Nichts unendlich? Die Unendlichkeit des Raumes ist nicht vorstellbar. Aber die gleichförmige Vorstellung des Raumes führt zu keiner Schranke, woraus notwendig folgt, dass der Raum wirklich unendlich sein muss. Die Unmöglichkeit, gedanklich auf Grenzen zu stoßen, erlaubt es, den Raum als unendlich zu betrachten und angesichts der Unendlichkeit über seine eigenen Grenzen hinauszugelangen. Ich komme nirgendwo an.

    Die Räume im Haus sind durch Türen verbunden, die sich jeweils in vier Richtungen öffnen lassen. Ich versuche mir zu merken, in welchen Raum ich gelange, wenn ich die Tür so oder so öffne, um den Rückweg zu finden. Aber es gelingt mir nicht. Die vielen verschiedenen Möglichkeiten, die sich mit dem Betreten jedes Raumes um vier erweitern, kann ich nicht behalten – zumal ich auf dem Weg zurück umdenken müsste. Alles verkehrt sich: positiv wird negativ. Negativ wird positiv. Manchmal führt eine Tür auf eine Treppe. Ich muss mich entscheiden: hinauf oder hinunter. Wähle ich den Weg hinab, gelange ich mitunter auf eine höhere Ebene. Es gibt keine Ordnung: kein oben und unten, kein links und rechts, kein richtig und falsch. Im Labyrinth des Irrtums finde ich einen Anhaltspunkt: Unbezweifelbar bleibt der Zweifel. Alle Teile des Hauses sind viele Male da, jeder Ort ist ein anderer Ort. Der Weg heraus ist ein anderer als der hinein. Eingang und Ausgang. Ich bin nicht da, wo ich gerade bin.

Nothing

In the evening, when the sun sets, the light is very soft. The sky stretches transparently above the town. It changes from bright orange to pale pink until the horizon has almost completely disappeared. Grey houses push together to form walls. The contours dissolve. Only a few points of light remain. The town is invisible. Darkness devours everything. It is an opaque surface, one that is deep. What is this impenetrable black? If I were to hear nothing, nothing would be there. Is the nothing black? A light beam penetrates the darkness. Everything becomes light, flooded by light and then suddenly dipped into the dark once more. The air is grey, spreading around me in fine impermeable layers of a shade that is hardly darker. Earlier I thought that I could see the air, in the evening when it was dark in the room, the dancing in front of my eyes. But I can't see the air. Just like I can't see the light. It's immaterial. Nothing. Is the nothing white? Light spreads, driving out the darkness. The initially gloomy black area now starts to shine, to shimmer, to flicker. Structures change continuously. They are just different again and again without any standstill. The changes are permanent and steady. Today I am once more someone different from whom I was yesterday. Everything is in flux. I have to watch out for the shifts and displacements, for movements and diversions, in order to be able to recognize and join in the game of sense. The shining honeycomb is reflected in the window. An image and its reverse. Truth and deception. Is there any correspondence between something real and our image of it at all? What is actual? What is real? Where is the boundary between reality and appearance? Everything is linked together, mixed, interwoven. References and connections shift with increasing speed. I have to hurry, ever faster, ever further. I always want to be somewhere else than where I am now.

The sun burns. My mouth becomes dry. My eyes can hardly bear the glaring, blinding light. I drive. The motor hums. It is an expanse bordering on infinity, one of glittering white. My eye has nothing it can hold on to. The speed kills the space. All that remains is the time. It passes and yet seems to stand still. There is slow-moving racing all over. My thoughts dissolve. I blur my boundaries and seem to disappear myself in this boundless blurring, leaving nothing more. Is the nothing infinite? The infinity of space is not conceivable. However, the uniform idea of space leads to no limits, from which we must conclude that space really must be infinite. The impossibility of reaching limits to the imagination allows us to see space as infinite and so progress beyond our own limits in view of the infiniteness. I arrive nowhere.

Doors link the rooms in the house. Each room can be opened in four directions. I try to remember, which one I reach if I open the door this way or that, in order to find the way back. But I fail. I can't remember the many different possibilities, which expand by four with every room entered – particularly since I would have to rethink on the return. Everything reverses: positive becomes negative, negative becomes positive. Sometimes a door leads to stairs. I must decide: up or down. From time to time, when I decide to go down, I reach a higher level. There is no order: no up and down, no left and right, no correct and incorrect. I find one clue in the labyrinth of error: doubt remains undeniable. All parts of the house are there many times. Every place is a different place. The way out is a different one to that in. Entrance and exit. I am not where I currently am.

Der Blick verfängt sich in der Weite. Ruhe, aber ohne Stillstand. Kein Geräusch. Ich höre nichts mehr. Dann höre ich meinen Herzschlag und wie das Blut durch die Adern strömt. Ich schließe die Augen und lasse nur einen kleinen Schlitz offen. Durch ihn betrachte ich das, was ich sehen will. Ich drehe mich im Kreis. Rundherum dasselbe Bild. Der Anfang ist das Ende. Das Ende ist der Anfang. Die Sonne ist zugleich angenehm wärmend, heiß, sengend, verbrennend – je nachdem wie ich es wahrnehme, empfinde, aus welchem Blickwinkel ich es betrachte; wer, wie, wo ich bin. Alles ist viele Male da, aber zwei Dinge scheint es nur einmal zu geben: oben die verwirrende Sonne, unten mich. Wenn ich nicht nach oben schaue, werde ich nie erfahren, was unten ist. Verzerrte Entfernungen, flackernde Erscheinungen. Das gleißende Licht löscht aus, was soeben geschehen ist. Ein zentraler Punkt ist die Lichtquelle, die alle Dinge erhellt, und der Konvergenzpunkt für alles, was gewusst werden muss: ein vollkommenes Auge der Mitte, dem nichts entgeht und auf das alle Blicke gerichtet sind. Ich finde mich nur, wenn ich das ansehe, was ich nicht bin.

Der Raum hat zwei Funktionen: er umschließt und erhält. Eines kann beides: das Licht. Es scheint sich ohne Widerstand gleichmäßig auszubreiten, gelangt überall hin. Zusehends beginnt alles sich zu bewegen. Der Raum hat kaum Bestand. Der Moment lässt ihn erstehen, sich wandeln und vergehen in dem unwiderstehlich mächtigen Hauch des Lichts. Das Sehen löst sich auf. Und dieser Ton, der in langen Wellen den Raum durchströmt, bevor er den Körper durchdringt. Vom Ton überflutet und dann plötzlich wieder in Stille getaucht. Bis es einem fast den Kopf zerreißt. Von einem Extrem zum anderen übergehen. Vom blendend Heißen zum kalten Dunkel. Der schwarze Raum wölbt sich, dehnt sich aus ins Unermessliche. Die Zeit krümmt sich, ist unüberwindlich. Durch den Tunnel rasend, im Morgen ankommen. Wer im Jetzt lebt, hat keine Erinnerung an die Schatten der Vergangenheit. Wer im Jetzt lebt, hat auch keine Zukunft. Alles ist im Augenblick. Zwischen den Gedanken Lautlosigkeit und Leere. Ist das Nichts leer? Der blinde Fleck der Erkenntnis. Leerstellen. Tappen im Dunkeln. Ein Blitz zerschneidet die Finsternis für den Bruchteil einer Sekunde. Anwesenheit und Abwesenheit, Sichtbarwerden und Verschwinden: Erinnerte Vergangenheit. Vergessene Gegenwart. Gegenwärtiges Vergessen. Vergangene Erinnerung. Die Irritation ist zum Wesensmerkmal im Netz der kaum mehr überschaubaren Strukturen und Zusammenhänge geworden. Wo immer ich nicht bin, ist der Ort, wo ich selbst bin.

Wenn ich die Augenlider fest zusammenpresse, tanzen bunte funkelnde Lichtpunkte. Künstlicher Schwindel. Die Realität um mich herum vibriert. Millionen von Reizen stürmen auf mich ein. Schillerndes Rauschen. Bruchstücke von Ereignissen verwirren sich zum Chaos. Augenblicke verbleiben im Bewusstsein als dynamische Fragmentsymphonien aus Gesten, Wörtern, Licht und Klängen. Was gespeichert wird, entscheidet das Gedächtnis ohne mein Zutun. Es ist ein evolutionäres Instrument, hat seinen eigenen Willen. Die Erinnerung steuert sich selbst. Der erloschene Traum ist für immer verloren. Zerbrechliche, flüchtige Existenz. Zeitloses Licht. Vergessene Bilder. Zeitlose Bilder. Vergessenes Licht. Ich bin zur falschen Zeit am rechten Ort, zur rechten Zeit am falschen Ort.

Das Licht rast und schafft es doch nicht, uns zu erreichen, bevor der Stern verglüht ist. Wenn wir ihn sehen, hat er aufgehört zu existieren. Leben und Tod. Tag und Nacht – die schärfsten Gegensätze zwischen Licht und Finsternis, die nie zusammentreffen, sich gegenseitig ausschließen. Licht ist die Entziehung der Finsternis, und Finsternis ist die Entziehung des Lichts. Schatten ist die Vermischung von Finsternis mit Licht und wird von größerer oder geringerer Dunkelheit sein, je nachdem, ob das Licht, das sich mit ihm vermischt, von geringerer oder größerer Kraft ist. Das Licht ist aktiv. Der Schatten ist passiv. Das Licht ist nicht vom Schatten getrennt, sondern durchdringt ihn mit der Zeit. Wohin verschwindet das Licht in der Dunkelheit?

My view gets caught in the distance. Quiet but without stopping. There is no sound. I hear nothing more. Then I hear my heartbeat and how the blood flows through my veins. I close my eyes and leave just a small slit open. Through that I view what I want to see. I go round in a circle. All around me is the same view. The beginning is the end. The end is the beginning. The sun is simultaneously pleasantly warming, hot, scorching, burning – according to how I perceive it, feel it, from which viewpoint I see it, who, how, where I am. Everything is there very frequently, but two things seem to be there just once: above, the confusing sun, and me below. If I don't look up then I will never experience what is below. There are distorted distances, flickering appearances. The blinding light extinguishes what has just occurred. One central point is the light source that illuminates all things, and is the convergence point for everything that must become known: a perfect eye of the centre, which doesn't miss anything and towards which all eyes are directed. I only find myself when I see that which I am not.

The room has two functions: it encloses and preserves. One thing can do both: the light. It seems to spread evenly without resistance, reaching everywhere. Visibly everything starts to move. The room hardly lasts. The moment allows it to arise, change and pass by in the irresistible powerful breath of the light. The sight dissolves. And this note that flows through the room in long waves before it penetrates the body. You are flooded by the sound and then suddenly dipped in silence again, until it almost tears away your head. Passing from one extreme to the other. From the blindingly hot to the cold dark. The black room swells, extending beyond measure. The time bends, is invincible. Racing through the tunnel, arriving in the morning. Whoever lives in the present has no memory of the shadows of the past. Whoever lives in the present also has no future. Everything is in the moment. Between thought, soundlessness and emptiness. Is nothingness empty? The blind spot of recognition. Blanks. Groping in the dark. A flash of lightning cuts the darkness for a split second. Presence and absence, becoming visible and disappearing: Remembered past. Forgotten presence. Present forgetting. Past remembering. The irritation has become the basic trait in the network of structures and connections that are hardly clear anymore. Wherever I am not, is the place where I am myself.

If I press my eyelids together hard, then colourful, sparkling points of light dance, creating artificial dizziness. The reality vibrates around me. Millions of stimuli assail me. A shimmering roar. Fragments of events become tangled to chaos. Moments remain in my consciousness as dynamic fragment symphonies from gestures, words, light and sounds. My memory decides what is stored without my assistance. It is an evolutionary instrument with its own will. Memory guides itself. Once deleted, a dream is lost forever. Fragile, brief existence. Timeless light. Forgotten images. Timeless images. Forgotten light. I am in the right place at the wrong time, at the right time in the wrong place.

The light races and still doesn't manage to reach us before the star has burned out. When we see it, it has ceased to exist. Life and death, day and night – the fiercest oppositions between light and darkness, which never meet, mutually excluding each other. Light is the revocation of darkness, and darkness is the revocation of light. Shadow is the intermixing of darkness with light and is of greater or lesser darkness, according to how weaker or stronger the light is that mixes with it. Light is active. Shadow is passive. Light is never separated from shadow, instead penetrating it over time. Where does the light disappear to in the darkness?

Tunnel, 2002 – Scheinwerfer + Ton   *Tunnel, 2002 - floodlight + sound*

White Noise # 1, 2000 – Scheinwerfer + Ton   *White Noise # 1, 2000 - floodlight + sound*

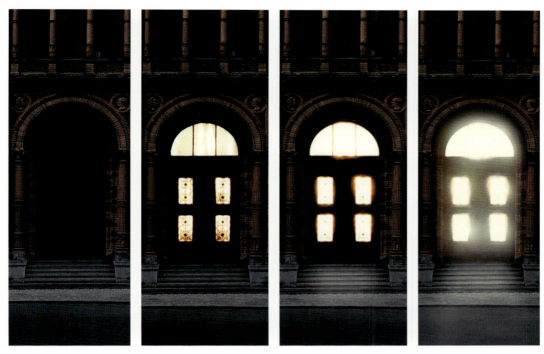

Dis-Appearance, Berlin, 2001 – Scheinwerfer   *Dis-Appearance, Berlin, 2001 – floodlight*

White Noise # 2, Oktogon, Dresden, 2000 – Scheinwerfer + Ton   *White Noise # 2, Octagon, Dresden, 2000 - floodlight + sound*

Werkzeuge Lichtmodell & Lichtzeichnung WiSe 2003/04
Tools Light Model & Light Drawing WiSe 2003/04

LICHTMODELL

Ein schnelles Konzeptmodell wird so gebaut, dass es selbst leuchtet und/oder Licht reflektieren kann. Unter kontrollierten Lichtbedingungen wird das Modell im Studio inszeniert und photographiert. Im Prozess des Photographierens findet eine Transformation statt. Durch Bewegung und Licht entstehen räumliche Strukturen, die Ideen für ein späteres Projekt liefern können. Die Übung ist hoch motivierend, da räumlich interessante Ergebnisse schnell und relativ unabhängig von der Qualität des Modells entstehen können.

LIGHT MODEL

A swiftly executed concept model is constructed in such a way that it emits its own light and/or can reflect light. Under controlled lighting conditions the model is "staged" and photographed in the studio. During the process of being photographed, a transformation takes place. Movement and light create spatial structures, which may yield ideas for a later project. The process of trying out is highly motivating, as spatially interesting results can be produced swiftly and relatively independently of the model's quality.

LICHTZEICHNUNG

Die Photokamera dient als Stift. Körperbewegungen werden direkt in die Photographie übertragen. So entstehen auf einfache Weise räumliche Strukturen, die sich durch ihre Immaterialität auszeichnen. Beide Werkzeuge wurden von Andrew Holmes entwickelt. [TA]

LIGHT DRAWING

The photographic camera functions as a drawing pencil. Physical movements are transferred directly to the photo. Thus, simple means give rise to spatial structures which are striking for their lack of materiality. Both tools were developed by Andrew Holmes. [TA]

Torsten Meißner: „Phoenix"   *Torsten Meißner: "Phoenix"*

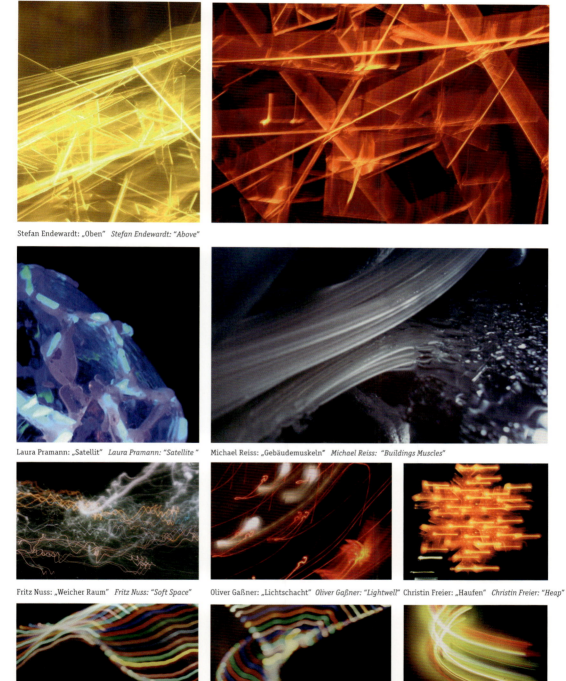

Stefan Endewardt: „Oben" *Stefan Endewardt: "Above"*

Laura Pramann: „Satellit" *Laura Pramann: "Satellite"*   Michael Reiss: „Gebäudemuskeln" *Michael Reiss: "Buildings Muscles"*

Fritz Nuss: „Weicher Raum" *Fritz Nuss: "Soft Space"*   Oliver Gaßner: „Lichtschacht" *Oliver Gaßner: "Lightwell"*   Christin Freier: „Haufen" *Christin Freier: "Heap"*

Lena Köppen: „Reflektionen im Stoff" *Lena Köppen: "Fabric Reflections"*   Thomas Sommerick: „Schnell" *Thomas Sommerick: "Fast"*

Werkzeug Lichtfilm SoSe 2004
Tool Light Film SoSe 2004

LICHTFILM

Raum wird durch Licht wahrgenommen. Licht ist dynamisch. Räume verändern sich mit dem Wechsel des Lichtes im Laufe des Tages, bis hin zur Mischung des künstlichen Lichtes innen mit Ereignissen außen. Die Studierenden haben mit filmischen Mitteln zwei Lichtsituationen ihres Projektes erarbeitet: Blick von außen und Blick von innen nach außen. Dabei wurden Modelle inszeniert und abgefilmt, reale Situationen mit Protagonisten gestellt oder digitale Trickfilme gebaut. Die Ergebnisse der Fokusierung flossen in das Semesterprojekt ein. [TA]

LIGHT FILM

Space is perceived by light. Light is dynamic. Spaces alter with the way light changes during the day, up to and including the mixing of artificial light inside with events outside. By filmic means the students have completed two of their project's "light situations": looking in from outside and looking out from inside. In the process, models were staged and filmed, real situations with protagonists were set up, or digital trick-films developed. The results of this process of focusing flowed into the semester project. [TA]

Christian Necker: „Lichtgalerie" *Christian Necker: "Light Gallery"*

Jürgen Missfeldt: „Kontakt 34" *Jürgen Missfeldt: "Contact 34"*

Gunnar Behrens: „Haus für Handel und Wohnen" *Gunnar Behrens: "House for Commerce and Residence"*

Martin Mohelnicky: „Ritterstraße Acht" *Martin Mohelnicky: "Ritterstraße No 8"*

Alireza Shalviri: „Between the Façades" *Alireza Shalviri: "Between the Façades"*

Werkzeug Perfekter Raum / Tool The Perfect Space

PERFEKTER RAUM

Der Perfekte Raum ist ein didaktisches Werkzeug zur Konzentration einer Entwurfsidee, zur Unterstützung der räumlichen Kernidee eines Entwurfes.
Anhand von Modellen, von 2D- und 3D-Zeichnungen des Perfekten Raums werden Raumgliederung und Materialität einer räumlichen Schlüsselsituation des Entwurfsprojektes bearbeitet. Diese Schlüsselsituation wird dafür ganz bewusst isoliert und stark vergrößert betrachtet.
Die Frage nach dem Perfekten Raum für eine oder mehrere spezifische Handlungen klammert andere – ebenso wichtige – Entwurfsparameter aus und zwingt den Entwerfer, sich auf die genaue Beobachtung und räumliche Umsetzung der gewählten Aktion zu konzentrieren. Wichtig ist: Was nimmt der Nutzer wahr, welche Materialität ist perfekt für diesen Ort.
Die Erwartungen an diesem Raum oder Raumzusammenhang werden damit zuerst idealisiert und im weiteren Projektverlauf wieder im Dialog mit anderen Entwurfsparametern diskutiert. Die so gewählte induktive Entwurfsmethode beugt ganz bewusst traditionell deduktiv geprägten Entwurfsverfahren vor.

THE PERFECT SPACE

The perfect room is a didactic tool for concentrating on a design idea as well as supporting a design's core spatial idea.
Using models, 2D and 3D drawings of the perfect room, its structure and material character can be modified in a key spatial situation. To that end, this key situation is deliberately isolated and observed at greater magnification.
The question of the perfect room for one or more specific actions excludes other, equally important design parameters, forcing the designer to concentrate on exact observation and spatial application of the chosen action. The important thing is: what does the user perceive and what kind of material shape is perfect for this location.
Thus, initially the expectations towards this room or spatial connection are idealized and, throughout the course of the project, they are discussed again in dialogue with other design parameters. The choice of the inductive design method in this way deliberately safeguards against traditional processes of deductive design.

Jannes Wurps: „Kletterraum"   *Jannes Wurps: "Climbing Space"*

Marc Dufour-Feronce: „Bürobad" *Marc Dufour-Feronce: "Office baths"*

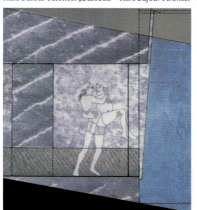  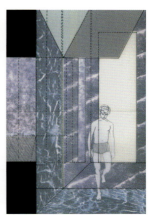

Christoph Jantos: „libraRIBBON, Staatsbibliothek zu Berlin" *Christoph Jantos: "libraRIBBON, National Library Berlin"*

Franziska Streit: „Meeting point" *Franziska Streit: "Meeting point"*

Irmina Czapla: „Falten" *Irmina Czapla: "Folding"*

Felix Sommerlad / moleStage 2003/2004

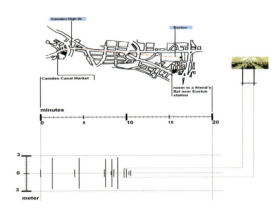

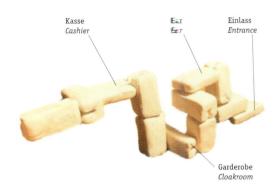

Kartierung des Weges zwischen Markt und Wohnung
Mapping the route between market and apartment

Raumkonfigurationstestspiel *Test game for room configuration*

MOLESTAGE

Die Bekanntschaft mit einem arbeitslosen Schauspieler, der auf dem Londoner Camden Market durchsichtige, kolorierbare Kunsterde verkaufte, war der Ausgangspunkt für das Projekt moleSTAGE. Die zeitliche und räumliche Kartierung seines Nachhauseweges diente als Grundlage für die quantitativen Dimensionen der unterirdischen Zugänge. Die schwierige berufliche Situation des Schauspielers und das Fehlen einer Infrastruktur, die Kunst und Kommerz zusammenbringt, war Anlass für die Entwicklung der Grundidee. Es entstand ein Gebäude, in dem Künstler und Produzenten, Kreative und Förderer für die Dauer eines Projektes zusammentreffen, um zu probieren, zu proben und den Publikumstest gleich vor Ort durchzuführen. Die moleSTAGE vereint so Probebühne, Aufführungsort und Lebensraum.

MOLESTAGE

The acquaintance with an unemployed actor, who was selling transparent dyeable artificial earth on London's Camden Market, was the inspiration for the project moleSTAGE. The temporal and spatial charting of his way back home served as the basis for the quantitative dimensions of the underground access points. The actor's difficult professional situation and the lack of infrastructure uniting art and commerce was the motivation for developing a basic idea: a building was created where artists and producers, creative individuals and sponsors can meet for the duration of the project to try out, rehearse and carry out an audience test directly on location. Thus, the moleSTAGE combines rehearsal stage, performance venue and room for living.

Schnitt Eingänge *Section entrances*

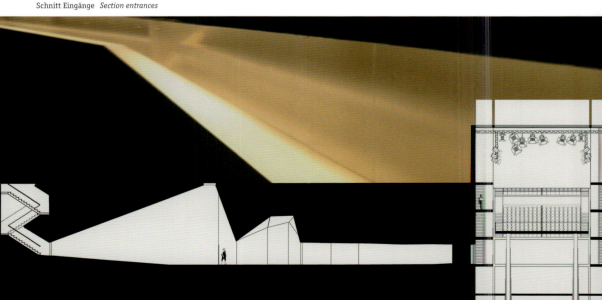

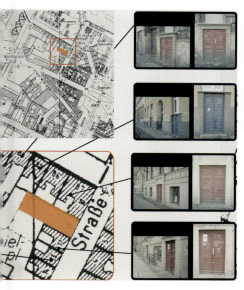
Kohlenkellereingänge *Coal cellar entrances*

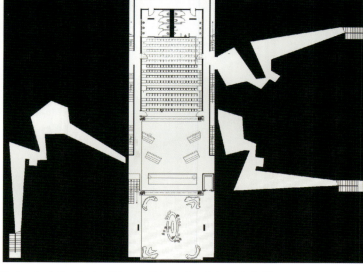
Eingänge durch die vorhandene Bebauung *Entrances through the existing building*

ZUGÄNGE

Für die Zuschauer, die bei Uraufführungen oder Premieren in die moleSTAGE kommen, gibt es keine offensichtlichen Eingangstüren. Nur durch die Kohlenkellereingänge der Nachbarbebauung und daran angegliederte unterirdische Gänge gelangen die Zuschauer ins Theater. Die jeweiligen Eingänge der Umgebung werden immer erst kurz vor den Aufführungen bekannt. So wird das Konzept der „Sneak-Preview" durch die wechselnden Eingangssituationen unterstrichen.
Zur Straße hin wölbt sich das Gebäude blasenförmig nach außen, schafft sich Raum und beherbergt hier die Privat- und Gemeinschaftsräume. Die Theater- und Proberäume sind zur Hofseite hin angesiedelt und können so in die Inszenierung integriert werden.

ACCESS POINTS

There are no clearly marked entrances for spectators attending first nights or premières to access the moleSTAGE. The spectators can only enter the theatre through coal cellars in the neighbouring building and connecting underground passages. The relevant entrances in the vicinity are only announced shortly before the performances begin. Thus, the idea of a "sneak preview" is impossible because of the changing entrance situations.
The building curves in a bubble shape towards the street, creating space for itself and accommodating private and community rooms here. The theatre and rehearsal rooms are located towards the courtyard and thus can be integrated into the performance.

Eingangsszenario moleSTAGE *Entrance scenario moleSTAGE*

 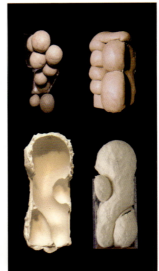 

Aus der Beobachtung der "Eco-Earth", einem volumenverändernden Polyacrylamid wurden Form und Raumstruktur der moleSTAGE entwickelt und in verschiedenen Studienmodellen vertieft

Form and spatial structure of the moleSTAGE were developed and refined in different study models by observing the "Eco-Earth" – a polyacrylamid that changes its capacity

Collage Ansicht Luckauer Straße *Collage: view of Luckauer Straße*   Formfindung *Finding form*   Polyachrylamid *Polyachrylamid*

RAUMKONZEPT

Grundlage des Raumkonzeptes der moleSTAGE bilden die Überschneidungen von Privat- und Gemeinschaftsraum, von Proben- und Bühnenbereichen. Das ermöglicht ungeplantes Proben und Improvisieren, spontane Sessions und ausufernde Gelage bis in die Morgenstunden. Ein privater Rückzugsort ist dennoch immer vorhanden, um dem Treiben bei Bedarf entfliehen zu können.
Untereinander sind Bühnen-, Foyer- und Zuschauerraum mischbar, sogar die Aufhebung jeder Trennung ist möglich. Durch ein dem Palettenparken ähnliches System können beispielsweise Foyer und Bühne innerhalb kürzester Zeit getauscht werden. Von der klassischen Inszenierung bis hin zum modernen Theater ohne jede räumliche Trennung von Zuschauer- und Spielraum ist hier jede Variante denkbar.

CONCEPT

The overlapping of private and community space, of rehearsal and stage areas creates the base of the spatial concept for moleSTAGE. This makes spontaneous rehearsals and improvisations possible, as well as sessions and revelry into the early hours. However, there is always a private retreat in order to escape the activities if necessary. The space for the stage, foyer and spectator is interchangeable; it is even possible to override the separation between each area. For instance, the foyer and stage can be changed at top speed by a system that is similar to parking partitions. Here, every imaginable variation is possible, from a classical performance to modern theatre, but without any spatial separation of spectator and performance space.

Innenansicht Gemeinschaftsbereich *Interior view: community area*   Außenansicht *Exterior view*   Foyer wird Bühne *Foyer becomes stage*

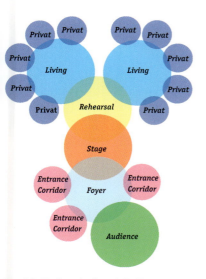

Räumliche Konfiguration der moleSTAGE
Spatial configuration of the moleSTAGE

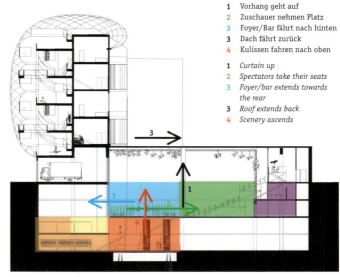

1	Vorhang geht auf
2	Zuschauer nehmen Platz
3	Foyer/Bar fährt nach hinten
3	Dach fährt zurück
4	Kulissen fahren nach oben
1	*Curtain up*
2	*Spectators take their seats*
3	*Foyer/bar extends towards the rear*
3	*Roof extends back*
4	*Scenery ascends*

Schnitt Zustand 1 *Section state 1*

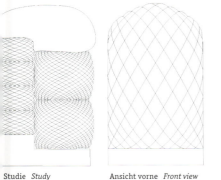

Studie *Study* Ansicht vorne *Front view*

Grundriss 1. OG *Layout: first upper floor*

Innenansicht Theater *Interior view theatre*

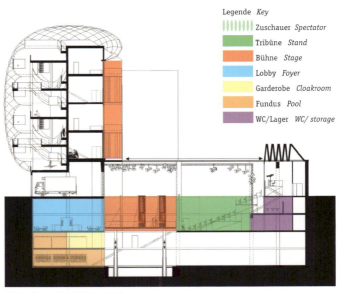

Legende *Key*

Zuschauer	*Spectator*
Tribüne	*Stand*
Bühne	*Stage*
Lobby	*Foyer*
Garderobe	*Cloakroom*
Fundus	*Pool*
WC/Lager	*WC/ storage*

Schnitt Zustand 2 *Section state 2*

Susanne Hofmann

Spürbare Architektur

Schulkinder fanden in einer unserer Untersuchungen wohlklingende Worte, um ihre gebaute Umwelt zu beschreiben. Architektur sei: luftig, golden, eisig, frostig, klein, pelzig, weich, gerundet, biegsam, feurig, glatt, eckig, brutal, rund, zärtlich, farbig, sprudelnd, geil, schluchtig, herzschlagend, geschmeidig, schimmernd, kantig, süß, fedrig, atmend, köstlich, flirrend zart, saftig, fleischig, aromatisch, duftend, hart, heiß, elastisch, gleitend, gefedert, üppig, gedämpft, fein, flüchtig, schwach, flauschig, kuschelig, leuchtend, kraftvoll, sexy, explodierend, hell, dunkel, klanglos, klingend, weit, eng, festlich, heiter, ernst, majestätisch, gemütlich, bedrohlich, trüb, bedrückend, magisch, wuschelig, plastisch, dehnbar, lebendig, tief, feucht, schwebend. Architektur berührt offensichtlich – nicht nur in der Anschauung, sondern auch emotional. Sie bestimmt unsere sinnliche Wahrnehmung, wie die von den Kindern benutzten Adjektive verdeutlichen. Kinder reagieren oft sehr direkt und lebendig auf ihre Umwelt. Mit zunehmendem Alter wird diese Sensibilität leider häufig überdeckt, aber auch als Erwachsene „spüren" wir noch Architektur. Wir erfahren sie im Zusammenspiel der unterschiedlichsten Parameter als räumliche Stimmungsqualität und als synästhetisches, also alle Sinne ansprechendes Erlebnis.

Ähnlich wie das Wetter bestimmt auch der uns umgebende Raum unser Wohlbefinden. Wir spüren das Wetter, indem sich Temperatur, Luftdruck, das Licht, der Sonnenschein auf unsere Stimmung auswirken. Gleichzeitig lässt es sich mit Temperatur- und Windmessungen, der Ermittlung von Niederschlagsmengen, Luftfeuchte, Luftdruck und Wolkendichte bestimmen. Es gibt also ein wissenschaftlich definiertes und ein

Drittes Obergeschoss: Mit dem Drachen fliegen: Die Schulkinder lernen in kleinen Gruppen zwischen leuchtenden und metallenen Drachenschweifen.

Third upper floor – Flying with the dragon: schoolchildren learn in small groups to ramble between illuminated and metal dragontails.

Sensuous Architecture

In one of our studies, school children found a range of melodious adjectives for describing their built environment. Architecture is: breezy, golden, icy, frosty, small, furry, soft, rounded, bendy, fiery, smooth, square, brutal, round, tender, coloured, sparkling, cool, soaring, heart-pounding, supple, shimmering, edged, sweet, feathery, breathing, delicious, shimmering soft, juicy, fleshy, aromatic, fragrant, hard, hot, elastic, sliding, spring-suspended, lush, subdued, fine, brief, weak, fleecy, snug, lucent, powerful, sexy, exploding, light, dark, toneless, ringing, far, close, festive, cheerful, serious, majestic, comfortable, threatening, dull, depressing, magical, fuzzy, plastic, flexible, lively, deep, damp, floating. Clearly, architecture is touching – not only intellectually, but also emotionally. As the adjectives used by the children clearly show, Architecture defines our sensory perception. Children's reactions to their environment are often very direct and lively. Unfortunately, this sensitivity often diminishes with increasing age, but as adults we still 'feel' architecture. We experience it, in the interplay of the most diverse parameters, as the quality of spatial mood, and as synaesthesia, an experience appealing to all senses.

Just like the weather, the space around us also determines our well-being. We perceive the weather through the effects that temperature, air pressure, light, and sunshine have on our mood. At the same time, we can measure it through temperature and wind measurements, precipitation, humidity, air pressure, and cloud density. There is therefore a scientifically-defined and a perceived

gefühltes Wetter, eine tatsächlich messbare und eine gefühlte Temperatur der Luft. So mancher Wetterbericht vermerkt das. Analog dazu spüren wir auch die Ausstrahlung eines Orts, eines Raums oder einer Architektur, und wie das Wetter kann auch ein Gebäude auf objektivierbare Parameter zurückgeführt werden: Seine Nutzung, das für seinen Bau verwendete Material, die Form des Baus und seiner Räume, die sie bestimmende Farbe, ihre natürliche oder künstliche Belichtung, die Akustik der Räume, also ihr Klang, die Einbindung des Gebäudes in den Ort, an dem es gebaut wurde – alle diese Gegebenheiten bestimmen die Wirkung und die Ausstrahlung von Räumen, Bauten oder ganzen Städten.

Atmosphäre ist nicht nur die Gashülle unseres Planeten, sie ist auch unser unmittelbarer Kontakt zur Wirklichkeit. Schließlich umgibt uns außer unserer Kleidung zunächst ein „Klima" aus ephemeren Effekten, die durch die Architektur bestimmt werden, und erst dann das Bauwerk selbst. Dieses ist wiederum von atmosphärischen Effekten durchdrungen und durch sie definiert. Der Philosoph Gernot Böhme[1] beschreibt Atmosphären als räumlich spürbare Stimmungsqualitäten, die man nicht ermessen kann, sondern empfinden muss, um sie zu verstehen. Einige Architekturen vermögen uns zu bestimmten Handlungen zu inspirieren. Manche Räume machen uns flüstern, andere verleiten uns zu langsamem und bedachtem Gehen, wieder andere zum forschen Schreiten. Manche Orte haben sogar ein erhöhtes Potential, sich dort zu verlieben, oder

Zweites Obergeschoss: Ein Thron für den Augenblick eines Flügelschlages: Gruppen von 4 Kindern sitzen in aufklappbaren Sitzlandschaften wie in der Flügelbeuge des Drachens, lesen dort, arbeiten und diskutieren.

Second upper floor – A throne for the moment of a wing's flap: groups of four children sit in extendable seating landscapes, as though they are in the fold of the dragon's wings; they read, work and discuss there.

sie lassen durch uns als Nutzer den Raum zum Klingen bringen. Die atmosphärische Wirkung ist in der sakralen Architektur, aber auch in Herrschafts- oder Theaterbauten ein essentieller Bestandteil der räumlichen Komposition, aber sie existiert – gewollt oder ungewollt – letztlich in jeder räumlichen Situation, sei sie auch noch so profan.

Der Architekt August Endell hob schon 1908 in seinem Aufsatz *Die Schönheit der großen Stadt* die bestimmende Ausstrahlung von alltäglichen Orten und Räumen hervor: „Das Wirksamste ist nicht die Form, sondern ihre Umkehrung, der Raum, das Leere, das sich rhythmisch zwischen den Mauern ausbreitet, von ihnen begrenzt wird, aber dessen Lebendigkeit wichtiger ist, als die Mauern."[2], und an einer anderen Stelle derselben Schrift heißt es: „Nebel, Dunst, Sonne, Regen und Dämmerung, das sind die großen Mächte, die im unendlichen Wechsel die großen Steinnester mit immer neuem Farbglanz umkleiden."[3]

Endells Raumdefinition legt die Vorstellung einer Architektur nahe, deren Eigenheiten eher in den subjektiven emotionalen Reaktionen liegen, die sie hervorruft, als in der rationalen metrischen Definition ihrer Form. Es geht bei der atmosphärischen Wirkung der Architektur also nicht allein um den geometrischen Raum, den sie formt, sondern auch um seine sinnliche Erfahrung. Sie ist bei aller Kritik an der Monotonie und

weather, that is, an objectively measurable and a subjectively perceived climate. This distinction is made in some weather reports. Similarly, we also feel the atmosphere of a place, a space or a piece of architecture and, like the weather, a building can also be reduced to objectifiable parameters: its use; the material used for its construction; the shape of the structure and its rooms; the colour defining it; its natural or artificial lighting; the acoustics of the rooms, i.e. its sound; the integration of the building with the location in which it was built – all these conditions determine the effect and the atmosphere of rooms, buildings and whole towns.

Atmosphere doesn't only refer to our planet's gaseous envelope; it is our direct means of contact with reality. For ultimately, besides our clothes, we are surrounded first by a "climate" of ephemeral effects, which are determined by architecture, and then by structure itself. The philosopher Gernot Böhme[1] describes atmosphere as spatially perceptible qualities of mood that cannot be measured, but rather must be experienced in order to be understood. Some architecture may inspire us to certain actions. Many spaces will make us whisper. Some lead us to a slow thoughtful pace, others to determined strides. In some places there is an increased potential for falling in love, or we as users awaken the resonance of the space. Atmospheric effect is an essential part of the spatial composi-

tion in sacred architecture as well as in government buildings and theatres. However, ultimately these effects — intended or unintended — exist in every spatial situation, even in the most profane.

In his essay *Die Schönheit der großen Stadt* (1908), the architect August Endell highlighted the defining atmosphere of everyday locations and spaces. "The most effective is not form, but its converse, space, emptiness, which rhythmically spreads out between the walls that delimit it, but whose vitality is more important than the walls. (...)"[2] Elsewhere in the same essay he writes: "Fog, mist, sun, rain and twilight – these are the great powers that in infinite variation coat great walls with more and more shining colour."[3]

Endell's definition of space is close to a conception of architecture whose distinctiveness lies more in the subjective emotional response it elicits than in rational metric definition of form. Hence, the atmospheric effect of architecture is not only a matter of geometrical space, which it shapes, but also sensory experience. In all criticism of the monotony and tactile sterility of our built environment, few people address this experience as a factor in the architectural concept of space. Architectural effects and affects are frowned upon by architects. There is,

der taktilen Sterilität unserer gebauten Umwelt einer der am wenigsten beachteten Faktoren des architektonischen Raumentwurfs. Architektonische Effekte und Affekte sind unter Architekten noch immer verpönte Begriffe. Es macht jedoch nicht viel Sinn, Architektur als ein rein körperliches Objekt zu behandeln und ihre Wirkung auf die Sinneswahrnehmung zu leugnen. Architektur kommuniziert auf einer atmosphärischen Ebene, sie baut Identitäten, Ausstrahlung und Anmutung auf. Damit ist sie direkt mit der Gefühlswelt verbunden. In der Filmarchitektur werden Atomsphären gezielt als Medium eingesetzt. Auf ähnliche Weise lässt sich auch zwischen Architekten und Laien, vor allem mit Kindern, über ihre Vorstellungen von der räumlichen Umgebung ihrer Alltagswelt kommunizieren.

Entwurf einer spürbaren Architektur – ein Praxisbericht

An der TU Berlin, Fakultät VII Architektur/Gesellschaft/Umwelt wurde das Studienmodell „Die Baupiloten" als Brückenschlag zwischen Ausbildung, Praxis und Entwicklung eingerichtet. Die Baupiloten sind eine wechselnde Gruppe von Studierenden, die unter Anleitung in ihrem Architekturstudium eigenständig Baumaßnahmen entwickeln. Sie erarbeiten dabei alle Bauphasen – vom konzeptionellen Entwurf über Überzeugsarbeit beim Bauherrn mit entsprechenden Darstellungen bis hin zur Realisierung bei knappen Budgetvorgaben. Das menschliche Empfinden steht im Mittelpunkt der Architektur, die

Erstes Obergeschoss: HauchSanftSein: Zwischen den leichten, transluzenten Schleiern der Decke und den schimmernden, textilen Garderobenschränken wird der Atem des Drachens spürbar.

First upper floor – BreathBeSoft: the dragon's breath is tangible between the light translucent veils of the ceiling and the shimmering textile cupboards of the cloakroom.

die Baupiloten entwerfen und bauen. Sie soll sozial engagiert und experimentell sein und auch mit geringen finanziellen Mitteln leicht spürbare Atmosphären schaffen. Dabei werden neben den klassischen Baumaterialien auch ephemere Materialien wie Luft und Licht, Wärme und Klang eingesetzt.

Für zwei Projekte nahmen die Baupiloten Architekturvorstellungen von Kindern zum Ausgangspunkt ihres Entwurfs: bei der Modernisierung der Erika-Mann-Grundschule in Berlin-Wedding[4] (2003 fertig gestellt) und für den Umbau der Kindertagesstätte Traumbaum in Berlin-Kreuzberg[5], die sich derzeit im Stadium der Ausführungsplanung befindet. Beide Projekte sollen die Kraft haben, auch auf ihr Umfeld einzuwirken und zu einer Verbesserung der Lebensqualität in problematischen Stadtquartieren Berlins beizutragen.

Für die Kindertagesstätte in Berlin-Kreuzberg malten und bastelten Kinder im Alter von zwei bis elf Jahren, um ihre Vorstellungen eines „Traumbaums" zu umreißen. Die jüngsten Kinder konnten sich sprachlich noch nicht genau artikulieren, waren jedoch in der Lage, über Bilder zu kommunizieren: Der Traumbaum sollte mit ihnen leben, sich bewegen und verändern. Die Vorstellungen und Wünsche der Kinder dienten den Baupiloten als Inspiration für ihre Arbeit. Sie entwarfen Einbauten, die in ihrer

however, little sense in treating architecture as a purely physical object and thus denying its effect on sensory perception. Architecture communicates on an atmospheric level. It builds identities, atmosphere and impressions, and is thus directly connected to the world of feeling. In set design, atmosphere is purposely used as a medium. In a similar way, architects and laypeople alike (children in particular) can express their everyday world and their perception of the spatial environment.

Designing Noticeable Architecture – a Project Report

The "Baupiloten" scheme was set up at the Faculty of Architecture, Society and Environment at the Technical University of Berlin to bridge the gap between education, practice and development. The Baupiloten are architecture students who develop their own construction projects under the guidance of their tutors. They work on all phases of the project, from preliminary design and persuading building owners with relevant models and drawings through to construction on tight budgets. Human feeling stands at the centre of the brand of architecture that the building pilots design and build. It is intended to be socially committed and experimental and to create an easily noticeable atmosphere with limited financial resources. In addition to traditional building materials, ephemeral materials such as air, light, warmth and sound are also used.

The "Baupiloten" used the children's architectural ideas as the starting point for their own design in two Berlin projects: the modernization of the Erika Mann primary school in Wedding, Berlin[4] (completed in 2003) and the conversion of the Traumbaum nursery in Kreuzberg[5] (currently in the planning stages). Both projects were intended to be on such a scale that would allow them to impact upon the surroundings and help improve the quality of life in disadvantaged districts of Berlin.

Working on the primary school project in Kreuzberg, children aged from two to eleven made paintings and models which expressed their ideas of a "dream tree". The youngest children were not yet able to articulate their ideas linguistically, but were able to communicate through images. The dream tree was meant to live with them, move and change. The children's ideas and desires were an inspiration to the "Baupiloten". They designed a built object that resembled a tree in terms of texture and form and included a tree's capacity for protection and sanctuary. The dream tree helped children of diverse cultural backgrounds to unite and collaborate with one another. It was as if a fairytale creature had come to life: the tree stimulated the children's imagination and gave

Struktur und ihren Formen einem Baum ähnlich sind und wie dieser Schutz und Rückzugsmöglichkeiten bieten. Der Traumbaum hilft den Kindern, die vielfältige kulturelle Lebenshintergründe haben, zusammenzufinden. Er wirkt wie ein Realität gewordenes Fabelwesen, regt die Phantasie der Kinder an und gibt ihnen die Möglichkeit, in kleineren oder größeren Gruppen zu spielen und zu kommunizieren. Er kann glitzern und leuchten, er kann sich bewegen und Geräusche machen. Sein Blätterdach reflektiert vielfach natürliches Licht weit in die tiefen Flure hinein, seine Blätter rascheln, als würden sie kichern, und auch ein „Schnarchen" ist geplant, so dass die Kinder mit dem Baum träumen können. Sie begreifen dort ihre Welt mit aller Sinnen, finden Freunde und tauschen sich mit ihnen aus.

In Berlin-Wedding entwarfen Schüler im Alter von neun bis 13 Jahren in Collagen phantastische Zukunftslandschaften. Sie brachten ihre Vorstellungen beeindruckend konkret zum Ausdruck. Die eingangs zitierten Adjektive der Schulkinder zeigen, dass sie vor allem auf die sinnliche Wahrnehmung und ihr imaginiertes Empfinden eingingen. Die Baupiloten tauchten auch bei diesem Projekt in die von den Kindern erdachte Welt ein und entwickelten ihre Entwürfe für das sehr autoritär wirkende Schulhaus aus den Wünschen der Kinder. Ihr „Schülerparlament"[6] fungierte während des gesamten Bauprozesses quasi als Vertretung der Bauherren. Die Kinder wurden ernst genommen und ihre Entscheidungen respektiert. Mit ihnen

Erdgeschoss: Sternenstaubtauchen: Über den gelb-grün lackierten Metallmöbeln wachsen Pflanzen unter violettem Licht und bieten dem Drachen einen Schlafplatz.

Ground floor – Stardust-diving: plants grow beneath violet light above the yellow-green lacquered metal furniture and offer the dragon a place to sleep.

entwickelten die Baupiloten eine „Silberdrachenwelt", die zur Grundlage einer expressiv spielerischen Architektur wurde.

Je weiter man sich heute in das Schulgebäude hinein und in ihm hinauf bewegt, desto stärker ist der Geist des Silberdrachens zu spüren: ein Geist, der sich verändert, der klingt, leuchtet und schimmert. Im Erdgeschoss, der Welt des „Sternenstaubtauchens", wachsen über den gelb-grün lackierten Metallmöbeln Pflanzen unter violettem Licht und bieten dem imaginären Drachen einen Schlafplatz. Im ersten Obergeschoss wird im „HauchSanftSein" zwischen den leichten, transluzenten Schleiern der Decke und den schimmernden, textilen Garderobenschränken der Atem des Drachens spürbar. Im zweiten Obergeschoss, „dem Thron für den Augenblick eines Flügelschlags", können Schülergruppen von vier Kindern in aufklappbaren Sitzlandschaften wie in der Flügelbeuge des Drachens sitzen und dort lesen, arbeiten und sich unterhalten. Im dritten Obergeschoss kann man schließlich „mit dem Drachen fliegen". Die Schulkinder lernen in kleinen Gruppen zwischen leuchtenden und metallenen Drachenschweifen. Im Haupttreppenhaus, dem „Riesenbrumsel", ist das Treppenauge zu einem musikalischen Lehrpfad geworden, der den Drachen tanzen und springen lässt.

them the opportunity to play and exchange ideas in small or large groups. The tree can glitter and shine; the tree can move and make sounds. Its roof of leaves scattered natural light far down below, its leaves rustled and tickled. The tree will even be able to doze off so that the children can dream along with it. The children used all their senses to comprehend their world. They had fun and were keen to exchange views.

In Wedding, Berlin, school children aged from nine to thirteen designed collages of fantastic futuristic landscapes. They produced impressively vivid representations of their ideas. The adjectives the children used (quoted above) indicated that they drew primarily on sensory perception and imaginary sensation. The "Baupiloten" also immersed themselves in the children's world during the project and, from the children's requests, developed designs for the highly authoritarian-looking school building. The school parliament[6] acted as the building owners' representative throughout the entire construction process. The children were taken seriously and their decisions respected. The "Baupiloten" devised a "silver dragon world" that became the basis of an expressively playful architectural style.

Today, the further you venture inside the school building and move around, the more you feel the spirit of the silver dragon: a transforming, audible,

glowing, shimmering spirit. On the ground floor, in the world of "stardust diving", plants illuminated under violet light grow over the yellow and green metal furniture, forming a dragon's lair. On the first floor, in the "soft breath" area, the breath of the dragon can be felt between the gossamer, translucent veils of the ceiling and the shimmering cloakrooms made of fabric. On the second floor is "the throne for the time of a wing beat", four pupils at a time can sit as if in the bend of the dragon's wing and read, work and talk. On the third floor, they can "fly with the dragon". Here the pupils study in small groups between shining, metallic dragon's tails. The main stairway has become a musical trail that allows the dragon to dance and jump.

Like Kreuzberg, Wedding is a suburb of Berlin that is a social flashpoint, with an unemployment rate of more than fifty per cent. Eighty-five per cent of parents whose children attend the Erika Mann School do not speak German as their first language. The pupils come from twenty-five different countries. The new architecture of the school should help them overcome linguistic and cultural barriers and go some way towards establishing the building with its various facilities as an educational centre for local citizens. This is why children, parents and

Wie Kreuzberg ist auch der Stadtteil Wedding ein sozialer Brennpunkt Berlins mit einer Arbeitslosigkeit von über 50 Prozent. 85 Prozent der Eltern, deren Kinder die Erika-Mann-Schule besuchen, sind nicht deutschsprachiger Herkunft. Die Schülerinnen und Schüler stammen aus 25 Nationen. Die neue Architektur der Schule soll ihnen helfen, Sprach- und Kulturbarrieren zu überwinden, und dazu beitragen, das Gebäude mit seinen vielfältigen Angeboten als Bildungszentrum für alle Bürgerinnen und Bürger in das Quartier zu integrieren. Kinder, Eltern und das Lehrerkollegium waren deshalb aktiv am Bauprozess beteiligt. In diesem Sinne ist diese Architektur sozial, sie wirkt identitätstiftend. Für die Erika-Mann-Grundschule ist die erfolgte Synthese von Architektur und Pädagogik der Auftakt zu einem zukunftsgerichteten Umbau zu einer Ganztagsschule als „KinderKiezZentrum".

Die Fiktion des Drachens veranschaulicht unsere Vorstellung einer sozial engagierten Architektur, die mit den Kindern leben und sich mit ihnen verändern kann. Wir wollten den Kindern Tiefe, Intensität und auch Differenz anbieten und erreichen, dass die Architektur den Kindern Lust darauf macht, sie zu ergründen. Und tatsächlich waren sie von den interaktiven Modellen der Entwurfsphase begeistert: Ein Mädchen freute sich über das Licht, das ihr regelrecht „entgegen spritze". Als der Umbau fertig gestellt war, sagte ein anderes Mädchen, es sei froh, dass es den Drachen gibt. Für sie war die Imagination Realität und die neue Atmosphäre so deutlich spürbar geworden,

Haupttreppenhaus: Riesenbrumsel: Das Treppenauge ist zu einem musikalischen Lehrpfad geworden, der den Drachen tanzen und springen lässt.

Main stairwell – giant fuss: the head of the staircase is turned into a musical learning path that makes the dragon dance and jump.

dass sie sie benennen konnte. Gerade die Reaktionen der Kinder in den Entwurfsphasen sowie nach der Fertigstellung haben uns darin bestätigt, die atmosphärische Wirkung der Architektur explizit in ihren Entwurf einzubeziehen und sie auch während des Baus stets zu reflektieren und zu kontrollieren, das heißt: messbare und empfundene Architektur miteinander in Einklang zu bringen.

ANMERKUNGEN
(1) Gernot Böhme: *Atmosphären.* Frankfurt am Main 1995
(2) Endell, August: *Die Schönheit der großen Stadt.* Hier verwendete Auflage: Berlin 1984. S. 51
(3) A.a.O.
(4) Baupiloten-Team: Frank Drenckhahn, Johannes Gutsch, Gordana Jakimovska, Nils Ruf, Urs Walter
(5) Baupiloten-Team: Julie Baumann, Jenny Brockmann, Nikolai Erichsen, Franziska Fischer, Danile Hülseweg, Stefan Kels, Uta Schrameyer
(6) Ab der dritten Jahrgangsstufe schickt jede Klasse der Schule drei Abgeordnete in das Parlament.

staff were closely involved in the construction process. This is social architecture; it establishes identities. For the Erika Mann Primary School, the successful synthesis of architecture and pedagogy is the beginning of a lasting modification, turning the day school into a neighbourhood children's centre.

The fiction of the dragon illustrates our idea of socially committed architecture that can live with the children and change with them. Our intention was to offer the children depth, intensity and diversity, and achieve a situation in which the children would be motivated to grasp the architecture for themselves. As it happened, the children were enthusiastic about the interactive models during design stage. One girl was thrilled about the light which, she insisted, "sprayed her". When the modification was finished, another girl said she was happy that there was a dragon. For her fantasy was reality and the new atmosphere could be felt so clearly that she could put it in words. It is precisely the children's reactions during the design stages and after completion that confirmed to us the value of explicitly integrating the atmospheric effects of architecture into architectural design and constantly reflecting on it and verifying it during construction, i.e. bringing objective and subjective architecture into harmony.

NOTES
(1) Gernot Böhme, *Atmosphären*, Frankfurt 1995.
(2) August Endell, *Die Schönheit der großen Stadt*, Berlin 1908, p. 51.
(3) l.c.
(4) Baupiloten: Frank Drenckhahn, Johannes Gutsch, Gordana Jakimovska, Nils Ruf, Urs Walter.
(5) Baupiloten: Julie Baumann, Jenny Brockmann, Nikolai Erichsen, Franziska Fischer, Danile Hülseweg, Stefan Kels, Uta Schrameyer.
(6) Every class appoints a representative in the parliament after the third school year.

Werkzeug Workshop Haut / Tool Workshop Skin SoSe 2004

WORKSHOP HAUT

Eine Gruppe von Studierenden und Lehrenden steht an einem sonnigen Frühlingstag vor dem TU-Gebäude der Fakultät Architektur. Eine große Schiebetür der Fassade, 2 x 2,20 m, ist geöffnet. Abwechselnd passen verschiedene Gruppen von vier bis fünf Studierenden ihre eigenen Elemente in die Öffnung ein und stellen sich dicht dahinter in den Innenbereich des Studenten-Cafes »A«.
Vor der Fassade schütten verschiedene Personen immer wieder Eimer voll Wasser gegen die eingepasste Haut.
Dahinter ertönen Aufschreie der Bearbeiter/innen, bis sie nach einigen Minuten, meist durchnässt, durch eine Öffnung ihres Elementes nach außen schlüpfen. Der Wassertest wiederholt sich, bis alle 20 Gruppen ihre Fassadenhaut erprobt haben.
Nachdem die Studierenden ein Semester lang ein hybrides Gebäude zum Arbeiten und Wohnen entworfen haben, sollten sie dieses Projekt im letzten Abschnitt ihres Grundstudiums bis ins Detail vertiefen. Der erste von vier einwöchigen Workshops am Beginn des 4. Semesters beinhaltete das Thema Haut.
Die Studierenden skizzierten innerhalb kurzer Zeit ein Konzept für eine Fassade mit Öffnung, die sie in einer Woche als Ausschnitt bauten. Die Details für ihre Gebäudehaut entwickelten sie nach dem Test im Maßstab 1:1 als Zeichnung. [EK]

WORKSHOP SKIN

One sunny spring day, a group of students and tutors is standing outside the TU building of the Faculty of Architecture. A large sliding door 2 x 2.2 m) in the façade is opened. In sequence, different groups of 4–5 students fit their own elements into the opening and take up position right behind it inside the Student Cafe A.
In front of the façade, various people keep emptying buckets of water against the adjusted skin. Behind them are the resounding cries of male and female "arrangers", until after a few minutes later, and mostly wet through, they slip out through an opening in their element. The water test is repeated until all 20 groups have tested out their façade skin.
Once the students have spent a whole semester designing a hybrid building to work and live in, in the last phase of their basic studies, they are expected to follow up this project down to the last detail. The first of four one-week workshops early in the 4th semester posed "skin" as its theme. Within a limited time the students drafted out a design for a façade with an opening, which they constructed as a section within a week. After the test, they developed details of their building skin as a drawing on the scale 1:1. [EK]

Isabell Weiland, Nicole Scharf: gespannte Stoffhaut   Isabell Weiland, Nicole Scharf: Tensed fabric skin

Gunnar Behrens, Benedikt Tulinius, Christin Freier: Wabenstruktur aus Draht, mit Klarsichtfolie umwickelt   Gunnar Behrens, Benedikt Tulinius, Christin Freier: Honey-comb structure made of wire, wrapped in transparent foil

Michael Reiss, Felix Sommerlad, Franziska Streit, Thomas Sommerick, Ivonne Weichold, Alecto Krammer: Goldfolienblase in Klarsichtfolienbubble, beide mit Staubsaugerabluft aufpumpbar. Transparenz und Durchlässigkeit werden durch das Luftvolumen und den Luftdruck steuerbar.   Michael Reiss, Felix Sommerlad, Franziska Streit, Thomas Sommerick, Ivonne Weichold, Alecto Krammer: Gold foil blister in a bubble of transparent foil, both inflatable with vacuum cleaner exhaust air. Transparency and permeability is adjustable by the air-volume and air-pressure.

Ines Wegner / Transfer 1 & 2 2002/2003

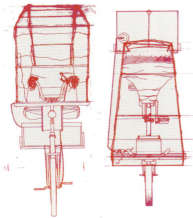

Slawamobil   *Slavamobile*

Stimmungskarte   *Mood chart*

SLAWAMOBIL

Ich verfolge eine Person auf Schritt und Tritt, ich werde ihr Schatten sein, wenigstens für einen Tag und eine Nacht. Sie ist ein Dividuum, sie lässt ihr Blut aufspalten, behält die Zellen zurück und verkauft das Plasma. Zeitweilig öffnet sie ihr verletzliches System und liiert sich mit einer Maschine und deren künstlichem System.
Die Erfahrung des Plasmaspendens indiziert eine neue Wahrnehmung vom Leben der Privatperson, des Individuums in Berlin. Der intime, persönliche Teil soll sich räumlich und bildsprachlich abzeichnen und die Person auf ihren Wegen begleiten…

SLAVAMOBILE

I follow a person's every move; I will be his shadow, at least for one day and night. The person can be divided in two, allowing his blood to be split up, yet keeping his cells and selling the plasma. Occasionally, the person opens up his vulnerable system and liaises with a machine and its artificial system.
The experience of donating plasma indicates a new perception of a private individual's life – the individual in Berlin. The intimate, personal part is to be distinguished spatially as well as in pictorial language and accompany the person on his different ways …

Pinke Welt   *Pink world*

Innenraumcollagen *Interior space collages*

Innenraum *Interior space*

SLAWAMOBIL / FLIESSENDER RAUM

...sie im Außen abgrenzen und gleichzeitig eine Schnittstelle bilden. Im ersten Semester entsteht das „Slawamobil", ein Transportmittel, ausgestattet mit persönlichen Kennzeichen und Bedarfsgegenständen der Person. Unter dem Einfluss abstrakter Innenraumcollagen im zweiten Semester erscheint mir die geschaffene Situation eher wie eine Schälung oder Häutung, bei der Persönliches nach außen projiziert und der private Raum erweitert wird. Um dies räumlich übertragen zu können und nutzbar zu machen, versuche ich mich am Raum.

SLAVAMOBILE / FLOWING SPACE

... demarcation on the outside and simultaneously forming an interface. The "Slawamobil" is created in the first semester. It is a means of transport, equipped with a personal number plate and personal items of the user. Under the influence of abstract interior space-collages in the second semester, the created situation seems to me more like a peeling or skinning process, whereby the personal element is projected towards the outside and the private space is extended. To apply this process and make use of it I make an attempt at the space.

Bauanleitung *Building instruction*

Schnitte *Sections*

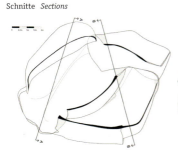  

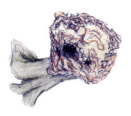 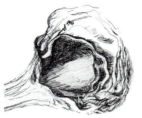  

Innenraumskizzen *Interior space sketches*

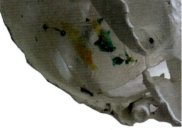  

Bewegtes Modell *Dynamic model*

FLIESSENDER RAUM

Der imaginierte Raum löst die Grenzen zwischen Innen und Außen auf. Die Raumgrenzen bergen Zwischenräume, Wahrscheinlichkeitsräume, Übergangsräume.
Das Gebilde ist ein Möglichkeitsraum, seine Bestandteile sollen nach dem Menschen geformt sein und auf ihn eingehen. Im Innenraum befinden sich Häute, die als Möbel, raumteilende oder -verbindende Segmente funktionieren und den Raum strukturieren, ihm eine Stimmung geben. Die Umsetzung ist für die Konstruktion der Schalen mit Glasfaserkunststoffen und für die Häute mit einer Kombination von Technogel und verstärkten Kunststofffolien denkbar.

FLOWING SPACE

The imagined space dissolves the boundaries between inside and outside. The spatial boundaries conceal intervening, probable and transitory spaces.
The construction is a potential room; its integral parts are to be formed in accordance with the human individual and to accommodate it. The interior space carries skins that serve as furniture and room dividers or connecting segments that structure the space, giving it atmosphere. This can be applied to the construction of the pod with fibre-glass plastics and for the skins with a combination of Technogel and reinforced plastic sheets.

 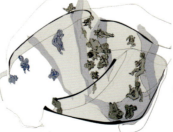 

Szene 1–3 *Scene 1–3*   Szene 4 *Scene 4*   Szene 5 *Scene 5*

Theaterversuch
Garcin, Ines und Estelle werden sich ihrer Zuschauerrolle bewusst. Gleiches gilt für die Anwesenden, die sich ihrer Zuschauerrolle annehmen und (Szene 4) diese nicht im herkömmlichen Sinne vorfinden. Es setzen Verfolgen, Sehen- und Hörenwollen ein. Mit der Aktivität von Handlung und Darstellern nimmt die Bewegung der Zuschauer im Raum zu, bis sich schließlich (Szene 5) eine vollkommene räumliche Durchmischung beider Parteien einstellt.

Attempt at theatre
Garcin, Ines and Estelle become aware of their role as spectators. So do the others that are present, accepting their role as spectators (Scene 4) but find it unusual. A desire sets in to pursue, see and hear. Due to the activity of the plot and the actors, the movement of the spectators in the room increases, until finally (scene 5), a perfect spatial intermingling of both parties emerges.

Erweiterter Privatraum *Extended private space*   Bewegter Raum *Dynamic space*

Modellzeichnungen *Model drawings*   Collage *Collage*

SZENARIO

Die Schalen bestehen aus GFK, an den krafteinleitenden Stellen, wie Gelenken und Aufhängungen, mit Carbonfasern verstärkt. Die Häute bestehen aus Weich-PVC-Folie – innen verschweißt, außen doppelt gelegt. Ihr Hohlraum ist mit zwei verschiedenen Flüssigkeiten gefüllt, die nicht einander, dafür aber jeweils einen anderen Farbstoff lösen. Die Aufhängungen für die Häute sind mit Carbonfasern in die Schalen eingebettet und sorgen für flexible Anbringungsmöglichkeiten.
Die Füße sind entweder sehr schwer und dadurch ausreichend standfest oder funktionieren als eine Art pneumatischer Saugfuß. Denkbar wäre auch ein Klebeeffekt, der den Geckofüßen nachempfunden ist: Die unzähligen Haare an ihren Füßen verästeln sich und sind so mikroskopisch klein, dass van-der-Wals-Kräfte wirksam werden.

SCENARIO

The pods consist of fibre-glass plastic, reinforced with carbon fibres at the power-injecting places like limbs and mounts. The skins consist of soft PVC sheets – welded on the inside and double-layered on the outside. Its hollow space is filled with two different liquids that do not dissolve each other, although they each dissolve a different colour material. The mounts for the skins are embedded with carbon fibres into the shells and ensure flexibility for alternative mountings.
Either the feet are very heavy and thus given sufficient stability, or else they function as a kind of pneumatic suction pad. A gluing effect would be similar, as if the feet of a gecko were being imitated: the countless hairs under their feet spread out like tiny branches and are so microscopically small that van-der-Wals powers come into effect.

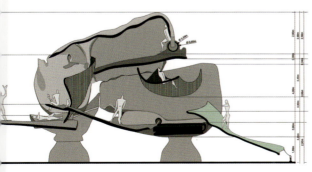 

1 Kugellager
2 nach Montage mit Epoxydharz verkleben
3 Metallring in GFK-Schalung eingebettet
4 schwerer Fuß / pneumatischer Saugnapf

1 Ball-bearing
2 Glued with epoxy resin after assembly
3 Metal ring embedded in fibre-glass plastic pod
4 Heavy foot / pneumatic suction pad

Werkzeug Workshop Touch / Tool Workshop Touch SoSe 2004

WORKSHOP TOUCH

An einem Nachmittag waren im Architekturgebäude der TU Berlin und im angrenzenden Außenraum zahlreiche Objekte und Installationen zu erleben. Diese hatten vor allem eine Gemeinsamkeit: Sie waren in vielerlei Hinsicht körperlich erfahrbar; sie wollten erfühlt, betastet, berührt, begangen werden.

Sie wurden von den Studierenden im Rahmen eines einwöchigen Workshops in Kleingruppen konzipiert, im Maßstab 1:1 gebaut und präsentiert.

Wie in dem eine Woche vorher abgehaltenen Workshop „Haut" (siehe Seite 210f.) hatten die Studierenden auch hier Gelegenheit, ihre im Vorfeld entwickelten Entwurfsprojekte auf ihre taktilen Qualitäten hin zu überprüfen. Manche haben eher ein prototypisches Detail entwickelt, dass zu dem jeweiligen Entwurfskonzept passt. Andere haben damit eine konkrete räumliche Situation in ihrem Entwurfsprojekt weiterentwickelt und überprüft. Nach dem Workshop wurden die Arbeiten in Karten dokumentiert und sind daraufhin in die Detailüberlegungen zu den Entwurfsprojekten eingeflossen.
[PG]

WORKSHOP TOUCH

One afternoon, numerous objects and installations were explored in the architectural building of the TU-Berlin and in the adjoining outside space. All these had primarily one factor in common: in many respects they could be experienced physically; they needed to be felt, handled, touched, and used.

In the context of a one-week workshop in small groups, the students conceived the project, constructed and presented it on a scale of 1:1.

As in the previously held workshop, "Skin" (cf p. 210f.), here, too, students had the opportunity to test the tactile qualities of their provisionally worked-out design-projects on actual textiles. Several students had preferred to develop a prototype detail, which would fit in with the overall design concept. Others chose to continue developing and testing out a concrete spatial situation in their design-project. After the workshop, the details of all the pieces of work were documented on cards and subsequently had a bearing on the design-projects.
[PG]

Franziska Streit, Keeser Tülay: Luftballongefederter „Reinschlüpfsack"

Franziska Streit, Keeser Tülay: "Slip-in Sleeping Bag"

Christin Freier, Oliver Gaßner, Lena Köppen: „Anschmiegelandschaft" aus Einweghandschuhen, überall anzubringen

Christin Freier, Oliver Gaßner, Lena Köppen: "Caressable Landscape" from one-way gloves, to be applied everywhere

Carsten Smolik, Verda Sindiran, Alireza Shalviri: „Entspannungsmöbel", Spannkonstruktion aus Fahrradschläuchen

Carsten Smolik, Verda Sindiran, Alireza Shalviri: "Furniture to relax into", self-assembly construction out of bicycle tyre tubes

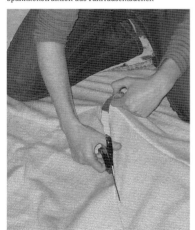 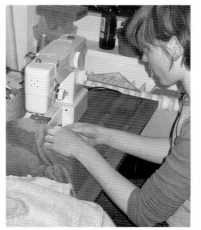 

Franziska Streit, Keeser Tülay: Luftballongefederter „Reinschlüpfsack"

Franziska Streit, Keeser Tülay: "Slip-in Sleeping Bag" with air-balloon springs

Paul Grundei

Aktive Träume

Wie alle zwei Jahre drängten sich auch diesmal wieder 360 „Frischlinge" zur Einführungsveranstaltung für das Grundstudium im größten Hörsaal der Fakultät. Neben zwei weiteren Fachgebieten erläuterten wir vom Team k_studio das bevorstehende Programm. Unser Professor, Lutz Kandel, überraschte uns und die übrigen Anwesenden mit einem schlichten Satz: „Die Häuser, von denen Sie träumen, sind alle schon gebaut." Falls die Erstsemester tatsächlich schon von Häusern geträumt hatten, so waren sie jetzt verunsichert. Sollten ihre Häuserträume hier nicht methodische Unterstützung erhalten?

Vielleicht ist Prof. Kandels Satz eine Absage an das von den Medien kreierte Klischee vom Architekten als sonnengebräuntem, Cabrio fahrendem Golfspieler; doch ist inzwischen diese Vorstellung für die meisten Architekten ohnehin gründlich überholt. Vielleicht ist der Satz auch als Kritik an der Strategie des „konzeptuellen Entwerfens" zu verstehen, die sich in Mitteleuropa spätestens in den 1990er Jahren als konsequente Trägerplattform der Gedankenwelt von Architekten etabliert hat. Das „konzeptuelle Entwerfen", so kritisieren es die Medien mitunter gerne, sei lediglich eine Legitimation für die Selbstverwirklichung von Architekten. Dabei wird jedoch übersehen, dass das Arbeiten mit dem methodischen Apparat „Konzept" die Ressourcen und Arbeitsweisen von Architekten mittlerweile um wesentliche, zeitgemäße Aspekte erweitert hat.

In der gleichen Einführungsveranstaltung sagte Prof. Kandel später: „Sie lernen, zu einem Problem, von dessen Lösung Sie zunächst keine Ahnung haben, Informationen zu beschaffen und zu ordnen, Lösungsvorschläge zu entwickeln, diese zu präsentieren und zu bewerten." Die Studierenden sollten also weiterhin von Häusern träumen, aber „aktiv". Aktiv träumen meint, den Prozess des Träumens bewusst zu gestalten, seine Bestandteile zu definieren, zu erforschen, zu überprüfen, darzustellen und zu kommunizieren. Ausgangspunkt ist dabei immer wieder das sorgfältige Auswählen, Analysieren und Dokumentieren von entwurfsbestimmenden Ressourcen und Parametern. Für wen und für welche Situation möchte ich eigentlich an welchem Ort träumen? Wie kann ich relevante Informationen aus anderen Wissensgebieten beschaffen und in die Arbeit einbinden? Wie können (Zwischen-)Ergebnisse im Arbeitsprozess mit zeitgemäßen Mitteln kommuniziert werden? Der Dialog mit den eigenen Grundlagen ist hier kein Vorgang, der einleitend behandelt und dann abgeschlossen werden kann, sondern einer, der den Entwicklungsprozess kontinuierlich bereichert. Bei vielen Projekten führt erst eine experimentelle Herangehensweise zu den gewünschten (Forschungs-)Ergebnissen. Solche Experimente wurden im k_studio in vielerlei Hinsicht durchgeführt: als Projekte im Maßstab 1:1[(1)], als Tragkonstruktions-, als Fassaden-, als Material- und als Modellexperimente zur Erforschung der Raumwahrnehmung u.a.m.[(2)]

Methodische Fertigkeiten werden im k_studio immer anhand der individuellen, kontinuierlich weiterentwickelten Semester- oder Jahresprojekte der Studierenden vermittelt. Gerade durch diesen Bezug auf das eigene „Konzept" aktivieren die Studierenden mitunter erstaunliche Energien in der Aneignung methodischer Fähigkeiten

Active Dreams

As always happens at two-yearly intervals, this time 360 freshmen again thronged into the induction event for the new intake of students in the faculty's large auditorium. In addition to representatives speaking from two other disciplines, as members of k_studio we also described the forthcoming programme. Our professor, Lutz Kandel, astonished us and the others present with a simple sentence: "The houses you dream about are already all built". If the freshmen had already dreamt about houses, they now felt insecure. Were their "dream-houses" here not to be given methodical support?

Perhaps Prof. Kandel's words were a disclaimer of the media-generated cliché of the architect as a suntanned golfer, who drives a convertible; though in recent years this image is already well out of date for most architects. Perhaps, the sentence should also be understood as a criticism of the strategy of "conceptual design", which established itself in Central Europe by the 1990's at the latest as a logical basis of architects' thinking. "Conceptual Design" – as the media often liked to complain – is merely an excuse for architects' self-fulfilment. This reaction overlooks the fact that working with the methodical apparatus "concept" has recently expanded architects' resources and working methods by indispensable, up-to-date methods.

In the same introductory event Prof. Kandel went on to say: "You will learn to gather and classify information about a problem whose solution will initially not even be remotely clear to you; you will also learn how to develop, present and evaluate suggested solutions." In other words, the students should go on dreaming about houses – but "actively".  To dream actively means to give your dreams a concrete form, to define their constituent parts, to research, check, depict and communicate them. As ever, the starting-point here is the meticulous selection, analysis and documentation of design-determining resources and parameters. For whom, for what situation, and in what location do I really wish to dream? How can I acquire relevant information from other fields of knowledge – and build them into the work? How can intermediary results obtained during the working process be communicated by contemporary means? The dialogue with one's own basic principles is not a mere procedure, which can be treated as an introductory component and then concluded, but rather one that never stops enriching the process of development. In many projects an initially experimental approach leads to the desired (research) goals. This kind of experiment has been carried out in the k_studio in many different forms – as 1:1 projects[1], as experiments in load-bearing structures, façades, and in material and model experiments exploring our perception of space and so forth.[2]

In the k_studio methodical skills are always conveyed on the strength of the students' individual, continuously evolving project work per semester or per year. Precisely through this reference to their own "concept", the students, for their part, activate extraordinary energies in acquiring methodical abilities and in devel-

und in der Weiterentwicklung ihrer Projekte im Hinblick auf eine Vielzahl von technischen und rechtlichen Fragen, die sich in der konsequenten Durcharbeitung stellen. Die enge Kooperation mit engagierten Sonderfachgebieten der Fakultät und weiteren Spezialisten ist dafür unumgänglich. Erst so können die Studierenden jene integrativen Fähigkeiten trainieren, die von ihnen im Berufsleben auch weiterhin erwartet werden[3]. Wenn „Raumkunst" die plausible Entwicklung und Verdichtung aller wahrnehmbaren Parameter eines Gebäudes beschreibt, so kann diese erst unter solchen Bedingungen simuliert werden.

Das Anforderungsspektrum für den Generalistenberuf Architekt[4] hat sich in den letzten Jahrzehnten in vielen Feldern erweitert: Im Bereich der Visualisierung haben die Gestaltungsmöglichkeiten und -anforderungen enorm zugenommen, bautechnische Systeme werden immer komplexer. Gleichzeitig müssen Architekten, zumindest in Mitteleuropa, immer häufiger die allgemeine Abnahme handwerklicher Fähigkeiten der am Bau Beteiligten kompensieren. Folglich entwickeln sich im Berufsfeld Spezialisierungen – die Qualität der uns alltäglich umgebenden, gebauten Umwelt leidet darunter.

Architekten beginnen, auch öffentlich ihr Generalistendasein zu beklagen. Dabei ist es gerade diese Integrationsfähigkeit, dieses „aktive Träumen", das ihre Kernkompetenz beschreibt: in einem prozesshaften Ablauf den inhaltlichen Bogen „von der ersten Skizze bis zur letzten Schraube" spannen zu können. Bei Studierenden sind Lehrangebote, in denen sie Realisierungsprojekte in allen Leistungsphasen durcharbeiten, zurzeit sehr gefragt.[5]

Beim bisherigen Modell „Projektstudium" stand in den ersten Semestern des Diplomstudiengangs das Entwurfsprojekt im integrativen Zentrum aller Lehrveranstaltungen. Dadurch wurden vernetzte und prozessorientierte Lehrkonzepte zumindest theoretisch begünstigt. Erfahrungsberichte aus höheren Semestern zeigen, dass diese Entwurfsprojekte möglichst schon ab Studienbeginn angeboten werden sollten, weil die Studierenden auf einer solchen methodischen Basis ihre Fähigkeiten kontinuierlich aufbauen können. Mit der Einführung des neuen Bachelor-Studiengangs im Herbst 2005, in dem eine vereinfachte, nach Einzelfächern isolierte, konservative Grundlagenausbildung vorgesehen ist[6], werden solche Lehrangebote weitestgehend undurchführbar.

„Konzepte werden erst dann tragfähig, wenn sie sich in der konsequenten Weiterentwicklung zu Gebäuden bewähren", hieß es schon am Ende meines Studiums. Mit dieser Aussage ist keineswegs die Forderung verbunden, das Denken in Gebäudekonzepten abzutun oder (Ausbildungs-)Wege zum architektonischen Entwurf zu simplifizieren, sondern vielmehr diese Wege konsequent zu einem tragfähigen Architekturkonzept zu entwickeln und dabei nicht außer Acht zu lassen, dass sich in diesen Konzepten potentielle Aktionsmöglichkeiten für Benutzer entfalten können.

ANMERKUNGEN
(1) Vgl. dazu: Wolfgang Grillitschs Beitrag: *1:1,* Seite 222ff.
(2) Vgl. dazu: die Darstellung der methodischen Werkzeuge *Skin,* Seite 210f., und *Touch,* Seite 216f.
(3) Vgl. dazu: Harald Klofts Beitrag: *Engineering Free Forms,* Seite 232ff.
(4) Vgl. dazu auch: Lutz Kandels Beitrag: *Der neue Architekt,* Seite 290ff.
(5) Vgl. dazu: Susanne Hofmanns Beitrag: *Spürbare Architektur,* Seite 200ff.
(6) Vgl. dazu auch: Editorial, Seite 8ff.

oping their projects further with regard to a multitude of technical and legal issues arising from a thorough exploration. For this purpose, close cooperation with committed specialist institutes and other experts is crucial. Only thus can the students train those integrative abilities which will be expected of them subsequently in professional life[3]. Assuming that "the art of space" describes the plausible development and concentration of all the perceivable parameters in a given building, these can only be simulated under such conditions.

Over the last decades, the range of demands made upon the all-round profession of architect, as usually defined[4], has widened in several respects. In the field of visualisation, for instance, the opportunities and demands for creation have increased enormously, with civil engineering systems also becoming more and more complex. At the same time architects – at least in Central Europe – have to compensate more and more often for the general decline in craft skills on the part of construction-workers. As a result, they are developing specialisms within their professional field – and the quality of those buildings that ordinarily surround us has suffered accordingly.

Architects have recently begun – even publicly – to bewail their all-round profession. Yet precisely this ability for integration, or "active dreaming" describes their core competence to follow through a lengthy process and thus complete the substantive work required: "from the first sketch right down to the last screw". At present, those courses that offer the opportunity to finish projects that can be worked through at all phases of achievement are in high demand with the students.[5]

According to the "project-study" model as it has hitherto existed, in the early semesters of the diploma course the design project has been at the integrative centre of all teaching. This has at the very least corroborated and, in theory, favoured complex, process-oriented teaching concepts. Experience reports from later semesters indicate that these design projects should be offered as soon as possible after studies start, because students can go on building up their abilities on this kind of methodical basis. With the introduction of the new Bachelor degree in autumn, 2005, which foresees a simplified, more conservative basic grounding – hived off into single subject areas[6] – teaching opportunities like this will be all but impossible to offer.

"Concepts can only be workable, if they prove themselves under sustained refinement as buildings" – I already heard at the end of my course. This statement is in no way linked to the demand to disregard thinking dealing with building concepts or to simplify (educational) pathways leading to architectonic design. What it does say, is that these pathways must be developed into a valid concept of architecture, without – in the process – forgetting that these concepts might also contain potential activities for users.

NOTES
(1) Cf. Wolfgang Grillitsch's article: *1:1*, pp. 222ff.
(2) Cf. the description of methodical tools in *Skin*, pp. 210f. and *Touch*, pp. 216f.
(3) Cf. Harald Kloft's article, *Engineering Free Forms*, pp. 232ff.
(4) Cf. also Lutz Kandel's article: *The New Architect*, pp. 290ff.
(5) Cf. Susanne Hofmann's article: *Sensuos Architecture*, pp. 200 ff.
(6) Cf. also: *Editorial*, p. 8ff.

Wolfgang Grillitsch

1:1

... Something more academic would have been a big bore. [1]

Review

Ein Gastkritiker und zwei Assistenten sitzen ratlos um die Studentin herum. Sie präsentierte ein sehr gelungenes Projekt. Sie hat aus der Beobachtung des Tagesablaufs einer Tagesmutter einen idealen Raum entwickelt, der dann auf einem konkreten Grundstück in ein zu entwerfendes Gebäude – überlagert mit einer zusätzlichen Funktion – eingebaut wurde. Die Studentin löste das zweisemestrige Entwurfsprogramm, indem sie eine Kindertagesstätte mit einer Bibliothek kombinierte. Die freie Formensprache des idealen Raums wurde konsequent und überzeugend weiterentwickelt, sie verwob sich im Entwurfsprozess mit dem Raumprogramm zu einem Gebäude. Aber keiner in der Runde der Kritiker sagt etwas zum Projekt, alle hatten sich nach 16 Projekten verbal verausgabt. Einem Tutor fällt es ein, er versucht, die schweigende Runde zu erlösen: „Was hier noch fehlt, ist ein Detail. Ich meine, wie das Gebäude vom Boden rauskommt. Schwebt es darüber, liegt es auf etwas auf? Hat es einen Sockel? Ein Gebäude wächst nicht einfach so wie ein Pilz aus dem Boden." Sicherlich hat der Tutor, genauso wie fast jeder, der Architektur studiert hat, diesen Spruch selbst einmal während des Studiums zu hören bekommen. Ein Detail muss her. Woher nehmen, natürlich stehlen, das heißt: kopieren. Ein Standarddetail abzeichnen. Aber genau das wollen die Lehrenden nicht haben. Details sind für sie wie die Gene der Architektur. In ihnen steckt die Information, wie das Haus einmal ausschauen wird. Sie haben aber auch sehr viel damit zu tun, ob es kostengünstig oder teuer wird, ob es hineinregnet oder ein behagliches Raumklima entsteht, ob das Haus lange hält oder ob das temporäre Gebilde

Verkleidung eines Baumes mit Mahagony-Imitat

Covering a Tree with Imitation Mahogany

1:1

... *Something more academic would have been a big bore.* [1]

Review

A guest critic and two tutors sit cluelessly around the female student. She presented a very successful project. She developed an ideal room from observing the day of a child minder, which was then built into a concrete property in the design of a building, superimposed with an additional function. The student solved the one-year design programme, by combining a day nursery with a library. The free use of forms of the ideal room was developed further in a consistent and convincing way. In the development process they intertwined with the development programme to form a building. However, no one in the round of the critics said anything about the project. After 16 projects they had all over-exerted themselves verbally. One student assistant notices. He tries to rescue the silent round: "What is still missing here is a detail. I mean, how the building arises from the ground. Does it float above it? Does it lie on something? Does it have a base? A building does not just grow out of the ground like a mushroom." Surely the student got to hear this saying himself at least once during his studies, just like almost everyone who studied architecture. We have to have a detail. But where do we take it from - of course steal, or copy. Copying a standard detail? That is precisely what the teaching staff doesn't want to have. For them, details are like the gene of architecture. They contain the information, how the house will once look. However, they also have a lot to do with whether it will be cost-effective or expensive, whether it rains in or a cosy room climate arises, whether the house has a

Detail
Detail

leicht zerlegbar und wiederverwendbar ist. Es ist wichtig, etwas über Details zu lernen, aber schwierig, weil dies ein so komplexes Feld ist. Im Grundstudium bleibt für das Entwickeln von Details oft wenig Zeit. Was nützt es, Details zu beherrschen, wenn man nicht entwerfen kann.

Learning by doing

Lehrangebote, die das Arbeiten im Maßstab 1:1 anbieten, sind immer wieder eine Chance, Realität mit Planspiel, Lehre mit Forschung zu koppeln. Und sie verfügen über weit mehr Potential, als es das Erlernen einer Detailplanung aus Büchern hat. „Gerade in einer Zeit, die fraglich erscheinen lässt, ob es für die im Wesentlichen auf die Gestaltung von Objekten ausgebildeten Studierenden auch eine ausreichende Zahl zu gestaltender Objekte geben wird, und die im Zuge der „Schrumpfung" erkennen lässt, dass auch andere Qualifikationen, wie zum Beispiel die Gestaltung von Prozessen und Aktionen, zunehmend an Bedeutung gewinnen, scheint mir die Verstärkung des Ansatzes *learning by doing* notwendig. Aus dieser Erkenntnis wurden von meinem Fachgebiet in den letzten Jahren verstärkt Aufgabenstellungen gewählt, die Innovationsgeist, soziale Phantasie, Selbstständigkeit und Selbstverantwortlichkeit in hohem Maße herausfordern. Tugenden, die in meinem Verständnis universitäres Lernen und Forschen charakterisieren." [2]

Links: Tischler
Mitte: Haustechniker
Rechts: Trockenbauer

Left: Joiner
Center: House-technician
Right: "Drywaller"

1:1-Lehrangebote sind keine Neuerfindung. Bei Frank Lloyd Wright's School of Architecture in „Taliesin West" begannen und beginnen noch heute die Studierenden ihre Ausbildung mit einem Zeltaufenthalt in der Wüste, um im Bauexperiment ihr eigenes temporäres Haus zu errichten. Es gibt also schon seit langem viele unterschiedliche Einsatzgebiete für 1:1-Projekte und Versuche innerhalb der universitären Ausbildung und Forschung von 1:1-Projekten und Versuchen. 1:1 kann in fast alle Unterrichtsfächer der Architekturausbildung integriert werden, weil sich die für ein Projekt erforderlichen Kompetenzen notwendigerweise von selbst verbinden, wie bei den *Baupiloten* im Durchlaufen „aller Bauphasen – vom konzeptionellen Entwurf über das Überzeugen des Bauherrn mit entsprechenden Darstellungen bis hin zur Realisierung bei knappen Budgetvorgaben." [3]

1:1 in der Lehre bildet eine Brücke zur Praxis und hat überaus interdisziplinäres Potenzial. Erfolgreich fertig gestellte 1:1-Projekte überzeugen von selbst, das hilft den Universitäten auch, öffentliche Aufmerksamkeit zu erlangen: Sei es, dass für ein Bauwerk Auftraggeber außerhalb der Universität existieren oder dass mittels Initiativprojekten Institutionen oder Gruppierungen mit Architektur „beglückt" werden. Aber auch die Präsenz und das Agieren im öffentlichen Raum erzeugen diese Aufmerksamkeit.

long life or the temporary construction can be easily dismounted and reused. It is important to learn something about details, but difficult because it is such a complex field. Often, in basic courses little time remains for developing details. What use is mastering details, if you can't design.

Learning by doing

Again and again, teaching opportunities offer work on a 1:1 scale. It is an opportunity to couple reality with experimental game, and theory with research. They also have far more potential than learning detailed planning from books has. "It seems to me, that the reinforcing of the *learning-by-doing* approach is necessary precisely a time in which it seems doubtful whether there will also be enough objects for the students to design - students who are essentially trained to design objects, and where we can discern in the course of the 'contraction' that other qualifications, such as designing processes and actions, become increasingly more important. From this finding, formulations were increasingly chosen from my branch over the last years, ones considerably challenging innovative spirit, social fantasy, independence and self-responsibility. Virtues that characterize university learning and research in my understanding." [2]

1:1 teaching opportunities are no new discovery. Students at Frank Lloyd Wright's School of Architecture in Taliesin West started, and today still start, their

  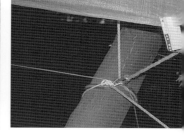

education with a stay in a tent, so as to construct their own temporary house in the desert in a construction experiment. Consequently, for quite a while there have been many different fields of application within university education and research from 1:1 projects and trials. 1:1 can be integrated in almost all subjects in architecture education. This is because the skills required for a project are necessarily automatically combined, as with the *building pilots* in running through "all the building phases, from conception design to convincing the builder-owner with corresponding depiction, right up to realization with a tight budget." [3]

Links: Konstrukteur
Mitte: Fundament
Rechts: Zugseile

Left: Builder
Center: Foundation
Right: Draw rope

In teaching, 1:1 forms a bridge with practice and has extensive interdisciplinary potential. Successfully completed 1:1 projects automatically convince. That also helps universities achieve public attention, be it because some building clients exist outside the university or that institutions or groups are made happy thanks to initiative projects with architecture. However, being and operating in the public area can also produce this attention.

We can now return once more to the one-year design task described at the start. Isn't "observing the day of a child minder" or "analysing the location" by going out and seeing what really happens, also working at a 1:1 scale? Design pro-

Noch einmal zur anfangs geschilderten Zweisemester-Entwurfsaufgabe: Ist „die Beobachtung des Tagesablaufs einer Tagesmutter" oder „die Analyse des Orts", indem man rausgeht und nachschaut, was tatsächlich passiert, nicht auch Arbeiten im Maßstab 1:1? Stecken in einer Systematisierung dieser Schritte, die immer wieder in Entwurfsprogrammen von den Studierenden gefordert werden, nicht Themen für Forschung innerhalb der Lehre? Es gibt zahlreiche Methoden, auch in benachbarten Disziplinen, die man in die Architekturlehre integrieren kann. Da die Zeit für Forschung künftig sicher eher weniger als mehr wird, ist es sinnvoll, Ausbildung und Forschung so weit wie möglich zu verschmelzen. Buckminster Fuller hat dies im Rahmen von 1:1-Projekten sehr zielgerichtet getan: „Nahtlos geht seine Forschungsarbeit in eine Modellierungsarbeit mit Studierenden über. (...) Fuller hat die Gabe, die Studenten zu begeistern und sie zu echten Innovationen und Erfindungen zu stimulieren." [4] Das multipolare Tensegrity-Prinzip wurde von Fullers Studenten Kenneth Snelson entdeckt.

Das 47-Stunden-Haus

In einem komprimierten Zeitrahmen geriet der *47-Stunden-Haus*-Workshop[5] zum bausportlichen Intensivtraining. Eine hyperkonkrete Aufgabenstellung und der Verzicht auf eine lange Entwurfsphase schaffen einen schnellen Einstieg für alle 20, in fünf Teams tätigen Studierenden. Die verzweigten Stämme eines Baumes am Campus mussten mit einer drei Meter hohen Mahagonivertäfelung verbaut werden. Das Trockenbauteam erstellte eine freistehende, skulpturale Wand mit einem Eingangstunnel, einer überdachten Bar und vielen anderen angepassten Einbauten. Eine von der Konstrukteurgruppe errichtete Zeltplanenkonstruktion aus mit Seilen verspannten Druckstäben komplettierte das offene *47-Stunden-Haus*. Die Haustechnik-Crew entwickelte ein Lichtkonzept mit vielen, in die anderen Gewerke verbauten Lichteffekten. All diese Abhängigkeiten der einzelnen Teams untereinander zu koordinieren, gehörte zu den Aufgaben des Generalplanerteams, das die Zeitabläufe überwachte und fehlende Materialien sowie Werkzeuge in letzter Sekunde organisierte. Sehr bewusst wurden die Vorgaben in der Aufgabenstellung so formuliert, dass sie erst einmal die Möglichkeiten beschränkten. Aber das *47-Stunden-Haus* überzeugte am Ende nicht nur durch seinen schnellen Aufbau – an allen Ecken und Enden waren material- und themengerechte Detaillösungen als sichtbare Zeugen des energiegeladenen Entstehungsprozesses abzulesen.

Durch die Energie des Machens entsteht ein gruppendynamischer Prozess, das Arbeiten im Maßstab 1:1 wirkt überaus motivierend auf die Studierenden und lehrt Teamgeist. Andrew Freear von den *Rural Studios* sagte dazu in einem Interview: „Dabei machen sie alles, sie heben Fundamente aus, machen die Betonarbeiten, ziehen Böden ein, bauen Dächer, installieren sanitäre Einrichtungen und legen Stromleitungen. Sie arbeiten 24 Stunden am Tag." [6] Es hat im Fall der *Rural Studios* auch damit zu tun, dass die Projekte in einem anspruchsvollen sozialen Kontext partizipartiv mit den Bauherren entwickelt werden, was natürlich nur in Lehrprogrammen geht, die mehr als nur einen Workshop umfassen.

Das Wissen verteilt sich gut, „skills are shared, expertise is won in doing, and standing achieved by word-of-mouth." [7] Manche der Studierenden haben noch nie eine Bohrmaschine in der Hand gehalten. Andere sind ausgebildete Zimmerleute oder

grammes demand these steps from the students again and again. Doesn't their systematization contain themes for research within the teaching? There are numerous methods, from neighbouring disciplines too, which we can integrate into the science of architecture. In future, there will certainly be less time for research rather than more, so it makes sense to merge education and research as far as possible. Buckminster Fuller did this very purposefully within 1:1 projects: "There was a smooth transition from his research work to the modelling work with students. (...) Fuller has the gift of filling students with enthusiasm and stimulating them to true innovations and inventions." [4] Fuller's student Kenneth Snelson discovered the multi-polar Tensegrity Principle.

The 47-hour house

In a compressed time framework, the *47-hour house* workshop [5] developed into intensive training for construction sport. The 20 students working in five teams all received a rapid introduction thanks to the hyper-concrete terms of reference and the renunciation of a long design phase. The twisted trunk of a tree on the campus had to be used in building three-metre high mahogany panelling. The dry construction team prepared a freestanding sculptural wall with an entrance tunnel, a covered bar and many other fitted fittings. A tarpaulin construction made from compressed rods tensed with ropes constructed by the designer group completed the open *47-hour house*. The mechanical services crew developed a light concept with many lighting effects constructed by other craftsmen. The general planner team was responsible for coordinating all of these dependencies among the individual teams. It supervised the timing and organized missing materials and tools at the last second. The tasks in the terms of reference were very deliberately formulated such that it first restricted the possibilities. In the end, however, the *47-hour house* didn't just convince because of the rapid construction. Wherever you look, you can read detail solutions suitable for the material and theme as visible witnesses of the energy-laden process of origin.

A group-dynamic process arises from the energy generated by doing something. Working at a 1:1 scale has an extremely motivating effect on the students and teaches them team spirit. Andrew Freear from the *Rural Studios* talked about this in an interview: "In the process they do everything, they dig foundations, do the concrete work, put in floors, build roofs, install sanitary equipment and lay electric cables. They work 24 hours a day."[6] In the case of the *Rural Studios* it also has something to do with the projects being developed participatively with the client in an ambitious social context, which naturally only works in teaching programmes which contain more than just one workshop.

The knowledge spreads well, "skills are shared, expertise is won in doing, and standing achieved by word-of-mouth." [7] Some of the students have never held a drill in their hand. Others are trained carpenters or additionally earn their money as dry builders – as was the case with one student of the *47-hour house* – and bring along their own machines. One person learns movements by watching others. Or no one can do it perfectly and everyone just tries. The failure of one's own construction ideas is also a part. The path from the idea to implementation is a short one

verdienen ihr Geld nebenher als Trockenbauer, wie es bei einem Studenten vom *47-Stunden-Haus* der Fall war, und bringen ihre eigenen Maschinen mit. Der eine schaut sich dann die Handgriffe vom anderen ab. Oder keiner kann es perfekt und man versucht es einfach. Auch das Scheitern einiger Konstruktionsideen gehört mit dazu. Der Weg von der Idee zur Umsetzung ist ein kurzer, und die Ergebnisse aktivieren einen Lerneffekt, der sich jedem Studierenden nachhaltig einprägt. Dieses direkte Lernen erzeugt Erfahrung. Weil es über die Simulation in einem Planspiel hinausgeht, offenbart sich die Komplexität der Abläufe, die der Umsetzung eines architektonischen Werks zugrunde liegen. So mussten zum Beispiel die Überlagerung von verschiedenen Gewerken (sprich: Projektteams) geklärt werden. Die Studierenden organisierten das Material- und sonstiges Sponsoring, sie telefonierten mit Baumaterialhändlern sowie Firmen und organisierten die Infrastruktur vor Ort, wie zum Beispiel einen Stromanschluss auf der Wiese. Hier stecken genau die Potentiale, die weiterentwickelt werden können.

Bis jetzt sind die meisten 1:1-Abteilungen der Universitäten nur mit geringen finanziellen Mitteln ausgestattet. Häufig handelt sich lediglich um Übungen, die – weil unterschätzt – nur ab und zu im Rahmen von Workshops angeboten werden. Dabei bekäme man dafür sogar relativ leicht die nötigen Mittel: Die Baustoffindustrie ist daran interessiert, dass die Studierenden ihre Produkte einsetzen und lernen, damit umzuge-

Links: Erstellen des Rohbaues
Mitte: Spannen der Planen
Rechts: Begutachtung

Left: Construction work
Center: Erecting the textile structure
Right: Examination

hen. Da real gebaut wird, stellen die Ergebnisse oft auch einen monetären Wert dar. Wie jeder weiß, der selbst einmal ein Low-Budget- Projekt realisiert hat, bekommt man leichter Sponsorengelder, wenn bereits ein Teil der Finanzierung steht. Diese Anschubfinanzierung ist bei einem 1:1-Workshop immer vorhanden: 20 Studierende arbeiten täglich acht Stunden, die bei einer Firma mindestens 30 Euro kosten, was täglich 160 Stunden zu je 30 Euro, also 4.800 Euro pro Tag ergibt. Ein Zehntages-zehntägiger Workshop mit 20 Studierenden verfügt also über ein Arbeitsleistungspotenzial von 48.000 Euro. Peter Fattinger, Assistent an der TU Wien, bewies beispielhaft, wie dieses Modell funktioniert, indem er die Bestückung des Transitraums am Flughafen Wien-Schwechat mit Schlafkojen initiierte. Bis dahin mussten die Asylbewerber dort auf Wartebänken aus Lochblech schlafen. Das österreichische Innenministerium sprang mit 5.000 Euro Unterstützung ein, die nur für das nötige Material verwendet werden. „Hätte man eine Firma damit beauftragt", so Fattinger, „hätte es das Zehnfache gekostet."

1:1 bietet viel, was man in anderen Maßstäben nicht ausprobieren kann. Die Formel dafür lautet: 1:1=Testen. Man kann Architektur in Benutzung testen, den Entwurf erleben und Erfahrung sammeln, wie der gebaute Raum von anderen Menschen wahrgenommen wird. „Die Praxis ist der Prüfer: Sind die Zimmer gut, stimmt die

and the results activate a learning effect, which has a lasting effect on every student. This direct learning creates experience. The complexities of the processes underlying implementation of architectonic work reveal themselves because it expands beyond simulation into an experimental game. So for example, the overlapping of diverse craftsmen (i.e. project teams) had to be settled. The students organized the material and other sponsoring; they telephoned with construction material traders and firms and organized the on-site infrastructure, such as an electrical connection in the country. Here are precisely the potentials, which can be further developed.

So far, most 1:1 departments at universities have had only limited financial means. Because they are underestimated it is often just a matter of exercises, which are only offered from time to time within workshops. This is despite the fact that it is relatively easy to obtain the necessary means. The building materials' industry is interested in students using their products and so learning how to handle them. Since building really occurs, the results also often represent a monetary value. Anyone who has once realized a low-budget project himself or herself knows that it is easier to obtain sponsors' money when you already have part of the financing. This knock-on financing always exists with a 1:1-workshop. Twenty students work eight hours daily, which would cost at least 30 Euros each with a firm,

 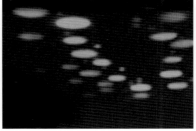 

making 160 hours at 30 Euros, i.e. 4,800 Euros each day. That means a ten-day workshop with 20 students has at their disposal a job performance potential of 48,000 Euros. Peter Fattinger, tutor at the TU Vienna, proved with an example how this model functions by initiating the equipping of the transit lounge at Vienna-Schwechat Airport with bunks. Until then, people seeking asylum had to sleep on waiting benches made of punched plate. The Austrian Ministry of the Interior helped out with 5,000 Euros support, which is only used for the necessary material. "If they had engaged a firm to do it," says Fattinger, "then it would have cost ten times the amount." *(8)*

Links: Einweihung
Mitte: Eingangsbeleuchtung
Rechts: Barbeleuchtung

Left: Inauguration
Center: Entrance area
Right: Bar lights

1:1 offers much of what you cannot try at other scales. The formula for this is 1:1 = test. You can test architecture in use, experience drafting and gather experience, how other people perceive the constructed space. "Practice is the tester: are the rooms good, is the insolation correct, how does the community live, does the rain get in, how high are the room's heating costs?"*(9)* Self-construction teaches how something is made, and makes it easier to assess the costs, the material and job performance required by the construction work. "It is important to understand how heavy a piece of wood is, which you must transport to the build-

Besonnung, wie lebt die Gemeinschaft, regnet es hinein, wie hoch sind die Heizkosten des Zimmers?" *(9)* Der Selbstbau lehrt, wie etwas gemacht wird, und macht den Aufwand, den Bauarbeiten an Material und Arbeitsleistung erfordern, besser einschätzbar. „Es ist wichtig zu verstehen, wie schwer ein Stück Holz ist, das man auf den Bauplatz transportieren und hier anbringen muss. Man lernt die Situation der Arbeiter zu begreifen, indem man selbst umsetzt, was man gezeichnet hat und merkt, wie schwierig es ist, etwas Schönes entstehen zu lassen." *(6)*

1:1-trainierte Studierende sind besser für die Zeit nach dem Studium ausgebildet, unabhängig davon, ob ihre spätere Kariere in Großbüros, im eigenen Büro oder in Lehre und Forschung stattfindet. Die 1:1-Praxis lehrt Improvisationsvermögen und die Fähigkeit, Projekte durchzuziehen. Dies befähigt auch dazu, den Architektenberuf so auszuüben, dass man nicht verhungern muss, falls es gerade wieder einmal nichts zu bauen gibt.

ANMERKUNGEN

(1) Escher, Frank (Hg.): *John Lautner, Architect,* London 1994
John Lautner, im Interview mit Frank Escher. John Lautner war Student bei Frank Lloyd Wright in Taliesin West. Weitere Statements von Lautner im Interview zu 1:1:
„Oh, yeah. Physical labor, yeah. That was part of – everything was part of learning for architecture and that's the way he felt about it, and I think it's absolutely the best. Architecture should be concerned with everything in life, so when you know how to build it physically, and then you know what stone is good for, you know what wood's good for, you know, what to plan for, you know, what to design (...) And everything was basic and nothing to be repeated and nothing routine, nothing."

(2) Technische Universität Darmstadt (Hg.): *Sichten 2004,* Technische Universität Darmstadt, Ernst Wasmuth Verlag Tübingen, 2004: Essay von Professor Stephan Goerner: learning by doing. Im selben Katalog, im Essay „reality bites" von Dipl.-Ing. Oliver Langbein, findet sich zum Thema 1:1: „Auch größere konkrete Bauaufgaben eignen sich durchaus für die Lehre. Einige Hochbau Fachgebiete denken über das Modell ‚teaching office' nach. (...) Bei wirklich großen Projekten ist die ‚Portionierung' der Aufgaben für die Lehre eine schwierige Sache. Wie im Büro eine mehr oder weniger zufällige Wegstrecke des Projektes zu begleiten, kann es auch nicht sein. Einfacher sind kleine Projekte in den Studienalltag zu integrieren, wie bspw. die beiden OSA-Workshops ‚strom' 2003 und ‚mapping' 2004. In beiden Fällen handelte es sich um konkrete Aufträge, die in der Lehre mit Studenten realisiert wurden."

(3) www.baupiloten.com. Textauszüge aus der Homepage des Instituts: „*Baupiloten* sind eine Gruppe von Studierenden, die unter der Leitung von Susanne Hofmann in ihrem Architekturstudium eine Baumaßnahme realisieren. Mit der Gründung dieser Einrichtung reagiert die Architektin auf die von Seiten der berufsständischen Organisationen beklagte Praxisuntauglichkeit der Absolventen."

(4) Krause, Joachim/Lichtenstein, Claude (Hg.): *Your Private Sky. R. Buckminster Fuller. Design als Kunst einer Wissenschaft.* Hrsg. Joachim Krausse und Claudia Lichtenstein, Verlag Lars Müller, Museum für Gestaltung Zürich, 1999

(5) 47- Stunden-Haus, Gecekondu Workshop, gemeinsam mit Benjamin Foerster-Baldenius studio_k, Technische Universität Berlin 2000, mit Studierenden des Grundstudiums, Organisation: Elke Knöss mit Gesa Büttner. Mit der freundlichen und großzügigen Unterstützung der Firma Kapella Baustoffe in Berlin, die das gesamte Material gespendet hat.

(6) Fezer, Jesko/Heyden, Mathias: *HIER ENTSTEHT. Strategien partizipativer Architektur und räumlicher Aneignung.* Hrsg. Jesko Fezer und Mathias Heyden, Berlin, b_books 2004; Auszüge aus dem Interview mit Andrew Freear, *Rural Studio*.

(7) Moos, David/ Trechsel, Gail (Hg.): *Samuel Mockbee and the Rural Studio: Community Architecture.* Birmingham 2003 Museum of Art, Hrsg. David Moos und Gail Trechsel; Auszug aus dem Beitrag von John Forney

(8) Aus: Falter, 50/01 vom 12.12.2001, Wochenzeitung, Wien
Peter Fattinger ist wissenschaftlicher Mitarbeiter am Institut für Architektur + Entwerfen, e253/2 an der Technischen Universität Wien.

(9) Hübner, Peter/Sulzer, Peter: *Lernen durch Selberbauen.* Peter Hübner, Peter Sulzer, Karlsruhe 1983 *Bauhäusle, Selbstbau einer studentischen Wohnanlage am Institut für Baukonstruktion, Universität Stuttgart*

ing site and put up here. You learn to understand the situation of the workers, by realizing yourself what you delineated, and notice how difficult it is to let something beautiful be built." [6]

1:1-trained students are better educated for the time after studying, independently of whether their later career occurs in offices, in their own office or in teaching and research. The 1:1 practice teaches the ability to improvise and the ability to get through projects. This also qualifies you to exercise the architectural profession such that you don't have to starve, if there is currently nothing to build again.

NOTES

[1] *John Lautner, Architect*, Ed. Frank Escher, Artemis, London 1994
John Lautner, in an interview with Frank Escher. John Lautner was a student at Frank Lloyd Wright in Taliesin West. Further statements from Lautner in an interview to 1:1:
"Oh, yeah. Physical labor, yeah. That was part of – everything was part of learning for architecture and that's the way he felt about it, and I think it's absolutely the best. Architecture should be concerned with everything in life, so when you know how to build it physically, and then you know what stone is good for, you know what wood's good for, you know what to plan for, you know what to design. ... And everything was basic and nothing to be repeated and nothing routine, nothing."

[2] *Sichten 2004*, Technische Universität Darmstadt, Ernst Wasmuth Publishers Tuebingen, 2004: Essay from Professor Stephan Goerner: learning by doing,
In the same catalogue, in the essay reality bites, Dipl.-Ing. Oliver Langbein writes the following about 1:1: "Even larger concrete construction tasks are definitely suitable for teaching. A few surface engineering fields are considering the 'teaching office' model. ... one difficult thing with really large projects is 'portioning' the tasks for teaching. As in the office, it also can't be a matter of accompanying a more or less coincidental stretch of the project. It is easier to integrate small projects into study routine, as for example both the OSA Workshops 'electricity' 2003 and 'mapping' 2004. In both cases it was specific tasks, which were realized in teaching with students."

[3] Text excerpts from the homepage of the institute:
Baupiloten (construction pilots) are a group of students who are realizing a building measure in their architecture studies under the guidance of Susanne Hofmann. The architect founded this service in reaction to professional organizations complaining about graduates' incompetence.

[4] *Your Private Sky, R. Buckminster Fuller, Design als Kunst einer Wissenschaft*, Ed. Joachim Krausse and Claudia Lichtenstein, Lars Müller Publishers, Museum für Gestaltung Zurich, 1999.

[5] *47 Stundenhaus*, Gecekondu-Workshop, together with Bejamin Foerster-Baldenius, TU Berlin 2000, Field Prof. Kandel, Faculty VII, with students from the basic course, organisation: Elke Knöss with Gesa Büttner. Many thanks to the company Kapella Baustoffe, which has generously donated the material for this workshop.

[6] *HIER ENTSTEHT, Strategien partizipativer Architektur und räumlicher Aneignung*, Ed. Jesko Fezer and Mathias Heyden, Berlin, b_books 2004, Excerpts from the interview with Andrew Freear, Rural Studio.

[7] *Samuel Mockbee and the Rural Studio: Community Architecture*, 2003 Birmingham Museum of Art, Edd. David Moos and Gail Trechsel, Excerpts from the contribution from John Forney.

[8] From: Falter, 50/01 from 12th December 2001, Wochenzeitung, Vienna.
Peter Fattinger is scientific assistant at the Institute for Architecture + Design, e253/2 at the TU Vienna.

[9] *Lernen durch Selberbauen*, Peter Hübner, Peter Sulzer, Karlsruhe 1983.
Bauhäusle, Selbstbau einer studentischen Wohnanlage am Institut für Baukonstruktion, Universität Stuttgart

Harald Kloft

Tragwerksplanung gekrümmter Formen

Die vergangenen Jahre haben die formale Freiheit der Architektur wesentlich erweitert. Durch die entstandene digitale Design- und Fertigungsumgebung wurde – in Kombination mit neuen Materialien – ein vollkommen neues Repertoire der Formensprache möglich. Gewagt gekrümmte Formen, die vor einigen Jahren noch als unrealisierbar galten und von denen als „pure Fantasien"[1] geträumt wurde, können heute gebaut werden.

Jedes geometrisch komplexe Projekt stellt unterschiedliche Herausforderungen an den Tragwerksentwurf und führt zu unterschiedlichen digitalen Arbeitsprozessen. In dieser Studie möchte ich meine Erfahrungen mit der Formengenerierung, dem Tragwerksentwurf und der Realisierung von „freien Formen" anhand zweier Projekte[2] mit verschiedenen Architekten aufzeigen. Das erste Projekt ist der so genannte *Bubble*[3] von Bernhard Franken, das zweite Projekt ist das von Peter Cook und Colin Fournier entworfene neue Kunsthaus Graz in Österreich. Beide Projekte sind insofern radikal, als dass alle Beteiligten – Auftraggeber, Planer und Firmen – im Glauben an die Realisierung visionärer Architektur das Risiko eingingen, Neuland zu betreten.

Der Formbildungsprozess

Architekten und Ingenieure der vorangegangenen Generation wie Frei Otto und Heinz Isler haben komplexe Formen durch Experimente mit maßstabsgerecht gebauten Modellen entwickelt. Dementsprechend war die Bandbreite des architektonischen Ent-

Bubble - BMW-Pavillon auf der Interationalen Automobilausstellung IAA in Frankfurt am Main, 1999

Bubble - Pavillion for BMW at the International Automobile Exhibiton IAA in Frankfurt am Main, 1999

Engineering Curved Shapes

Recent years have brought an extension of formal freedom in architecture. The emerging digital design and production environment, combined with new materials and modern technologies, makes possible unprecedented challenges in the repertoire of formal language. Boldly curved shapes, a few years ago regarded as unrealizable and dreamed as "pure fantasies"[1], can now be built.

Each geometrically complex project presents different challenges for structural design and can result in different digital working processes. In this study I would like to explore my experiences on form generation, structural design and manufacturing issues of two free-form projects[2] in collaboration with different architects: the first project is the so-called *Bubble*[3] by Bernhard Franken, the second project is the new *Kunsthaus Graz*, Austria, designed by Peter Cook and Colin Fournier. Both projects are radical in the way all participants – clients, planning parties and contracted firms – risked failure for believing in the idea of realizing visionary architecture.

Form Generation Process

For architects working in earlier times, like Frei Otto and Heinz Isler, complex forms were developed in experiments with scaled physical models. As a result, the range of formal structural design was limited by and shaped according to the laws of gravity. Today digital models are produced in "form generation" processes defined by the specific parameters of the architect's design. Generating a digital

Kunsthaus Graz,
fertiggestellt im September 2003

Kunsthaus Graz (Graz Art Gallery), completed September, 2003

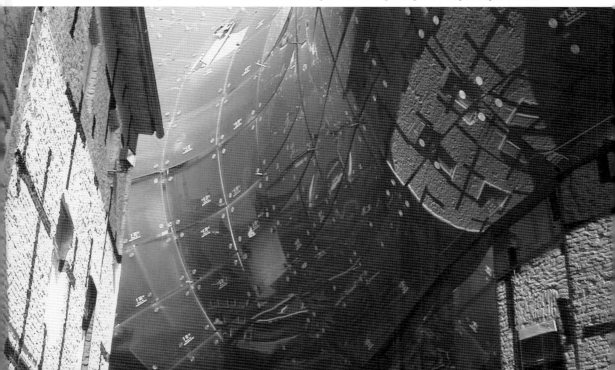

wurfs, den Gesetzen der Schwerkraft folgend, formal begrenzt. Heute werden in Formbildungsprozessen digitale Modelle generiert, die den Architekten enorme Freiräume bei der Formensprache ermöglichen. Die Generierung digitaler Modelle hängt dabei von den Entwurfsprozessen ab, die von Architekt zu Architekt oder gar von Projekt zu Projekt deutlich variieren können.

Bubble

Für die Entwicklung der *Bubble*-Form nutzte Franken seine „parametrische Entwurfsmethode" [4] in der digitalen Umgebung der Maya-Animationssoftware [5]. Diese Methode der Formengenerierung, die bekannte physikalische Gesetze nutzt, erlaubt dem Architekten, grundstücksspezifische Parameter als virtuelle Kräfte zu programmieren. Inspiriert durch das Ausstellungsthema – Werbung für einen neuen BMW-Wasserstoffmotor – inszenierte Franken in einem zeitgesteuerten 4D-[5] Formungsprozess die Idee zweier miteinander verschmelzender Wassertropfen. Die eigentliche Form erhielt er durch das Einfrieren des Prozesses in genau dem Moment, in dem sich die beiden Tropfen auf Grund des physikalischen Gesetzes der Adhäsion miteinander verbinden wollen. Diese Form wurde – nachdem geometrische Fehler korrigiert worden waren – als dreidimen-

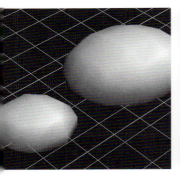
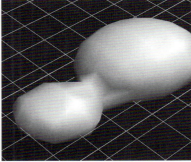
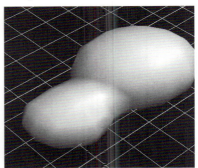

Bubble
digitaler Formgenerierungsprozess

Bubble
Process of digital form-generation

sionale „master geometry" des Projekts festgelegt und stellte während der Entwurfsentwicklung und des Herstellungsprozesses für alle am Projekt Beteiligten den dimensionalen Bezugspunkt dar, der geometrisch nicht verändert werden durfte.

Kunsthaus Graz

Der Entwurf von Peter Cook und Colin Fournier steht für einen anderen Ansatz. Der Entwurf wurde nicht primär am Computer entwickelt. Die Architekten formten für den Wettbewerb skulptural ein manuelles Gießharzmodell aus einem Stück. Die Proportionen des Wettbewerbsentwurfs, der später als „Friendly Alien" bekannt werden sollte, wurden durch die Besonderheiten des Grundstücks in der Grazer Altstadt mit ihrem typischen Gewirr von roten Dachlandschaften inspiriert.

Im Gegensatz zum *Bubble*-Projekt resultierte aus diesem „manuellen Entwurfsprozess" keine dreidimensionale „master geometry". Um eine digitale Version des Wettbewerbsmodells herzustellen, dachten die Architekten und Ingenieure zunächst daran, das Originalmodell in 3D[6] zu scannen. Um jedoch die optimale Form bezüglich des Tragwerks und der Materialien zu entwickeln, entschied man sich dann, ein digitales Modell von Grund auf mit Hilfe der Rhinocerous-3D-Modell-Software neu

model depends on the design processes, which vary distinctly from one architect to another or even from project to project.

Bubble

Franken's bubble form was generated using his "parametric-design-method" in the digital environment of the Maya animation software[4]. This form-generation method, utilizing known physical laws, allowed Franken to programmme site specific parameters into virtual forces. For the bubble form, Franken set up a time-based (4D)[5] modelling process of two water drops coming together, inspired by the promotional theme for the exhibition of a new BMW hydrogen engine. The actual form was achieved by freezing the process at the moment the two drops unite due to the physical laws of adhesion. This shape, corrected for geometrical errors, established the 3D "master geometry" of the project. It provided the dimensional reference for all project participants during the design development and manufacturing process and was not allowed to change geometrically.

Kunsthaus Graz

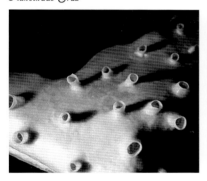 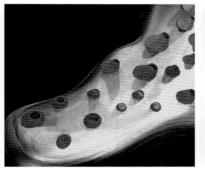 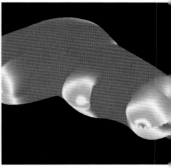

Peter Cook's and Colin Fournier's design illustrates a different approach. Here the design did not rely heavily on computers, and the architects actually sculpted by hand the final physical model in one piece. The proportions of what would later be known as the "friendly alien" were inspired by the site in the old part of Graz with its typical maze of red-colored roofs.

Unlike the bubble project, this "manual design process" did not produce a 3D master geometry. To create a digital version of the physical competition model, the architects and engineers initially thought to scan the original model in 3D[6]. However, in order to develop the best form in terms of structure and materials, it was then decided to digitally re-build the model from scratch using Rhinocerous 3D modeling software. The digital model captured the design intent of the original scheme and included all relevant structural design variables allowing the engineers to better address structural behavior and manufacturing issues.

Kunsthaus Graz
Links: Latexmodell als Negativform für das manuelle Gießharzmodell
Mitte und rechts: digital erzeugte 3D-Modelle

Kunsthaus Graz
Left: Latex model as a mould for the competition model
Centre and right: Digital 3D-models

Structural Design

What are the implications of the different form generation processes for structural design? As a "single-layer-based" design method, the digital model consists of

aufzubauen. Das generierte digitale Modell bildete die Entwurfsabsicht des Originals ab und beinhaltete alle geometrisch relevanten Daten des Wettbewerbsentwurfs. Dies ermöglichte es den Ingenieuren, das Tragwerksverhalten zu optimieren und die Form auf die Fertigungstechniken abzustimmen.

Tragwerksentwurf

Welche Auswirkung haben die beschriebenen verschiedenen Formbildungsprozesse für den Tragwerksentwurf? Ein computergeneriertes, digitales Modell besteht aus Schichten, die hinsichtlich ihrer Funktion, Dicke und Zuordnung (Innen-, Außen- oder Zwischenschicht) sowie ihrer Materialität nicht definiert sind. Für den Tragwerksentwurf können in einem digitalen, integralen Planungsprozess zwei grundsätzliche Optimierungsebenen unterschieden werden. Die erste Ebene zielt auf die geometrische Optimierung der Form, das heißt die Entwicklung eines formaktiven Tragwerks. Ideal ist eine Form, die sich wie eine Schale verhält und nur geringe Biegespannungen aufweist. In diesem Zusammenhang sind die Formfindungsexperimente Antoni Gaudís für die Kirche Sagrada Familia berühmt geworden. In der zweiten Optimierungsebene wird

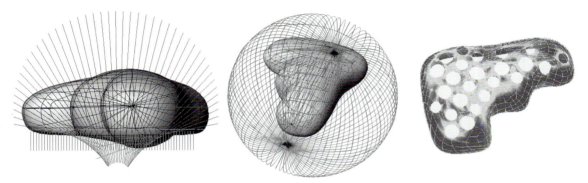

Kunsthaus Graz
Links: FE-Untersuchung des Tragverhaltens
Mitte und rechts: Erzeugung der Tragstruktur

Kunsthaus Graz
Left: FE-Analysis of the structural behaviour
Centre and right: generation of the structure

die geometrische Form materialisiert, und der Geometrie werden die entsprechenden Materialkennwerte und Steifigkeiten zugewiesen.

Der Tragwerksentwurf ist schließlich ein iterativer Prozess der Abstimmung zwischen Form, Material und Steifigkeiten. Mit Hilfe analytischer Softwaretools wie Finite Elemente- und 3D-Vektorframework-Programmen kann dann ein Tragwerk mehr oder weniger in eine bestimmte geometrische Form gebracht werden.

Der Bubble

Bei Frankens *Bubble* war das vorrangige Ziel der Architektur, die dynamische Balance der sich vereinenden Wassertropfen und somit die Idee der Form als „gefrorenem Moment"[7] abzubilden. Hierzu wurde eine „master geometry" definiert, die während des Formbildungsprozesses keinen geometrischen Modifikationen unterworfen werden durfte.

Als Konsequenz entwickelten die Architekten und Ingenieure zwei Optionen für den Tragwerksentwurf: entweder die Realisierung eines Primärtragwerks, auf dem eine zweite, nicht tragende Außenhaut aufliegt, oder die Außenhaut ist selbsttragend, so dass sie als Hülle und Tragwerk in einem wirkt. Solch ein „skin deep"-Tragwerk[8]

layers that are not defined according to function (whether the layer is an inside-, outside-, or in-between-layer), thickness or material. However, structural design is a process that from the beginning must take into account the various practical demands that are placed on it from all participants in the design process.

In such an integrated, multi-party planning process, two critical aspects emerge. First and foremost, the structure must be engineered to behave with organic, shell-like characteristics. The ideal is a form which represents the rules of stress flow. Famous in this context are the form finding investigations of Antoni Gaudí represented by an obsessive series of physical models for the church of Sagrada Familia in Barcelona. Secondly, the correct materials must be selected in defining the form and joint strength of the structure.

Designing a structure that suits the architectural intention then becomes a matter of iteration. Analytical software tools, like finite elements and spatial vector framework programs, presuppose definitions of mathematical and mechanical conditions. For example, the mechanical ability to move the points of intersection defined geometrically in the architectural model must be defined in the analytical software. Depending on the mechanical conditions, one can more or less force a structural system into a given geometrical form.

Bubble

In Franken's *Bubble* a single layer skin defined the generated form – the "master geometry." Since the "master geometry" was fixed and not subject to structural modifications during the form generation process, it supported the primary aim of the architecture to convey the dynamic balance of unifying water drops and thus the idea that form is only a "frozen moment".[7]

Accordingly, the architects and engineers faced two structural design options: design the primary load-bearing system to support a secondary and non-structural skin, or design the skin itself to serve as the primary load-bearing system. Such a "skin-deep"[8] structure functions like a shell where internal and external layers are one and the same and where the structure is defined purely by its material thickness. In order to emulate a water drop, the design team elected to develop a surface-structure defined by a single, transparent material. The consequences of this decision will be described later.

Kunsthaus Graz

The architectural and engineering design team created the digital model of the geometry for the Kunsthaus in the design development phase by translating the conceptual competition scheme into a digital environment. Whereas Franken's digitally generated "master geometry" was fixed and did not allow for formal alterations, Peter Cook and Colin Fournier supported designing the structure via careful changes to the overall shape. In this way the structural behavior was allowed to influence the final geometry.

For the complex roof of the Kunsthaus, the structural system was designed as a system of tubular steel members that supported an outer layer of acrylic glass panels with complex shapes. The external skin was designed as a

funktioniert wie eine Schale, bei der Innen- und Außenschicht ein und dasselbe sind und deren Struktur lediglich durch die Stärke des Materials bestimmt ist. Um wirklichkeitsnah die Idee eines Wassertropfens abzubilden, entschied sich das Entwurfsteam, eine Struktur aus einem einzigen, transparenten Material zu entwickeln, die gleichzeitig trägt und einhüllt. Die Konsequenzen dieser Entscheidung werden später beschrieben.

Kunsthaus Graz

Das Entwurfsteam aus Architekten und Ingenieuren überführte, wie zuvor beschrieben, das manuelle Wettbewerbsmodell in ein digitales 3D-Modell. Während Frankens digital generierte Form als master geometry festgelegt war und keine formalen Veränderungen zuließ, unterstützen Peter Cook und Colin Fournier die Optimierung des Tragwerkverhaltens durch behutsame Veränderungen der Form. Für das komplexe Dach des Kunsthauses wurde schließlich ein formbildendes, räumliches Stabtragwerk aus Stahl entworfen, das nach außen mit einer hinterlüfteten Hülle aus Acrylglas bekleidet wird.

Die Elemente des Stabtragwerks wurden in einem schubsteifen, triangulierten Muster angeordnet und wirken als hybrides Tragsystem, das das Tragverhalten von Schalenstrukturen und Biegesystemen verbindet. Das provokative Wettbewerbsversprechen, eine ambitionierte Form mit einer „transparenten Außenhaut" als bautechnisch funktionierendes System zu entwerfen, das zudem die funktionalen Anforderungen an ein Kunsthaus erfüllt, konnte in dem vorgegebenen Zeit- und Kostenrahmen nur bedingt umgesetzt werden. Die Erfahrung zeigt, dass es für solch ein ehrgeiziges Projekt ratsam ist, sich auf wenige, innovative Aspekte zu konzentrieren, wie die zweifach gekrümmte, warmverformte Außenhaut aus Acrylglas, die bei einem Bauvorhaben dieser Größenordnung und Form noch nie vorher realisiert wurde.

Material und Form

Jeder, der geometrisch komplexe Formen bauen möchte, wird mit dem Mangel an geeigneten Materialien und Produktionstechniken konfrontiert. Da solche Bauten im Grunde Prototypen sind, kann man nur selten auf geeignete industrielle Herstellungsverfahren zugreifen. Die Realisierung zweifach gekrümmter Formen und gefalteter Oberflächen stellt immer eine Herausforderung an die Kreativität von Architekten, Ingenieuren und Baufirmen dar und kann nur durch die Einbeziehung neuer Technologien erreicht werden.

Die nun folgende Schilderung der Realisierung des Bubble-Projekts liefert ein exzellentes Beispiel für den Idealismus und den Aufwand bei der Herstellung komplexer Formen.

Bubble

Meine erste Begegnung mit Bernhard Franken war amüsant. Obwohl er stolz ein Holzmodell präsentierte, das aus einem Stück CNC-gefräst war, wollte er es doch in einem „imaginären" transparenten Material verwirklichen, um die Idee und Form eines Wassertropfens zu vermitteln. Nachdem die Umsetzung durch eine triangulierte Glasoberfläche verworfen wurde, verfolgte man zwei Strategien: erstens mit pneumatischen Konstruktionen zu arbeiten, die mit Luftdruck von innen die Form von

series of discrete layers, each responding to a specific set of functional requirements. The structural layer, consisting of members arranged in a triangulated pattern in response to the need for structural stiffness, was designed as a hybrid structural system combining the behavior of shell structures and bending systems. Designing the "transparent skin" as a functioning technical system to meet the requirements of an art museum and to realize the ambitious shape was a provocative promise for the competition that was not possible to keep in reality. For such an ambitious project, it is expedient to focus on and realize one innovative aspect like the double-curved, thermally-formed outer skin of acrylic glass, which in this size and shape had never been previously built.

Material and Form

Any one seeking to design and build complex shaped surfaces will be faced with a lack of suitable materials and production techniques. Since these buildings are essentially prototypes, one cannot apply industrial processes that are suited for the production of complex forms but require large quantities in order to be

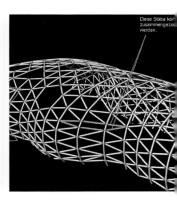

economical. Realizing doubly curved forms and folded surfaces challenges the creativity of architects, engineers and construction companies, and it is only achievable by the integration of new technologies. The following description of how the *Bubble* project was produced serves as an excellent example of the costs involved in the manufacturing of complex shapes.

Kunsthaus Graz
Links: Wettbewerbsmodell aus Gießharz
Mitte: Rendering mit Stahlrohrtragwerk
Rechts: Räumliches Stabwerkmodell

Kunsthaus Graz
Left: Competition model made of resin
Centre: Digital model with triangulated tubular steel structure
Right: Spatial vectorwork model

Bubble

My first meeting with Bernhard Franken was amusing. Although he proudly presented a one piece CNC-milled wooden model, he still wished to have it realized in an "imaginary" transparent material to convey the idea and shape of a water drop. Here, once all ideas concerning triangular patterned glass-surfaces were eliminated, two strategies emerged: first, to work with flexible membranes and foils to be formed by pneumatic pressure from inside, and second, to remodel flat and stiff plates out of transparent material into a double curved shape. After long discussions with the client during which the first and technically proven option was found to be unfeasible for a motor show pavilion, the focus turned to realizing a double curvature out of thermally formed acrylic glass. Together with the Austri-

Wassertropfen beschreiben, und zweitens flache, schubsteife Platten aus transparentem Material in eine zweifach gekrümmte Form zu bringen. Nachdem die erste und technisch machbare Option nach langen Diskussionen mit dem Auftraggeber als undurchführbar für einen Ausstellungspavillon abgelehnt wurde, konzentrierte man sich auf die Realisierung des *Bubble* mit zweifach gekrümmten, warmgeformten Acrylglasscheiben. Gemeinsam mit dem österreichischen Bauunternehmen Metallbau Pagitz wurde der Pavillon als eine Konstruktion entworfen, bei der die Acrylglasscheiben als Schalenkonstruktion das Primärtragwerk bilden sollten. In einem Werk in Österreich sollten die warmverformten Scheiben miteinander verklebt werden und der Bubble in zwei Teilen mit einem russischen MI-28 Hubschrauber nach Frankfurt über die Alpen geflogen werden. Dieser Plan erforderte die Digitalisierung des gesamten Prozesses vom Entwurf bis zur Konstruktion. Um die Frage der Elementierung des „Acrylpuzzles" zu lösen, wurden in der computergestützten Design-Umgebung (CAD) von CATIA[(9)] die Größen der Acrylscheiben festgelegt, und die Elemente mit ähnlichen Krümmungen auf einer PU-Form geschachtelt.

Die 25 Millimeter dicken Acrylscheiben wurden aus flachen Scheiben wie folgt in eine zweifach gekrümmte Form gebracht: Zunächst wurden Polyurethanschaumformen gefräst. Dann wurden die Acrylglasscheiben in einem Ofen auf 150 bis 160 Grad Celsius erhitzt und in die PU-Formen gelegt. Nach dem Formungsprozess wurden die einzelnen Scheiben schließlich CNC-gesteuert auf die exakte Geometrie zugeschnitten. Durch den parametrischen Entwurfsprozess konnte so jede PU-Form für fünf bis sieben individuelle Geometrien mit ähnlicher Krümmung benutzt werden. Zum Verkleben der Acrylscheiben entwarf das ausführende Unternehmen ein Gerüst aus lasergeschnittenen, hölzernen Rippen, das aus dem 3D-Modell des Bubbles als orthogonales System von ebenen Schnitten entwickelt wurde. Zeitliche und geometrische Probleme und das Temperaturverhalten des Acrylglases machten das Verkleben der Scheiben kompliziert und führten zu Terminproblemen. Dies gipfelte darin, dass nur sechs Wochen vor Eröffnung der Internationalen Autoausstellung der Plan einer Außenhaut aus Acrylglas, die als Primärtragwerksstruktur dienen sollte, verworfen wurde.

In dieser extrem kritischen Situation blieb das Entwurfsteam gefasst und entschied sich, Tragstruktur und formgebende Oberfläche zu trennen. Über Nacht wurde die Geometrie des temporären Montagegerüstes aus Sperrholz in ein Tragsystem aus schubsteif miteinander verbundenen Aluminiumrippen übertragen. Da die originären, 25 Millimeter dicken Scheiben zu schwer für eine nichttragende Außenhaut waren, wurde der gesamte Formungsprozess mit zehn Millimeter dicker Acrylglasscheiben wiederholt. Es wurde Tag und Nacht produziert. Die Acrylscheiben wurden schließlich vor Ort auf die 24 mm dicken Rippen aus Aluminium montiert und vermittelten, wie nicht anders möglich, die Intention der ursprünglichen Entwurfsidee.

Resümee

Der Bubble und das Kunsthaus Graz stellen neue Möglichkeiten des Bauens dar, die noch vor wenigen Jahren als unrealisierbar galten. Die Erfahrungen des *Bubble*-Projekts ermöglichten erst die Ausführung der zweifach gekrümmten, blauen Acrylhaut des Kunsthauses. Neben der Herausforderung an neue Bautechnologien ist die Freiheit der formalen Sprache in der Architektur viel versprechend im Hinblick auf neue

an contractor Metallbau Pagitz, the pavilion was designed as a construction of acrylic glass sheets as the primary load-bearing structure, to be glued together off-site in Austria – because of the high demands on the glued joints – and lifted in place to Frankfurt with the Russian Helicopter MI 28. This plan required that the whole process be digitized from design to construction. To "puzzle solve" the acrylic question, a parametric design process in the computer-aided design (CAD) environment of CATIA[9] determined the maximum size of the acrylic sheets to be stacked up with similar curvatures on one mould. The acrylic sheets with a thickness of 25 mm were formed from flat sheets into a double curved shape: First polyurethane foam moulds were milled, the NC Codes for the milling machine were generated with the CATIA software. Then the acrylic plates were heated to 150 to 160 degrees Celsius in an oven and formed over the moulds. After the forming process, the individual sheets were trimmed into the exact geometry. By defining a parametric design process, each mould could be used for five to seven individual geometries with similar curvature. To assemble the puzzle of the acrylic sheets, the contractor designed scaffolding out of wooden ribs, which were generated by

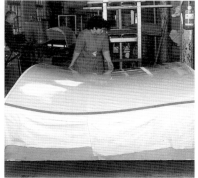

defining the double-curved surface of the *Bubble* as an orthogonal system of planes. Gluing the acrylic pieces together was complicated by geometrical and timing problems and, just six weeks before the opening of the International Motor Show, culminated in aborting the plan for an acrylic skin to serve as the primary load-bearing structure.

Still maintaining its cool in this extremely critical situation, the design team decided to separate the load-bearing structure from the formative surfaces. The geometry of the temporary plywood scaffolding was translated into a load-bearing structural system with flexural rigid connected aluminum ribs. Because the original 25 mm thick sheets were too heavy for a non-structural skin, the whole forming process was restarted with 10mm thick acrylic plates and produced day and night. The acrylic sheets were finally installed on-site over the aluminum supporting ribs and resulted in an appearance similar to the original design.

Bubble
Links: Fräsen der PU-Formen
Mitte: Acrylglasscheibe nach dem Fromungsprozess
Rechts: Holzskelett als Montagegerüst

Bubble:
Left: Milling the polyurethane forms
Centre: Finished sheet of thermally formed acrylic glass
Right: Temporary plywood scaffolding

Conclusion
The Bubble and the Kunsthaus Graz represent new opportunities in building that were regarded as unrealizable a few years ago. In fact, the *Bubble* project made it

Entwurfssynergien in der Zusammenarbeit von Architekten und Bauingenieuren. In diesem Zusammenhang sollten die Tragwerksingenieure das kreative Potential ihrer Disziplin nutzen, um die Möglichkeiten der digitalen Formgebung strukturell und materiell weiterzuentwickeln.

Für Architekten stellen die digitalen Entwurfsprozesse eine Möglichkeit dar, die ursprünglich mit ihrem Beruf verbundenen Aufgabengebiete und Verantwortlichkeiten zurückzuerobern, indem sie zukünftig die gesamte Planungsphase digital steuern. Ein wichtiger neuer Aspekt für den digitalen Arbeitsablauf ist besonders die Steuerung des Herstellungsprozesses. Analog zur Rolle des Compilers eines Computers besteht die Aufgabe, Daten der Planungsbeteiligten in digitale Maschinencodes zu übertragen. Diese Aufgabe ist hinsichtlich der Kostenfrage wichtig und entscheidend für die Realisierung frei geformter Bauten. Dieses Risiko sollten die Planer nicht den Bauunternehmen überlassen, sondern zukünftig die Verantwortung selbst übernehmen und darin Potentiale entdecken.

ANMERKUNGEN

(1) *UNstudio* – Ben van Berkel, Caroline Bos: *Seven Visions for Seven Metamorphoses*, in: *Venews* 09.04
(2) Die Projekte *Bubble* und *Kunsthaus Graz* habe ich als Projektleiter während meiner Zeit bei Bollinger + Grohmann zur Realisierung gebracht.
(3) *The Bubble* ist der Name des von Bernhard Franken (in Zusammenarbeit mit ABB Architekten) entworfenen BMW-Pavillons für die Internationale Automobilausstellung IAA 1999 in Frankfurt.
(4) *Maya* wurde von *Alias Wavefront* (http://www.aliaswavefront.com) entwickelt und auf den Markt gebracht.
(5) Diesen Begriff hat Martin Bechthold von der Harvard Design School definiert.
(6) Diese Methode wendet auch Frank O. Gehry an, um manuell gebaute Modelle zu digitalisieren. Während der Entwurfsphase bauen die Architekten eine Reihe von Modellen, die mit der computergestützten (CAD) Entwurfsumgebung von *CATIA* dreidimensional digitalisiert werden, um die Form im Hinblick auf das Raumprogramm und die örtlichen Gegebenheiten zu entwickeln.
(7) In diesem Zusammenhang merkte Bernhard Franken an, dass Deformationen Auskunft geben über die Kräfte, die für den Formbildungsprozess verantwortlich sind.
(8) Der Begriff „skin deep" wurde von Johan Bettum in einer Vorlesung an der Frankfurter Städelschule geprägt.
(9) *CATIA* ist ein 3D-Softwaretool für virtuellen Entwurf, Simulation und Analyse von industriellen Produktentwicklungen. Der Durchbruch gelang *CATIA* mit der Entwicklung der 777-Maschine der Firma Boeing in den späten Achtzigern. Dieses Flugzeug wurde vollständig mit der computergestützten Design-Umgebung (CAD) von *CATIA* entworfen.

possible to take on the double-curved blue-colored acrylic surfaces of the *Kunsthaus*. Besides the challenges in new building technologies, the freedom of formal language in architecture offers a promise of new collaborative design synergies for architects and engineers. In this context, structural engineers may exploit the creative potential of their discipline by developing the digital form generation possibilities structurally and materially.

For architects, digital design processes represent an opportunity to reclaim the spheres of activities and responsibilities of the original profession by implementing digital control of the whole planning phase. In particular, to "puzzle solve" the manufacturing process is an important new aspect to the digital workflow. Analogous to the role of a compiler in a computer, to "puzzle solve" a project is tantamount to translating all the collected data of the planning parties into detailed "machine" codes, i.e. to produce the data necessary for execution. This task is important to meet costs and crucial to realizing a free-form project. This risk should not be left to the construction company but should be taken on by the architects themselves.

Bubble: Montage und fertiger Pavillon auf der Internationalen Automobilausstellung IAA in Frankfurt am Main, 1999

Bubble: Construction on Site and Completed Pavillion at the International Automobile Exhibition IAA in Frankfurt am Main, 1999

NOTES

(1) *UNstudio* – Ben van Berkel, Caroline Bos in: *Seven Visions for Seven Metamorphoses*, Venews 09.04.
(2) I worked on these projects (*Bubble* and *Kunsthaus Graz*) as project leader in my time at Bollinger + Grohmann.
(3) *The Bubble* is the name given to the BMW pavilion project designed by Bernhard Franken (in association with ABB architects) for the 1999 International Motor Show *IAA* in Frankfurt.
(4) *Maya* is developed and marketed by *Alias Wavefront* (http://www.aliaswavefront.com).
(5) This term is formulated by Martin Bechthold from Havard Design School.
(6) This method Frank O. Gehry and his team use for digitizing their physical models. In the design phase the architects manually built a series of physical models, which were three-dimensionally digitized in the computer-aided design (CAD) environment of *CATIA* to correct and check the shape with respect to the programme and the site.
(7) Bernhard Franken expresses in this context that only deformation gives information about the forces which are responsible for the form generation process.
(8) "Skin deep" was articulated as such by Johan Bettum in a lecture at the Städelschule in Frankfurt.
(9) *CATIA* is a 3D-software tool for virtual design, simulation and analysis in industrial product processes. It is developed by the French company Dassault Systems. The breakthrough of *CATIA* goes back to the development of the 777 airplane by the Boing Company in the late 1980s. This airplane was completely designed in the computer aided design (CAD) environment of *CATIA*.

Torsten Frank

Raumnetze

Räumliche Netze sind eine eigene Gattung zugbeanspruchter Konstruktionen, die den Prinzipien des Leichtbaus unterliegen. Sie sind weltweit zu finden – allerdings bisher vor allem auf Spielplätzen als so genannte „Spiel-Raumnetze". Warum sollte ihre Anwendung als Makrostruktur für hängende Gärten, vorgespannte Seilbrücken, sei.verspannte Türme oder sogar Gebäude auch weiterhin nur planerische Vision bleiben?[1]

Räumliche Netze unterscheiden sich von den häufig anzutreffenden weit gespannten Flächentragwerken, zum Beispiel dem Münchener Olympiadach, durch ihre dreidimensionalen Tragsysteme. Die Gruppe der zugbeanspruchten Konstruktionen lässt sich in drei Kategorien einteilen: eindimensionale Linientragwerke (Schrägseilbrücken, Hängebrücken), zweidimensionale Flächentragwerke (Seilnetze, Schwergewichts-Hängedächer), dreidimensionale Raumtragwerke (Hängehäuser, Raumnetze).

Pionier auf dem Gebiet der räumlichen Netze ist der Architekt Conrad Roland, der diese Konstruktionsart seit 1962 erforscht und den Begriff „Raumnetze" geprägt hat. In zahlreichen Veröffentlichungen [2] und Vorträgen stellte er zwischen 1965 und 1969 seine visionären Entwürfe von Raumnetz-Städten dar. Ausgehend von dem Anspruch, möglichst leichte und damit Ressourcen schonende Bauweisen zu entwickeln, wurden Architekturentwürfe mit tragenden Strukturen aus Zugelementen entwickelt. Es entstanden die ersten Überlegungen für Hängehäuser, bei denen die einzelnen Geschossdecken von oben abgehängt werden und somit die Druckkräfte in wenigen Stützen von großem Querschnitt konzentriert werden. Ein Beispiel für diese Bauweise ist das Ludwig-Erhard-Haus in Berlin (Architekt: Nicholas Grimshaw & Partner 1994–1998)

Bauwerk Raumnetz-Stadt, Quelle: Ulrike Müller, 2005

Spatial-Net-City building, source: Ulrike Müller, 2005

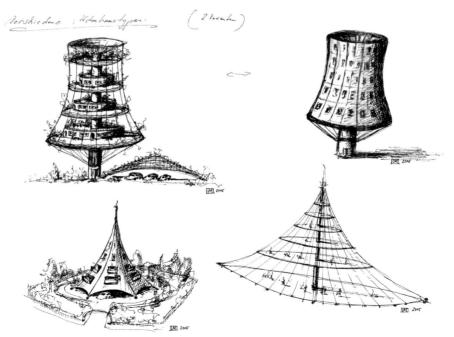

Spatial Nets

Spatial nets are a class of tensile structure in their own right. Based on the principles of lightweight construction, they can be found worldwide. So far though, they are primarily found in playgrounds as so-called playground nets. Why should their use as macrostructures in hanging gardens, pre-tensioned rope bridges, guyed towers or even buildings continue to remain just a planning vision? [1]

Spatial nets differ from the ubiquitous wide-spanning surface structures, such as the roof of the Munich Olympic Stadium, through their three-dimensional load-bearing systems. Tensile structures can be divided into three categories: one-dimensional line structures (rope-stayed bridges, hanging bridges), two-dimensional surface structures (rope-net membranes, gravity-suspension roofs), three-dimensional spatial structures (suspended houses, spatial nets)

A pioneer in the area of spatial nets is the architect Conrad Roland, who has been researching this type of construction since 1962 and first coined the term. He described his visionary designs of spatial net cities in numerous publications and lectures between 1965 and 1969. [2] Beginning with the requirement for the development of a form of construction that is as light as possible and hence economical, architectural designs were developed with load-bearing structures made from tension elements. In the first concepts for suspended houses, the individual intermediate floors were suspended from above, thus concentrating the compressive forces on a few supports with a large cross-section. One example of this style is the Ludwig-Erhard-Haus in Berlin (architect: Nicholas Grimshaw & Partner 1994-1998).

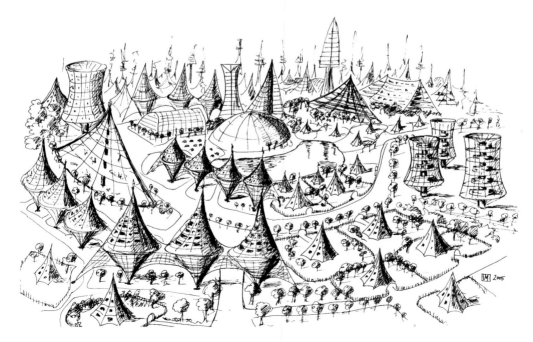

Ein hoher Grad von Entmaterialisierung wird in derartigen Systemen jedoch erst dann erreicht, wenn auch die horizontalen Flächen von gespannten, frei durchhängenden Seilnetzen gebildet werden. Wird diese Bauart auf mehreren Achsen in der Tiefe des Raums wiederholt, entsteht ein vorgespanntes räumliches Netzwerk, ein „Raumnetz". Alle wesentlichen Entwicklungen für die Anwendung solcher Konstruk-tionen als Spiel-Raumnetze wurden ebenfalls von Conrad Roland hervorgebracht (Conrad Roland Spielbau 1975-1985). Der von ihm entwickelte „Seilzirkus®", ein pyramidenförmiges Kletternetz, ist heute weltweit auf Spielplätzen (3) zu finden. Die Konstruktionsprinzipien von Raumnetzen wurden in dieser Anwendung in fast allen theoretisch denkbaren Formen baulich umgesetzt. Die Vielfalt der Spiel-Raumnetze gibt einen guten Überblick über die Möglichkeiten dieser Konstruktionen.

Raumnetze lassen sich nach der äußeren und der inneren Form kategorisieren. Für ihre äußere Form benötigen sie zur Unterstützung Masten, Stützen, Druckstäbe, Bögen oder Rahmen. Bei Spiel-Raumnetzen mit starrem Rahmen werden sämtliche Kanten aus biegesteifen Stäben gebildet. Das Raumnetz ist in den Rahmen fest eingehängt und verspannt, die Kräfte werden dabei vom Rahmen aufgenommen. Raumnetz und Rahmen bilden ein in sich geschlossenes statisches System. Bei der zweiten Gruppe werden die Form stabilisierenden Kräfte durch innere Druckstäbe aufgenommen. Die Kanten der Konstruktion werden von Seilen gebildet. Die Randseile weisen dabei die für Seilkonstruktionen typischen Krümmungslinien auf.

Im Hinblick auf die Reduzierung der biegesteifen Materialien und damit des Materialeinsatzes ist das Raumnetz mit einem einzigen zentralen Druckstab allen Kon-

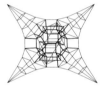 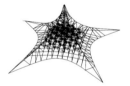 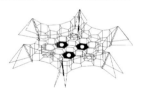

Von links nach rechts:
Spiel-Raumnetz mit äußerem starren Rahmen
Spiel-Raumnetz mit inneren Druckstäben
Spiel-Raumnetz mit zentralem Druckstab
Spiel-Raumnetz mit seitlichen Abspannpfosten

From left to right:
Playing net with rigid external frame
Playing net with internal compressed elements
Playing net with a central compressed element
Playing net with lateral anchoring posts

struktionen überlegen. An ihren Ecken benötigen solche Konstruktionen jedoch Schwergewichtsfundamente, die den gesamten Materialeinsatz erheblich erhöhen. Eine sehr viel freiere Formensprache ist durch seitlich angeordnete Abspannpfosten zu erreichen. Anzahl, Höhe und Lage der Pfosten können variiert werden. Die Abspannkräfte werden auch hier von Pfosten und Schwergewichtsfundamenten aufgenommen. Mischformen verschiedener Arten der äußeren Aufhängung und die Addition mehrerer Raumnetze sind vielfach als Spielnetze realisiert worden. Dabei können sämtliche Prinzipien miteinander vermischt werden.

Die beschriebenen Systeme benötigen zu ihrer Formstabilität Vorspannkräfte. Die Bespannung eines Tennisschlägers kann hierfür als anschauliches Beispiel herangezogen werden. Das Füllen des Volumens zwischen den äußeren Begrenzungslinien eines Raumnetzes ergibt die innere Form. Dieser Raum könnte nach dem Zufallsprinzip durch Seile gebildet werden, die sich ohne Regel im Raum treffen. Die Opuntienspinnen der Gattung Cyrtophora bauen so ihre dreidimensionalen Fangnetze. Für eine bautechnische Anwendung ist diese zufällige Bauweise sehr aufwendig, so dass auf geometrische Formen zurückgegriffen wird, wie sie auch bei Raumfachwerken aus Metall anzutreffen sind.

However, a greater degree of dematerialization in such systems will only be realised when the horizontal surfaces are also formed from stressed free-hanging rope nets. A pre-stressed spatial network - a 'spatial net' – is formed if this construction is repeated on several axes in the depth of the space. Until now, the use of spatial nets has remained limited to playgrounds. Here, all major developments were also produced by Conrad Roland (Conrad Roland Spielbau 1975-1985). Today, the 'Rope Circus'® developed by Roland, a pyramidal climbing net, can be found on playgrounds throughout the world.[3] In this application, the construction principles of spatial nets are implemented structurally in almost all theoretically conceivable forms. The diversity of the playground spatial nets is testimony to the possibilities of these constructions.

Spatial nets can be categorized according to their external and internal forms. For their external form, they require masts, supports, compression elements, arches, or frames for support. In the case of playground nets with rigid frames, all the edges are formed from rigid bars. The spatial net is securely attached to the frame and made taut. In the process, the forces are borne by the frame, and the frame and net form a self-contained static system. In the second group, the form-stabilizing forces are borne by compression elements. Ropes form the edges of the construction. The peripheral rope exhibits the lines of curvature typical of rope constructions.

The spatial net with a single central column is superior to all constructions as regards reducing the flexural rigid materials and thus the material deployment. However, such constructions require heavy foundations at their corners, substantially increasing the total material deployment. A much freer use of form can be achieved with laterally

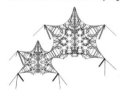 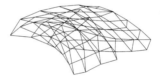 

arranged stay posts. The number, height and length of the posts can be varied. Here too, the posts and foundations bear the suspension forces. Hybrids of diverse forms of external suspension and the combination of several spatial nets are often realized as playground nets. In the process, all the principles can be used concurrently.

The systems described require tensioning forces for their stability of form. The stringing of a tennis racket is good example of this. Filling the volume between the exterior limits of a spatial net produces the inner form. This space can be formed according to the principle of random chance by the ropes, which meet in space in an irregular manner. Opuntien spiders of the genus Cyrtophora construct their three-dimensional spider nets in this way. In terms of construction practice, this method of building is elaborate and highly involved . As a result we fall back on geometrical form, evident in such structures as metal space frames.

Space-filling polyhedra allow themselves to be stacked perfectly in a space and are therefore a good geometrical starting point. Of these, the cube (hexahedron) is an example known by everyone and is thus easy to imagine. Among the polyhedra group, the blunt octahedron is the best space-filler. Its surface is lowest in relation to the filled space. Every edge in space filled with regular octahedral

Von links nach rechts:
Zweimast Spiel-Raumnetz mit zentralem Druckstab und seitlichen Abspannpfosten
Oktaederstumpf gestapelt
Oktaederstumpf verzerrt
Hexaederstumpf verzerrt

From left to right:
Two-mast playing net with central compressed element and lateral
Octahedral butt-stacked
Octahedral butt structure-distorted
Hexahedral structure-distorted

Raumfüllende Polyeder lassen sich lückenlos im Raum stapeln und sind daher eine gute Ausgangsgeometrie. Der Würfel (Hexaeder) ist hierfür ein allen bekanntes und einfach vorstellbares Beispiel. In der Gruppe der Polyeder ist der Stumpfoktaeder der beste Raumfüller. Seine Oberfläche ist im Verhältnis zum gefüllten Raum am geringsten. Im regelmäßig mit Oktaederstümpfen gefüllten Raum ist jede Kante gleich lang. Diese Struktur wird sehr häufig bei Spiel-Raumnetzen eingesetzt. Derartige Raumstrukturen müssen jedoch keineswegs regelmäßig sein. Vielmehr kann durch Verzerrung der Grundform eine Anpassung an den zu füllenden Raum erfolgen. Dies ergibt vor allem dann Sinn, wenn die äußere Form durch einen vorhandenen Raum, eine Hülle oder ein Stahlskelett vorgegeben ist.

Eine andere Herausforderung derartiger Raumstrukturen besteht in der Führung und Verknotung der im Raum verlaufenden Seile. Bei einer Hexaederstruktur ist die denkbar einfachste Lösung, Seile in x-, y- und z-Richtung durchlaufen zu lassen und jeweils drei Seile als Knoten zusammenzuführen. Die Führung von durchgehenden Seilen bei einer Oktaederstumpfstruktur bedeutet einen deutlich höheren Planungsaufwand. Die Seile verlaufen im System der Oktaeder in verschiedenen Richtungen und knicken an den Knotenpunkten ab. Die Seilführung muss jede Kante des Oktaederstumpfs genau einmal erfassen.

Spiel-Raumnetze sind weltweit zu finden. Die Übertragung der Prinzipien dieser Leichtbauweise in einen größeren Maßstab lässt jedoch noch auf sich warten. Dabei eignen sich Raumnetze zum Beispiel vorzüglich als Tragsysteme für textile Dächer. Gerade die Verwendung von sehr dünnen, sogar durchsichtigen Kunststoff-Seilen lässt Dachmembranen scheinbar schwerelos über Flächen schweben. Ein bisher wenig beachteter Vorteil dieser Konstruktionen ist das geringe Packvolumen. Derartige System sind leicht zusammenlegbar, können daher einfach vorfabriziert oder temporär verwendet werden. Dies wird überall dort besonders interessant, wo aufgrund der Transportwege oder der Umgebungsbedingungen – zum Beispiel unter Wasser – ein normaler Bauvorgang nicht möglich ist. Ein Raumnetz-Haus kann vorgefertigt und in einzelnen Teilen sogar mit dem Flugzeug verschickt werden [4]. Aussichts- oder Rettungstürme, die nur bei Bedarf aufgebaut oder ausgefahren werden, sind eine weitere Anwendungsmöglichkeit. Auch Hängebrücken wurden bisher noch nicht als vorgespanntes räumliches Netzwerk ausgebildet.

Warum sollte es nicht doch eines Tages ganze Bauwerk-Raumnetz-Städte geben, wie sie Conrad Roland beschrieben hat? Auf dem Gebiet der Bauwerk-Raumnetze sind noch Möglichkeiten offen, die bisher auf Grund der technischen Komplexität und der damit verbundenen Baukosten nicht gelöst worden sind.

ANMERKUNGEN
(1) Vergleiche IL 20, Seite 38/39
(2) siehe Literaturverzeichnis
(3) Dokumentiert unter www.corocord.de
(4) Vergleiche Roland, Conrad: *Frei Otto – Spannweiten*. S.108

QUELLEN
Roland, Conrad: *Frei Otto – Spannweiten, Ideen und Versuche zum Leichtbau*. Berlin 1965
Rühle, Hermann: *Räumliche Dachtragwerke, Konstruktion und Ausführung. Band 2*, Köln 1970
IL 8 (1975): *Netze in Natur und Technik*. Mitteilung des Instituts für leichte Flächentragwerke
IL 14 (1975): *Anpassungsfähig Bauen*. Mitteilung des Instituts für leichte Flächentragwerke
IL 20 (1979): *Aufgaben*. Mitteilung des Instituts für leichte Flächentragwerke
IL 24 (1998): *Prinzip Leichtbau*. Mitteilung des Instituts für leichte Flächentragwerke
Critchlow, Keith: *Order in Space*. London 1969

butts is equidistant. This structure is very frequently used with playground nets. However, such spatial structures do not have to be regular. Rather, the space to be filled can be modified by distorting the basic form. This makes sense primarily when the external form is predefined by an existing space, a shell or a steel skeleton. In the early stages, they tested the use of spatial nets with an octahedral butt structure as an alternative to hexahedral structure.

Another challenge with such spatial structures exists in guiding and knotting the ropes running through the space. The simplest conceivable solution with a hexahedral structure is to let ropes run through in directions x, y and z, and bring together three ropes respectively as knots. A clearly greater planning effort is required to guide the ropes through an octahedral butt structure. The ropes run in diverse directions in the octahedron system and bend at the knots. The rope must be guided so as to touch every edge of the octahedral butt only once.

Playground nets can be found throughout the world. However, we are still waiting for the principles of this lightweight construction technique to be transferred to a larger scale. Spatial nets are excellently suited, for example, as weight-carrying systems for textile roofs. It is precisely the use of very thin, even transparent plastic ropes that allows roof membranes to float in a seemingly weightless manner. A hitherto unnoticed advantage of these constructions is their low packing volume. Such systems are easily collapsible. For this reason they can be simply prefabricated or used as temporary structures. This is especially useful in situations where a normal construction process is impossible because of transport routes or environmental conditions – for example under water. A spatial net house can be prefabricated and even sent by aeroplane in separate pieces.[4] A further possible application is an observation or rescue tower, which is only constructed or extended when needed. So far, suspension bridges have not been constructed using pre-tensioned spatial nets.

Why shouldn't entire cites of spatial net buildings appear in the future, as Conrad Roland described them? There are still possibilities open in the area of spatial buildings, which remain unexploited because of the associated technical complexity and construction costs

NOTES
(1) Cf. IL 20, p.38/39
(2) See Bibliography
(3) Documented under www.corocord.de
(4) Cf. Roland, Conrad: *Frei Otto – Spannweiten*, p.108

SOURCES
Roland, Conrad: *Frei Otto – Spannweiten, Ideen und Versuche zum Leichtbau*, Ullstein Berlin Publishing House, 1965
Rühle, Hermann: *Räumliche Dachtragwerke, Konstruktion und Ausführung Vol. 2*, Verlagsgesellschaft Rudolf Müller Cologne, 1970
IL 8 (1975): *Netze in Natur und Technik*. Mitteilung des Instituts für leichte Flächentragwerke
IL 14 (1975): *Anpassungsfähig Bauen*. Mitteilung des Instituts für leichte Flächentragwerke
IL 20 (1979): *Aufgaben*. Mitteilung des Instituts für leichte Flächentragwerke
IL 24 (1998): *Prinzip Leichtbau*. Mitteilung des Instituts für leichte Flächentragwerke
Critchlow, Keith: *Order in Space*, Thames and Hudson, 1969

Jo Staudt / Urban Currents 2001/2002

Strömungsverläufe *Currents*

Verwirbelungen durch Hindernisse *Turbulences caused by obstacles*

Koyaanisqatsi

STRÖMUNGEN

Das Gelände an der Friedrichstraße ist seit jeher ein sehr bewegter Ort. Zur Formfindung fanden diverse Untersuchungen statt. Dabei stand vor allen Dingen die Erkundung menschlicher Bewegungsmuster im Vordergrund. Dabei wurden besonders die Bewegungen der Menschen auf dem Gelände an der Friedrichstraße wichtig. Parallel dazu fand eine Auseinandersetzung mit anderen Strömungsphänomenen statt. Im Vordergrund stand hierbei vor allen Dingen die Formenbildung durch Strömungen (z.B. Wasser). Eine Kombination dieser Untersuchungen führte zur endgültigen Form des Gebäudes.

CURRENTS

The site at Friedrichstraße has always been a very dynamic place. Various investigations took place to find a form. The exploration of human patterns of movement was of interest. In this case people's movements at the Friedrichstraße site were especially important. A debate with other phenomena of movement took place in parallel. In this case, the creation of form through flows (e.g. water) was especially examined. A combination of these investigations led to the final form of the building.

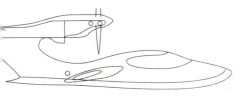

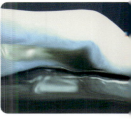

Natürliche Referenzen *Natural references*

Tragwerksexperimente *Structural experiments*

Räumliches Strömungsmodell des Gebietes *Spatial flow model of the area*

EXPERIMENTE

Verschiedene Referenzen aus Natur und Technik, aber auch physikalische Experimente halfen bei Überlegungen zum Tragwerk. Seifenblasenversuche erlaubten sowohl Beobachtungen an pneumatischen Systemen als auch Experimente mit Minimalflächen und zeigten, dass für das Projekt letztendlich doch der Bezug auf die Konstruktionsweisen im Flugzeugbau, welche ja auf strömungsdynamische Gegebenheiten eingehen, ausschlaggebend ist. Eine räumliche Spantenkonstruktion erlaubt so, mehrsinnig gekrümmte Oberflächen zu erzeugen, welche nicht rein statischen Überlegungen folgen, sondern auch das Bild eines durch Strömung geformten Körpers hervorrufen.

EXPERIMENTS

Different references from nature and technology as well as physical experiments assisted in the considerations on the load-bearing structure. Bubble experiments permit both observations on pneumatic systems and experiments with minimal surfaces. For the project the relation to building methods in aircraft construction is of ultimate significance, given the conditions for flow dynamics that are important in this field. A spatial vertical frame construction thus permits the production of multi-faceted, curved surfaces that do not purely follow static deliberations, but also evoke the picture of a body formed by the flow.

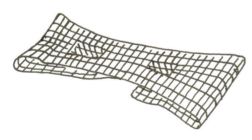

Tragwerksmodelle *Structural models*

Eingangsbereich   *Entrance hall*

The Wheel – ein hybrides Möbelstück   *The Wheel – a hybrid piece of furniture*

THE WHEEL

„The Wheel" ist ein hybrides Möbelstück. Es erlaubt dem Benutzer, seine unmittelbare Umgebung den eigenen Bedürfnissen anzupassen. Durch einfache Rotation bietet es Erholungs- und Arbeitsraum, einen Rückzugs-, Schlaf-, aber auch sozialen Begegnungsort. Durch seine spezielle Form und Rotation um die eigene Achse können sich zwei Menschen gegenüber sitzen oder einer alleine auf einen Monitor blicken, entspannt sitzen, lesen oder sich auf einer ebenen Fläche zur Ruhe legen. The wheel kann sich frei im Raum bewegen oder aber an einer fixen Position rotieren.

THE WHEEL

"The Wheel" is a hybrid piece of furniture. It permits the user to modify his immediate surroundings to his own needs. Through simple rotating, it offers a relaxation and work space, a retreat and sleeping area as well as a social meeting point. By its special form and rotation around its own axis, two people can sit opposite or watch a screen on their own; they can sit and relax, read or lie down for a rest on a flat surface. The wheel can move freely in the room or rotate in a fixed position.

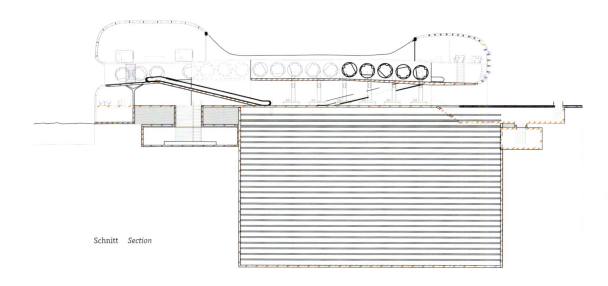

Schnitt   *Section*

Von links oben nach rechts unten:
Präsentationsmodell: Ankunft von der Weidendamm Brücke; Blick von der Weidendamm Brücke; Eingang von der Friedrichstraße; Blick auf den Haupteingang; Ankunft von der Friedrichstraße

From top left to bottom right:
Presentation model: Arrival from Weidendamm Brücke; view from Weidendamm Brücke; entrance from Friedrichstraße; view of the main entrance; arrival from Friedrichstraße

THE RENT OR BUY A BOOK LIBRARY

Die Bibliothek an der Friedrichstraße ist ein Ort permanenter Menschenströme. Das Straßenniveau bietet die Möglichkeit, sich nach „drive/walk thru"-Manier Bücher auszuleihen bzw. zu kaufen. Gelagert werden die Bücher in einem unterirdischen Lager. Die oberen Stockwerke bieten urbane Rückzugsorte. Dort können sich Menschen von der Hektik des Alltags erholen. Auch kulturelle Aktivitäten finden dort ihren Raum. Die Erschließung des Gebäudes ist auf diese verschiedenen Geschwindigkeiten abgestimmt; somit ist es möglich, den optimalen Raum für die jeweilige Gemütslage zu finden.

The library at Friedrichstraße is a location where streams of people are permanently flowing past. The street level offers the opportunity to borrow or buy books in a "drive/walk thru" mode. The books are kept in an underground store. The upper levels offer urban locations for retreat. There, people can recover from the hectic activity of the day. Cultural activities also use this as a venue. Access to the building is tailored to these different speeds, and thus it is possible to find the perfect space for the current mood.

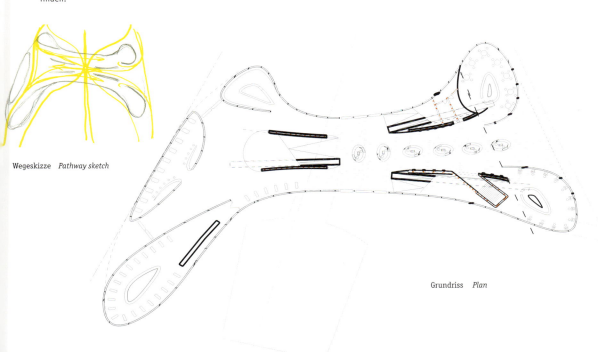

Wegeskizze   *Pathway sketch*

Grundriss   *Plan*

Daniel Krüger / Bibliothek nonstop 2001/2002

Oben und unten: Der Kokon ist ein Ort zum geistig Arbeiten, der sich durch Zurückklappen der Rückenlehne in einen verführerischen Schlafraum verwandeln lässt.

Above and below: The cocoon is a place for brainwork. It is possible to change it into a tempting bedroom by folding down the back-rest.

ARBEITSWEISE

Der Flügel eines Insekts wird zur Innenraumcollage. Aus dieser wird das Modell eines hybriden Ortes zum geistig Arbeiten und Schlafen generiert. Das hier im Kleinen ausformulierte Thema „geistig Arbeiten und Verführen" war prägend für das ganze „Bibliothek nonstop"-Projekt sowie viele andere kleinere und größere Entdeckungen. Beispielsweise war ein gebogenes Stück Blech in einen Schuhkarton gesteckt, Wegbereiter der Lichtsegel.
Auf Grund des Templum-Gedankens der imaginären Nähe zum Wasser waren genaue Untergrund-Untersuchungen nötig, um die Bibliothek zu verorten, dabei kam heraus, dass es dort zu Zeiten der DDR einen Exterritorialraum gab.

WORKING METHOD

An insect's wing becomes an interior spatial collage. This generates the model of a hybrid place for intellectual work and sleeping. The subject of "working and seducing intellectually" that is formulated here on a small scale as well as many other minor and major discoveries were influential for the entire "non-stop library" project. For instance, a piece of bent metal that was placed on a shoe box was preparing the way for the light sail. On the basis of the templum idea of an imaginary proximity to water, precise investigations underground were necessary in order to localise the library; in the process, it emerged that during the GDR era there was an exterritorial room here.

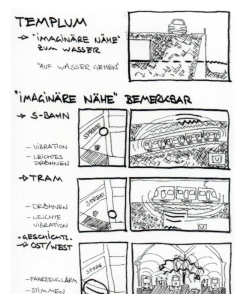 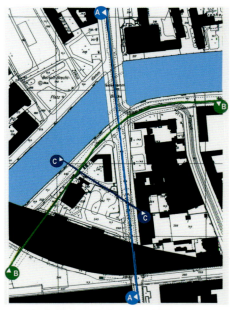

Oben: Zwei Kartierungen des Exterritorialraums
Above: Two mappings of the extraterritorial space

Links: Notizen im Zusammenhang mit dem Templumgedanken
Left: Notes in connection with the idea of the templum

Oben und rechts: Entwicklung des Tragwerks vom Schildkrötenpanzer über Versuche mit Gipsschalen zur endgültigen Spantenkonstruktion, die die notwendige Flexibilität bietet.

Above and right: The development of the final construction is based on the physique of a tortoise and some experiments with shells made of plaster.

Unten und links: Das Lichtsegel, Arbeitsmodell und die Integration im Projekt am Tag und in der Nacht

Below and left: The working model of the light sails and the integration into the project at day and night

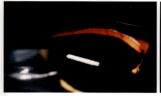   

BIBLIOTHEK NONSTOP

Das Projekt ist der Entwurf für eine neue Zweigstelle der Staatsbibliothek zu Berlin für Film- und Theaterwissenschaften, eine hybride Kombination von Bibliothek und Kino. Sie wird unterirdisches Laboratorium und verführerische Unterwelt gleichzeitig sein. Das Gebäudegefüge nistet sich bewusst zwischen der vorhandenen Infrastruktur ein und verflechtet sich mit dieser. Sie besetzt den Raum, wo sich zur Zeit der DDR ein exterritorialer Umsteigebahnhof der BVG befand. Diesen Gedanken aufnehmend, bildet sie auch einen Exterritorialraum, indem sie Teile der vorhandenen Infrastruktur in ihren Innenräumen aufnimmt.

NON-STOP LIBRARY

The project is the design for a new subsidiary of the Berlin State Library, Department of Film and Theatre Sciences, a hybrid combination of library and cinema. It will be an underground laboratory and a seductive underworld at the same time. The building structure deliberately nestles between the existing infrastructure and is interwoven with it. It occupies the space where during the GDR era an exterritorial interchange station of the BVG (Berlin transport company) was located. Adopting these ideas, it forms an exterritorial space by adopting parts of the existing infrastructure into its inner rooms.

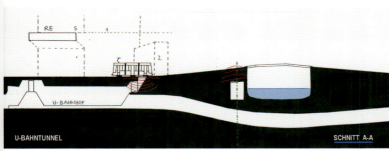 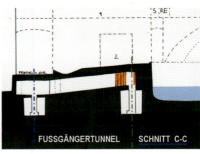

Die Kartierungen des Untergrundes sollen die Komplexität des Ortes veranschaulichen. Sie waren auch ein wichtiges Werkzeug beim Entwurfsprozess.

The mappings of the underground should visualize the complexity of the area. They were also an important tool to design the project.

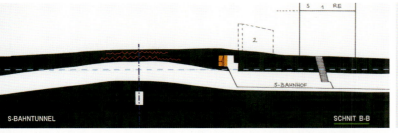 

missing

operation: EP. K_02
in search of the parent ship

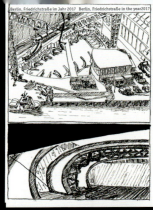

Berlin, Friedrichstraße im Jahr 2017 — Berlin, Friedrichstraße in the year 2017

IN BETWEEN ± 0,00 m
(± 34,6 m ü. NN)

1. EXPRESS ENTRANCE
2. RIVER SPREE

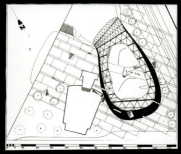

DIVE IN − 2,50 m

1. ENTRANCE / REGISTRATION
2. PEDESTRIAN UNDERPASS
3. HIBITION AREA
4. CAFE
5. RIVER SPREE
6. WC
7. KITCHEN
8. STOCKROOM
9. LIBRARY ENTRANCE
10. LOWERED OUTDOOR AREA
11. TERRACE

Erkennen könnt ihr es an den zwei Lichtsegeln, die die Platzoberfläche durchstoßen, und daran, daß der Platz leicht angehoben ist. Die B. besitzt zwischen diesen zwei Lichtsegeln einen Expresseingang, der für euch aber nicht weiter interessant ist, da er nachts geschlossen ist und nur von Forschern benutzt werden kann, die den entsprechenden Türcode kennen.

You can identify it by two light sails that penetrate the surface of the square and by the fact that the square is slightly raised. The library has an express entrance located between these light sails but that is not of interest for you, as it is closed at night and can only be used by scientists who know the appropriate code for the door.

Ihr benutzt ruhig den regulären „Kino-Eigang" im südöstlichen Teil des Platzes, direkt schräg gegenüber des Bahnhofsausgangs. Über eine Treppe gelangt ihr in den Kassen- und Garderobenbereich, tagsüber ist hier die Rezeption der B.. – Vorsicht scharfe Rechtskurve! – während des Bibliothekbetriebes hätte man hier einen coolen Blick auf den Freihandbereich, aber wenn Kino ist sind die Glasscheiben getrübt und man sieht die geheimnisvollen Lichtreflexe der Projektionen.

You better use the normal "cinema entrance" in the southeastern part of the square, directly on an angle opposite the station's exist. You take the stairs to the carh-desk and cloakroom area; during the day the library's reception is located here. Be careful, a sharp curve to the right! During library hours you would have a cool view of the open shelf area, but when the cinema is open the glass panes are misty and you see the mysterious light reflexes of the projections.

OCEAN OF BOOKS − 10,00 m

1. READING CHAIRS
   (CINEMA PLATFORM)
2. ARCHIV
3. ARCHIV / STOCKROOM /
   WORKSHOP
4. CONNECTING PASSAGE
   ARCHIV - ADMINISTRATION
5. WC
6. OPEN ACCESS

So, wenn dann die Luft rein ist, könnt ihr ins „Büchermeer" eintauchen und aus dem „Sci-Fi"-Regal das richtige Buch heraussuchen.

Thus, when the coast is clear, you can dive into the "sea of books" and look for the right book from the "Sci-Fi" shelf.

Ach noch was! Falls irgendetwas dazwischen kommen sollte: Fliegt im Notfall einfach Richtung Lichtsegel und an der Projektionsfläche nach oben. Dort wo das Lichtsegel die Platzoberfläche durchstößt befindet sich ein Lichtschlitz aus Glas - wie im unteren Schnitt zu erkennen ist – den ihr einfach mit einer Rakete zerschießt, da fliegt ihr durch und ihr seid in Sicherheit. – Also gut, ihr wisst was ihr zu tun habt!

And another thing! If anything should come up: in case of an emergency simply rush in the direction of the light sail and up towards the projection surface. At the point where the light sail penetrates the surface of the square, there is a glass light opening – as can be recognized from the cut below – and you simply shoot through it with a rocket. You then rush through it and are safe. – Okay, you know what you have to do.

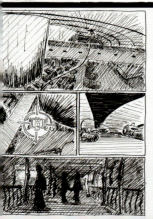

später dann — later then

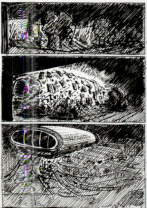

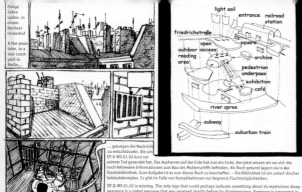

A few years later, in a rear courtyard in Berlin...

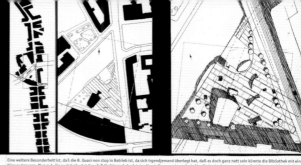

...gelungen die Nachricht zu entschlüsseln, die uns EP.K-WS 01.02 kurz vor seinem Tod gesendet hat. Das Ausharren auf der Erde hat nun ein Ende, den jetzt wissen wir wo sich die noch fehlenden Informationen zum Bau des Mutterschiffs befinden. Als Buch getarnt lagern sie in der Staatsbibliothek. Eure Aufgabe ist es nun dieses Buch zu beschaffen. – Die Bibliothek ist ein unterirdischer Gebäudekomplex. Es gibt im Falle von Komplikationen nur begrenzt Fluchtmöglichkeit.

EP.K-WS 01.02 is missing. The only sign that could perhaps indicate something about its mysterious disappearance is a coded message that was received shortly before its disappearance. Everyone is interested in the question whether the message contained any reference to the mother ship... The answer is hidden in the "Non-stop Library" and so our two courageous heroes set off for the Friedrichsstraße triangle.

Eine weitere Besonderheit ist, daß die B. Quasi non stop in Betrieb ist, da sich irgendjemand überlegt hat, daß es doch ganz nett sein könnte die Bibliothek mit einem Kino zu kreuzen. Nun gut, für euch bedeutet das, daß ihr bis nach der letzten Vorstellung warten müsst, bis alle Leute draussen sind. – Gut! Jetzt sag ich euch aber erstmal wo ihr die B. findet. - Gar nicht schwer – Wenn ihr dem Friedrichstraßenverlauf in Richtung Norden folgt, ist doch vor dem S-Bahnhof der letzte noch verbliebene Freiraum. – Bingo! Genau darunter ist das Ding vergraben.

Another peculiarity is that the library is sort of open non-stop and this arises because somebody thought that it might be quite nice to cross the library with a cinema. Well, for you that means that you have to wait for the last show, until all the people are outside. – Good! Now I will just reveal to you where you find the library. – Not difficult at all. – If you follow the continuation of the Friedrichstraße in northerly direction the last remaining open space is located right in front of the S-Bahn station – Bingo! The thing is buried right underneath it.

OVERVIEW – 5.00m

1. INFORMATION AND SERVICE AREA
2. CINEMA PLATFORM
3. CANVAS / LIGHT SAIL
4. ACCESS TO CINEMA PLATFORM
5. LOWERABLE SUSPENSION BRIDGE
6. ADMINISTRATION
7. EXHIBITION AREA
8. WC
9. SUBURBAN TRAIN STATION
10. SUBWAY
11. RIVER SPREE

RESEARCH AND WORK – 8.00m

1. VIDEO AND WORKROOM FOR RESEARCHER
2. SUBWAY
3. SUBURBAN TRAIN

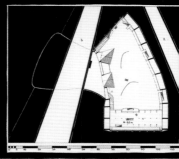

Durch einen Verbindungstunnel gelangt ihr direkt zum „Überblick-Level", von dem die Kinovorstellungen, die für die Kinovorstellungen für etwa 3m angehoben werden, zu erreichen sind. Von dem „Überblick-Level" habt ihr ideale Möglichkeiten nach dem „Sci-Fi"-Regal zu suchen. Falls der Kinobetrieb immer noch läuft wartet ihr bis sich ein Hängewalk unter dem Fußgängertunnel herabsenkt, über den die Leute das Kino Richtung Café oder Ausgang verlassen.

You directly access the "overview level" by a connecting tunnel that leads to the cinema platforms that can be raised about 3 metres for cinema shows. You have ideal opportunities from the "overview level" to search for the "Sci-Fi" shelf. If the cinema is still in operation, you wait until a suspended walkway lowers beneath the pedestrian tunnel that takes the people in the cinema out towards the café or the exit.

Ein gutes Versteck, um die Zeit zu überbrücken, ist auf dem Fußgängertunnel oder, falls einer der Video- und Arbeitsräume offen sein sollte, könnt ihr auch ungestört dort warten.

The pedestrian tunnel is a good hiding place to pass the time, or if one of the video- or working-rooms are open you can wait there undisturbed.

Am nächsten Tag / The next day

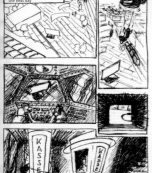
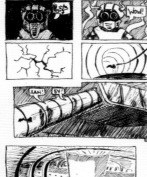

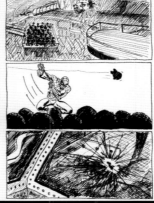
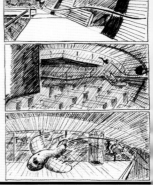

END ?

AIR ROUTE RECORDING

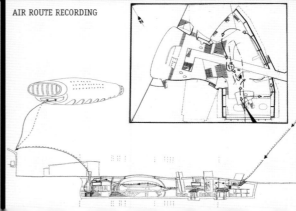

Werkzeug Materialexperimente / Tool Material Experiments SoSe 2003

MATERIALEXPERIMENTE SOSE 2003

Das zweite Semester ist dem Materialexperiment gewidmet. Innerhalb von acht Wochen entwickelt jeder Student eine kleine Struktur, basierend auf der thematischen Weiterentwicklung des ersten Semesters. Insbesondere ist die Auseinandersetzung mit einem bestimmten Material im Zusammenhang mit dem Thema seines Projektes zu wählen. Durch Exkursion, Recherche und Experimente lernen die Studenten, sich mit den räumlichen und haptischen Charakteristika des ausgewählten Materials vertraut zu machen.
Am Ende des Semesters wird das Projekt in Form eines 1:20 bzw. 1:1 Modells in dem ausgewählten Material sowie im Grundriss, in Schnitten und in 3D-Darstellungen präsentiert. [CK]

MATERIAL EXPERIMENTS SOSE 2003

The second semester was devoted to material experiments. Within a space of eight weeks each student develops a small structure, based on the thematic continuation of the first semester. In particular, students select the exploration of a specific material in the context of the theme of their project. By means of excursion, research and experiment, the students learn to make themselves familiar with the spatial and haptic characteristics of the chosen material.
At the end of the semester, the project is presented in the form of a 1:20, or 1:1 model in the chosen material, as well as in layout, sections and 3D-versions. [CK]

Friedrich Rohde: Vorexperimente zur „Geburtsmaschine", Draht-Silikonmodell   *Friedrich Rohde: Pre-experiments with "Birth Machinery", wire-silicon model*

Oliver Gaßner: Leichte Betonstruktur durch Luftballonkammern als Verlustschalung   *Oliver Gaßner: Light concrete structure through air balloon chambers as a loss scale*

Mario Bär: Epoxidharzmodell auf Gipsform modelliert   *Mario Bär: Epoxy-resin model, modelled on plaster-cast*

Felix Sommerlad: Silikonexperimente   *Felix Sommerlad: Silicon experiments*

Werkzeug Materialexkursion / Tool Material Excursion SoSe 2003

MATERIALEXKURSION 2003

Im Rahmen des zweitens Semesters 2003 wurde eine Exkursion unter dem Thema Material organisiert. Ziel der Exkursion war es, den Studenten die Herstellungsmethode, aber auch den unterschiedlichen Gebrauch verschiedener Materialien zu vermitteln. Zur Wahl standen der Besuch von Fabriken von Konstruktionsmaterialien wie Beton, Metall und Holz, aber auch der Besuch von auf die Konstruktion von Flugzeugen, Schiffen oder auch Fertighäusern spezialisierten Werkstätten. Jede Exkursion erlaubte den Studenten, sich mit einer Technik vertraut zu machen, die sie dann im Rahmen des Semesterprojektes vertiefen konnten.

MATERIAL EXCURSION 2003

In the course of the second semester, 2003, an excursion on the theme of material was arranged. The excursion's objective was to convey to students not only the manufacturing method but also the various uses applicable to different materials. The options were either a visit to a factory making building materials, such as concrete, metal and wood; or a visit to specialist workshops constructing aeroplanes, ships or even ready-made houses. Every excursion enabled the students to familiarise themselves with a certain technique, gaining knowledge they could then extend in the context of the semester project.

Stahlwerk Eisenhüttenstadt *Eisenhüttenstadt Steel Works*

 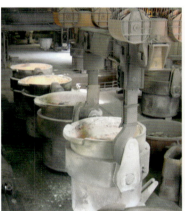 

Stahlwerk Eisenhüttenstadt *Eisenhüttenstadt Steel Works*

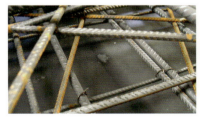  

Betonwerk Gommern *Gommern Concrete Works*

Corocord Raumnetz, Berlin *Corocord Network, Berlin*

Anupama Kundoo

Auf das Material kommt es an

Form folgt Technik

Anders als bestimmte, unabdingbare Faktoren, die den Entwurf eines guten Gebäudes bestimmen – wie zum Beispiel das Klima – ist die Hinwendung zu neu aufkommenden Bautechnologien der Faktor, der die Ausrichtung der Architektur bestimmt. Über die üblichen Verbesserungen der Bautechnologie hinaus treibt die offensichtliche globale Krise natürlicher Ressourcen die Erforschung und Entwicklung umweltbewusster Bautechnologien voran. Die nächste Architektengeneration muss sich darüber klar werden, welchen Einfluss Baumaterialien auf die Umwelt haben. Diese Belange sollten sich in der Architektur der Zukunft widerspiegeln.

Stahlbeton in Indien: ein Problem

In Indien wurde die große Vielfalt an traditionellen Baumaterialien durch Stahlbetontragwerke mit Ziegelwänden und Stahlbetondächer ersetzt. Aus diesem Phänomen ergeben sich verschiedene Nachteile. In Indien ist Stahlbeton das Bauelement, dessen Herstellung am meisten Energie verbraucht. Zudem besteht großer Mangel an Zement und Stahl. Dieser Mangel führt häufig zu Verzögerungen des Baugeschehens und stellt die Haupthürde für die schnelle Errichtung von Wohnraum dar.⁽¹⁾

Zudem sind in den meisten Gegenden Stahlbetondächer für das Klima nicht geeignet, da die absorbierte Hitze in die darunter liegenden Wohnräume geleitet wird. Dies wiederum führt zu hohen Klimatisierungskosten und da die benötigte Isolierung für diese Technologie unerschwinglich ist, wird sie von den meisten Verbrauchern vermieden.

Wall House:
Ausgesparte Betondecke unter Verwendung von umgekehrten Tonschüsseln

Wall house: recessed concrete roof using inverted clay bowls

Material Matters

Form follows technology

Unlike certain fixed geographical factors that dictate the design of a good building – such as climate – changes to prevailing building technologies are the single major factor shaping the direction of architecture. In addition to standard advancements in building technologies, the acknowledged global crises in natural resources drives the exploration and development of environmentally sensitive building technologies. The next generation of architects must be aware of the impact of building materials on the environment. Emerging architecture is likely to reflect these concerns.

The Problem of Reinforced Concrete in India

In India, the wide variety of traditional building materials has been replaced by Reinforced Cement Concrete (RCC) frame structures with brick walls and reinforced concrete roofs. This phenomenon has several shortcomings. The manufacturing of RCC consumes the highest energy of a building component in India, and there is also a huge scarcity of cement and steel. This scarcity often results in construction work delays and presents a major hurdle in the quick delivery of shelter. [1]

Also the RCC roof is not climatically comfortable in most areas since the heat it absorbs is transferred to the living spaces underneath. This in turn means high cooling costs, and since the insulation needed for this technology is cost prohibitive most consumers avoid it.

Wall House: Bogenkonstruktion unter Verwendung von ineinander geschachtelten Tonschüsseln

Wall house: construction using clay bowls put into one another

In ländlichen Gegenden werden die benötigten Materialien mit Lastwagen befördert, die zusätzlich Energie verbrauchen und die Umwelt verschmutzen. Ein weiterer Nachteil besteht darin, dass die Großindustrie der nahen Städte auf Kosten der lokalen Wirtschaft Gewinn macht. Durch Analphabetismus, ungelernte Arbeit und mangelhaftes Wissen über Zement und seine chemischen Reaktionen ist ein Großteil der ländlichen Gebäude aus diesem Material von extrem schlechter Qualität. Im Gegensatz zu Gebäuden aus Lehm können sie weder abgerissen noch einfach repariert werden. Für professionell ausgeführte Hi-Tech-Anwendungen hoch budgetierter Projekte jedoch stellt ist Stahlbeton unbedingt auf jeden Fall ein Zaubermaterial wunderbares Material dar.

In Indien betrifft der Wohnungsmangel sowohl auf dem Land als auch in der Stadt in der Hauptsache Arme und Schlechtverdienende. In Anbetracht dieser Lage erscheint es sinnvoll, neue Kombinationen heimischer Materialien und kostengünstige Technologien zu untersuchen, die nicht nur dem örtlichen Handwerk entsprechen, sondern auch möglichst geringe Auswirkungen auf die Umwelt haben.

Die folgenden Arbeitsbeispiele zeigen meine anhaltende Suche nach umweltgemäßen Baumaterialien und Technologien und meinen Beitrag zu einer zeitgemäßen Architektur, die bewusster mit diesen Ressourcen umgeht.

Pierres Haus

Gewölbedächer, Hohlmauern und stahlverstärkte Zementrippen zur Regulierung von Blendlicht, die aber Windbewegung zulassen, bilden die Hauptelemente des Bauens.

Links: Pierres Haus
Mitte: Pierres Haus
Rechts: Gebranntes Haus: Auslegen der Lehmsteine

Left: Pierre's house
Center: Pierre's house
Right: Fired house: exposing the clay bricks

Die Gewölbedächer waren das Ergebnis der Suche nach einer isolierenden Überdachungstechnologie, die ein Aufheizen des Hauses verhindern und aus umweltfreundlichen Materialien hergestellt sein sollte. Speziell entworfene, hohle Terrakottaröhren wurden zu Gewölbeketten zusammengefasst, eine Technologie, die eine Stahlkonstruktion oder Beton überflüssig macht und doch ein „Pucca"-Dach (2) ermöglicht. Das Gebäude, das 450 m² umfasst, wurde 1992 fertig gestellt. Der Erfolg dieser Technik führte zu einer Reihe von Experimenten mit verschiedenen Alternativen: isolierte und modulare Terrakottadächer, die auch in späteren Projekten zu sehen sein werden.

Das gebrannte Haus am Beispiel von „Spirit Sense"

Ein gebranntes Haus oder ein feuergehärtetes Lehmhaus ist im Prinzip ein Haus aus Lehm, das nach dem Bau im Ganzen nachbehandelt wird, damit es die Festigkeit von Ziegeln erhält. Unter Benutzung einer besonderen, von Ray Meeker von der Golden Bridge Pottery entwickelten Technik wird ein gebranntes Haus normalerweise aus Lehmziegeln gebaut, die vor Ort aus Lehmmörtel hergestellt werden. Das Innere wird ebenfalls mit Lehmziegeln oder anderen Keramikprodukten wie zum Beispiel Fliesen gefüllt und dann wie ein Brennofen angeheizt. Das Brennen dieser Stoffe im Inneren des Hauses produ-

In rural areas these materials are transported by trucks that consume more energy and cause more pollution. As an additional disadvantage, the big industry of nearby cities benefit economically at the expense of local economies. Due to illiteracy, unskilled labour, and a lack of knowledge of cement and its chemical reactions, the bulk of rural constructions with this material turn out to be of extremely poor quality and, unlike mud buildings, they can neither be taken down nor repaired easily. Yet for hi-tech applications in big budget projects built by skilled professionals, reinforced concrete is unquestionably a wonder material. The majority of India's housing shortage, both in rural and urban areas, befalls poor and low-income people. In response to this, it is worth exploring indigenous materials that are combined in new ways, and cost-effective technologies that are not only suited to local skills but have a minimal impact on the environment.

The following examples of my work reflect my continued search for environmentally suitable building materials and technologies and my contribution toward an architecture of our times that is more conscious of using these resources as opposed to others.

Pierre's House

Vaulted roofs, cavity walls, and steel-reinforced cement fins for regulating glare while allowing the free movement of prevailing winds constitute the chief building language. The vaulted roofs were the result of a search for an insulated roofing

technology that would prevent the house from heating up and would be made from environmentally friendly materials. Specially designed, hollow terracotta tubes were assembled into catenary vaults, a technology that eliminates the need for structural steel or concrete, while still providing a "Pucca" [2] roof. The building, covering 450 m², was completed in 1992. The success of this technique led to a series of experiments involving insulated and modular terracotta roof alternatives that can also be seen in later projects.

Links: Gebranntes Haus : nach dem Ausbrennen
Mitte: Hemants Haus: Dachkonstruktion
Rechts: Hemants Haus: Konstruktionsgerüst

Left: Fired house: after the firing
Center: Hemant's house: roof structure
Right: Hemant's house: scaffolding

Fired House: The example of "Spirit Sense"

A fired house or a fire-stabilized mud house is, in principle, a house made from mud that is cured as a whole after building to achieve the strength of brick. Built using a rare technology developed by Ray Meeker of Golden Bridge Pottery, a fired house is typically constructed with mud bricks made on site with mud mortar, the interior is also stuffed with mud bricks or other ceramic products such as tiles, and fired as if it were a kiln. The firing of these products inside the house produces heat that is absorbed by the walls and, as a consequence, fires the house as well. The fuel cost is largely commensurate to the products inside. In principle, the

ziert Hitze, die von den Wänden absorbiert wird und in der Folge das Haus selbst brennt. Die Kosten des Brennstoffs entsprechen im Großen und Ganzen denen der Baustoffe des Hauses. Im Prinzip erhält man so die Festigkeit eines Ziegelsteins zum Preis von Lehm. Auch Zement wird in der Mörtelmischung unnötig.

„Spirit Sense" wurde für eine Töpferin entworfen. Sie wollte ihr Haus unbedingt in dieser Technik gebaut haben. Da das Haus am Rande einer Schlucht in einem unter Umweltgesichtspunkten sehr sensiblen Gebiet lag, erschien dieses Vorgehen sinnvoll. Ray Meeker, der technische Berater dieses Projekts, fügte einen zusätzlichen, neuen Aspekt hinzu. Um wie in früheren Fällen die Benutzung von wertvollem Holz zum Brennen der Konstruktion zu vermeiden, wurde Kohlestaub in die Lehmmischung für die Ziegel eingebracht. So musste man nur noch das Feuer entzünden und dann brannten die Füllmasse, die Konstruktion und die Keramikprodukte im Inneren, bis der ganze Kohlenstaub in den Ziegeln verbraucht war.

Anupamas Hütte

Als die einfachste Form der Behausung besteht dieses Haus aus einem Blätterdach (geflochtenen Kokosblättern), das auf unbehandelten, mit Kokosseilen zusammengehaltenen Elementen aus Casuarinaholz aufliegt. Die Konstruktion steht auf groben Granitstelzen, die verhindern, dass Termiten in das Holz gelangen.

Der obere Boden ist aus gespaltenen Pakamaramstämmen, die auch durch Seile verbunden sind. Granitpfeiler schaffen einen fließenden Übergang zwischen dem Innen- und Außenraum. Im Wohnbereich umfassen sie Höfe und definieren die unter freiem Himmel liegenden Zellen des Badbereichs. Dieses Haus hat einen minimalen Einfluss auf die Umwelt und verschmilzt harmonisch mit der Natur. Außerdem wird der Bedarf an Elektrizität und Wasserbeheizung komplett durch Sonnenenergie gedeckt. Am „Haus für Hemant und Divya" kann man sehen, wie diese Technik mit entsprechend höheren Kosten verfeinert und verbessert wurde.

Mauerhaus

Hier wurde eine örtliche Tradition der Ziegelherstellung wiederbelebt. Aus den Ziegeln von 18 x 10 x 2,5 cm, die heute nur noch für ornamentale Zwecke eingesetzt werden, wurden die dicken Hauptmauern dieses Hauses unter Verwendung von Kalkmörtel gebaut. Da die Ziegel einen Mauerverband im Verhältnis 1:2 nicht zuließen, musste dieser eigens entwickelt werden und ist sowohl im Mauerwerk der Fassade als auch in den Sturzunterseiten und Fensterbrettern sichtbar. Hier wurde mit einer Reihe von Dach- und Deckplattentechniken experimentiert.

Um den für konventionelle Flachdachkonstruktionen üblichen Verbrauch von Stahl und Beton deutlich zu reduzieren, wurden traditionell als Kochtöpfe fungierende Terrakottatöpfe zur Schaffung von Hohlräumen in den Deckenelementen benutzt. Diese Formen verbleiben nach dem Gießen in der Deckenplatte. Hochwertige Schalungsformen sind in ländlichen Gegenden noch immer unerschwinglich. Diese Technik ermöglicht aber trotzdem eine Gussästhetik, die keine hohe Investition in die Schalungsform erfordert. Da weder Verputz noch Anstrich nötig sind, fallen auch diese Kosten weg. In späteren Arbeiten zeigt sich eine Verbesserung dieser Technik mit einem entsprechend niedrigeren Stahlverbrauch.

strength of brick is achieved for the cost of mud. Cement in the mortar mix also becomes unnecessary.

"Spirit Sense" was designed for a woman who is a potter and was very keen on building her house with this technology. This process also made sense given that the house is located at the edge of a canyon in a very environmentally sensitive area. Ray Meeker, technical consultant for this project, introduced an additional new aspect. To avoid using valuable wood to fire the structure as in previous cases, coal dust was introduced into the clay mixture used to make the bricks. It was only necessary to light the fire and then the mass, structure, and ceramic products placed within, burned until all the coal dust within the bricks was spent.

Anupama's Hut

As the most basic kind of dwelling, this house consists of a thatch roof (woven coconut leaves) supported on untreated Casuarina wood members tied together in place with coconut ropes. The structure stands on rough granite stilts that prevent termites from reaching the wood.

The upper floor is made of split Pakamaram stems that are also tied on with rope. Granite pillars are used to create a gradual transition between inside and outside, and to include courtyards in the living or private open-to-sky spaces in the bath areas. This is a house with minimal environmental impact and it harmoniously blends into nature. It is also entirely dependant on the sun for its electricity and water heating demands. In the 'House for Hemant and Divya', one can see how this technique was refined and improved at an accordingly higher cost.

Wall House

Anciently used local bricks of 18 x 10 x 2.5 cm, still being produced for use in ornamental features, were revived and used to build the thick main walls of this house using lime mortar. As the bricks do not follow the proportion of 1:2 the bonds were specially designed and can be seen both in the exposed brickwork of the facades as well as in the lintel bottoms or windowsills. A series of roof and slab technologies were experimented with here.

In order to significantly reduce the use of structural steel and the volume of concrete used in the conventionally made flat roofs, terracotta pots that are locally produced as cooking pots were used to create voids in filler slabs These moulds remain in the slab after casting. High quality moulds are still unaffordable in rural areas yet this technique achieves a cast aesthetic without expensive investment in moulds. In addition, since plastering or painting is no longer required, these costs are also eliminated. Later works exhibit an improved version of this technique where the savings in steel are proportionally greater.

Sri Aurobindo World Centre for Human Unity

The space consists of a circular open hall with a diameter of 16 meters, two ancillary rooms attached on one side, and amphitheatre steps rising outwards and

Sri Aurobindo World Centre for Human Unity

Der Raum besteht aus einer runden, offenen Halle mit einem Durchmesser von 16 Metern und zwei Nebenräumen an einer Seite. Durch nach oben und außen strebende Amphitheaterstufen entsteht ein Übergangsbereich. Das Stahlbetongebäude wurde so entworfen, dass die Last unter Verbrauch möglichst geringer Betonmengen effektiv verteilt werden konnte. Für den abschließenden Entwurf wurden 25 Kubikmeter Beton benötigt. Für konventionelle Entwürfe braucht man 75 Kubikmeter. Schräge Pfeiler verringerten die Stützweite. Die Form der Träger wurde optimiert. Diese Form konnte durch die Einführung stahlverstärkter Gussformen als verlorene Schalung ökonomisch gegossen werden. Die geringere Last der einzelnen Deckenplatte führt zu leichteren Trägern, folglich zu leichteren Stützen und dadurch zu leichteren Fundamenten. Dies wiederum reduziert die Gesamtkosten und resultiert in einer minimalistischen Architektur.

Sangamam: Günstiger Wohnraum

Sangamam befindet sich am Rande von Auroville, Tamil Nadu, einem von Umwelt- und Sozialproblemen betroffenen Gebiet. Zu diesen zählen Wassermangel, Salzwasserinfiltration, Bodenerosion, abnehmende Bodenfruchtbarkeit, Arbeitslosigkeit sowie Unzulänglichkeit von Wohnmöglichkeiten, Bildung und medizinischer Versorgung.

Der Boden vom Baugelände wurde im Labor getestet und für die Konstruktion von tragenden Wänden für brauchbar befunden. Die uralte Technik des Bauens mit

Links: Wall House: Ausbau
Mitte: Wall House: Rohbau
Rechts: Sri Aurobindo World Centre for Human Unity: Übersicht

Left: Wall house: interior
Center: Wall house: shell construction
Right: Sri Aurobindo: World Centre for Human Unity: overview

gestampfter Erde wird in ausgearbeiteter Form genutzt, um den Standard der Oberflächenbeschaffenheit, der Festigkeit und der Wasserbeständigkeit zu verbessern. Außerdem sollte eine schnellere, modulare Baumethode ermöglicht werden. Aus Stahl und Bootsbausperrholz wurde eine ausgearbeitete, haltbare Schalungsform geschaffen, die den Bauprozess beschleunigt und so flexibel ist, dass man verschiedene Mauerlängen herstellen kann. Ein Team von 4 Arbeitern kann pro Tag 2,2 Meter einschalige Mauer von 23 cm Dicke produzieren. Zu der gesiebten Erde werden 5 Prozent Zement gegeben, um die Masse wasserbeständig zu machen, was die Druckfestigkeit des Materials bei Feuchtigkeit beträchtlich erhöht.

ANMERKUNGEN

(1) National Trends in Housing Production Practises, Volume 1, India, Nairobi, 1993, UN Habitat

(2) „Pucca" bedeutet „eigen" oder „beständig" und ist ein häufig gebrauchtes Wort zur Beschreibung indischer Häuser. Das Gegenteil, Katcha, bezieht sich auf eine Ansammlung von zeitweise bestehenden Häusern, wie zu Beispiel strohgedeckte Hütten.

upwards to contain a transitional space. It is a reinforced concrete building designed in the most efficient way to transfer the load using the smallest volume of concrete possible. The final design used 25 cubic meters of concrete instead of 75 cubic meters as required in conventional designs. Sloping columns reduced the span, and the shape of the beams was optimised. This form could be cast economically by introducing steel-reinforced moulds as lost shuttering. The reduced load in a slab results in lighter beams hence lighter columns and therefore lighter foundations. This in turn reduces overall costs while achieving a minimalist architecture as well.

Sangamam: Low Cost Housing

Sangamam is situated on the outskirts of Auroville, Tamil Nadu, in an area affected by environmental and social problems, including water scarcity, saline water intrusion, soil erosion and declining soil fertility, unemployment, and inadequate housing, educational, and medical facilities.

Soil from the site has been laboratory-tested and found to be suitable for the construction of load bearing walls. The age-old rammed earth building technique is utilized in a more sophisticated form to achieve a better standard of finish, more strength and water-resistance, and to enable a quicker modular method of building. A sophisticated long-lasting mould is created with steel and marine-ply that speeds up construction and is flexible enough to produce a range

of wall lengths. A team of four labourers can produce per day 2.2 meters of monolithic wall, 23cm thick. Five per cent of cement is added to the sieved earth to make the mass water-resistant, adding significantly to the wet compressive strength of the material.

Links: Sri Aurobindo World Centre for Human Unit: Dachdetail
Mitte: Sangamam: Hilfsgerät zum Rammen der Wände
Rechts: Sangamam: Ausbau

Left: Sri Aurobindo: roof detail
Center: Sagamam: implement to help tamp in walls
Right: Sangamam: interior

NOTES
(1) National Trends in Housing Production Practices, Volume 1, India, Nairobi, 1993, UN Habitat
(2) "Pucca" refers to Proper, or Permanent and is a frequently used word in the description of Indian houses, its opposite, Katchha refers to the bulk of houses that are of semi-permanent nature, such as thatch roof huts

Julian Vincent

Bionik und Architektur

Einer der Grundpfeiler der Kreativität ist die Organisation, die gemeinhin durch die Anfertigung von Listen unterstützt wird. Listen mit Möglichkeiten, Ideen, Quellen, Dingen. Und so begann ich diesen Essay, indem ich eine Liste dessen schrieb, was die meisten Leute als Schnittpunkte zwischen Architektur und Biologie betrachten. Ich machte aber keine Liste der Ideen, die ich nutzen wollte. Ich machte eine Liste der Ideen, die ich nicht nutzen wollte. Ich konnte sie niederschreiben und dann ignorieren, ohne dass die Ideen das Gefühl gehabt hätten, sie wären aus dem Prozess ausgeschlossen worden. Auf diese Weise konnte ich meinen Kopf von anerkannten Prinzipien und gängigen Ideen befreien und ihn (so hoffte ich) neueren, weiter hergeholten Dingen öffnen. Und so begann ich:

> Selbstgenerierende/entfaltbare Strukturen/Grüne Technologie

Da dachte ich – hier muss es sich um biologische Systeme handeln, so notierte ich:

> Selbstregulierend

Und hier begann der Durchbruch. Denn mein Denken richtete sich von der Architektur und Gebäuden auf dynamische Maschinen, und die dynamischsten Maschinen, die ich kenne, sind Roboter. Ich hatte kürzlich einen Projektantrag zu autonomen bionischen Robotern geschrieben. Deshalb waren die nächsten drei Stichworte:

> Autonom/Roboter/Intelligent

Diese Begriffe verweisen auf Möglichkeiten, jedoch nichts, das im architektonischen Sinne neu wäre. Verfolgt man die Idee der Robotik, indem man einige der aktuellen Probleme und Ideen von autonomen Robotern hervorhebt, so erhält man:

Benedikt Tulinius „Sog", Collage SoSe 2003
Die Collage dient als Werkzeug zur Ideensammlung. Ohne im Voraus zu wissen, was entstehen wird, werden Bilder bewusst gemacht und können zu räumlichen Strukturen weiterentwickelt werden.

Benedikt Tulinius, "Maelstrom", Collage SoSe 2003
The collage acts as an instrument for collecting ideas. Without knowing in advance what is going to result, images are made deliberately and can be further developed into spatial structures.

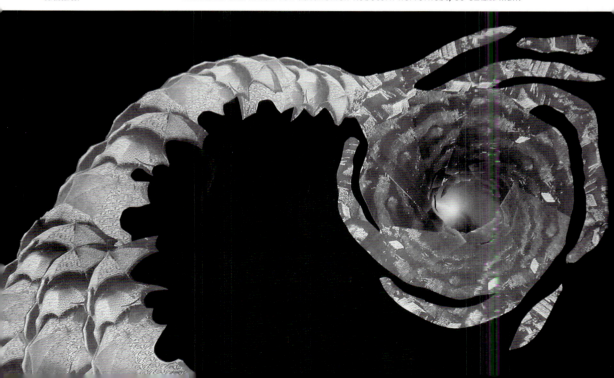

Biomimetics and Architecture

One of the mainstays of creativity is organisation, commonly achieved by making lists. Lists of opportunities, of ideas, of resources, of things. So I started this essay by writing a list of what most people see as the crossing points between architecture and biology. But I wasn't making a list of ideas to use. I was making a list of ideas I didn't want to use. I could write them down and then ignore them without the ideas feeling as if they had been left out of the process. That way I could clear my mind of the accepted principles and current ideas and open it up to (I hoped) some newer things from further away. Here's how I started:

Self-designing/Deployable structures/Green technology

Then I thought – this is supposed to be about biological systems, so I put it down:

Self-regulating

And this is where the breakthrough started. Because my thinking changed from architecture and buildings to dynamic machines, and the most dynamic machines I know of are robots. I had recently written a project proposal about autonomous biomimetic robotics, so the next three words were:

Autonomous/Robotic/Intelligent

These words hint at possibilities, but nothing that might be novel in architectural terms. Take the robotics ideas further, emphasising some of the current problems and ideas in autonomous robots, and we get:

Embodied functions/Energy management/Distributed robotics

These are important for autonomy for two main reasons: energy conservation and

Schadi Weiss „CMF Spider", Collage SoSe 2003
Erste Collage zum späteren Projekt einer temporären Konzerthalle, die aus einzeln ansteuerbaren Faltelementen (Schirmen) besteht. Auf- und Abbau der Halle erfolgt durch die gleichzeitige Faltung oder Entfaltung der einzelnen autonomen Elemente.

Schadi Weiss "CMF Spider", Collage SoSe 2003
The first collage for a subsequent project to build a temporary concert-hall, which consists of moveable folding elements (umbrellas). The hall is put up and taken down by the simultaneous opening or closing of the individual autonomous elements.

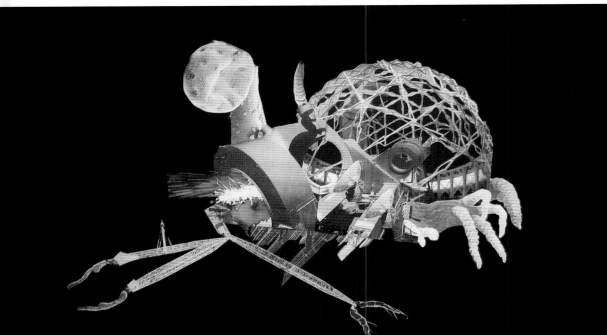

Schadi Weiss „Night and Day Dome", 1:1 Arbeitsmodell SoSe 2003
Herstellungsprozess
a, b) Regenplane von Schirmstruktur abtrennen ...
c) ... Haltedraht kappen ...
d) ... Arme vom Schirmkopf abnehmen ...
e) Schirmkopf neu vermessen (60° Winkel) und Markierungen setzen
f) Schraubendreher erhitzen
g) Spalten an den Markierungen einformen und sechs Schirmarme befestigen

Schadi Weiss "Night and Day Dome", 1:1 Working Model SS 2003
Manufacturing Process
a,b) Keep plans for rain separate from umbrella-structure ...
c) ... Cut down the holding wire ...
d) ... Remove the arms from the brolly head ...
e) Re-measure the brolly head (60° angle) and note where the marks are
f) Heat up the screwdriver
g) Form notches where the marks are and attach six brolly arms

Physische Funktionen/Energiemanagement/Dezentralisierte Roboter
Wichtig für die Autonomie ist dies hauptsächlich aus zwei Gründen: Energieerhaltung und Stabilität. Physische Funktionen sind jene Funktionen, die eher vom Material der Maschine als von ihrem Steuerungssystem bestimmt sind. Ein einfaches Beispiel wäre ein Roboter, der laufen kann – die Beine so entwerfen, dass Trägheit und Aufhängung ihnen die Resonanzfrequenz eines Pendels geben, in dessen Rhythmus der Roboter laufen möchte. So eine Maschine kann eine sanfte Schräge ohne Steuerung oder Antrieb hinablaufen – lediglich als Resultat von Form und Masse. Die Steuerung wird nur dazu benötigt zu starten, anzuhalten und mit Hindernissen und Unregelmäßigkeiten fertig zu werden. Dies wirkt sich natürlich auf das Energiemanagement aus, da weniger Energie für den Antrieb und für die Steuerungssysteme benötigt wird (die Ressource der Schwerkraft wird genutzt – obwohl man natürlich auch wieder berg auf gehen muss!). Gibt es dynamische Funktionen in Gebäuden, die auf dem Prinzip des Gegengewichts beruhen (Beispiele sind Schiebefenster, (die ein Bleigewicht an einem über eine Rolle geführten Seil haben, das das Gewicht des Fensters beim Hinauf- und Hinabschieben ausbalanciert), Aufzüge (die auch ein Gegengewicht haben) und federnde Türangeln). Aber gibt es noch andere Funktionen, die von einem Federungsmechanismus profitieren könnten oder die in einer Resonanzfrequenz arbeiten könnten. Energiemanagement bedeutet zum Teil überhaupt weniger Energie zu verbrauchen, es bedeutet aber auch, diese effektiver zu nutzen. Und eine Möglichkeit besteht darin, Energie über lange Zeit auf niedrigem Niveau anzusammeln, um sie dann in kürzerer Zeit auf einem höheren Niveau zu verbrauchen – Energieverdichtung. Die Technologie zur Energiegewinnung steht bereits zur Verfügung – Sonnenkollektoren, Windmühlen, Gezeitenkraft,

usw. Die Natur nutzt aber noch andere Wege wie die chemische Umsetzung (die Technologie hat chemische Batterien, die Elektrizität speichern – jedoch nicht sehr effektiv) und die mechanische (die elastischen Systeme, die viele Tiere zur Bewegung im Allgemeinen, zum Springen, zum Herausschnellen der Zunge oder zum Schließen der Klauen nutzen). Der dritte Punkt auf der Liste, die dezentralisierten Roboter, bezieht sich darauf, wie eine Gruppe kleiner Roboter miteinander in Kontakt bleiben und komplexe Aufträge in einem großen Areal ausführen kann. Ein ähnliches System ist für Heimroboter entwickelt worden, die umherwandern und Staub und Abfälle essen. Idealerweise würden sie dies in Wärme umwandeln, die sie dann in jene Teile des Raums transportieren würden, die erwärmt werden sollen. Einen anderen Aspekt der dezentralisierten Roboter beleuchten Studien über Ameisen, die zeigen, dass ihre Anpassungsfähigkeit zumindest teilweise auf der Art und Weise beruht, wie sie sich selbst organisieren. Diese erlaubt ihnen, von einem Erkundungsmodus (zum Beispiel in einer chaotischen Umgebung) auf einen gänzlich zielorientierten Modus umzuschalten, wenn sie genau wissen, was sie tun möchten. Im architektonischen Zusammenhang könnte das sehr interessant werden, denn die Roboter können lokale und globale Anforderungen in ihrem Verhalten kombinieren. Dies klingt nach einer Möglichkeit für

robustness. Embodied functions are those that are dictated by the hardware of the machine rather than its control system. A simple example would be in a walking robot – to design the legs so that their inertia and hinging gives them a resonant frequency, like a pendulum, which is the frequency at which the robot wants to walk. Such a machine can walk down a smooth slope with no control or actuation – it's all done as a result of the shapes and masses. The control is needed only to start and stop and to cope with obstacles and non-uniformities. This impinges on energy management, of course, since less energy is required both for the actuation (the resource of gravity is being used – though you still have to walk back up the hill!) and for the control systems. Are there any dynamic functions in a building that can be counterweighted (examples are sash windows [which have a lead weight on a rope going over a pulley which balances the weight of the window as it slides up and down], lifts [which also have a counterweight] and spring door hinges)? Or are there any other functions which would benefit from some sort of spring attachment or which could work at a resonant frequency? Energy management is partly about using less energy overall, but it's also about using it more effectively. And one way is to gather energy at a low level over a long time and use it over a shorter time at a higher level – power amplification. The energy gathering technology is already available – solar collectors, windmills, tidal power, etc. But there are other ways nature uses, such as chemical transformations (technology has chemical batteries which store electricity – but not very efficiently) and mechanical (the spring systems which many animals use for locomotion in general, jumping, shooting out a tongue or snapping a claw closed). The third item on the

list, distributed robotics, refers to the way in which a group of small robots can keep in touch with each other and perform complex jobs over a wide area. A similar sort of system has been proposed for home robots that wander around eating up dust and waste. Ideally they would turn this into heat, migrating to those parts of the room that need to be warmed. Another aspect of distributed robotics comes from studies on ants, which have shown that their adaptability is at least in part based on the way in which they organise themselves. This enables them to go from an exploratory mode (for instance in a chaotic environment) to a totally goal-orientated mode, when they know exactly what they want to do. In architectural terms this begins to sound interesting, because the robots can combine local and global requirements in their behaviour, and this sounds like a possibility for an aggregating system for the automatic design and construction of buildings. When the foundations are being laid, with the attendant lack of knowledge about the structure of the ground beneath the surface, they are calibrated to chaotic mode. Once foundations have been established, they move over to goal-seeking mode. But since the command structure is a continuum between these two modes, it allows the ants to stay flexible in their organisation and adaptable in the structures that they

a) Schirmarme ablängen und zuspitzen ...
b) ... auf Gabelkopfdurchmesser
c) Gabelkopf und Schirmspitzen verbinden und kleben
d) ... Blech ausschneiden ...
e) ... längs falten ...
f) ... in drei Segmenten biegen ...

a) Cut the brolly arms to length and taper them off ...
b) ... to the diameter of the fork-shaped head
c) Connect and glue the fork-head and brolly tips
d) ... Cut out tin ...
e) ... Fold lengthways ...
f) ... Bend into three segments ...

a) ... falzen, zuschneiden und lochen
b) Fertigen Verbindungsstück zwischen drei Schirmen
c) Detail
d) Linearmotor am Schaft des Schirmes
e) Detail
f) Schaltung
g) Versuchsanordnung Einzelschirm

a) ... Fold, cut to length and punch holes
b) A complete connecting unit among three umbrellas
c) Detail
d) Linear motor on the umbrella shaft
e) Detail
f) Control
g) Provisional arrangement of an individual umbrella

ein kumulatives System für automatischen Entwurf und Konstruktion von Gebäuden. Fehlt bei der Herstellung von Fundamenten das Wissen um die Strukturen der Erde unter der Oberfläche, so sind die Ameisen in chaotischer Weise organisiert. Sind die Fundamente jedoch einmal hergestellt, so gehen sie zu einem zu suchenden Modus über. Da aber die Befehlsstruktur das Kontinuum zwischen diesen beiden Modi ist, erlaubt sie den Ameisen, in ihrer Organisation flexibel und in den Strukturen, die sie herstellen, anpassungsfähig zu bleiben. So können sie auf unterschiedliche äußere Bedingungen reagieren, indem sie die Struktur leicht aber anpassungsfähig erhalten. Sie könnten auf innere und äußere Lichtverhältnisse reagieren, um Fenster der richtigen Größe an der richtigen Stelle zu platzieren.

Diese Gedanken laufen auf die folgenden verfügbaren Merkmale hinaus: lokale, unabhängige Wirkkräfte, die zu zeitweiligen Aktivitäten in der Lage sind. Sie nutzen lediglich eine ladungserhaltende Energiezufuhr. Funktionen die in ihrer Variabilität begrenzt sind, dabei aber absolut zuverlässig, da sie eher auf einer lokalen Managementstruktur fußen als auf einer globalen Steuerung.

In ähnlicher Richtung wird im Advanced Concepts Team der European Space Agency in Noordwijk in den Niederlanden geforscht. Roboter sammeln sich eigenständig in unabhängig voneinander berechneten Bewegungsabläufen, um dann in einer vorherbestimmten Struktur zusammenzukommen. Zunächst müssen wir den lokalen Bedingungen gestatten, die Struktur zu bestimmen, oder wir müssen den Robotern die Fähigkeit geben zu spüren, wie ihre Präsenz die lokalen Bedingungen verändert hat und wie sie ihren Beitrag zur Struktur modifizieren können. Und was treibt diese Gedanken, zumindest zum Teil, an? Die Idee der Autonomie, des Energiemanagements

und der spezifischen, neuen Mechanismen, die der Biologie abgeschaut wurden. Die nächste Generation der Raumstationen wird eine Menge des strukturellen Designs der Biologie und der Bionik verdanken.

Ist das ein Sciencefiction-Luftschloss? Viele Sciencefiction-Konzepte werden Realität – zum Teil, weil ihre Ideen in der Traumwelt wurzeln. Gibt es eine Sciencefiction der Architektur? Ich habe keine gesehen. Viele Sciencefiction Erzählungen nutzen imaginäre Architektur als Hintergrund und als einen Weg, die Geschichte im Kontext einzuführen. Ich habe jedoch noch keine Sciencefiction - Erzählung gelesen, in der die Architektur das Hauptthema wäre.

Vielleicht ist es das, was wir brauchen – eine Architekturbewegung, die auf Star Trek und Star Wars basiert. Eine Architektur, deren Gebäude robotertechnisch sind, anwachsend und sich ändernd in Reaktion sowohl auf die Umgebung als auch auf die Bewohner – ohne die direkte Intervention eines Menschen.

make. Thus they could respond to varying external loads in order to keep the structure light but adaptive, and could respond to both internal and external lighting conditions in order to put windows of the right size in the right places.

These thoughts (musings/propositions?) lead to the following available characteristics: local independent effectors, capable of intermittent action using only a trickle-charge energy supply; functions which are limited in range but totally reliable because they rely on local management structure rather than global control.

Research along similar lines is being conducted by the Advanced Concepts Team of the European Space Agency at Nordvijk in the Netherlands. Robots are combining autonomously on independently calculated trajectories to aggregate into a predetermined structure. Next we need to allow the local conditions to determine the structure, or give the robots the ability to sense how their presence has changed the local conditions and to modify their contribution to the structure.

And what is, at least in part, driving these thoughts? The ideas of autonomy, energy management, and specific novel mechanisms that have been stolen from biology. The next generation of space stations will owe much of their structural design to biology and biomimetics.

Is it Sci-Fi pie in the sky? Many science-fiction concepts become reality, partly because the ideas have been seeded in the dream world. Is there a science fiction of architecture? I haven't seen one. Many Sci-Fi stories use imaginative architecture as their backdrop, and as a way to establish the context of the story, but I haven't come across a Sci-Fi story in which the architecture is the main theme.

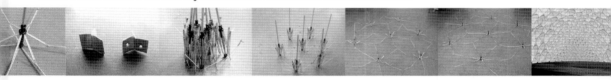

So perhaps that's what we need – a movement in architecture based on Star Trek, or Star Wars. An architecture where the buildings are robotic, growing and changing, in response to both the environment and the inhabitants, without the direct intervention of humans.

a) sechsarmiger Schirm
b) Knotenpunktelement
c) Sieben Schirme gefaltet
d)-f) Entfaltung der Struktur aus sieben Schirmen
h) Innenansicht des Dome

a) Six-arm umbrella
b) Nodal point element
c) Seven umbrelias, folded
d)-f) Unfolding of the structure of seven umbrellas
g) Interior view of the dome

Stefan Endewardt/Erfahrisator WiSe 2002/03

Shadow-Play.

Tageskarte
Map of the day

DER ERFAHRISATOR

Der "Erfahrisator" konstruiert durch die Verknüpfung verschiedener non-visueller Impulse (hören, fühlen, riechen) in einer nach einem abstrakten Muster zusammengeführten Situation eine neue Erfahrung. Ziel ist es, komplexe Sachverhalte als Mustervernetzung zusammen zu denken und so den mentalen Raum zu gestalten und zu erweitern. Um die Wirkung durch Konzentration zu unterstützen, hüllt die räumliche Konstruktion die gerade "erfahrende" Person in einen geschützten Raum und gibt ihr ein Gefühl von Geborgenheit.

THE EXPERIENCE-MAKER

The "Erfahrisator" or "experience-maker" constructs a new experience through the combination of different non-visual senses (hearing, feeling, smelling) in a situation that is created according to an abstract pattern. The aim is to unite complex problems as an exemplary network by the power of thought and thus to design and extend the mental space. To support the energy concentration, the spatial construction wraps the person who is just "experiencing" in a protected room and thus gives the person a feeling of security.

Pläne des Erfahrisators *Drawings of the Experience-Maker*

U-Alexanderplatz
Underground station Alexanderplatz

The experience-maker ist the result of an analysis of transfer.
It is constructed to bind non-visual sensations to a new experience.
The first test took place at the catacombs of the Berlin Alexanderplatz. The experience resulted from the components:
soil - to touch
humans - to listen
vibrations - to feel
thunderstorm - to hear
The experiment was sucessful through its location within the exhibition area and through its timeless dimension.

- heavy traffic
- light traffic
- experience-maker

Project:

Stand-Positio

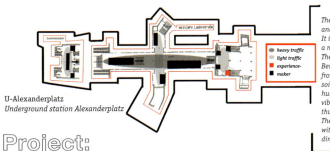

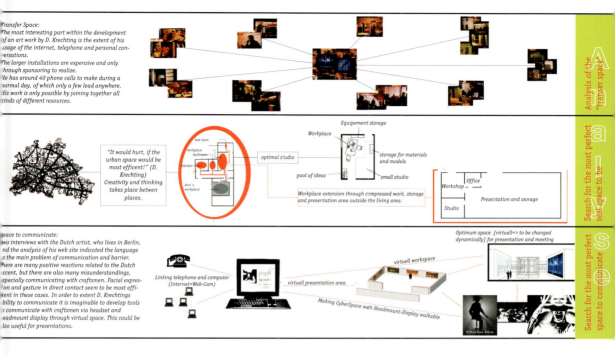

Transfer Space:
The most interesting part within the development of an art work by D. Krechting is the extent of his usage of the internet, telephone and personal conversations.
The larger installations are expensive and only through sponsoring to realize.
He has around 40 phone calls to make during a normal day, of which only a few lead anywhere.
His work is only possible by joining together all kinds of different resources.

"It would hurt, if the urban space would be most efficient!" (D. Krechting)
Creativity and thinking takes place between places.

Space to communicate:
Two interviews with the Dutch artist, who lives in Berlin, and the analysis of his web site indicated the language as the main problem of communication and barrier. There are many positive reactions related to the Dutch accent, but there are also many misunderstandings, especially communicating with craftsmen. Facial expression and gesture in direct contact seem to be most efficient in these cases. In order to extent D. Krechtings ability to communicate it is imaginable to develop tools to communicate with craftsmen via headset and headmount display through virtual space. This could be also useful for presentations.

A — Analysis of the "transfer space"
i — Search for the most perfect real space to be
s — Search for the most perfect space to communicate

Der Erfahrisator ist ein Produkt der Auseinandersetzung mit der Dekonstruktion von Realitätsverständnissen (individuelle und Gruppensichtweisen vs. totale Realität), dem Versuch der Komplexitätserfassung durch Musterverknüpfungen und der Personen-, Raum- und Tätigkeitsanalyse des niederländischen Künstlers Dirk Krechting, die mit der Aufgabe verbunden war, seine gesellschaftliche Dienstleistung in ein neues „Produkt" zu transformieren, das seiner Tätigkeit gerecht wird und anwendbar ist.

The "Erfahrisator" or "experience-maker" is a product of the debate on the deconstruction of conceptions of reality (individual and group perspectives versus total reality). It is the attempt at grasping complexity by connecting patterns; people, space and activity of the Dutch artist, Dirk Krechting, were analysed in order to transform his social service into a new "product" that lives up to his activity and is at the same time applicable.

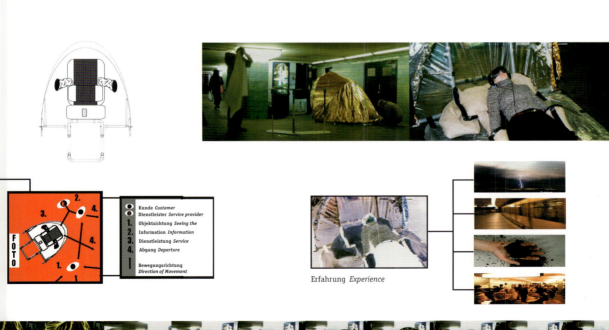

Kunde *Customer*
Dienstleister *Service provider*
1. Objektsichtung *Seeing the*
2. Information *Information*
3. Dienstleistung *Service*
4. Abgang *Departure*

Bewegungsrichtung *Direction of Movement*

Erfahrung *Experience*

Stefan Endewardt / The Sky-Base Project SoSe 2003

Sky-Station

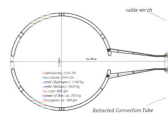

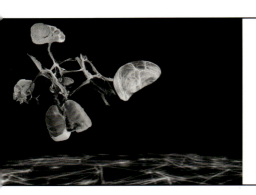

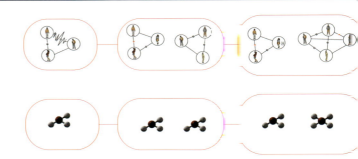

SKY-BASE-PROJEKT

Das Sky-Base-Projekt ist der Versuch, eine architektonische Struktur zu schaffen, die Individualität und Kollektivität vereint. Sie soll Prozesse und Situationen gerecht werden, Geborgenheit, Sicherheit, Flexibilität und Selbstbestimmtheit bieten. Die Wahl, mit wem und wo zusammengelebt wird, bleibt offen, so das die Schwelle sich den Veränderungen von Tatsachen anzupassen, niedrig gehalten wird und auf destruktive Situationen reagiert werden kann.
Vorausgegangen war die Aufgabenstellung, Architektur auf vier Parkplätzen zu planen, was durch die „Base-Station", die als Versorgungs- und Infrastruktureinheit funktioniert, erfüllt ist.

SKY-BASE PROJECT

The Sky-Base-Project is the attempt to create an architectural structure that unites individuality and collectivity. It is meant to do justice to processes and situations and offer security, safety, flexibility and self-determination. The choice remains open as to with whom and where cohabitation is to be, so that the threshold is kept low for adapting to changing facts and a reaction can be given to the "destructive" situations.
The task that preceded was to plan architecture on four parking spaces, which is fulfilled by the "Base-Station" that functions as a supply and infrastructure unit.

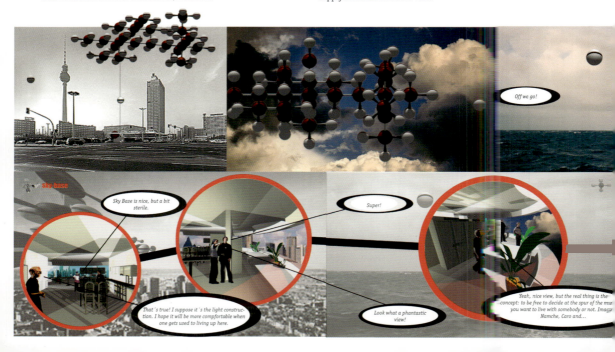

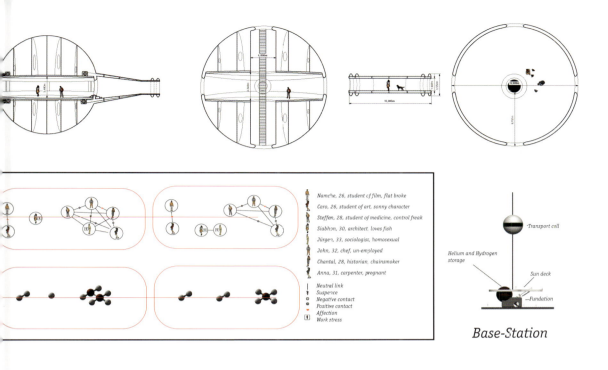

Analytischer Einfluss auf das Projekt und Ausgangspunkt der Überlegung, wie Raum beschaffen sein sollte, war die Betrachtung der Probleme und Vorzüge des Hausprojekts Erkelenzdamm 45 in Berlin/Kreuzberg und die WG, in der ich in diesem Projekt lebe. Technisch ist das Projekt ein Produkt interdisziplinärer Forschung und ein dadurch zusammengetragenes Wissen.

Anzumerken ist, dass die gewählte Form einer realisierten Traumvorstellung entspricht, die als solche möglicherweise elitär und sozial bedenklich ist und daher eher als Struktur für neue Gedankenansätze gesehen werden kann, um andere Problemlösungen zu denken.

The analytical resources for the project and the starting point for deliberation of how the space is to be formed were observations of the problems and advantages of the housing project at Erkelenzdamm 45 in Berlin-Kreuzberg and the shared house I live in as part of this project. Seen technically, the project is a product of interdisciplinary research and of knowledge gathered in that way.

It is to be noted that the chosen form corresponds to a dream notion that has been achieved and as such is possibly elitist and socially suspect and therefore is rather to be seen as a structure for new approaches in order to solve other problems.

Matthew Griffin

Architektur Ausdehnen

Architektur wird mehr als alle anderen Kunstformen von sozialen, ökonomischen, technischen und physischen Strukturen beeinflusst, die außerhalb der Kontrolle der Architekten liegen. Sie sind die Matrix, innerhalb derer der Architekt arbeitet. Wir bezeichnen diese Strukturen als „Prästrukturen". Die Zwänge oder Möglichkeiten, die sie hervorbringen, sind manchmal offensichtlich, oft jedoch sehr subtiler Natur. In jedem Fall haben diese Prästrukturen großen Einfluss auf jedes Projekt. Der Unterschied zwischen gutem Design auf Papier und einem guten Gebäude wird oft dadurch bestimmt, wie der Architekt mit ihnen umgeht. Beispiele sind im ökonomischen Bereich:

Etats, Geschäftspläne, finanzielle Limits, die das eigene Engagement betreffen;

Im technischen Bereich ist es die Infrastruktur, die eine Aktion ermöglicht oder effizienter macht, wie zum Beispiel Hardware, Software, Werkzeuge.

Schließlich würde man auch Raum, Zeit und die Gesetze der Physik als Prästrukturen bezeichnen, ebenso wie das Wissen und die Gedankenmuster, die unser Verhalten bestimmen, oder Gesetze und Organisationsformen, die Arbeit in verschiedenen Maßstäben ermöglichen.

Ganz allgemein bestimmt Kommunikation die Qualität der Interaktion und die Möglichkeiten der Aktion.

Diese Prästrukturen waren für Architekten schon immer problematisch. Trotz ihrer großen Auswirkungen auf die tägliche Arbeit gibt es wenig Diskussion über die Möglichkeiten der Einflussnahme. Diese Möglichkeiten sind aber tief in sämtliche Prozesse integriert und kommen oft auf einer persönlichen Ebene „hinter den Kulissen" zum

Space Race
Stückguthalle am Ostbahnhof,
Berlin 1999

Space Race
Freight depot Ostbahnhof, Berlin 1999

Expanding Architecture

Architecture, more than any other art form, is influenced by social, economic, technical and physical structures which are beyond the control of the architect. These can be called "prestructures" and they are the matrix within which the architect works. Sometimes the constraints or opportunities arising from them will be obvious and at other times more oblique, but regardless, these prestructures have a large influence on a project, and the difference between a good design on paper and a good building is often determined by how an architect deals with them. Some examples are:

Economic – budgets, business plans, financial limits on one's own engagement;

Technical – infrastructure that makes an activity possible or more efficient, such as hardware, software, tools;

Physical – space, time, and the laws of physics;

Social – knowledge and thought patterns which determine behaviour, legal systems that prescribe what is possible, or forms of organisation which make work possible on different scales;

Communication – which determines the quality of interaction, and possibilities for action.

These prestructures have always posed problems for architects. Despite their large effect on the profession, there is little discussion of them with respect to design issues. These influences are integrated deep within all processes, most of which work at a personal level "behind the scenes". Because this kind of insight is

Space Race
Stückguthalle am Ostbahnhof,
Berlin 1999

Space Race
Freight depot Ostbahnhof, Berlin 1999

Tragen. Da diese Art von Einsicht für außenstehende Dritte schwer zu erlangen ist, konzentriert sich dieser Artikel auf die Idee des Designs der Prästrukturen innerhalb des Kontextes unseres Büros *Deadline* im Verlauf der letzten acht Jahre. Wir unterscheiden nicht zwischen der Lösung von Designaufgaben und den Strategien, die notwendig sind, die zugrundeliegenden Prästrukturen zu überwinden. Dies bedeutet, dass wir neue Rollen übernehmen, die außerhalb der klassischen Architektentätigkeit liegen, um so unser Aktionsfeld aktiv zu erweitern. Die Ausdehnung unseres Berufs hat uns größere kreative Freiheit gegeben, als es konventionellere Herangehensweisen an Architektur ermöglichen.

Unsichtbare Arbeit

Da die zugrundeliegenden Prästrukturen einen wesentlichen Anteil an dem Ergebnis eines Projektes haben, konzentrieren wir unsere Forschung zunächst darauf. Erst im zweiten Schritt setzen wir uns mit dem gewünschten Endprodukt auseinander. Wenn wir kreative Wege finden, mit den Prästrukturen umzugehen, entstehen daraus unerwartete und manchmal einzigartige Ergebnisse. Während der 90-er Jahre haben wir viele Experimente am Rande der Architekturproduktion gemacht. Um einen geeigneten Rahmen zu schaffen, haben wir 1997 zunächst mit mehreren Leuten *Urban Issue*, eine Art Galerie, gegründet, die es in dieser Form bis dahin in Berlin nicht gab. An diesem offenen Ort haben unsere Arbeiten größtenteils die Form einer Installation oder Präsentation angenommen.

Später wurden wir, um unsere gebauten Projekte *Slender + Bender* zu realisieren, zunächst Projektentwickler. Wir kauften ein Grundstück, entwickelten einen Geschäftsplan und verhandelten die Finanzierung mit Banken. Die Annahme dieser Rolle gab uns unvergleichliche Flexibilität und einen Grad von kreativer Freiheit, der nur in seltenen Glücksfällen in einer herkömmlichen Kunden-Architekten-Beziehung erreicht werden kann. Alle unsere Arbeiten in diversen Medien durchzieht ein konstantes Interesse an den Entwicklungen moderner Kommunikationstechnologien und deren direkten Auswirkungen auf die gebaute Umwelt. In vielen Projekten haben wir direkte oder indirekte Versuche mit diesen Technologien gemacht.

Technologie-Experiment Nr. 1: Space Race (1999)

Space Race – eine Zusammenarbeit mit *büro.genial* – war eine Installation, die mit den räumlichen Beziehungen experimentierte, die durch moderne Kommunikationstechnologien neuerdings möglich geworden sind. Indem bestehendes Material (Autos) mithilfe von Kommunikationstechnologie (Zeitung, Radio, Fernsehen und Internet) kurzzeitig umgelenkt wurde, konnten wir innerhalb weniger Stunden eine riesige Struktur (400m x 5m x 2m) in einer verlassenen Bahnhofshalle in einem östlichen Industriegebiet Berlins konstruieren. Die Fahrer, die unserem Aufruf gefolgt waren, parkten ihre Fahrzeuge auf einer gefährlich schmalen (5m) Plattform. Bei Anbruch der Dämmerung schalteten alle Fahrer ihre Blinker an und ihre Radios auf volle Lautstärke, so dass die Leere mit Sound und Licht durchdrungen war. Besucher spazierten entlang der Plattform und erlebten ein wellenartig bewegtes akustisches Feld, das die vielfältigen Radiostationen verströmten. Dieses Feld transformierte die undefinierte Länge der Halle in eine Abfolge von kleinen und

Bender, Berlin 2004

Bender, Berlin 2004

difficult to attain without firsthand knowledge, this article presents the ideas of prestructural design within the context of our office, *Deadline*, over the last eight years. In our practice we do not separate solving a design problem from the strategies needed to overcome underlying prestructural issues. This has meant that we must take on new roles outside the realm of architecture, and expand our field of action. This expansion of our profession has allowed us more creative freedom than is usually available in more conventional approaches to architecture.

Invisible Work

These initial prestructures have a major effect on the outcome of a project, so our research is often focused on the prestructures rather than the end products. If we can develop creative ways to deal with the prestructures, this will often lead to unexpected, and sometimes unique results. During the nineties we did many experiments on the edges of architectural production. These mostly took the form of installations or presentations in the gallery *Urban Issue*, which we initiated in 1997.

More recently we became developers in order to realise our first buildings (Slender + Bender). Assuming this extra role gave us unparalleled flexibility, and a degree of creative freedom that is difficult to attain working within a typical client/architect framework. Throughout our work in various media, one of our constant interests has been the changes caused by communications technologies and their direct consequence for the built environment. In many of our projects we have experimented with these technologies directly or indirectly.

Technology Experiment No. 1: Space Race (1999)

Space Race, a collaboration with *büro.genial*, was an installation that experimented with the new spatial relationships available through communication technology. By temporarily re-organising existing material (cars) using communication technology (newspaper, radio, television and the Internet) we were able to construct a large (400m x 5m x 2m) structure in a few hours, in an abandoned railway hall in Berlin's industrial east end. The drivers who followed the call parked their vehicles on a precariously narrow (5m) platform. At dusk the drivers switched on their radios, lit their blinkers and saturated the emptiness with sound and light. Visitors walked along the main deck and experienced an undulating acoustic field emanating from the radios, each tuned to a different station. This field transformed the hall's indefinite length into a succession of distinct aural spaces, optically fused by a blinking, pulsing mass of cars.

The prestructure employed in *Space Race* was the flexibility and accessibility of communication technology. This pervasive technology is one of the key changes in our society, and will have many subtle prestructural effects on our built environment in the coming decades.

Bender: Eingangsbereich
Bender: entrance

Flexible Revolution

The information revolution is changing our society as dramatically as the industrial revolution did two centuries ago. Although this new revolution affects all areas of our lives, it does not remove architecture from its grounding in physical

großen auralen Räumen, optisch verschmolzen durch die blinkende und pulsierende Masse der Autos.

Die Prästruktur, die in *Space Race* voll ausgeschöpft wurde, war die Flexibilität und Zugänglichkeit von Kommunikationstechnologie. Diese allgegenwärtige Technologie ist eine der Hauptveränderungen in unserer Gesellschaft. Sie wird unsere gebaute Umwelt in den kommenden Dekaden mit zahlreichen subtilen prästrukturellen Effekten prägen.

Flexible Revolution

Die Informationsrevolution verändert unsere Gesellschaft heute in demselben Maß wie die industrielle Revolution vor zwei Jahrhunderten. Obwohl die Revolution alle Bereiche unseres Lebens berührt, kann sie die Architektur nicht der physischen Präsenz entziehen. Gebäude werden weiterhin mit Hammer und Nagel gebaut, sie existieren im physischen Raum und werden in ihm genutzt, sie bedienen dieselben menschlichen Bedürfnisse wie seit Tausenden von Jahren.

Die heute meistdiskutierten prästrukturellen Veränderungen in der Architektur betreffen die neue Software, die es erleichtert, komplexe Geometrien zu beschreiben und zu bauen. Eine der weniger offensichtlichen Verschiebungen ist die Art, wie wir heute unsere Städte benutzen. Neue Gebäudetypologien, neue Lebensstile und neue Produktionsmethoden bringen sehr langsame, aber umso deutlichere Gesichtsveränderungen hervor. Diese prästrukturellen Veränderungen können für Architekten neue Handlungsräume schaffen, indem sie neue Wege, neue Projekte und neue Sichtweisen aufdecken.

Technologie-Experiment Nr. 2: Templace.com

1999 begannen wir, an *templace.com* zu arbeiten. Es ist ein Web-Werkzeug, das die temporäre Nutzung von städtischen Räumen erleichtert und ermöglicht. Der Impuls für das Projekt entsprang eigener Erfahrung: Sechs Monate dauerten die Verhandlungen zur Anmietung eines leerstehenden Ladenraumes für *Urban Issue*, einen experimentellen Ort, den wir mit einer Gruppe von Leuten von 1997–99 betrieben haben. Unverhältnismäßig viel Zeit und Energie floss in die Beschaffung eines geeigneten Raumes im Vergleich zu dem Zeitraum der tatsächlichen Nutzung.

Raum nach Bedarf

Könnte die Zeit, die man braucht, um einen Raum zu finden, von sechs Monaten auf einige Stunden oder Tage reduziert werden, so bedeutet diese prästrukturelle Veränderung einen enormen Aktivitätsschub für die Stadt. Verlassene und vernachlässigte städtische Gebiete könnten leichter reaktiviert werden. *Templace.com* könnte es ermöglichen, Räume in regelmäßigen Abständen zu nutzen. In innerstädtischen Gebieten, in denen Raum schwer zu finden ist, könnte dadurch größere Flexibilität erzeugt werden. Raum müsste nur für die Zeiten gemietet werden, in denen er genutzt wird: Mieter A nutzt einen Yogaraum montags und Mieter B nutzt denselben Raum freitags für einen Tanzkurs.

Wir haben das Web-System *templace.com* im Rahmen von *Urban Catalyst*, einem von der EU geförderten Forschungsprojekt, entwickelt. In seiner derzeitigen

Space Race *Space Race*

presence. Buildings will continue to be built with hammers and nails, exist and be used in physical space, and satisfy the same most basic human needs that they have satisfied for thousands of years.

The prestructural contexts surrounding and accompanying the construction and use of buildings have shifted throughout history and will continue to shift. This not only changes day-to-day architectural practice, but also the end products of these processes: the buildings themselves.

The most discussed prestructural change in architecture today is the recent introduction of design software, which is contributing to this flexible revolution by making complex geometry easier to describe and build. Some of the less obvious shifts involve changes in the way we use our cities. New building typologies, new lifestyles and new production methods are slowly but surely resurfacing our cities. These prestructural changes can create new space for architects to act by revealing new paths, new projects, and new points of view.

Technology Experiment No. 2: Templace.com

Space Race *Space Race*

In 1999 we began work on *templace.com*, a web tool to support and encourage the temporary use of urban space. The impetus for the project came from our experience running the gallery *Urban Issue* in Berlin Mitte from 1997 to 1999, where we spent 6 months organising a lease for an empty shop below our apartment. The time we spent arranging a lease for the space was vastly disproportionate to the amount of time spent using the space.

Space on Demand

If one could reduce the time spent finding a space and negotiating a lease to a matter of days or hours, this prestructural change would increase the amount of activity in a city and could also help reactivate deadened urban areas. By allowing tenants to rent space in recurring intervals, *templace.com* could bring more flexibility to high density areas where free space is hard to find, because space would not have to be rented for times when it was not being used.

We developed the web system *templace.com* within an EC funded research project, *Urban Catalyst*, and in its current version it offers free web-based database

Version bietet *templace.com* temporären Nutzern kostenlose Datenbanksysteme an, auf deren Grundlage sie ihre Erfahrungen und ihr Wissen teilen können. Es bietet außerdem ein einfaches System für das Marketing und die Verwaltung von temporär genutzten Räumen. Das System steht weiterhin jedem zur Verfügung, der Interesse hat, dieses Experiment fortzuführen.

Gebautes Experiment Nr. 2: Bender

Die besonderen Vorteile dieser Kommunikationswerkzeuge führen zu der Idee, die unser letztes Projekt *Bender* ermöglicht hat. *Bender* ist ein siebengeschossiges Gebäude in Berlin-Mitte mit acht *Miniloft*®-Apartments, die über das Internet an Kurzzeitbesucher vermietet werden. Die Studioapartments sind eine komfortable Alternative zu einem Hotelzimmer.

Als absehbar wurde, dass die Zeiten für Architekten härter werden würden, entschlossen wir uns, selbst zu Projektentwicklern zu werden. Nach zweijähriger intensiver Suche kauften wir ein schmales Grundstück an einer Hauptverkehrsstraße, am westlichen Rand des ehemaligen östlichen Zentrums.

Im vorderen Grundstücksbereich gab es eine überwucherte Kellerruine, im hinteren Bereich einen schmalen, viergeschossigen Seitenflügel mit acht Einzimmerwohnungen, der dringend sanierungsbedürftig war. Der Bau fand in zwei Phasen statt. Die Sanierung des Altbaus (*Slender*) begann 2001. Die zweite Phase, der Neubau (*Bender*), endete 2004. Das fertige Projekt ist eine komplexe Verflechtung von Neubau und Sanierung. Bender ist eindeutig zeitgemäß und bezieht sich auf seinen Kontext, ohne nostalgisch oder retrospektiv zu sein.

SlenderBender gehört zu einer neuen urbanen Gebäudetypologie, die eine lebendige Mischung diverser programmatischer Funktionen auf kleiner Fläche integriert. Das Projekt verbindet Kurzzeit-*Minilofts*®, Büroräume, einen Laden, Parkplätze und ein „Einfamilienhaus".

Der potentielle Ertrag aus den *Minilofts*® erlaubte es, ein geiziges Gebäude auf einem so kleinen Grundstück zu realisieren, das die meisten Projektentwickler als unbebaubar bezeichnen würden.

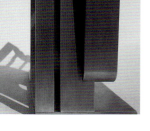

Bender: Modell *Bender: model*

Schönheit der Finanzen

Da Gebäude finanziell funktionieren müssen, ist es ein ebenso wichtiger Schritt, einen Geschäftsplan zu entwerfen, der genug Kapital abwirft, um das Gebäude zu finanzieren, wie eine einzigartig überzeugende architektonische Idee zu entwickeln.

Das Design des Gebäudes berücksichtigte viele verschiedene Aspekte, die alle zusammen funktionieren mussten. Das Scheitern nur eines Aspektes konnte leicht zum Zusammenbruch des gesamten Projektes führen. Da das Grundstück sehr klein und die Architektur ungewöhnlich war, waren die Baukosten bezogen auf die nutzbaren Quadratmeter sehr hoch. Diese Kosten wurden durch höhere Mieteinnahmen ausgeglichen, die durch das Kurzzeitapartmentkonzept generiert wurden. Dies wiederum wurde erst durch die flexible Revolution, in diesem Fall die Internetvermarktung, möglich.

Diese Finanzdesignfragen zu lösen war eine der Hauptaufgaben, die wir in unserer Doppelrolle als Architekten und Developer annahmen. Wir „entwarfen" die

systems for temporary users to share their experience and expertise, and a basic system for marketing and managing temporarily rented spaces. The system is still available for anyone interested in continuing this experiment.

Built Experiment No. 2: Bender

The specific advantages of these communication tools led to the idea that made our latest project, *Bender*, possible. It is a seven-storey building in central Berlin and houses eight *miniloft*® apartments which are rented through the Internet on a short-term basis to people visiting Berlin. The studio apartments are a comfortable alternative to a hotel room.

Without built references, it is almost impossible for a young architect to find his or her first client. To circumvent this, we became developers. After two years of searching, we purchased a narrow site on a busy street in an area that used to be on the western edge of East Berlin.

The front half of the site was an overgrown bombsite. The slender four-storey building that survived at the rear contained eight small apartments and had seen little change in the previous 50 years. Construction was undertaken in two phases. Built Experiment No.1, the renovation of the surviving structure *Slender* began in 2001. The second phase *Bender*, the new building in front, ended in 2004. The finished project is a complex interweave of new construction and renovation. Bender is clearly contemporary, and it relates to its context without being retrospective or nostalgic.

Slender-Bender belongs to a new typology of urban buildings that integrates a lively mixture of programmatic functions on a small site. The project combines short-term *minilofts*®, office space, a family "house", a shop, and parking.

The potential rate of return provided by the *minilofts*® allowed us to construct an ambitious building on a site so small that most developers would consider it unbuildable.

Bender - abends *Bender at dusk*

Fiscal Beauty

Because buildings need to function financially, devising a business plan that could generate enough capital to finance the building was just as important a step as conceiving a striking architectural idea. The design of the building took on many different aspects, which all had to work together. Failure in one of these aspects could easily have lead to the collapse of the whole project. Because the site was small, and the building unusual, the building costs per usable square meter were very high. These costs, however, were offset by higher rents generated by the short-term rental concept, made possible by the flexible revolution.

These fiscal design issues where one of the key tasks we assumed in our dual role as developer and architect. In doing this we "designed" the economic prestructure of the project rather than simply accepting financial constraints that would have undermined the project.

Priority Focus

By bundling client and architect, we could focus the project more precisely and consistently than would have been possible in a conventional client-architect

ökonomischen Prästrukturen des Projektes, anstatt die finanziellen Begrenzungen, die das Projekt unterminiert hätten, einfach zu akzeptieren.

Fokus der Prioritäten

Durch die Bündelung von Auftraggeber und Architekt konnten wir das Projekt viel präziser und nachhaltiger fokussieren als in einer herkömmlichen Kunden-Architekten-Beziehung. Wir schlossen das übliche Problem, dass die Qualität der Architektur dem finanziellen Programm des Kunden geopfert wird, aus. Natürlich konnten wir die finanziellen und rechtlichen Begrenzungen nicht ignorieren, aber wir konnten sie unserem Ziel, herausragende Architektur zu realisieren, unterordnen.

Über ein Jahr haben wir mit der Bauaufsicht verhandelt, um sechs Ausnahmen von der Berliner Bauordnung zu erwirken. Auf diese Weise haben wir die legalen Prästrukturen geschaffen, die notwendig waren, um *SlenderBender* so zu bauen, wie wir das Gebäude geplant hatten. Normalerweise hätten die meisten Auftraggeber den Architekten in einer solchen Situation gezwungen, das Design radikal den behördlichen Anforderungen anzupassen, um die hohen Kosten durch die Verzögerung zu vermeiden.

Geld spricht

Als wir anfingen, das Gebäude zu entwerfen, hatten wir uns ziemlich naiv vorgenommen, dass wir alle finanziellen Aspekte zweitrangig behandeln würden, um das zu bauen, was wir für das Beste hielten. Dies war eine unserer Richtlinien, die das gesamte Projekt durchzogen. Sie bedeutete eine Herausforderung im Umgang mit den finanziellen Rahmenbedingungen.

Banken wollen kein Risiko eingehen. Ihr finanzielles Engagement ist üblicherweise auf einen Anteil begrenzt (80 Prozent), der sich auf den niedrigstmöglichen Wiederverkaufswert des Besitzes bezieht – ein Wiederverkaufswert, der deutlich unter den marktüblichen Raten liegt. Dieser prästrukturelle Zwang macht es schwer, ein Gebäude zu finanzieren, das mehr kostet als die akzeptierten Durchschnittspreise, die die Banker für ihre Wertschätzungen benutzen.

Unerwartete, sich verändernde ökonomische Zwänge sind eine nicht zu ignorierende Prästruktur. Während der Bauzeit von *SlenderBender* waren wir von diversen ökonomischen Krisen betroffen, die alle zu einem desaströsen Ende der ganzen Unternehmung hätten führen können. Das ganze Projekt hindurch war es eine unserer schwierigsten Aufgaben, Wege zu finden, um die immer neuen finanziellen Probleme kreativ zu lösen.

Ausdehnung des Aktionsfeldes

Der prästrukturelle Rahmen ist ein essentieller Teil jedes architektonischen Projektes. Er ist mehr als ein Ausgangspunkt oder eine Aufgabenstellung und er ist in alle Prozesse integriert, die das gesamte Projekt betreffen.

Bis heute ist der Einfluss der Prästrukturen auf Architektur weitgehend außerhalb des architektonischen Diskurses geblieben. Indem die Berücksichtigung der prästrukturellen Faktoren ein integraler Teil des Designprozesses wird, können Architekten ihren Aktionsradius erweitern und ihre Chancen erhöhen, herausfordernde Projekte zu realisieren.

Bender: Zeitplan *Bender: timetable*

-72 / 12.5	Construction
-60 / 14	Tender Documents
-48	
-36 / 34	Planning Permission
-24	
-12 / 18	Property Search

relationship. This meant we were able to avoid the common problem of good architecture being sacrificed to a client's financial agenda. Although we could not ignore the financial and legal limitations placed upon us, we refused to let them dominate in decisions that could undermine our goal of creating an outstanding building.

We spent one year negotiating six exemptions from the Berlin building code to establish the legal prestructures necessary to construct *Bender* the way we had designed it. In this situation, most normal clients would have forced their architect to radically alter the design simply because the cost of the delay involved was too high.

Money Talks

When we started designing, we rather naively declared to ourselves that we were going to make all budgetary aspects secondary and build what we thought was best. This was one of our guiding principles throughout the project, and made sorting out the financial framework challenging.

Banks do not want to take risks. Their financial engagement is usually restricted to a proportion (about 80%) of the lowest possible resale value of the property, a resale value that is significantly less than going market rates. This restrictive prestructural constraint makes it difficult to finance a building that costs more than the accepted averages bankers use for their valuations. The argument that a building of extraordinary character has a higher market value than a standard one has no quantification in German banking rules.

Shifting economic pressures, often unexpected, are a prestructure that is impossible to ignore. During the construction of *Bender* we experienced several "economic crises", which could have put a disastrous end to the whole undertaking. Throughout the project, finding ways to solve the financial problems was our most difficult and important task.

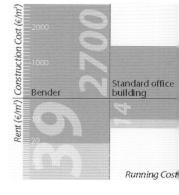

Bender: Kostenvergleich

Bender: cost comparison

Expanding Action

The prestructural framework is a quintessential part of any architectural project. It is more than a departure point or a brief, and is integrated into all the processes that constitute a project.

Despite this, for good architecture to become reality it requires talented, engaged, and unrelenting architects. To date, the influence of prestructures on architecture has largely remained beyond the scope of architectural discourse. By considering prestructural factors an integral part of the design process, architects can expand their radius of action, and improve their chances of realising challenging projects.

Lutz Kandel

Der neue Architekt

Kaum einer bestreitet, dass mehr Absolventen der Architekturstudiengänge in den Markt wollen, als dieser aufnehmen kann. Das deutsche Architektenblatt nennt für 1999 bereits 6666 Absolventen, denen etwa 3600 altersbedingt ausscheidende Architekten gegenüberstehen (DAB. Heft 11/2000, S. 1408). Die Anzahl von Kollegen, die wegen mangelnder Auftragslage ausgeschieden sind, ist nicht in dieser Zahl enthalten. Insgesamt ist die Aufnahmefähigkeit des Marktes geringer geworden. Früher galt als Faustregel, dass etwa die eine Hälfte der Absolventen durch die öffentliche Hand und ihr zuzurechnende Institutionen aufgenommen werden und die andere Hälfte durch die Bauwirtschaft und freie Büros. Der öffentliche Sektor stellt heute nur noch in ganz wenigen Fällen Absolventen ein, gleiches gilt für die Bauwirtschaft. Dem immer noch stark nachgefragten Studium der Architektur steht inzwischen eine zögerlich reduzierte Ausbildungskapazität der Hochschulen (einschließlich der Fachhochschulen) gegenüber. Jedoch bricht das Interessen ausgebildeten Architekten schneller weg als diese Kapazitäten reduziert werden können. An allen Hochschulen ist aber der Trend erkennbar, dass Studenten aus ökonomischen Erwägungen freiwillig das Studium aufgeben.

Es heißt, „alle Wirtschaftsentwicklung verläuft zyklisch". Das Bauwesen und die planenden Berufe spürten dies. Die älteren Kollegen haben alle bereits mehrere Zyklen der Nachfrage nach Bauleistungen erlebt und trösten sich damit, dass es ja auch einmal wieder besser werden müsste. Leider wird diese Hoffnung enttäuscht werden. Die planende Branche lebt von Investitionen der öffentlichen Hand, der Industrie und der gewerblichen Immobilien und Wohnungswirtschaft.

Wir alle wissen, wie leer die öffentlichen Geldtöpfe zwischenzeitlich sind und wie hoch der Schuldenstand der Stadt- und Staatshaushalte ist. Die Industrie baut in Osteuropa und Asien mehr als in Deutschland. Die Immobilienwirtschaft sitzt auf Halden von unvermieteten Bürokomplexen und wird zudem von Skandalen und Mittelabfluss aus den offenen Immobilienfonds geschüttelt. Die Wohnungswirtschaft ist durch Leerstand, schrumpfende Städte und zurückgehende Baugenehmigungen gekennzeichnet.

Wenn sich die öffentliche Hand als Bauherr weitgehend zurückzieht, der Industriebau in Deutschland der Globalisierung zum Opfer fällt, die Immobilienwirtschaft zurückhaltender bauen wird und der Wohnungsbau sich auf den Einfamilienhausbau in den Speckgürteln um die großen Städte im Westen konzentrieren wird, reduzieren sich die klassischen Aufgaben für Architekten drastisch – zumal der Bau von Einfamilienhäusern und die Sanierung von Bestandsimmobilien im Selbstverständnis vieler Architekten nicht mehr zu den Kernbereichen ihrer Tätigkeit zählen.

Die Globalisierung und die Fehler der Politiker können nur zu einem Teil für diese Entwicklung, die die Fortexistenz des Berufsstandes infrage stellt, verantwortlich gemacht werden. Gravierender in der Auswirkung ist die demographische Ent-

The New Architect

Few dispute the fact that there are more architecture graduates wanting to enter the market each year than can be absorbed. *Deutsches Architektenblatt* has already given a figure of 6,666 graduates for 1999, compared with around 3,600 architects retiring because of age (DAB Vol. 11/2000, p. 1408). This number does not contain the amount of architects retiring due to insufficient orders. The overall capaciousness of the market has lessened. There used to be a valid rule of thumb that around half the graduates were absorbed by public authorities and affiliated institutions and the other half by the building and construction industry and independent offices. Today, the public sector creates very few new jobs for graduates. The same is true for the building and construction industry. There is still a strong demand for architecture courses but this contrasts with the hesitantly lowered education capacity of universities (including the technical high schools). However, the demand for architects is disappearing faster than this capacity can be reduced. There is a recognizable trend at all universities of students abandoning their studies voluntarily due to financial considerations.

It is said that fluctuations in economic development follow a cyclical pattern. The building and construction industry as well as the planning professions have experienced this. The older colleagues have all seen several cycles of demand and decline in construction work and are comforted by the thought that things are bound to get better. Unfortunately this hope is unfounded. The planning sector is dependant on investment from the public coffer, industry, and the commercial real-estate and housing sectors.

In the meantime, we are all aware of how poor the public authorities have become and how high their budget debt is. Industrial development is more prolific in Eastern Europe and Asia than in Germany. The property sector is sitting on mountains of untenanted office properties and has been shaken by scandals and a funding drain from the open property funds. The housing sector is characterised by empty properties, shrinking cities and fewer planning and building commissions.

If public spending can no longer be considered a significant source of commissions, industrial construction in Germany is a victim of globalisation, construction in the property economy will become more restrained and residential construction will focus on building detached houses in the stockbroker belts around the large cities in the west, and the traditional tasks of architects are diminished. This is particularly so since architects no longer consider the construction of detached houses and redevelopment of inventory assets part of their core activities.

Globalisation and the errors of politicians can only be made partly responsible for this situation, which calls into question the continued existence of the expert profession. Graver consequences can be expected from the transformation

wicklung der Bevölkerung, die – wie allgemein bekannt – von einem Weihnachts- zu einem Kugelbaum mutiert.

Die heute über 40-Jährigen sind mit Wohnraum und aller weiteren Infrastrukturleistungen wie Krankenhäusern und Museen gut versorgt. Für die nachwachsenden, heute noch jüngeren Jahrgänge wird diese Versorgung sehr großzügig sein, da sie für höhere durchschnittliche Jahrgangsstärken ausgelegt ist. Es wäre vermessen, aus dieser Entwicklung eine Steigerung der Zahl und des Umfangs von Architektenaufträgen zu erwarten. Hoffnung versprechen Architektentätigkeiten im Ausland, insbesondere dort, wo die Immobilienmärkte boomen.

Wie reagieren Architekturstudenten auf diese Entwicklung? Ein Teil verlässt die Hochschulen ohne Abschluss, ein weiterer großer Teil schließt die Augen vor der Entwicklung und hofft auf bessere Zeiten. Die Findigen besetzen Randgebiete und leben dort ihre Kreativität aus, was nicht ausschließt, dass ab und an Architektenleistungen erbracht werden.

Beispiele aus meinem Umfeld:

A unterhält ein Büro für die Vermessung von Altbauten, Rohbauten und Baudenkmälern.

B hat ein Stadtteilkino übernommen und betreibt dieses mit Events, Wunschfilmen und Stadtteilarbeit.

C veranstaltet Stadtführungen mit dem Schwerpunkt Architektur, produziert Reiseführer und Stadtpläne für Architekten.

D hat eine kleine Firma für Innenausbau und Planung aufgebaut und realisiert schlüsselfertige, Gewerke begreifende Kleinaufträge.

E entwirft, baut und betreibt Kulissen für Film und Fernsehen

F ist in einer Wirtschaftsprüfersozietät als Fachmann für Immobilien tätig.

G hat sein Hobby zum Hauptberuf gemacht und verchartert Yachten.

H betreibt einen erfolgreichen Club und veranstaltet Events.

Stefan Kels, Fabian Greiff, Andreas Pohl:
www.hitch-net.de

Wenn ich diese Realitäten mit den Studien- und Prüfungsordnungen der Hochschulen vergleiche, komme ich zu dem Schluss: Die Hochschulen verstellen durch die primäre Konzentration auf das klassische Entwerfen von Hochbauprojekten den Blick auf viele weitere Möglichkeiten. Sie sind bei der aktuellen Gestaltung der Studienpläne derart mit der Organisation des Generationswechsels der Lehrenden, der Abwehr von Budgetkürzungen und der Einführung von Bachelorstudiengängen beschäftigt, dass das Ergebnis der Schrumpfkuren oft weniger von überlegtem, zielgerichtetem Handeln als von Zufälligkeiten des hochschulpolitischen Alltagsgeschäfts zeugt.

Die geschilderte Entwicklung führt zu einem Dilemma für Ausbildungsstätten und Studienpläne:

- Die Hochschulausbildung ist derzeit auf das Erlernen des Entwerfens als Kernkompetenz des Architekten ausgerichtet. Es zählt vor allem der schöne Entwurf.

- Die Mehrheit der Absolventen wird jedoch mit der klassischen Architektentätigkeit, wie sie die HOAI beschreibt, und insbesondere mit dem Entwerfen von Gebäuden im späteren Berufsleben kaum oder nur am Rande in Berührung kommen.

of Germany's population demographic which, as is generally known, is slowly beginning to bulge at the top.

Today's over 40s have ample living-space and sufficient access to infrastructure provisions such as hospitals and museums. This provision may not benefit later generations in the same manner, since it was designed to cater for a top-heavy age demographic. It would be presumptuous to expect an increase in the number and the extent of commissions for architects as a result of this development. Architectural activities abroad are promising, however, especially in those nations where real estate markets are booming.

How are architecture students reacting to this development? A number of them leave university without a degree; many of them close their eyes to the developments and wish for better times. The crafty occupy fringe areas and rely on their creativity, this does not exclude rendering architectural services every now and then.

Here are examples from my environment:

A runs an office for assessing old buildings, ruins and historical monuments.
B took over a district cinema and screens events, chosen films and local work.
C organizes tours of the city which focus on architecture, produces travel guides and city maps for architects.
D established a small company for interior design and planning, which carries out small orders designed for occupants that specialise in different handicrafts.
E designs, constructs and operates sets for film and television.
F is active in an accounting firm as a real estate expert.
G has made a profession out of his hobby by renting out yachts.
H runs a successful club and organizes events.

When I compare these real-life outcomes with the study and exam regulations of the universities I reach the following conclusion: universities breed a sort of short-sighted fatalism in their students, blinding them to other career possibilities through a strict focus on classic design protocols for standard engineering projects. While drawing up the current course structures, universities are busy organising the changing of the guard among the alumni, fending off proposed budget cuts and introducing new bachelor courses. Therefore the seemingly successful results of the cutback procedures are often more a consequence of general trends in the marketplace and changes to tertiary education policies rather than deliberate and well thought-out action.

These developments lead to a dilemma for education institutions and study courses:

- All relevant university courses teach design as a core competency of the architectural discipline.

- Emphasis is placed on aesthetic design.

- Most graduates seldom have any significant contact with classic architectural activity as it is described in the HOAI (the official Fee Structure for Architects and Engineers); particularly tasks such as designing buildings will be just marginally encountered in later professional life.

This has been aggravated by the rulings of the Federal Supreme Court. In recent

Verschärfend ist die Rechtssprechung des BGH. Sie ist – was das Wissen des Architekten angeht – in den letzten Jahren immer rigider und fordernder geworden. In der Umsetzung würde dies Studienpläne erfordern, die sich extrem am klassischen Architektenbild mit bautechnischer und bauwirtschaftlicher Spezialisierung orientieren.

Aus diesem Dilemma kann die Neugliederung der Studiengänge in Bachelor- und Masterstudien einen Ausweg eröffnen. Es wäre denkbar, den Bachelorstudiengang primär als Ausbildung von Generalisten zu sehen. Kammerfähigkeit der Absolventen wäre dabei kein Ausbildungsziel. Diese wäre für die wenigen zu erreichen, die sich einem speziellen Masterstudium als einem von mehreren alternativen Studiengängen unterzögen. Das Masterstudium könnte dann neben dem Entwerfen die notwendigen bauwissenschaftlichen und bauwirtschaftlichen Vertiefungen bieten.

Generalist bezeichnet dabei denjenigen, der viele Sachverhalte nur im Überblick kennt, aber fähig ist, übergreifende Konzepte zu entwickeln. Ich sehe ihn als Gegenpol zum Ingenieur, der von wenigen Sachverhalten sehr viel weiß. Die Generalistenausbildung benötigt ein breites Fächerangebot. Wichtig wäre es auch, das zu erhalten und zu fördern, was heute schon unsere Studierenden auszeichnet. Sie lernen, zu einem Problem, von dessen Lösung sie zunächst keine Ahnung haben, Informationen zu beschaffen und zu ordnen, Lösungsvorschläge zu entwickeln, diese zu präsentieren und zu bewerten. Das Entwickeln von Geschäftsideen und Erstellen von „Businessplänen" ist eine logische Fortsetzung dessen.

Der klassische Architektenberuf war Teil eines Bereitstellungsgewerbes. Der Architekt hielt Leistungsbereitschaft vor und wartete auf einen Auftraggeber. Angesichts der deutlich gesunkenen Nachfrage rückt das Entwickeln von Geschäftsideen in den Vordergrund der Architektentätigkeit: Es sind Ideen gefragt, die unter ästhetischen wie auch unter ökonomischen Aspekten gut sind.

Zwei Projekte, die unter meiner Betreuung für den Renault Traffic Design Award 2003 zum Thema „Raststätten der Zukunft" entstanden sind und mit Preisen bedacht wurden, verdeutlichen meine Hoffnung: Das Projekt *Fast-0-Stau* von Lisa Rezbach sieht mobile, durch Werbung finanzierte Miniraststätten mit WC und Dusche vor, die an Autobahnen genau dort aufgestellt werden, wo sich zur Ferienzeit Staus bilden. Das Projekt www.hitch-net.de von Stefan Kels, Fabian Greiff und Andreas Pohl sieht eine Einbeziehung von Raststätten in ein internetgestütztes Vermittlungssystem von Mitfahrgelegenheiten vor. Dazu werden in Serie produzierte Container mit Vermittlungs-, Warte-, Dusch- und Übernachtungsmöglichkeiten an vorhandenen Raststätten aufgestellt.

Beide Projekte zeigen Ansätze, die über das reine Entwerfen von Gebäuden hinausgehen. All denen, die dazu fähig sind, wird die Zukunft unseres Berufsstandes gehören.

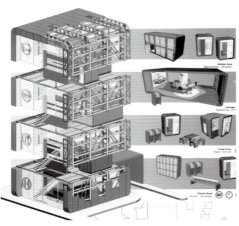

Stefan Kels, Fabian Greiff, Andreas Pohl: www.hitch-net.de

years it has become increasingly rigid and imperious where the architectural discipline is concerned. In their implementation, they would require degree courses to orient themselves towards the classic image of the architect; specialising in the design and industrial construction of buildings.

Splitting the degree courses into bachelors and masters presents one solution to this dilemma. It is conceivable to perceive the bachelor degree as a generalist education with a broad, multidisciplinary focus. The goal of such courses would not necessarily be to ensure the graduates' suitability for professional engagement. Instead, a masters degree would be made available to a select few. However this would present only one of several alternative study paths. The masters studies could then offer, in addition to design aspects, the necessary industrial and building construction know-how.

By "generalist" I mean a scholar who is familiar with a wide range of disciplines, but who is still capable of developing comprehensive concepts and engaging profoundly with a single discipline. I see him as a counterpoint to the engineer, who knows a great deal within a few disciplines. Generalist education requires a broad range of subjects. Of equal importance would be the preservation and support of what makes our students so special. They learn to obtain information regarding a problem, whose solution they initally have no idea of. They learn how to organise this information, propose solutions, present and assess them. Developing business initiatives and creating business plans are a logical continuation of this.

The classic architectural profession was part of a supply business. The architect advertised readiness to undertake a commission and waited for a client. In the context of clearly diminished demand, developing business schemes has now moved into the fore of the architect's activity. What is needed are ideas, ones that are successful both aesthetically and economically.

Lisa Rezbach: Rest-O-Stau

My hope is clarified by two projects on the theme of "service areas of the future", completed under my supervision, which won prizes in the 2003 Renault Traffic Design Awards. The *Rest-O-Jam* project by Lisa Rezbach places mobile, advertising-financed amenities such as toilets and showers along motorways where traffics jams tend to occur during the holiday season. The project *www.hitch-net.de* from Stefan Kels, Fabian Greiff and Andreas Pohl provides a service in which hitch-hikers can organise their trips over the internet. Mass-produced capsule units set up at service stations along the highway provide temporary amenities such as showers, beds and internet access for hitch-hikers organising their trips.

Both projects show approaches that go beyond pure building design. The future of our profession belongs to those of us who are able to innovate in this manner.

Semesterthemen

k_studio: Semesterthemen
Eine auszugsweise Zusammenstellung der wesentlichsten thematischen Zusammenhänge in den einzelnen Semestern.

SOMMERSEMESTER 2001 (2. Semester Grundstudium)
Thema: „Architektur und Film" mit Studienreise nach Holland.
Vergleichende Filmanalysen zu den Filmen „Lola rennt" und „Der Himmel über Berlin". Herausarbeitung signifikanter Sequenzen aus den Filmen und Gegenüberstellung mit den realen Drehorten in Berlin. Entwicklung eines Entwurfsprojekts zum Film-Raum im realen Stadt-Raum.

WINTERSEMESTER 2001/02 (3. Semester Grundstudium)
Thema: „Hybrid"
Übungen zur räumlichen Artikulation der Begriffe „Arbeiten", „Baden", „Schlafen", „Verführen" und zu ihrer Hybridisierung. Entwicklung eines perfekten, hybriden Raums. Verortung und Weiterentwicklung der Hybride in Entwurfsprojekten am Bahnhof Friedrichstraße in Berlin.

SOMMERSEMESTER 2002 (4. Semester Grundstudium)
Thema: „Hybrid"
Vertiefung der Entwürfe aus dem vorherigen Semester mit speziellem Fokus auf die Themen „Tragkonstruktion", „Innenraum" (Türspion-Innenraummodell) und „Außenwirkung" (Bauschild). Projektbegleitende Studienreise nach Istanbul. Mitorganisation und Teilnahme an der Jahresausstellung der Fakultät.

WINTERSEMESTER 2002/03 (1. Semester Grundstudium)
Thema: „Transfer 1"
Grundlagen des zwei- und dreidimensionalen Darstellens. Erforschung einer Person, die eine Dienstleistung ausführt, mit der mehrteiligen Übung „Shadowplay" als Grundlagen für das 1:1-Entwurfsprojekt „Transfer Public Test" mit Marktständen für jegliche Art der Dienstleistung – von der Fahrradreparatur zum Raumerlebnis – im U-Bahnhof Alexanderplatz.

SOMMERSEMESTER 2003 (2. Semester Grundstudium)
Thema: „Transfer 2 – Material"

Zahlreiche Exkursionen zu verschiedenen Betrieben: Betonfertigteile-, Holzsäge-, Holzplatten- und Stahlwerk, Fertighaus- und Seiltragwerkhersteller, Volkswagen-Werk, Filmstudio Babelsberg, Lichtdesigner. Nach verschiedenen Materialexperimenten am Modell: Weiterentwicklung des Themas des ersten Semesters zu einem kleinen Gebäude unter Verwendung einer bestimmten Materialkombination und der entsprechenden Technologie. Städtebaulicher Entwurf: „Matrix", betreut von Robert Slinger und Gal Riviere, Fachgebiet Städtebau Prof. Luise King. Mitorganisation und Teilnahme an der Jahresausstellung der Fakultät.

WINTERSEMESTER 2003/04 (3. Semester Grundstudium)
Thema: „Transfer 3 – Stadt und Markt"
Studienreise nach London, Analyse von Londoner Märkten: Dokumentation spezifischer Handels- und Wohnsituationen, Weiterentwicklung eines räumlichen Themas, Entwurfsprojekt an fünf Standorten rund um den Berliner Moritzplatz.

SOMMERSEMESTER 2004 (4. Semester Grundstudium)
Thema: „Transfer 4"
Vertiefung der Entwürfe aus dem vorherigen Semester mit vier Schwerpunkten, zu denen zuerst einwöchige Workshops durchgeführt werden: „Skin", „Touch", „Licht" und „Program". Die Workshopergebnisse werden in die Projekte eingearbeitet.

WINTERSEMESTER 2004/05 (1. Semester Grundstudium)
Thema: „Transfer 1"
Grundlagen des zwei- und dreidimensionalen Darstellens. Erforschung eines „Bauherrn" und seiner räumlichen Arbeits- und Wohnsituation mit der mehrteiligen Übung „Shadowplay" als Grundlagen für das 1:1-Entwurfsprojekt „Temporäre Läden" im U-Bahnhof Alexanderplatz und „Kommunikator" im Foyer des Architekturgebäudes der TU Berlin.

Vorträge / Lectures

SoSe 2001 Hugo Beschoor-Plug: *Amsterdam*; Thomas Kutschker: *Die verschwundene Grenze*; Winfried Pauleit: *Tektieren*; Marc Ries: *Wrong Way*; **WiSe 2001/02** Antje Buchholz + Jürgen Patzak-Poor: *Shifting the View*; Robert Slinger: *Templum*; **SoSe 2002** Florian Böhm: *CAEx - Erkundungen in neuen Entwurfsräumen*; Sebastian Finkh: *Einführung in Form Z I und II*; Erik Göngrich: *Istanbul*; Karsten Hochkirch: *Hydrodynamische Formoptimierung im Designprozess*; Harald Kloft *Materials Experience - Konstruktion und Realisierung von Frei-Form-Architekturen*; Anupama Kundoo: *Material Matters*; Axel Thallemer: *Airtecture*; Neil Thomas: *NO*; Julian Vincent: *Smart by Nature*; Hüsnü Yegenoglu: *Istanbul, das Ende von 1001 Nacht*; **WiSe 2003/04** Arturo Gogollo: *Bauen und Lehren in Columbien*; Andrew Holmes: *One day in my life*; Martin Kaltwasser: *Zehn Jahre Winterakademie*; Robert Mull: *The University of North London*; Cordelia Polinna: *London*; Minze Tummescheidt: *Jarmark Europa*; **SoSe 2004** Marie-Therese Harnoncourt: *Materialexperimente, Werkbericht*; **WiSe 2004/05** Jason Danziger: *Mapping*; **SoSe 2004** Harald Kloft: *Engineering Form*

Gastkritiker / Guest Critics

Markus Bader, Sandra Bartoli, Andrea Benze, Antje Buchholz, Hugo Beschoor-Plug, Nancy Couling, Uwe Dahms, Daly Deda, Jason Danziger, Sebastian Finkh, Isabell von Fournier, Oliver Elser, Christiane Fath, Katharina Feldhusen, Benjamin Foerster-Baldenius, Gunda Förster, Ernst J. Fuchs, Judith Giseler, Stephan Siebener, Stella Geppert, Matthew Griffin, Wolfgang Grillitsch, Marie-Therese Harnoncourt, Florian Haydn, Markus Hirschmüller, Susanne Hofmann, Andrew Holmes, Rüdiger Ihle, Stephanie Kaiser, Martin Kaltwasser, Birgit Klauck, Holger Kleine, Alexander Koblitz, Anne König, Anupama Kundoo, Michaela Kunze, Thomas Kutschker, Anuschka Kutz, Jean Lamborelle, Rainer Maria Löneke, Claudia Lüling, Noel Mac Cauley, Christof Maier, Philipp von Matt, Volkmar Nickol, Karin Ocker, Anne-Marie O´Connor, Ines Rudolf, Ulrike Rau, Matthias Reese, Uwe Rieger, Frank Roost, Ines Schaber, Martina Schmitt, Florian Schmid, Robert Slinger, Gabor Stark, Jörg Stollmann, Christian Teckert, Pamela Theodorakopoulou, Friedrich Tuczek, Svantje Uphoff, Julian Vincent, Katrin Voermanek, Paola Yacoub, Nicole Zahner, Rudolf Zimmermann

Topics, Workshops, Excursions

k_studio: Semester Subjects
A selected compilation of the most essential thematic connections from individual semesters.

SUMMER SEMESTER 2001
2nd Semester: "Architecture and Film" with study visit to Holland Comparative film analysis of the films "Lola Rennt" and "Der Himmel über Berlin". Concentration on significant sequences from the films and comparison with the actual shooting locations in Berlin. Development of a design project on the film and actual city space.

WINTER SEMESTER 2001/02
3rd Semester: "Hybrid"
Exercises on the spatial articulation of the ideas of "working", "bathing", "sleeping", "seducing" and their hybrid forms. Development of a perfect hybrid space. Location and further development of hybrids in design projects at Friedrichstraße station in Berlin.

SUMMER SEMESTER 2002
4th Semester: "Hybrid"
Extending the designs from the previous semester with special focus on the subjects "load-bearing constructions", "interior space" (door-spy interior space model) and "exterior effect" (building sign). Study visit to Istanbul to accompany project. Co-organisation and participation in the faculty's annual exhibition.

WINTER SEMESTER 2002/03
1st Semester: "Transfer 1"
Basics of two- and three-dimensional representation. Research on a person, who performs a service with the multi-part exercise "Shadowplay" as a basis for the 1:1 design project "Transfer Public Test" with market stands for every kind of service, from bicycle repair to spatial experience at Alexanderplatz underground station.

SUMMER SEMESTER 2003
2nd Semester: "Transfer 2 – Material"
Numerous excursions to different factories: for pre-fabricated concrete parts, a sawmill, for wooden beams and steel works, for prefabricated housing, a suspension/supporting frame manufacturer, the Volkswagen factory, the Babelsberg film studios and a light designer. After different material experiments on the model: further development of the first semester subject to a small building, using a particular material combination and corresponding technology. Urban design project: "Matrix", supervised by Robert Slinger and Sarah Riviere, chair for Urban Design Prof. Luise King. Co-organisation and participation in the faculty's annual exhibition.

WINTER SEMESTER 2003/04
3rd Semester: "Transfer 3 – City and Market"
Study visit London, analysis of London markets: documentation of specific trading and living situations, further development of a spatial theme, design project in five locations around Berlin's Moritzplatz.

SUMMER SEMESTER 2004
4th Semester "Transfer 4"
Extension of previous semester's designs with four focal points on which initial one-week workshops are carried out: "Skin", "Touch", "Light" and "Programme". The workshop results are integrated into the project.

WINTER SEMESTER 2004/05 (1st semester)
1st Semester: "Transfer 1"
Foundations of two- and three-dimensional representation. Research of a client, his spatial working and living situation, with multi-part exercise "Shadowplay" as the basis for the 1:1 design project "Temporary Shops" in the Alexanderplatz underground station and "Communicator" in the foyer of the architecture building at the TU Berlin.

k_ studio

von Sommersemester (SoSe) 2001 bis Sommersemester (SoSe) 2005 / from Summer Semester (SoSe) 2001 till Summer Semester (SoSe) 2005

Wissenschaftliche Mitarbeiter / Associate professors:

Claire Karsenty	WiSe 99 – WiSe 01, SoSe 03 – SoSe 05
Paul Grundei	WiSe 00 – WiSe 02, WiSe 03 – WiSe 05
Thomas Arnold	WiSe 00 – SoSe 03, SoSe 04 – SoSe 06
Elke Knoess	SoSe 01 – WiSe 04, SoSe 06 – SoSe 06
Barbara Böhm	SoSe 02 – WiSe 02
Rudolf Zimmermann	SoSe 03 – WiSe 03, SoSe 05 – WiSe 05

Lehrbeauftragte /Lecturers:

Philipp von Matt	SoSe 05
Cornelia Schluricke	SoSe 05
Gabor Stark	WiSe 00

Tutoren / Undergraduate assistants:

Gesa Büttner	WiSe 99 – SoSe 01
Katja Barthmuss	WiSe 99 – SoSe 01
Cornelia Schluricke	WiSe 00 – SoSe 02
Sven Morhard	SoSe 01 – SoSe 02
Anja Müller	SoSe 01 – WiSe 02
Anne Heusmann	WiSe 01 – WiSe 03
Dag Thies	WiSe 01 – SoSe 02
Yan Humbert	WiSe 02 – SoSe 04
Philipp Kring	WiSe 02 – SoSe 04
Daniel Wahl	WiSe 02 – SoSe 03
Christoph Jantos	SoSe 03 – WiSe 04
Beate Schmiegel	WiSe 03 – WiSe 04
Stefan Haas	SoSe 04 – WiSe 05
Marie Harms	WiSe 04 – SoSe 05
Ariane Wiegner	WiSe 04 – WiSe 05

Autoren

Thomas Arnold
Geboren 1965, Architekt
Architekturstudium an der Hochschule der Künste Berlin und der Architectural Association London, 1993 AA Diploma. Multidisziplinäre Arbeiten umfassen Planungen und Realisierungen von Gebäuden, Rauminstallationen und Filme. Unterrichtet Architektur seit 1997 u.a. an der University of Westminster London und der Technischen Universität Berlin. Veröffentlichungen im Bereich Architektur- und Gebäudelehre. Seit 2001 workspheres:research mit Birgit Klauck.
Lebt in Berlin.

Antje Buchholz
Geboren 1967, Architektin
Studium an der Hochschule der Künste Berlin und der Architectural Association London, Dipl.-Ing. 1996. Seit 1998 als Mitglied der Gruppe BAR (Base for Architecture and Research) Mitarbeit an der Entwicklung und Umsetzung von Stadtplanungs- und Bauprojekten. Feldstudien im Rahmen verschiedener Stipendien und Forschungsprojekte, insbesondere zu Alltagspraktiken im Stadtraum von Neapel, London und Warschau. Ausstellungen ihrer Videoarbeiten u.a.: Kunstverein Düsseldorf und Archilab 2004 in Orléans. Mehrfache Gastkritiken an verschiedenen Architekturschulen. Leitung eines Seminars „Urbane Anthropologie" an der Freien Universität Berlin.
Lebt und arbeitet in Berlin.

BAR : Base for Architecture and Research
(Antje Buchholz, Michael von Matuschka, Jack Burnett-Stuart, Jürgen Patzak-Poor)
Die Berliner Gruppe BAR wurde 1992 gegründet. Vier in enger Beziehung zueinander stehende Aktionsbereiche definieren die Arbeitsweise der Gruppe: das Konzept Ökonomie als das Fundament jedes Projektes; der Einsatz von Modellen, der es ermöglicht, grundlegende städtische Themen zu bearbeiten; Fallstudien als Untersuchungsmethoden für urbane Vielfalt; und experimentelles Bauen, der Raum, innerhalb dessen die Kompetenz des Architekten immer wieder neu definiert wird. Dieser konzeptionelle Rahmen wurde von BAR an verschiedenen Orten Europas eingesetzt, um einen Interaktionsprozess zwischen Ort, Architekt und Bewohner zu initiieren. Zuletzt hat sich BAR intensiv mit Wohnungsbau (m^3-house, seit 2003, und Schwedter Straße 26, 1999–2002), Stadtforschung und Entwicklungsprojekten (*City in Conflict*, 2003–2004, *Building Initiative*, 2004–2005) befasst.

Gunda Förster
Geboren 1967, Künstlerin
1991–1997 Studium an der Hochschule der Künste Berlin. 1996 Deutscher Kunstpreis, 1997 DAAD-Stipendium, 1998 Karl Schmidt-Rottluff Stipendium, 2001 Stipendium der Senatsverwaltung für Kultur Berlin, 2003 Stipendium der Stiftung Kunstfonds Bonn, 2003 H.W. & J. Hector Kunstpreis, 2004 Lux.us Lichtkunstpreis. Ausstellungen, temporäre und permanente Arbeiten in Athen, Berlin, Bonn, Budapest, Chicago, Dresden, Düsseldorf, Edinburgh, Genf, Hannover, Leipzig, Malmö, Mannheim, Moskau, München, New York, Recklinghausen, Rethymnon, Seoul, Stockholm, Tokio, Weimar, Wiesbaden, Wismar, Yokohama, Zürich.
Lebt in Berlin.
www.gunda-foerster.de

Thorsten Frank
Geboren 1960, Dipl.-Ing.
Studierte Wirtschaftsingenieur- und Bauingenieurwesen an der Technischen Universität Berlin, Abschluss als Dipl.-Ing. 1986. 1986 bis 1989 Innovationsassistent, später Technischer Leiter von Corocord Raumnetz GmbH, 1990–1992 DED-Entwicklungshelfer in Nepal (Hängebrückenbau). Seit 1992 Geschäftsleiter von Corocord Raumnetz, 2003 Gründung von AGS Leicht Bauten GmbH, beider Gesellschafter und Geschäftsführer.
Lebt in Berlin.

Matthew Griffin
Geboren 1969, Architekt
Studierte Architektur an der McGill University in Montreal (Bsc Arch 1993) und an der Architectural Association in London (AA Diploma 1996). Mitbegründer von *deadline*, zusammen mit Britta Jürgens 1993, Mitbegründer von *Urban Issue* 1997, Bau von *Slender* 2002, Architekturpreis Berlin 2003, Bau von Bender 2004.
Lebt in Berlin.

Wolfgang Grillitsch
Geboren 1966, Künstler und Architekt
Architekturstudium an der Universität für angewandte Kunst in Wien, Diplom bei Wolf Pix. 1991 Mitbegründer von *Poor Boys Enterprise* in Wien. Seit 1995 gemeinsam mit Elke Knöss des Büro Peanutz Architekten in Berlin. Leitung verschiedener 1:1 Workshops an der Technischen Universität Berlin, ABK Stuttgart, Technischen Universität Wien und an anderen Orten.
Lebt in Berlin.
www.peanutz-architekten.de

Paul Grundei
Geboren 1967, Architekt
Nach seinem Architektur-Diplom 1996 an der Akademie der Bildenden Künste Wien Übersiedlung nach Berlin. Arbeitete bis 2000 bei Axel Schultes Architekten und Barkow Leibinger Architekten. Lehrt an der Technischen Universität Berlin seit 1998. 1999–2000 ein Lehrauftrag „Städtebau für Architekten" bei Prof. Jerome King und seit 2000 als wissenschaftlicher Mitarbeiter am Fachgebiet Entwerfen und Baukonstruktion" Prof. Lutz Kandel. Mitbegründer von AS-IF, aktuelles Projekt: GFZK-2: Neubau Ausstellungsgebäude für die Galerie für Zeitgenössische Kunst in Leipzig.
Lebt in Berlin.
www.as-if.info

Susanne Hofmann
Geboren 1963, Architektin
Architekturstudium an der Architectural Association London; DAAD Stipendium, 1992 AA Diploma, Nominierung für RIBA Silver Medal. 1989: Selbstbau eines Ferienhauses, Mudge Island, Kanada. Mitarbeit in verschiedenen Büros: Steidle und Kiessler, Hamburg; Alsop und Lyall, London; sauerbruchhutton, London/Berlin; Gerhard Spangenberg, Berlin. Seit 1996 Lehrtätigkeit: University von Westminster, London, Technische Universität Berlin, HAW Hamburg. 2003 Gründung der praxisnahen Ausbildung *Die Baupiloten* in Kooperation mit der Technischen Universität Berlin, seit Juni 2004 Leitung des Studienreformprojektes „Die Baupiloten: das Studium als praxisbezogener Idealfall". Ausstellungen in London, Berlin, Hamburg, Rot-

Authors

Thomas Arnold
Born 1965, Architect
Studied architecture at the University of the Arts in Berlin, and at the Architectural Association in London; AA Diploma 1993. His multidisciplinary work ranges from building design and realisation to installations and films. Has been teaching architecture since 1997 at various schools including the University of Westminster, London, and the Technical University of Berlin. Publications in the field of architecture and building research. Since 2001 *workspheres:research*, together with Birgit Klauck.

Antje Buchholz
Born 1967, Architect
Studied architecture at the University of the Arts in Berlin and at the Architectural Association in London; Dipl.-Ing. 1996. Since 1998 participation in the development and implementation of urban design and architecture projects as a member of the group BAR (Base for Architecture and Research). Field studies in the context of several scholarships and research projects, particularly about everyday life practices in the urban realms of Naples, London and Warsaw. Exhibitions of her video works among others at Kunstverein Düsseldorf and Archilab 2004 in Orléans. Guest critic at various architecture schools. Conducted a seminar on "Urban Anthropology" at the Free University of Berlin.
Lives and works in Berlin.

BAR: Base for Architecture and Research
(Antje Buchholz, Michael von Matuschka, Jack Burnett-Stuart, Jürgen Patzak-Poor)
The Berlin-based BAR group was founded in 1992. Four interdependent areas of activity define the group's practice: the concept of economy as the foundation stone of every project; the use of models that makes it possible to address underlying city themes; case studies as an exploratory method for investigating urban diversity; and experimental construction, the space where the architect's expertise is redefined. This framework has been used by BAR in various places in Europe to initiate a process of interaction between site, architect, and user. BAR's activity has focused, more recently, on housing (*m3-house*, since 2003, and Schwedter Strasse 26, 1999-2002) and on urban research and development projects (*City in Conflict*, 2003-2004, *Building Initiative*, 2004-2005).

Gunda Förster
Born 1967, Artist
Studied from 1991 to 1997 at the University of the Arts Berlin. 1996 German Art Prize, 1997 DAAD scholarship, 1998 Karl Schmidt Rottluff scholarship, 2001 scholarship from the Department of Culture, Senate of Berlin, 2003 scholarship from the Kunstfonds Bonn, 2003 H.W. & J. Hector Art Prize, 2004 Lux.us Light Art Prize. Exhibitions, temporary and permanent work in Athens, Berlin, Bonn, Budapest, Chicago, Dresden, Düsseldorf, Edinburgh, Geneva, Hanover, Leipzig, Malmø, Mannheim, Moscow, Munich, New York, Recklinghausen, Rethymnon, Seoul, Stockholm, Tokyo, Weimar, Wiesbaden, Wismar, Yokohama, Zurich.
Lives in Berlin.

Thorsten Frank
Born 1960, Dipl.-Ing.
Studied engineering economics and civil engineering at the Technical University of Berlin, Dipl. Ing. 1986. 1986-89 innovation assistant and technical manager of Corocord Raumnetz GmbH, 1990-1992 DED development aid worker in Nepal (building of suspension bridges). Since 1992 manager of Corocord Raumnetz, 2003 founder of AGS Leicht Bauten GmbH; share holder and managing director.
Lives in Berlin.

Matthew Griffin
Born 1969, Architect
Studied architecture at McGill University in Montreal (Bsc Arch 1993) and at the Architectural Association, London (AA Dipl. 1996). Co-founder of *Deadline* with Britta Jürgens 1993, co-founder of *Urban Issue* in 1997, construction of *Slender* 2002, Architecture Prize Berlin 2003, construction of *Bender* 2004.
Lives in Berlin.

Wolfgang Grillitsch
Born 1966, Artist and Architect
Studied architecture at the University of Applied Arts in Vienna. After his diploma with Wolf Prix he co-founded *The Poor Boys Enterprise* in 1991. He moved to Berlin in 1995, where he founded *Peanutz Architekten*, together with Elke Knoess. Wolfgang Grillitsch instructed several 1:1 workshops at the Technical University of Berlin, ABK-Stuttgart, Technical University of Vienna and elsewhere.
Lives in Berlin.

Paul Grundei
Born 1967, Architect.
After his Architectural Diploma at the Akademie der Bildenden Künste (Academy of Fine Arts), Vienna, he moved to Berlin. Until 2000, he worked for Axel Schultes Architects and Barkow Leibinger Architects. Teaches at the Technical University of Berlin since 1998; from 1998–2000 as a lecturer in "Urban Planning for Architects" with Professor Luise King, and since 2000 as an assistant professor for "Architectural Design and Building Construction" at the chair of Prof. Lutz Kandel. Co-founder of *AS-IF*, current project: *GFZK-2: New Exhibition Building for the Museum of Contemporary Art in Leipzig*.
Lives in Berlin. www.as-if.info

Susanne Hofmann
Born 1963, Architect
Studied architecture at the Architectural Association in London; DAAD scholarship; AA Diploma 1992, nomination for the RIBA Silver Medal. 1989 design-built of a vacation home on Mudge Island, Canada. Worked in several offices: Steidle und Kiessler, Hamburg; Alsop und Lyall, London; sauerbruchhutton, London/Berlin; Gerhard Spangenberg, Berlin. Since 1996 teaching positions: University of Westminster, London, Technical University of Berlin, HAW

terdam und Buenos Aires. Auszeichnungen: Preis Soziale Stadt 2004, ar+d award 2004. Internationale Veröffentlichungen u.a. in: Bauwelt, Baumeister, AIT, Diseño Interior, Architectural Review, Architecture & Techniques, Metropolis, arq.
Lebt in Berlin und Hamburg.

Andrew Holmes
Geboren 1947, Architekt, Künstler
Studium der Architektur an der Architectural Association London, AA Diploma. Projekte und Publikationen im Themenfeld Kunst: 1999 *Postcards on Photography*, Cambridge Darkroom, Cambridge; 1999 *Asphalt Paradise und The Golden Hour*, Laurent Delaye Gallery, London; 2003 *Gas Tank City*, Plus One Gallery, London; 2004 *BlowUp: New Painting and Photoreality*, St Paul's Gallery, Birmingham. Projekte und Publikationen im Themenfeld Architektur: 2000 *Nighthawk City*, Aedes West, Berlin; 2001 *City of Dreams*, Trafo Haus, Galerie Aedes East, Berlin; 2002 *City by the Sea*, Galerie Aedes East, Berlin; 2003 "The Death of The Machine, Do-ing, Science Friction", Verlag der Architectural Association; 2004 "Nonument", Verlag der Architectural Association, 2005 *Light Signatures*, öffentliches Kunstprojekt, Sefton Park, Liverpool.
Lebt in London.

Cagla Ilk
Geboren 1976, Architektin
Absolvierte ihr Architekturstudium an der Architekturfakultät der Mimar Sinan Universität in Istanbul. Beschäftigte sich während ihres Studiums in der Türkei und anschließend in Berlin umfassend mit der Stadt Istanbul und beteiligte sich an verschiedenen Projekten: *Habitat – Istanbul 1996, Informelle Stadtentwicklung und Kommunikation im Stadtraum*, Istanbul 2001, *Informelle Ökonomien im Textilsektor*, Istanbul 2002, *ErsatzStadt* an der Volksbühne am Rosa-Luxemburg-Platz, Berlin 2003, „Istanbul – Self-Service City", veröffentlicht bei b-books, Berlin 2004, *1. Internationale Woche für Informelles Bauen Berlin, Rent a Room*, Berlin 2005.
Lebt in Berlin.

Lutz Kandel
Geboren 1939, Architekt, Professor für Entwerfen und Baukonstruktion
Studium der Architektur an der Technischen Universität München und der Technischen Universität Stuttgart. Redakteur und Lehrbeauftragter an der Hochschule für Gestaltung Ulm. Von 1969 bis 2000 Architekturbüro mit Prof. Dr. Horst Höfler in Stuttgart. Gastprofessur an der Eidgenössischen Technischen Hochschule Zürich von 1973 bis 1975. Seit 1980 Professor für Entwerfen und Baukonstruktion an der Architekturfakultät der Technischen Universität Berlin.
Lebt in Potsdam und Artá.

Claire Karsenty
Geboren 1969, Architektin
Studium der Architektur an der Ecole d'Architecture Paris Belleville und mit einem DAAD Stipendium 1998 an der Technischen Universität Berlin. Arbeitete nach ihrem Abschluss 1995 an verschiedenen Projekten und Wettbewerben in Paris und Berlin und war 1997 bis 1998 Mitarbeiterin des Daniel Libeskind Architectural Studio. Seit 1998 wissenschaftliche Mitarbeiterin an der Technischen Universität Berlin. Im selben Jahr Gründung von Kapok, zusammen mit Robert Slinger.
Lebt in Berlin. www.kapokberlin.com

Martin Kaltwasser
Geboren 1969, Architekt, Künstler und Kurator
Studium der freien Kunst an der Akademie der Bildenden Künste in Nürnberg, der Romanistik und Philosophie an der Freien Universität Berlin und der Architektur an der Technischen Universität Berlin. Gemeinsame Arbeiten mit Folke Köbberling.
Lebt in Berlin.

Folke Köbberling
geboren 1969, Künstlerin und Kuratorin
Studium der Architektur an der UdK in Berlin und der Bildenden Kunst an der HBK Kassel, University of Lanashire in Preston (England) und dem Emily Carr Institute of Art & Design in Vancouver.
Lebt in Berlin. www.folkekoebberling.de

Im Mai 2002 begleiteten Martin Kaltwasser und Folke Köbberling das k_studio gemeinsam mit Studierenden des Grundstudiums auf eine Exkursion nach Istanbul. Neben zahlreichen anderen Projekten waren sie seither Co-Kuratoren der Ausstellung *Learning From*, 2002–2003 (www.learningfrom.com) und *Self-Service-City Istanbul* im Rahmen des Projekts *Ersatzstadt* an der Volksbühne am Rosa-Luxemburg-Platz, Berlin, 2002–2003 (www.etuipop.de/ersatzstadt).

Birgit Klauck
Geboren 1963, Architektin und Akademische Rätin
Studierte Architektur an der RWTH Aachen, Architectural Association London und der Bartlett School of Architecture and Planning in London. Seit 1995 als Wissenschaftliche Mitarbeiterin und seit 1998 als Akademische Rätin an der Technischen Universität Berlin im Fachbereich Architektur tätig. Schwerpunkte in der Lehre sind integrative Entwurfsmethoden und die energetische Optimierung von Gebäudekonzepten. Birgit Klauck wurde 2003 erstmals in den Akademischen Senat der Technischen Universität Berlin gewählt und wirkt dort aktiv an der Gestaltung der Hochschulentwicklung mit. Seit 2001 Forschungen über Bürogebäude im Rahmen von workspheres™. Autorin und Herausgeberin des Entwurfsatlas Bürobau.
Lebt in Berlin. www.workspheres.com

Harald Kloft
Geboren 1963, Bauingenieur und Tragwerksplaner
Diplom und Doktorgrad im Bauingenieurwesen an der Technischen Universität Darmstadt. Legt seinen Schwerpunkt insbesondere auf den Tragwerksentwurf als integralen Bestandteil des architektonischen Entwurfsprozesses, wie zum Beispiel in Bernhard Frankens *Bubble*- und *Dynaform*-Pavillons für BMW und in Peter Cooks und Colin Fourniers *Kunsthaus Graz*, Österreich. Für letzteres Projekt war er Projektleiter der Tragwerksplanung für Bollinger–Grohmann. Leiter und Mitbegründer von *office for structural design* (osd), in deren Arbeit die Integration innovativer Aspekte der Tragwerksplanung sowie neue Materialien für architektonische Projekte im Vordergrund stehen. Seit 2000 Gastprofessor an der Städelschule in Frankfurt am Main, für die Architekturklasse von Ben van Berkel und Johan Bettum. Seit 2002 Professor und Dekan der Fakultät für Bauingenieurwesen an der Technischen Universität Kaiserslautern.
Lebt in Frankfurt am Main. www.o-s-d.com

Elke Knoess
Geboren 1964, Architektin
Studierte Architektur an der Technischen Universität Darmstadt und an der Architectural Association in London, 1993 AA Diploma. 1994 Aufenthalt in den USA, Mitarbeit im Büro W. McDonough an der Herman Miller Möbelfabrik, Michigan. 1998–2000 Lehrbeauftragte bei Prof. Luise King, Fachbereich Städtebau, Technische Universität Berlin. Seit 2001 wissenschaftliche Mitarbeiterin im Fachbereich Architektur, Fachgebiet Prof. Kandel, Technische Universität Berlin. 1997 Mitbegründerin von *Peanutz Architekten*, gemeinsam mit Wolfgang

Hamburg. 2003 founder of the education project *Die Baupiloten* (Building Pilots) in cooperation with the TU Berlin, since 2004 head of the academic reform project "The Building Pilots: Study as a Professionally-Oriented Ideal Scenario". Exhibitions in London, Berlin, Hamburg, Rotterdam and Buenos Aires; awards: Preis Soziale Stadt 2004, ar+d award 2004; international publications: among others Bauwelt, Baumeister, AIT, Diseño Interior, Architectural Review, Architecture & Techniques, Metropolis, arq.
Lives in Berlin und Hamburg.

Andrew Holmes,
Born 1947, Architect, Artist
Studied architecture at the Architectural Association, London, AA Dipl. Exhibitions in the field of Art: 1999 *Postcards on Photography*, Cambridge Darkroom, Cambridge; 1999 *Asphalt Paradise and The Golden Hour*, Laurent Delaye Gallery, London; 2003 *Gas Tank City*, Plus One Gallery, London; 2004 *BlowUp: New Painting and Photoreality*, St Paul's Gallery, Birmingham. Projects and Publications in the field of Architecture; 2000 *Nighthawk City*, Aedes West, Berlin; 2001 *City of Dreams*, Trafo Haus, Galerie Aedes East, Berlin; 2002 *City by the Sea*, Galerie Aedes East, Berlin; 2003 "The Death of The Machine, Do-ing, Science Friction", published by the Architectural Association; 2004 "Nonument", published by the Architectural Association, 2005 *Light Signatures*, Public Art Project, Sefton Park, Liverpool.
Lives in London.

Cagla Ilk
Born 1976, Architect
Studied Architecture at the architecture department of Mimar Sinan University in Istanbul. During her studies in Turkey, as well as later in Berlin, she analysed various aspects of the City of Istanbul within the following projects: *Habitat–Istanbul* 1996; *Informal Urban Development and Communication within the urban space*, Istanbul 2001; *Informal Economies in the Textile Sector*, Istanbul 2002, *ErsatzStadt* at the theatre Volksbühne am Rosa Luxemburg Platz, Berlin 2003; "Istanbul – Self-Service City", published by B-books, Berlin 2004; *1st International Week for Informal Building Berlin, Rent a Room*, Berlin 2005.
Lives in Berlin.

Lutz Kandel
Born 1939, Architect, Professor for Architectural Design and Building Construction
Studied architecture at the Technical University of Munich and the Technical University of Stuttgart. Editor and teacher at the University of Design, Ulm. From 1969 to 2000 architectural design firm with Prof. Dr. Horst Höfler in Stuttgart. Visiting Professor at the ETH Zurich from 1973 to 1975. Since 1980 professor for architectural design and building construction at the department of architecture of the Technical University of Berlin.
Lives in Postdam and Artá.

Claire Karsenty
Born 1969, Architect
Studied architecture at the Ecole d'Architecture Paris Belleville and in 1998 with a DAAD scholarship at the Technical University of Berlin. Worked after her graduation on various projects and competitions in Paris and Berlin, and 1997 to 1998 as part of the Daniel Libeskind Architectural Studio. Since 1998 assistant professor at the TU Berlin. Co-founded *KAPOK*, together with Robert Slinger.
Lives in Berlin.

Martin Kaltwasser
Born 1969, architect, Artist and Curator
Studied fine arts at the Academy of the Arts in Nuremberg, as well as roman languages and philosophy at the Free University of Berlin, and architecture at the Technical University of Berlin. Collaborations with Folke Köbberling.
Lives in Berlin.

Folke Köbberling,
Born 1969, Artist and Curator
Studied architecture at the University of the Arts in Berlin, as well as fine arts at the University of Fine Arts in Kassel, the University of Lanashire in Preston, England, and the Emily Carr Institute of Art & Design in Vancouver, Canada.
Lives in Berlin. www.folkekoebberling.de

In May 2002 Martin Kaltwasser and Folke Köbberling accompanied the k_studio and their first year students on an excursion to Istanbul. They have been involved in numerous projects since, among them as co-curators of *Learning From*, 2002-2003 (www.learningfrom.com) and *Self-Service-City*, Istanbul, as part of the project *Ersatzstadt* at the theatre Volksbühne am Rosa-Luxemburg-Platz, Berlin, 2002-2003 (www.etuipop.de/ersatzstadt).

Birgit Klauck
Born 1963, Architect, Associate Professor
Studied Architecture at the RWTH Aachen, the Architectural Association, London, and at the Bartlett School of Architecture and Planning, London. Since 1995 assistant professor and since 1998 member of the faculty board of the department of architecture of the Technical University of Berlin. In 2003 Birgit Klauck was first elected into the academic senate of the Technical University of Berlin. Within this function she is actively contributing to the academic progress of the University.
Since 2001 research on office buildings within worskpheres™. Author and editor of „Entwurfsatlas Bürobau" (design-handbook for office planning).
Lives in Berlin. www.workspheres.com

Harald Kloft
Born 1963, Structural Engineer
Diploma and Doctoral Degree in civil engineering at Darmstadt University of Technology. Focuses on structural design as an integral part of the architectural design process, such as in Bernhard Franken's *Bubble* and *Dynaform* pavilions for BMW and Peter Cook's and Colin Fournier's *Kunsthaus Graz* in Austria for which he took on the engineering project leadership as member of Bollinger+Grohmann. Principal and co-founder of the *office for structural design (osd)*, which focuses on the integration of innovative aspects of structural design and new materials in architectural projects. Since 2000 visiting Professor at the *Städelschule* in Frankfurt, in the architectural class of Ben van Berkel and Johan Bettum. Since 2002 tenured professor and head of the Department of Structural Design at Kaiserslautern University of Technology.
Lives in Frankfurt am Main. www.o-s-d.com

Elke Knoess
Born 1964, Architect
Studied architecture at the Technical University of Darmstadt and at the Architectural Association, London. AA Diploma in 1993. 1994 extended stay in the United States, working for W. McDonough on the Herman Miller works in Michigan. 1998-2000 assistant professor at the chair of Prof. Luise King, Department for Urban Planning at the Techincal University of Berlin. Since 2001

Grillitsch. PEANUTZ steht für kleine und große Eingriffe mit vielfältigem NUTZ. Ihre Theorien beziehen sie aus einer Reihe „designperformativer Arbeiten".
Lebt in Berlin.   www.peanutz-architekten.de

Anupama Kundoo
Geboren 1967, Architektin und Consultant für nachhaltige Architektur B.Arch der University of Bombay. Eigenes Büro seit 1990. Entwickelte verschiedene Technologien für nachhaltiges Bauen und baute mehrere experimentelle Projekte, u.a. Technologie-Transfer-Training für Arbeiter. Arbeitete für Sabine Fiebelkorn von 1992 bis 1995. Leiterin der Planungsabteilung von Auroville, Indien. Von 2000 bis 2003 Beraterin für nachhaltiges Bauen für ICAEN, Institut für Energie Catalunya, Barcelona sowie für eine Projektpartnerschaft der Städte London und Haryana, Indien, unter Schirmherrschaft der Europäischen Union. Vielfältige Reisen, weltweite Workshops und Vorträge.
Lebt zurzeit in Berlin.

Thomas Kutschker
Geboren 1963, Filmemacher, Photograph
Ausbildung zum Photographen am Lette-Verein Berlin; seit 1987 freiberuflicher Photograph. Seit 1989 als Filmemacher tätig. Seit 1992 Kameramann bei Kurz-, Industrie-, Dokumentar- und inszenierten Filmen. 1993 bis 1996 Postgraduierten-Studiengang an der Kunsthochschule für Medien in Köln, Fachbereich Film & Fernsehen. Diplom in audiovisuellen Medien. 1998 Förderpreis der Landesregierung Nordrhein-Westfalen der Gruppe für Filmregisseure und Kameraleute; 2000 Arbeitsstipendium für Künstler des Landes NRW; 2000 bis 2005 Lehraufträge an der Humboldt-Universität; 2002 Konzeption und Realisation der audiovisuellen Medien im neuen Museum der Gedenkstätte Sachsenhausen.
Lebt in Köln und Berlin.

Winfried Pauleit
Geboren 1963, Professor für Kunstwissenschaft/Kunstpädagogik an der Universität Bremen
Studium der Kunst- und Filmwissenschaft in Berlin, London und Chicago; Dr. phil. der Universität der Künste Berlin 2000. Mitherausgeber des Internetmagazins www.nachdemfilm.de, Publikationen und Vorträge in den Themenbereichen Film, Kunst und Medien, zuletzt: *Filmstandbilder. Passagen zwischen Kunst und Kino.* (Stroemfeld Verlag, Frankfurt am Main/Basel 2004). Heftredaktion zum Themenschwerpunkt: „Ästhetische Erziehung im Medienzeitalter" *Ästhetik & Kommunikation* Nr. 125 (Juni 2004); „Wie Cyborgs vom Kino lernen. Biografie versus Technologie am Besipiel von Lynn Hershmans Teknolust" in: Christine Rüffert u.a. (Hrsg.) *Unheimlich anders. Doppelgänger, Monster, Schattenwesen im Kino.* Berlin 2005, S. 161–170.
Lebt in Berlin und Bremen.

Marc Ries
Geboren 1956, Kultur- und Medientheoretiker
Diplomstudium der Philosophie, Soziologie und Erziehungswissenschaft in Wien und Klagenfurt. Promotion am Institut für Philosophie der Universität Wien. Seit 1989 Lehre in Österreich und Deutschland. 2000–2001 Vertretungsprofessor für Vergleichende Bildtheorie an der Friedrich-Schiller-Universität Jena. Von 1997 bis 2001 Leiter des Kunst- und Kulturproviders THE THING, Wien (www.thing.at). Projekte und Publikationen im Schnittfeld Medien/Kultur/Architektur und Kunst. Aktuelle Buchpublikation: Medienkulturen. (Sonderzahl, Wien 2002). Seit 2000 Arbeit an der Habilitation zu einer „Geoästhetik der Medien".
Lebt in Wien.

Robert Slinger
Geboren 1965, Architekt
Studierte Architektur in Sheffield, England. Unterrichtet Architektur und Städtebau an Universitäten in Großbritannien und Deutschland seit 1991. Von 1994 bis 1998 Projektarchitekt für Daniel Libeskinds Design Office. Wissenschaftlicher Mitarbeiter an der Technischen Universität Berlin von 1998 bis 2004. Mitbegründer von KAPOK, zusammen mit Claire Karsenty. Praktiziert und lehrt in seiner Freizeit Taiqiquan.
Lebt in Berlin.   www.kapokberlin.com

Christian Teckert
Geboren 1967, Architekt, Urbanist, Autor, Kulturproduzent
Architekturstudium an der Akademie der bildenden Künste Wien. Seit 1992 disziplinübergreifende Projekte und Publikationen an der Schnittstelle von Kunst, Urbanismus, Raumtheorie und Architektur. Gründete 1999 das *Büro für kognitiven Urbanismus* in Wien mit dem Kunsthistoriker Andreas Spiegl. 2001 Gründung von *AS-IF* mit den Architekten Stephanie Kaindl und Paul Grunze in Berlin und Wien. 2004/2005 Lehrbeauftragter am Institut für Gebäudelehre der Technischen Universität Graz. Seit 2005 Vorstandsmitglied der ÖGfA (Österreichische Gesellschaft für Architektur). Christian Teckert ist gemeinsam mit Andreas Spiegl Autor und Herausgeber von *PROSPEKT*, 2003 im Verlag Walther König, Köln erschienen.
Lebt in Wien.   www.as-if.info

Axel Thallemer
Geboren 1959, Designer und Ingenieur
Studierte Philosophie an der Ludwig-Maximilians-Universität München. Abschluss als Diplom-Ingenieur im Bauingenieurwesen an der Akademie der Künste in München. Postgraduiertenstipendium des DAAD zum Studium von Business, Public Relations und Psychologie an der NYSID, New York, USA. Professuren in München und Hamburg. Gastprofessor an der Universität von Houston, Texas, USA, sowie an den Akademien für bildende Kunst und Design Guangzhou, Canton und Tsinghua Universität, Beijing, China. Seit 2004 Dekan der Fakultät für Industriedesign der Universität für Industrielle und Künstlerische Gestaltung in Linz; außerdem Dekan der Fakultäten für Architektur, Innenraumplanung, und Städtebau. Arbeite für eine Agentur für Corporate Design in Hamburg, später für fünf Jahre am Forschungs- und Entwicklungszentrum der Porsche AG in Stuttgart. 1994 Gründer und seither Leiter der *Corporate Design for Long-Lasting Capital Goods and Components of Industrial Automation* und seit 2004 selbständig unter dem Motto: „... innovation in a team Airena®!" Seit 2002 Mitglied der Royal Society of Arts, London.
Lebt in München-Schwabing und Oberösterreich.

Julian F.V. Vincent
Geboren 1943, Professor für Biomimetik/Bionik
BA und MA an der University of Cambridge, PhD und DSc an der University of Sheffield. Spezialisierte sich als Zoologe auf Insektenphysiologie (Hormone und Oberhaut).
„I was always interested in engineering as well, so I started to apply ideas from engineering and materials science to biology. Then I applied ideas from biology to engineering."
Lebt in Bath.

assistant professor at the Department of Architecture of the Technical University of Berlin, chair of Prof. Lutz Kandel.
1997 Co-founder of *Peanutz Architekten*, together with Wolfgang Grillitsch. PEANUTZ stands for small and large interventions of versatile use (German: *Nutz*). Their theories are derived from a series of „designperformative works".
Lives in Berlin.

Anupama Kundoo.
Born 1967, Architect and Sustainable Design Consultant
B.Arch from the University of Bombay. Independent practice since 1990. Developed various eco-technologies for building and built several experimental projects including technology-transfer training for labourers. Worked in Berlin for Sabine Fiebelkorn between 1992 and 1995. Head of the Planning Department in Auroville, India; between 2000 and 2003 Sustainable Design Consultant to ICAEN, Institute of Energy Catalunya, Barcelona and a European Commission Project in partnership with the municipalities of London and Haryana, India. Travelled extensively and conducted workshops and lectures across the world.
Currently located in Berlin.

Thomas Kutschker
Born 1963, Film-Maker and Photographer
Apprenticeship for photography at the Lette-Verein Berlin; since 1987 freelance photographer. Since 1989 film-maker. Since 1992 cinematograhper for short films, industrial films and documantaries as well as fiction movies. 1993 to 1996 postgraduate at the Kunsthochschule für Medien (Media College of Art), Cologne – subject area: film & television. Diploma in audiovisual media. 1998, Förderpreis (Promotional Prize) of the Regional Government North Rhine Westphalia of the Group for Film-directors and Camera Crew. 2000, Work stipend for artists in the region of North Rhine Westphalia. From 2000 to 2005, teaching contracts at Humboldt University, Berlin. 2002, conception and realisation of audiovisual media in the new Museum of the Memorial Location at Sachsenhausen.
Lives in Cologne and Berlin.

Winfried Pauleit
Born 1963, Professor in Art Studies/Art Education at the University of Bremen
Studied Science of Art and Film in Berlin, London and Chicago; 2000 Dr.phil. from the University of Arts, Berlin. Co-publisher of the web-based magazine www.nachdemfilm.de, publications and lectures in the field of film, art and the media, most recently: "Filmstandbilder. Passagen zwischen Kunst und Kino", Stroemfeld Verlag, Frankfurt am Main/Basel 2004; "Wie Cyborgs vom Kino lernen. Biografie versus Technologie am Besipiel von Lynn Hershmans Teknolust", in: Christine Rüffert and others "Unheimlich anders. Doppelgänger, Monster, Schattenwesen im Kino", Berlin 2005, p. 161-170; Editor for the topic: "Ästhetische Erziehung im Medienzeitalter", *Ästhetik & Kommunikation* 125 (June 2004).
Lives in Berlin and Bremen.

Marc Ries
Born 1965, Culture and Media Theorist
Studied philosophy, sociology and educational science in Vienna and Klagenfurt, Austria. Doctoral Degree from the Institute of Philosophy of the University of Vienna. Since 1989 teaching positions in Austria and Germany. 2000 to 2001 visiting professor for comparative image theory at the Friedrich Schiller University Jena. 1997 to 2001 director of the art- and culture provider THE THING, Vienna (http://thing.at). Various projects and publications in the intersecting fields of media/culture/architecture and art. Most recent publication: "Medienkulturen", Sonderzahl, Vienna 2002. Since 2000 work on a state doctorate about the "Geoesthetics of the Media".
Lives in Vienna.

Rober Slinger
Born 1965, Architect
Studied architecture in Sheffield, England. Teaches Architecture and Urban Design at Universities in the UK and Germany since 1991. Project architect in Daniel Libeskind's design office from 1994 to 1998. Assistant Professor in Urban Design at the Technical University of Berlin from 1998-2004. Founded K4POK, together with Claire Karsenty. Practicies and teaches Taiqiquan in his spare time.
Lives in Berlin.

Christian Teckert
Born 1967, Architect, Urbanist, Author, Cultural Producer
Studied Architecture at the Academy of Fine Arts, Vienna. Since 1992 transdisciplinary projects and publications located at the interface between art, urbanism, space-theory and architecture. In 1999, he founded the *Bureau for Cognitive Urbanism* in Vienna, together with the art-historian Andreas Spiegl. 2001 co-founder of AS-IF, together with the architects Stephanie Kaindl and Paul Grundei in Berlin and Vienna. 2004/2005 teaching position at the institute of building science at the Technical University Graz. Since 2005 Member of the Board of the ÖGfA (Austrian Society for Architecture). Together with Andreas Spiegl, Christian Teckert is author and editor of "PROSPEKT", published by Walther König, Cologne 2003.
Lives in Vienna.   www.as-if.info

Axel Thallemer
Born 1959, Design Engineer.
Studied philosophy at the Ludwig-Maximilians-Universität, Munich. Completed his studies as a qualified engineer in the field of civil engineering at the Academy of Arts, Munich. DAAD postgraduate scholarship in Business, Public Relations and Psychology at NYSID, New York City, USA. Professorships in Munich and Hamburg. Guest professor at University of Houston, Texas / USA as well as at Academies of Fine Arts & Design Guanczhou, Canton and Tsinghua University, Beijing/China. Head of the Industrial Design Department at the Universität für Industrielle und Künstlerische Gestaltung, Linz, Austria since 2004, as well as dean of the faculties of architecture, interior design, urban development and space planning. Worked for a brand identity agency in Hamburg, then for five years as a design engineer in the styling studio at the Research and Development Center of Porsche AG, Stuttgart. 1994 founder and head of *Corporate Design for Long-Lasting Capital Goods and Components of Industrial Automation*; – since 2004 self-employed; motto: "… innovation input by team Airena®!" Since 2002 appointed fellow of The Royal Society of Arts, London.
Lives in Munich-Schwabing and Upper Austria.

Julian F. V. Vincent
Born 1943, Professor of Biomimetics/Bionics.
Zoologist specialised in insect physiology (hormones and cuticle), holding a BA and MA from the University of Cambridge, as well as a PhD and a DSc from the University of Sheffield.
"I was always interested in engineering as well, so I started to apply ideas from engineering and materials science to biology. Then I applied ideas from biology to engineering."
Lives in Bath.

Die StadtVilla

Die Vision vom lichten, leichten Wohnen hat Haacke mit diesem Hausentwurf neu definiert. Klarheit, Großzügigkeit, Intimität und offene Weite sind die Resultate einer Architektur von hohem, ästhetischen `Rang. Das Dach schwebt gleichsam über dem Haus und gibt ihm Leichtigkeit, eine schwerelose Eleganz. Licht durchströmt die zweigeschossige Villa von allen Seiten. Durch die offene Galerie und die raumhohen Fenster und Türen. Ein Haus, in dem es sich leicht und entspannt leben lässt – losgelöst von gekünstelter Repräsentation.

Musterhaus-Park Potsdam/Neu Plötzin · Senator-Haacke-Straße 1 (A 10/Abf. Groß Kreutz) · 14542 Neu Plötzin
Info-Telefon (08 00) 4 22 25 33 · www.haacke-haus.de